THE CAMBRIDGE COMI
AND

MW00813828

The Cambridge Companion to Shakespeare and Race shows teachers and students how and why Shakespeare and race are inseparable. Moving well beyond *Othello*, the collection invites the reader to understand racialized discourses, rhetoric, and performances in all of Shakespeare's plays, including the comedies and histories. Race is presented through an intersectional approach with chapters that focus on the concepts of sexuality, lineage, nationality, and globalization. The collection helps students to grapple with the unique role performance plays in constructions of race by Shakespeare (and in Shakespearean performances), considering both historical and contemporary actors and directors. *The Cambridge Companion to Shakespeare and Race* will be the first book that truly frames Shakespeare studies and early modern race studies for a non-specialist, student audience.

AYANNA THOMPSON is Director of the Arizona Center for Medieval and Renaissance Studies (ACMRS) and a Regents Professor at Arizona State University. She is the author of *Blackface* (2021), *Shakespeare in the Theatre: Peter Sellars* (2018), *Teaching Shakespeare with Purpose: A Student-Centred Approach* (2016), *Passing Strange: Shakespeare, Race, and Contemporary America* (2011), and *Performing Race and Torture on the Early Modern Stage* (2008). She wrote the Introduction for the Arden Third Series *Othello: Revised Edition* (2016), and is the editor of *Weyward Macbeth: Intersections of Race and Performance* (2010) and *Colorblind Shakespeare: New Perspectives on Race and Performance* (2006). She was the 2018–19 President of the Shakespeare Association of America, and served as a member of the Board of Directors for the Association of Marshall Scholars. She was one of Phi Beta Kappa's Visiting Scholars for 2017–18. She has conceived and organized large-scale interdisciplinary conferences like RaceB4Race.

THE CAMBRIDGE COMPANION TO SHAKESPEARE AND RACE

EDITED BY

AYANNA THOMPSON
Arizona State University

CAMBRIDGE
UNIVERSITY PRESS

CAMBRIDGE
UNIVERSITY PRESS

University Printing House, Cambridge CB2 8BS, United Kingdom

One Liberty Plaza, 20th Floor, New York, NY 10006, USA

477 Williamstown Road, Port Melbourne, VIC 3207, Australia

314–321, 3rd Floor, Plot 3, Splendor Forum, Jasola District Centre, New Delhi – 110025, India

79 Anson Road, #06–04/06, Singapore 079906

Cambridge University Press is part of the University of Cambridge.

It furthers the University's mission by disseminating knowledge in the pursuit of education, learning, and research at the highest international levels of excellence.

www.cambridge.org
Information on this title: www.cambridge.org/9781108492119
DOI: 10.1017/9781108684750

© Cambridge University Press 2021

First published 2021

A catalogue record for this publication is available from the British Library.

ISBN 978-1-108-49211-9 Hardback
ISBN 978-1-108-71056-5 Paperback

Cambridge University Press has no responsibility for the persistence or accuracy of URLs for external or third-party internet websites referred to in this publication and does not guarantee that any content on such websites is, or will remain, accurate or appropriate.

Contents

Figures

Contributors

PATRICIA AKHIMIE is Associate Professor of English at Rutgers University – Newark. She is the author of *Shakespeare and the Cultivation of Difference: Race and Conduct in the Early Modern World* (2018). She is co-editor, with Bernadette Andrea, of *Travel and Travail: Early Modern Women, English Drama, and the Wider World* (2019). She is currently at work on a new edition of *Othello* and a monograph about women's travel.

DENNIS AUSTIN BRITTON is Associate Professor of English at the University of New Hampshire. His research interests include early modern English literature, Protestant theology, critical race theory, and the history of emotion. He is the author of *Becoming Christian: Race, Reformation, and Early Modern English Romance* (2014), co-editor of *Rethinking Shakespeare Source Study: Audiences, Authors, and Digital Technologies* (2018), and co-editor of "Spenser and Race," a special issue of *Spenser Studies* (2021).

URVASHI CHAKRAVARTY is Assistant Professor of English at the University of Toronto and works on early modern literature, critical race studies, queer studies, and the history of slavery. Her first book, *Fictions of Consent: Slavery, Servitude and Free Service in Early Modern England*, will be published by the University of Pennsylvania Press, and her articles have appeared in journals and collections including *English Literary Renaissance*, *Shakespeare Quarterly*, and the *Journal for Early Modern Cultural Studies*.

AMBEREEN DADABHOY is Assistant Professor of Literature at Harvey Mudd College. Her research focuses on cross-cultural encounters in the early modern Mediterranean and race and religion in early modern English drama. She investigates the various discourses that construct human differences and how they are mobilized in the global imperial projects of the early modern period. Currently, she is working on a project that explores early modern anti-blackness from the Mediterranean to the Atlantic.

MATTHEW DIMMOCK is Professor of Early Modern Studies at the University of Sussex. His research focuses on the interaction of peoples and ideas that took place as a consequence of early modern England's "expansionary thrust" in the late sixteenth century. As well as extensive editorial work, his publications include *New Turkes: Dramatizing Islam and the Ottomans in Early Modern England* (2005), *Mythologies of the Prophet Muhammad* (2013), and *Elizabethan Globalism* (2019).

MILES GRIER is Assistant Professor of English at Queens College, City University of New York. He has published on the history of racial profiling, Joni Mitchell's blackface pimp alter ego, and the trope of racial blackness as illiteracy in early modern English theatre and culture. His essays have appeared in *Politics and Culture, Genders, Journal of Popular Music Studies, William and Mary Quarterly,* and the edited volumes *Scripturalizing the Human* and *Early Modern Black Diaspora Studies.*

ANDREW HADFIELD is Professor of English at the University of Sussex, and visiting professor at the University of Granada. He is the author most recently of *Shakespeare and Republicanism* (2005), *Edmund Spenser: A Life* (2012), and *Lying in Early Modern English Culture* (2017). *John Donne: In the Shadow of Religion* will appear in 2021. He is currently completing a study of literature and class and is co-editing the works of Thomas Nashe.

FARAH KARIM-COOPER is Head of Higher Education & Research at Shakespeare's Globe and Professor of Shakespeare Studies at King's College London. She has published over thirty articles and chapters in books, has edited four essay collections, and has written two books, *Cosmetics in Shakespearean and Renaissance Drama* (2006) and *The Hand on the Shakespearean Stage: Gesture, Touch and the Spectacle of Dismemberment* (2016). She is currently writing a book called *Shakespeare and Race.*

Actor and director ADRIAN LESTER, CBE, started his career with a string of award-winning performances in West End productions including *Company* and *Sweeney Todd.* He played *Hamlet,* directed by Peter Brook, *Henry V,* and *Othello* at the National Theatre and Ira Aldridge in *Red Velvet* in London and New York. Major TV roles include *Hustle,*

Undercover, Trauma, and *Riviera.* Movies include *Primary Colors, Day after Tomorrow,* and Oscar-nominated *Mary Queen of Scots.*

ARTHUR L. LITTLE, JR. is Associate Professor of English at the University of California, Los Angeles. His research works very much at the intersections of gender, sexuality, and race both in the early modern period as well as in more contemporary times. His publications include *Shakespeare Jungle Fever: National-Imperial Re-Visions of Race, Rape, and Sacrifice* (2000) and (in process) *Shakespeare and Race Theory* and *White People in Shakespeare.*

JOYCE GREEN MACDONALD, Associate Professor of English at the University of Kentucky, is the author of *Shakespearean Adaptation, Race, and Memory in the New World* (2020), and of several other studies of early modern performance and racial representation.

CAROL MEJIA LAPERLE is Professor and Honors Advisor for the English Department of Wright State University. She teaches and writes about Renaissance rhetoric, philosophies of will, theories of affect, and constructions of race and gender in early modern culture. She is editing a forthcoming collection of essays entitled *Race and Affect in Early Modern English Literature.* Her monograph-in-progress, *Dark Will: Race, Affect, and Volition in William Shakespeare,* examines philosophies of will and formations of race.

NOÉMIE NDIAYE is Assistant Professor of English at the University of Chicago. She works on representations of race and gender in early modern English, French, and Spanish theatre and performance culture. She has published several articles in peer-reviewed journals (including *Renaissance Drama, Early Theatre,* and *English Literary Renaissance*) and various edited collections. She is currently at work on her first monograph tentatively entitled *Racecraft: Early Modern Repertoires of Blackness.*

SCOTT NEWSTOK is Professor of English at Rhodes College and founding director of the Pearce Shakespeare Endowment. He is author of *How to Think Like Shakespeare* (2020) and *Quoting Death in Early Modern England* (2009); editor of *Paradise Lost: A Primer* (2020) and *Kenneth Burke on Shakespeare* (2007); and co-editor (with Ayanna Thompson) of *Weyward Macbeth* (2010).

MELISSA E. SANCHEZ is Donald T. Regan Professor of English and Comparative Literature and Core Faculty in Gender, Sexuality, and

Women's Studies at the University of Pennsylvania. She is the co-editor of *Rethinking Feminism in Early Modern Studies: Gender, Race, Sexuality* and the author of *Erotic Subjects: The Sexuality of Politics in Early Modern English Literature, Shakespeare and Queer Theory,* and *Queer Faith: Reading Promiscuity and Race in the Secular Love Tradition.*

AYANNA THOMPSON is Director of the Arizona Center for Medieval and Renaissance Studies (ACMRS) and a Regents Professor at Arizona State University. She is the author of *Blackface* (2021), *Shakespeare in the Theatre: Peter Sellars* (2018), *Teaching Shakespeare with Purpose: A Student-Centred Approach* (2016), *Passing Strange: Shakespeare, Race, and Contemporary America* (2011), and *Performing Race and Torture on the Early Modern Stage* (2008). She wrote the Introduction for the Arden Third Series *Othello: Revised Edition* (2016).

ALDEN T. VAUGHAN, Professor Emeritus of History at Columbia University and Affiliate Professor of History at Clark University, wrote *Roots of American Racism: Essays on the Colonial Experience* (1995) and *Transatlantic Encounters: American Indians in Britain, 1500–1776* (2006), among many works on early America. His publications on Shakespeare include *Shakespeare's Caliban: A Cultural History* (1991) with Virginia Mason Vaughan; together they edited *The Tempest* in the Arden Third Series (1999, rev. 2011).

VIRGINIA MASON VAUGHAN, Professor Emerita and Research Professor of English at Clark University, is the author of *Othello: A Contextual History* (1994), *Performing Blackness on English Stages, 1500–1800* (2005), *Antony and Cleopatra: Language and Writing* (2016), and *Shakespeare and the Gods* (2019). With Alden T. Vaughan she wrote "Before Othello: The Elizabethan Image of Sub-Saharan Africans," *William and Mary Quarterly* (1997), and *Shakespeare in America* (2012).

SANDRA YOUNG is Professor of English Literary Studies at the University of Cape Town. Her new book, *Shakespeare in the Global South: Stories of Oceans Crossed in Contemporary Adaptation* (2019), examines innovative adaptations that engage Shakespeare to tell new stories of dispossession across the Global South. Her first book, *The Early Modern Global South in Print: Textual Form and the Production of Human Difference as Knowledge* (2015), traces the emergence of a racialized 'South' in early modern geographies.

Note on Shakespeare Editions

All texts of Shakespeare quoted or referred to in this volume are from the New Cambridge Shakespeare, unless otherwise specified.

CHAPTER I

Did the Concept of Race Exist for Shakespeare and His Contemporaries?

An Introduction

Ayanna Thompson
Arizona State University

If there's a book you really want to read, but it hasn't been written yet, then you must write it.

– Toni Morrison[1]

When I was in university over thirty years ago, the answer to the question – did the concept of race exist during Shakespeare's lifetime – was an emphatic no. This answer was delivered in both explicit and implicit ways. Explicitly I was told that "Moor" did not mean "black," "African," and most especially it did not mean "sub-Saharan African." My Shakespeare professor said that I was being anachronistic when I attempted to link Shakespeare's inclusion of Moors, like Aaron, Othello, and the Prince of Morocco, with the burgeoning transatlantic slave trade of the seventeenth century; he said, to look at race in early modern texts is to misapply modern concepts to them.

At the same time, the editions of Shakespeare's plays I was reading routinely fell silent at certain moments. Claudio's rejoinder in *Much Ado about Nothing* that he is so repentant over Hero's death that he will do anything to marry her cousin, even "hold my mind were she an Ethiope" (5.4.38), receives no gloss in the Arden Second Series edition published in 1981.[2] Romeo's remark that Juliet's beauty "hangs upon the cheek of night / As a rich jewel in an Ethiop's ear" (1.5.44–45), is not explained by the editor of the 1980 Arden edition. Instead, the editor notes the similarity of the phrase to one used by Christopher Marlowe in *Hero and Leander*: "Rich iewels in the darke are soonest spide."[3] The implicit message of these and other observances was that race did not exist in Shakespeare's cultural and creative imagination. That there was no difference between Marlowe's "dark" and Shakespeare's "Ethiope" – that Shakespeare's employment of "Ethiope" was not a reflection of a growing awareness of Africans.

I'll provide one last editorial example, although I can't claim to have been in university when this was first published in 1997. Cleopatra's status as an Egyptian queen, and what exactly Shakespeare and his audiences would have imagined Egyptians to look like physically, have led to some interesting editorial maneuvering. The first lines of the play, after all, announce that Antony is so besotted with Cleopatra that his "goodly eyes," which should be focused on war, "now bend, now turn, / The office and devotion of their view / Upon a tawny front" (1.1.4–6). While the note in the first edition of the Norton Shakespeare explains, "A face or forehead of dark complexion (referring to Cleopatra; see the Introduction)," the introduction waffles on how this "tawny front" actually appears: "*Antony and Cleopatra* also renders problematic the object of desire. Presumably that object is Cleopatra ... It is unclear what they literally see in Cleopatra."[4] If race is not a part of one's interpretative lens, then it may be unclear why, how, and in what material ways Cleopatra appears. As many early modern race scholars have gone on to note, Cleopatra's assumed tawniness has ebbed and waned over the 400 plus years of the play's editing and staging, more an indication of the time of the publication or production than of Shakespeare's own historical moment.[5] The New Variorum edition of *Antony and Cleopatra*, a volume devoted to showing editorial trends, demonstrates the vicissitudes succinctly:

> **Tawny**] COTGRAVE (1611, Tanné): "Also, duskie, swart." WHITE (ed. 1883): "Cleopatra was a Greek, the daughter of Ptolemy, and was probably fair, although not with Teutonic fairness." WILSON (ed. 1950, pp. xi f.) reflects the consensus: "Shakespeare had thought of her as an African beauty."[6]

In other words, as early as 1611 (i.e., during Shakespeare's lifetime) tawny was understood to mean dusky and swarthy in complexion, but by the late nineteenth century the idea that Antony would love a dark-skinned African was an impossibility: Cleopatra had to be Greek and fair, but not quite all the way white, not Germanic white. While the New Variorum editor assumes that John Dover Wilson's 1950 proclamation that Shakespeare imagined Cleopatra to be an "African beauty" is now the "consensus" among modern editors, by 1997 her appearance is "unclear." No consensus then, I guess.

If you ask today in the 2020s if the concept of race existed for Shakespeare and his contemporaries, the answer is an emphatic yes. Yes, the concept of race existed. Yes, racialized epistemologies existed and were employed and deployed. And, yes, Shakespeare himself engages in both the

Figure 1.1   Despite prior scholarly claims that there were few to no blacks in early modern England, archival evidence shows the contrary, including this engraving of a black trumpeter which first appeared in print in a 1518 almanac and was reprinted regularly for almost seventy years.

symbolic and materialistic elements that comprise race-making. Yes, Shakespeare and race are coeval; they grew up as contemporaries. So, what has changed from 1990, the year I started university, to today, 2020, when I write this introduction? The history has not changed (although some new archival materials have been unearthed – see Figure 1.1), but the ways that scholars are trained to search the archives, read the texts, and analyze their significances has. While the critics writing in the 1980s and 1990s were trained primarily as new critics, post-structuralists, and Marxists, with a smattering of feminists among them, the scholars working and writing today have benefited from the birth, growth, and influence of African American studies, critical race theory, post-colonial studies, queer studies, and more recently critical white studies. My work is informed by a deep dive into both African American studies and post-colonial studies when I was in university. When I took the required

Shakespeare course in my final year of university, I had an analytical toolkit that was completely different, foreign, and unfamiliar to my well-esteemed professor.[7] I saw race and race-making; he saw anachronisms.

The book that you are holding and reading, *The Cambridge Companion to Shakespeare and Race*, would have been nearly impossible to create – and, sadly, even impossible to conceive – when I was in university, because it requires scholars who know not only Shakespeare's works, the historical and cultural milieu of the fifteenth, sixteenth, and seventeenth centuries in England and Europe, and the archives that hold the historical documents from these time periods, but also the history of imperialism, alternative archives that reveal more about the various lives of people of color in the early modern world, and the history of Shakespeare's employment in various theatrical, educational, and political moments in history – from the seventeenth century to the twenty-first century. Post-colonial studies, African American studies, critical race studies, and queer studies allow scholars to employ new methodologies for Shakespeare and his contemporaries.

What you are holding is the book that I would have wanted to read when I was in university. It opens up the man, the author, and his works to a much larger and more dynamic portrait of the universe in which he played and thrived. This book introduces readers to the various ways Shakespeare and race can be read, performed, and analyzed together, moving readers from the early modern period in which Shakespeare created to the present moment in which Shakespeare's works are studied, performed, and appropriated. The collection provides an historical overview, offering insights into the extant historical materials that document early modern constructions of race and racial difference. Moving well beyond *Othello*, it invites readers to ponder the specifics of racialized discourses, rhetoric, and performances in all of Shakespeare's plays, including the comedies and histories. Challenging the usefulness of the generic category of "Other" through the book's disaggregated chapters on Moors, Turks, and Jews, it presents an intersectional approach with other chapters that focus on the concepts of sexuality, lineage, nationality, and globalization. And finally, the collection invites the reader to grapple with the unique role performance plays in constructions of race by Shakespeare (and in Shakespearean performances), bringing the reader into the current moment with actors and directors who work with Shakespeare onstage. *The Cambridge Companion to Shakespeare and Race* is the first book that frames Shakespeare studies and early modern race studies for a non-specialist, student audience.

Imperial History

One of the major changes in perspective from the 1990s to today is an understanding that the world in which Shakespeare was living, observing, and creating was an imperial one: one in which European countries, including England, were not only exploring parts of the world that were new to them, but also creating exploitative systems that worked to diversify and bolster their economies at the expense of others. The literary theory New Historicism, which was developed in the 1980s, sought to understand Shakespeare not as a singular author but as a product of the historical, cultural, and material environs around him. Undergirded by Marxism, New Historicists were the first scholars to put pressure on the imperial conditions of Shakespeare's world. The fact that his theatre was called the Globe, for instance, serves as a reminder that while Shakespeare never traveled outside of England (as far as we know), the larger world was a part of his creative consciousness.[8] New Historicists explicitly argued that an imperial background informed Shakespeare's life and work.

Nonetheless, New Historicists were loath to take up the concept of race, racialized epistemologies, and/or the notion of race-making as central elements in this newly expanding imperial world. In fact, like my well-esteemed Shakespeare professor at university, New Historicists routinely claimed that an examination of race in the early modern period was anachronistic. To be fair to the New Historicists, scholars at the forefront of post-colonial studies and critical race studies were arguing that race was a modern concept developed primarily during the Enlightenment.[9] There was an odd chicken-and-egg phenomenon occurring, however, in which the scholars at the forefront of post-colonial studies and critical race studies were taught by early modernists who did not see race in Shakespeare's works (remember the there's-nothing-to-be-glossed-here notes); they, in turn, created new fields of study that argued that race was a modern phenomenon; and these new fields, consequently, influenced another generation of early modern and Shakespeare scholars, who continued to believe that race-making was a modern occurrence.[10]

There were a few scholarly voices who helped to open the door for early modern race studies. The Sierra Leonean scholar Eldred Jones, for example, published *Othello's Countrymen: The African in English Renaissance Drama* in 1965.[11] His book made it clear that early modern drama not only included references to Africa and Africans symbolically, but also included African characters materially, reflecting a burgeoning interest in the world outside of Europe. Then in 1969 Elliot H. Tokson published an article in *Modern Language Quarterly* called "The Image of the Negro in Four Seventeenth-Century Love Poems," in which he argued that "even though these four poems might well be the results of witty assaults on conventional love poetry and not reflect the poets' own racial views at all, they do contribute to the Negro's image as it was being shaped during this century."[12] Again, the argument relies on the idea that concepts of racial difference were being shaped in the seventeenth century. Tokson expanded on this argument in his 1982 monograph, *The Popular Image of the Black Man in English Drama, 1550–1688*.[13] One final example comes from the Trinidadian scholar Errol Hill, whose 1986 book *Shakespeare in Sable: A History of Black Shakespearean Actors*, was the first examination of performances of Shakespeare by actors of color.[14] As post-colonial theorists would later pun, the empire was writing back with race fully in the center of their frames of analysis.[15] For scholars like Jones, Tokson, and Hill, the concept of race and the process of race-making were evident in Shakespeare's time – one only had to look at the texts differently. As Tokson wrote in 1969, "Against a background of racial confrontation, these four poems ... add to the texture of conceptions that divided the races then, and still to some degree keep them apart today."[16] In other words, there were early scholarly voices that explicitly linked the past to the present with regards to notions of race.

As Geraldine Heng painstakingly details in her brilliant book *The Invention of Race in the European Middle Ages*, beginning in the eleventh century Europeans engaged in religious crusades which brought them in contact with various other nations and peoples, and she analyzes how Jews, Muslims, Africans, Native Americans, Mongols, Romani, and others were racialized in the process. Around Shakespeare's lifetime, the European world experienced increased and sustained encounters with an expanding world, including the arrival of the first large group of Africans in Portugal in 1444, the first voyage to the Americas by Christopher Columbus in 1492, and the first influx of Africans into England in 1554.[17]

At this exact moment, England's first freestanding, commercial, secular theatres were being built in London, and on those stages the globe and its people were being constructed, embodied, and enacted. One scholar tabulates that between 1579 and 1642 there were at least fifty plays with racialized figures, and another counts at least seventy productions with black characters.[18] It is important to realize not only that the early modern theatre was reflecting back English ideas about race, but also that these plays were creating new concepts, stereotypes, and visions for race. On the early modern stage, race-making is partially constructed rhetorically –

through, for example, rhetorical patterns, rhetorical "errors," figures of speech, metaphors, colloquialisms, and/or idioms – and partially constructed materially – through, for example, costumes, prosthetics, wigs, moustaches, physical gesture, vocal timbre, and/or accent.[19] In this way, early modern English theatre in general, and Shakespeare's plays in particular, provide a treasure trove of evidence of the ways race was being constructed in the period. Not in a singular, stable, and consistent way, but rather in multiple, erratic, and contradictory ways.

What Is Race?

So, what exactly is race? Let me begin by saying that race is *not* a biological, scientific, or genetic reality. Race is a fiction. I'll repeat: race is not a real thing. Nor is race a stable category that refers solely to skin color, somatic aspects, or phenotypes (think, for example, of all the stories of racial passing; how can one pass if race is tied solely to skin color?). The idea that race is a stable, identifiable biological trait comes from pseudo-scientific arguments that were created in the Enlightenment. These late seventeenth-century arguments were subsequently adopted and weaponized throughout much of the world to create disparities based on these pseudo-scientific notions of essential differences. Again, race is a fiction, but as Ann Stoler argues, race-making is a systemic reality and "a critical feature of racial discourse may be its 'polyvalent mobility.'"[20] In other words, the process of race-making is flexible so that it can be mobilized at different historical moments to create structural and material inequalities. Focusing on the systemic nature of race-making, Stoler claims, "The point is that these racial discourses were both new and renewed, well-worn and innovative, protective of the past and geared to limiting the entitlements of specific populations in the future."[21] Race-making, then, relies on both a fictional idea of a homogeneous social past and a fantastical idea of an aspirational future in which privileges will be limited to the non-raced. As Geraldine Heng explains, "race has no singular or stable referent" because "race is a structural relationship for the articulation and management of human differences, rather than a substantive content."[22]

The assumption that underlies this collection, then, is that race is neither a reality, nor a stable content – it is not skin, genes, nor invisible essential qualities. Rather, race is constructed by a social process that one might call race-making or "racecraft," to use a term coined by Karen E. Fields and Barbara J. Fields.[23] Race does not exist, but racism does. "Racism is first and foremost a social practice, which means that it is an action or a rationale for action, or both."[24] Racism produces race as a concept. Racism produces race to ensure an uneven distribution of goods, wealth, power, rights, etc. As Fields and Fields observe, "Racism and those other forms of inequality are rarely tackled together because they rarely come into view together. Indeed, the most consequential of the illusions racecraft underwrites is concealing the affiliation between racism and inequality in general."[25] Race-making, or what Fields and Fields call race-craft, is the underlying imaginative horizon, belief system, or individual and collective mental landscape that seeks to divide humans along unequal lines. They argue

> Distinct from *race* and *racism, racecraft* does not refer to groups or to ideas about groups' traits … It refers instead to mental terrain and to pervasive belief... [R]acecraft originates not in nature but in human action and imagination; it can exist no other way. The action and imagining are collective yet individual, day-to-day yet historical, and consequential even when nested in mundane routine.[26]

So, what does this mean for Shakespeare and his early modern world? It means that we can look to Shakespeare's works for examples of both racism and racecraft. This is not to malign Shakespeare as an individual – his individual, personal beliefs are not the goal of this type of analysis. Instead, this collection examines Shakespeare's plays and poems for moments when racecraft is visible, the moments when the "mental terrain" and "pervasive belief" of differences are visible, the moments when inequalities are being constructed, the moments when exclusions based on those constructed inequalities are being performed. Sometimes these moments announce themselves readily – Aaron the Moor in *Titus Andronicus*, for example, presents a highly visible moment of Shakespeare's racecraft – but sometimes these moments are more subtle – what underpins the Dromios' distinct difference from the Antiphili in *The Comedy of Errors*? And potentially more unsettling is the fact that Shakespeare's racecraft is unstable, inconsistent, erratic, unbalanced, mercurial, and seemingly capricious. In the past some scholars have argued that the malleability and inconsistency of racialized discourses in the early modern period are evidence that Shakespeare and his con-temporaries were not engaged in a racialized epistemology. In their formulation, inconsistency is a negative indicator of racecraft. Let me be clear, critical race theory has slain this dragon. Constructions of race are inconsistent and opportunistic; that is one of the hallmarks of race-making and racecraft.

It is also important to observe that whiteness is neither a biological reality nor a stable genetic identity either. Like race in general, whiteness is constructed in different ways at different historical moments. Shakespeare's works, in fact, provide fascinating snapshots of the ways that both whiteness and Englishness are created and recreated at different moments. Sometimes gender is a defining feature, sometimes class, sometimes religion, sometimes regional accent, and sometimes other factors are called into service to create the fantasy that whiteness or Englishness are real, stable, biological, and essential. Nonetheless, the work is all race-making and racecraft in the service of racism, whose aim is to create justifiable systemic, structural, and material inequalities. The essays in this collection are good at maintaining an intersectional lens so that we can see the ways that class, gender, sexuality, physical ability, etc. are instrumentalized at different times in the service of racecraft.

The Evidence and the Archives

As I have indicated, this volume demonstrates the ways that we read differently when detecting racializing epistemologies, race-making, and racecraft are a part of one's analytical toolkit. For the most part, the archives that the scholars in this collection consult have been known to scholars of previous generations; it is just that the tools available for the analyses of these sources are now different. There are a few crucial, new archival sources that I would like to highlight, however. First, Imtiaz Habib's 2008 book, *Black Lives in the English Archives, 1500–1677*, provides an invaluable database for the documentary evidence pertaining to the presence of blacks – African, American, and Indian – in sixteenth- and seventeenth-century England.[27] In the past, it was common to be told that Shakespeare would not have seen, let alone known, any black people when he was living and writing in Stratford-upon-Avon and London. Writing in 1978, for instance, G.K. Hunter argued, "The Elizabethans also had a powerful sense of the economic threat posed by the foreign groups they had daily contact with – Flemings or Frenchmen – but they had little or no continued contact with 'Moors,' and no sense of economic threat from them."[28] Habib's book challenges the certainty of these assertions. Finding 448 separate archival records for black individuals in early modern England, Habib argues:

> the substantial archival evidence of black people in England between 1501 and 1676 ... contributes significant, irreversible, and hitherto unavailable materialities to current understandings of racial discourse in

sixteenth- and seventeenth-century England. These records mark the empirical intimacy of the English construction of the racial other, and of the national-imperial drive that is its most immediate occasion."[29]

Moreover, Habib created a map for a cover of an academic journal that shows the proximity of specific black figures from the Tudor and Stuart periods to the freestanding early modern theatres on the South Bank of London.[30] Shakespeare may well have seen or known blacks in London.

Second, Nabil Matar's work translating early modern Arabic texts about their interactions with the English has opened an entirely new archive to Shakespeare scholars. While Queen Elizabeth I's interactions with the Moroccan ambassador, for example, were relatively well known to scholars, the Moroccan view of Elizabeth and England was not. Framing England in a global context, Matar's work palpably demonstrates that there are always (at least) two sides to every economic, diplomatic, and religious encounter in the early modern world.[31] The early modern Islamic texts that he has translated into English provide a new archive for Shakespeare scholars.

And finally, historians continue to identify earlier instances of slavery in the Mediterranean and the transatlantic.[32] While it was once argued that (1) the English did not participate in the slave trade until after Shakespeare's death and (2) there were no enslaved Africans in England, the new archival information about the number of blacks in early modern England coupled with the new historical data about the widespread use of slavery in premodern Europe allows one to read Shakespeare's texts in a different way. The English may not have been trading during Shakespeare's lifetime, but he clearly would have had knowledge about the burgeoning market for forced, unpaid human labor and the burgeoning system of race-making that attended it.

As will become clear the further one reads into this collection, there is still a lot of scholarly detective work to be undertaken. If one accepts the premise that race-making and racecraft are ways of thinking and structuring the world to create inequalities, then the archives have to be read in new ways – ones that address the erasures and inherent inequalities of the archives themselves. It should not be a surprise, for instance, that performance archives are particularly challenging when looking for actors of color, especially women of color. Archives, and what they preserve, value, erase, write over, and leave scant traces of, are racecraft.[33] As we collectively learn to discern and analyze racecraft in new ways, I am hopeful that in thirty years this collection will seem as outdated as the way I was first taught Shakespeare.

How to Read this Collection

Obviously, the best way to read *The Cambridge Companion to Shakespeare and Race* is cover-to-cover, beginning on page 1 and ending on page 293. All of the contributions are informative, and collectively they challenge the supposed neutrality of a color-blind approach to teaching, reading, and/or performing Shakespeare. The collection is unrelenting in its focus on racecraft. The first part of this book, however, provides an historical overview of the ways racecraft reveals itself in early modern England. Farah Karim-Cooper's essay, "The Materials of Race: Staging the Black and White Binary in the Early Modern Theatre," outlines how whiteness and blackness were constructed in both symbolic and material ways in early modern literature and theatre. Beginning with the poetic constructions, Karim-Cooper ends with the materials used to perform racial difference on the early modern stage – from lead paint (for whiteness) to dyed clothes and burnt cork (for blackness). Ambereen Dadabhoy fills in the historical context with her essay, "Barbarian Moors: Documenting Racial Formation in Early Modern England," which explores how England's national and imperial ambitions were not only tied to each other but also tied to racializing epistemologies. Her essay also demonstrates how early modern plays provide historical evidence of race-making.

If you are looking for specific examples of how an attention to racecraft informs an analysis of Shakespeare's plays, then the second section of this collection will appeal to you. Moving from analyses of genre to analyses of specific plays, this section provides the most examples of close readings of Shakespeare's works in this book. While many students and scholars assume that race is primarily a factor in tragedies like *Othello*, Shakespeare's comedies are riddled with racial jokes and references. Patricia Akhimie's essay, "Racist Humor and Shakespearean Comedy," argues that comedy, like racecraft, works through an us-versus-them worldview – group activities that operate through the construction of inequalities. This essay shows how a shift in focus reveals an entirely new way of reading. Next Andrew Hadfield takes us into a deep analysis of the race-craft inherent in constructions and discourses of bloodlines and lineage. In his essay, "Race in Shakespeare's Histories," Hadfield argues that constructions of Englishness are a racializing endeavor that is never pure. While plays like *Titus Andronicus* and *Othello* announce their race-making explicitly, many of Shakespeare's tragedies have characters who question what it means to be racialized (think, for example, of Malcolm's quip that Macbeth is "black," 4.3.52). Carol Mejia LaPerle's essay, "Race in

Shakespeare's Tragedies," argues that race-making is important to the early modern tragic genre precisely because the genre is obsessed with outward signs that either reveal or conceal interiority. For her, Shakespeare's tragedies repeatedly worry over the relationship between the symbolic and the material in a way that reveals the power of race-making.

Through a close reading of *Othello*, Matthew Dimmock's essay, "Experimental *Othello*," explores how Shakespeare's construction of the Moor of Venice radically departed from the "Turk play" genre in early modern England. Capitalizing on the early modern fascination with religious and racial differences, Shakespeare's play explores new forms of racecraft. While many overviews of the history of Jews in England point to their expulsion from England in 1290, the historical reality was much more complex. Dennis Britton's essay, "Flesh and Blood: Race and Religion in *The Merchant of Venice*," like Andrew Hadfield's essay on the history plays, delves into the specific ways that the constructions and discourses of flesh, blood, and lineage reveal a racialized epistemology. Moreover, Britton's analysis shows how race-making works through constructions of gender and sexuality. Sexuality studies has transformed the ways we approach Shakespeare's works. Through a close reading of *Antony and Cleopatra*, Melissa Sanchez's essay demonstrates an intersectional approach that works through the ways race, gender, and sexuality were entwined in the early modern English imagination. Challenging many assumptions, Sanchez argues that white chastity is the most perverse and disturbing sexuality in *Antony and Cleopatra*. Virginia Mason Vaughan and Alden T. Vaughan's essay, "*The Tempest* and Early Modern Conceptions of Race," argues that a historical contextualization of *The Tempest* demonstrates that race-making was never monolithic and always contingent. Their essay analyzes a rich transatlantic archive to understand *The Tempest*. The final essay in the second section, Noémie Ndiaye's "Shakespeare, Race, and Globalization: *Titus Andronicus*," argues that early modern globalization and capitalism necessitated a strategic and contingent racialized society that was hierarchized. *Titus Andronicus* presented in a global context shows how racecraft travels and mutates.

The third section of this book delves into the way race-making works in performance. This section is intended for those who are interested in the history of actors of color on Shakespearean stages and the ways that theatre-craft necessarily affects racecraft. Scott Newstok starts the section with "How to Think Like Ira Aldridge," an essay that provides the unique history of the nineteenth-century American actor through an analysis of seven strategies that marked his success. Urvashi Chakravarty's essay,

"What Is the History of Actors of Color Performing in Shakespeare in the UK?," takes us beyond the history of Ira Aldridge to provide a brief performance history of actors of color in the UK from the nineteenth century on. She uses alternative archives like legal archives and arrest warrants to read the faint traces of their histories. Looking specifically at female actors, Joyce MacDonald argues that the historical traces are even more difficult to detect for them. In "Actresses of Color and Shakespearean Performance: The Question of Reception," MacDonald notices that while Othello provides a performance touchstone for male actors, female actors of color have no similar role, rendering them even less visible. Nonetheless, she unearths fascinating records for some unsung leading women. This section ends with an incredible first-person account of an actor who has had to grapple with Othello. The award-winning actor Adrian Lester, who starred in the National Theatre's 2013 production, explores the challenges he faced in "*Othello*: A Performance Perspective." Fascinatingly, the essay includes quotes from interviews Lester conducted with some of his fellow cast members and other famous actors who have played Othello, including James Earl Jones.

The fourth and final section of this collection brings us squarely into the twenty-first century. These essays demonstrate how one can ask questions about Shakespeare's uses today and where we might go in the future. The section begins with Miles Grier's essay, "Are Shakespeare's Plays Racially Progressive? The Answer Is in Our Hands," which shows how the politics of Shakespeare's plays are entirely contextual. Arguing that there is nothing inherently progressive nor reactionary in Shakespeare's works, Grier warns that the dominant historical tide has been an alignment of Shakespeare with white supremacy and political and cultural imperialism. Grier challenges the reader to fight that tide. Widening the lens to a global and post-colonial scale, Sandra Young's essay, "How Have Post-Colonial Approaches Enriched Shakespeare's Works?," argues that interpretation is never neutral and is always contextual. A post-colonial framework allows Young to argue that resistant reading is a methodology that can be studied, taught, and adopted. Her essay offers a plethora of inspiring examples. And finally, Arthur L. Little, Jr. concludes the collection with his essay, "Is it Possible to Read Shakespeare through Critical White Studies?" Completing the circle that was started by Farah Karim-Cooper's analysis of the symbolic and material constructions of white and black, Little's essay highlights how racecraft not only creates black as a race but also creates white as one too – one that can and should be analyzed as unnatural, man-made, and as systemically implicated as blackness. His readings of the ways whiteness eludes some of Shakespeare's characters is eye-opening (e.g., his brief analysis of Phebe in *As You Like It*).

Potential Futures

I began this essay remembering the disconnect I felt when I was a university student from the ways Shakespeare was being analyzed, explored, and taught. Influenced by post-colonial and African American studies, I knew there must be other ways to read, interpret, and even perform Shakespeare. I started by looking at texts that seem to announce their interest in race most explicitly – *Titus Andronicus, Othello, The Merchant of Venice, Antony and Cleopatra,* and *The Tempest* – the plays that are sometimes referred to as his "race plays." This line of investigation was part and parcel of the first wave of early modern race scholars, who sought not only to reveal the black presence in early modern England and Europe but also to re-edit the plays with the new historical evidence informing the glosses (remember Cleopatra's "tawny front"). Early modern race studies has evolved in the intervening thirty years to engage more comprehensively and critically with both archival history (e.g., early modern Atlantic studies and African diaspora studies) and theories (e.g., critical race theory, critical white studies, performance studies). The way that race is defined in this collection, for instance, was not an available rhetoric or theory thirty years ago.

So where will you take Shakespeare in the next thirty years? Like Laurent Dubois, whom Sandra Young cites in her essay, this collection asks: "Whose history are you telling?"[34] In his essay, Miles Grier succinctly and powerfully declares, "To align Shakespeare with global white supremacy and political or cultural imperialism is to work with the tide of history. To turn the tide is not impossible, but it also requires reorienting work on economic, material, and ideological fronts – often from what appears to be scratch." How will you purposefully turn the tide, reorient the work, and alter Shakespeare studies? What archives, histories, or theories will push Shakespeare studies away from an alignment with white supremacy and imperialism? What viewpoints have we ignored, obfuscated, and/or erased? What book do you really want to read about Shakespeare? It's up to you to write it. In the meantime, I hope *The Cambridge Companion to Shakespeare and Race* inspires you to push our field into even more inclusive places in the future.

Notes

1 Quoted in Ellen Brown, "Writing Is Third Career for Morrison," *Cincinnati Enquirer,* 27 September 1981, F11.
2 *Much Ado about Nothing,* ed. A.R. Humphreys, Arden Second Series (London: Methuen, 1981), 214.

3 *Romeo and Juliet*, ed. Brian Gibbons, Arden Second Series (London: Methuen, 1980), 116 n.45.

4 Walter Cohen, "Antony and Cleopatra," *The Norton Shakespeare*, ed. Stephen Greenblatt (New York: W.W. Norton, 1997), 2629n2, 2621.

5 See, Francesca T. Royster, *Becoming Cleopatra: The Shifting Image of an Icon* (New York: Palgrave Macmillan, 2003); Celia Daileader, "The Cleopatra Complex: The White Actresses on the Interracial 'Classic' Stage," in *Colorblind Shakespeare: New Perspectives on Race and Performance*, ed. Ayanna Thompson (London: Routledge, 2006), 205–20.

6 *Antony and Cleopatra*, ed. Marvin Spevack, New Variorum (New York: Modern Language Association, 1990), 6n10.

7 Ayanna Thompson, "Response: Shakespeare, My Sparring Partner," *Early Modern Culture* 14 (2019): 183–86.

8 Richard Halpern, "Shakespeare in the Tropics: From High Modernism to New Historicism," *Representations* 45 (Winter 1994): 1–25.

9 See Michael Omi and Howard Winant, *Racial Formation in the United States: From the 1960s to the 1990s* (New York: Routledge, 1986); Anthony Appiah, "Race," in *Critical Terms for Literary Study*, ed. Frank Lentricchia and Thomas McLaughlin (University of Chicago Press, 1990); *Critical Race Theory: The Key Writings That Formed a Movement*, ed. Kimberlé Crenshaw, Neil Gotanda, Gary Peller, and Kendell Thomas (New York: New Press, 1996).

10 Kimberly Anne Coles, Kim F. Hall, and Ayanna Thompson, "BlacKKKShakespearean: A Call to Action for Medieval and Early Modern Studies," *Profession* (Fall 2019): https://profession.mla.org/blackkkshakespear ean-a-call-to-action-for-medieval-and-early-modern-studies.

11 Eldred Jones, *Othello's Countrymen: The African in English Renaissance Drama* (London: Oxford University Press on behalf of Fourah Bay College, the University College of Sierra Leone, 1965).

12 Elliot H. Tokson, "The Image of the Negro in Four Seventeenth-Century Love Poems," *Modern Language Quarterly* 30/4 (December 1969): 508–22 (at 509).

13 Elliot H. Tokson, *The Popular Image of the Black Man in English Drama, 1550–1688*, Perspectives on the Black World (Boston: G.K. Hall, 1982).

14 Errol Hill, *Shakespeare in Sable: A History of Black Shakespearean Actors* (Amherst: University of Massachusetts Press, 1986).

15 Bill Ashcroft, Gareth Griffiths, and Helen Tiffin, *The Empire Writes Back: Theory and Practice in Post-Colonial Literatures* (London: Routledge, 1989).

16 Tokson, "Image of the Negro," 522.

17 Kate Lowe, "Introduction: The Black African Presence in Renaissance Europe," in *Black Africans in Renaissance Europe*, ed. Thomas Foster Earle and Kate Lowe (Cambridge University Press, 2005), 1–14; Kate Lowe, "The Stereotyping of Black Africans in Renaissance Europe," in *Black Africans in Renaissance Europe*, ed. Earle and Lowe, 17–47; Emily Weissbourd, "'Those in Their Possession': Race, Slavery, and Queen Elizabeth's 'Edicts of Expulsion,'" *Huntington Library Quarterly* 78/1 (2015): 1–19.

18 Jonathan Burton, *Traffic and Turning: Islam and English Drama, 1579–1624*
    (Newark: University of Delaware Press, 2005), 92; Matthieu A. Chapman,
    "The Appearance of Blacks on the Early Modern Stage: *Love's Labour's Lost's*
    African Connections to Court," *Early Theatre* 17/2 (2014): 77–94 (at 86).

19 Ian Smith, *Race and Rhetoric in the Renaissance: Barbarian Errors* (New York
    and Basingstoke: Palgrave Macmillan, 2009); Virginia Mason Vaughan,
    Performing Blackness on English Stages, 1500–1800 (Cambridge University
    Press, 2005).

20 Ann Laura Stoler, "Racial Histories and Their Regimes of Truth," *Political
    Power and Social Theory* 11 (1997): 183–206 (at 200).

21 Stoler, 191.

22 Geraldine Heng, *The Invention of Race in the European Middle Ages*
    (Cambridge University Press, 2018), 19.

23 Karen E. Fields and Barbara J. Fields, *Racecraft: The Soul of Inequality in
    American Life* (London: Verso, 2014).

24 Fields and Fields, 17.

25 Fields and Fields, 261.

26 Fields and Fields, 18–19.

27 Imtiaz Habib, *Black Lives in the English Archives, 1500–1677: Imprints of the
    Invisible* (Aldershot and Burlington, VT: Ashgate, 2008).

28 G.K. Hunter, *Dramatic Identities and Cultural Tradition: Studies in
    Shakespeare and His Contemporaries* (New York: Harper & Row, 1978), 32.

29 Habib, 9–10.

30 Imtiaz Habib, cover of *Shakespeare Quarterly* 67/1 (2016).

31 Nabil Matar, *Turks, Moors, and Englishmen in the Age of Discovery* (New York:
    Columbia University Press, 2000); Gerald MacLean and Nabil Matar, *Britain
    and the Islamic World, 1558–1713* (Oxford University Press, 2011).

32 Hannah Barker, *That Most Precious Merchandise: The Mediterranean Trade in
    Black Sea Slaves, 1260–1500* (Philadelphia: University of Pennsylvania Press,
    2019).

33 Jennifer L. Morgan, "Accounting for 'The Most Excruciating Torment':
    Gender, Slavery, and Trans-Atlantic Passages," *History of the Present* 6/2
    (2016): 184–207.

34 Laurent Dubois, ""Atlantic Freedoms," *Aeon*, https://aeon.co/essays/why-haiti-
    should-be-at-the-centre-of-the-age-of-revolution (accessed 6 April 2020).

CHAPTER 2

The Materials of Race
Staging the Black and White Binary in the Early Modern Theatre

Farah Karim-Cooper
Shakespeare's Globe and King's College London

In his *Tracte Containing the Artes of curious Painting, Carving and Building*, published in English in 1598, Giovanni Paolo Lomazzo explains the symbolism of colors, including black and white. He first tells us that "cold produceth white, whereunto much light is required. Heat engendereth Black, proceeding from a small quantity of light and much heat." An early version of climate theory (the notion that race is defined and determined by environments and temperature), this definition of color, as Lomazzo calls it, echoes broader philosophies about color symbolism or color-concept. Lomazzo goes on: "some think blackness is a sign of madness and folly ... because fools and madmen are over-charged with black choler." He tells us "black is taken for a token of unhappiness"; he then reminds his reader, in fact, these associations originated much earlier: "Pythagoras was wont to say, that black appertained to the nature of evil. And Ovid in his invectives used the same, as also Horace ... Alecto and the three Furies were represented in black, according to Virgil."[1] What is curious about Lomazzo's notion of blackness is its implicit theatricality; the semiotics of blackness draw upon a range of character traits, such as "madness" or "folly." It was viewed as a "token" of unhappiness, particularly when we consider its humoral connections to melancholy. As Lomazzo states, even the Furies were "represented" in black, which highlights more ominous associations (the Furies of Greek and Roman antiquity were goddesses of vengeance). The color black, therefore, when it served as a racial signifier onstage in the commercial theatres of London would have been loaded with this diverse range of negative associations for audiences.

When Lomazzo goes on to define white, he suggests it is "apt to receive all mixtures, [and] signifieth simplicity, purity, and elation of the mind." Virgil had attributed the color to the garments of "chaste priests, good poets, [and] witty men," while Persius "saith," Lomazzo continues, "that a white man is interpreted to be a good and sincere man."[2] White is further associated in Lomazzo's text with faithfulness, good habits, cleanliness, angels, mirth, and joy – but not just any joy, the kind of joy or elation felt at the resurrection of Christ. Whiteness too is representable, but its essence – "joy," "purity" – is what Lomazzo is interested in emphasizing. These definitions found in a Renaissance artists' manual demonstrate a fundamental premise of critical race theory at work here: race is linguistically, symbolically, socially, and culturally constructed, not a consequence of biology or more spuriously, climate. These more dubious theories were embedded in European thought so early that it is no wonder that the works of the Western canon have perpetuated and reinforced racist assumptions about the meanings made by color.

To consider how early modern theatre companies represented race (in black *and* white) onstage in material terms, it is important first to understand how this binary is at work within the early modern cultures of conduct, beauty, and visual representation.

Renaissance Constructions of Black and White

In premodern texts related to beauty, behavior, and courtesy, whiteness is figured as an ideal in interior as well as exterior terms. As Lomazzo's text in the opening paragraph shows, whiteness is linked to a network of qualities associated with virtue and all that is good. This discourse influenced the ways the English considered difference. How one appeared in their demeanor, behavior, and physical complexion would have been viewed as a reflection of the inner self. Patricia Akhimie has described the process of cultivating difference as a "culture of conduct," defining conduct as "a set of socially meaningful behaviors which can be prescribed or prohibited, enacted or eschewed" and as a "key idiom for negotiating social difference in early modern English culture."[3] In many of these foundational texts on conduct as well as in the love poetry of the medieval and Renaissance periods, a white and shimmering complexion in particular is positioned as an ideal and as an essential component in the construction of womanhood. I have argued elsewhere that the ideals of beauty that are heavily invested in white or "fair" complexions derive in part from classical paradigms, but it is important to note that the emphasis on fairness as signifying both beauty and virtue is amplified during the Renaissance period.[4] In this period, whiteness and blackness are constructed as not just colors or complexions but also entire systems of value codified to produce a dubious but enduring sense of difference.

Richard Dyer has identified the persistent motif of the beautiful white body in Western European tradition as part of a "cult of whiteness," which worshipped "unsullied femininity" but always at the expense of darker-hued women, who in many literary contexts, are dismissed as sexually appetitive and threatening, such as in the "dark lady" sequence in Shakespeare's sonnets.[5] The assumption that whiteness is not only the superior ideal but "natural" is evident in courtesy manuals, including Baldassare Castiglione's dialogue *The Book of the Courtier*, translated into English by Thomas Hoby in 1561. When "The Count" discloses his awareness that Italian women want to be beautiful, he states:

> How much more attractive than all others is a pretty woman who is quite clearly wearing no make-up on her face, which is neither too pallid nor too red, and whose own colouring is natural and somewhat pale (but occasionally blushes openly from embarrassment or for some other reason) . . .[6]

Taking for granted that a "pale" complexion means "natural," texts like the one cited above establish that white bodies dominated the cultural imaginary and were therefore the "norm," thus emptying it of its racial meaning; this example also illustrates how the construction of the white or "fair" ideal is very often gendered. Kim Hall has shown just how ubiquitous the black/white binary is in Renaissance culture and texts, while also observing that this polarity is often figured in terms of female beauty:

> and these terms most often refer to the appearance of moral states of women . . . the terms acquire a special force when they are turned to women and . . . they are most frequently used in relation to women.[7]

The focus on gender in the context of staging early modern difference is significant because of the ways in which cosmetic technology makes meaning onstage in intersectional terms: we have to read black and white faces in ways that are not only motivated by constructions of femininity but more urgently in ways that consider the network of racial meanings they both produce.

But how did the early modern English acquire their ideas about black and white? One way was through the visual culture of the period. Royal portraits deliberately projected an image of the Tudor monarchs as icons of white privilege, divinity, and power (see Figure 2.1). In her essay on teaching race and gender, Hall recommends analyzing such images in order to get at the heart of racial construction. She observes that "in these portraits Elizabeth [for example] is excessively white in a way that becomes representative of a group identity"; particularly, Hall suggests, "the

Figure 2.1   George Gower's 1579 "Sieve" portrait of Queen Elizabeth I is a good example
of the way her whiteness was constructed.

whiteness of her bejeweled dress and 'cosmetically enhanced' features
combine in the Ditchley portrait to evoke virgin purity and Christian
grace and thus associate Elizabeth with 'the good'".[8] Portraits of Elizabeth
are linked to the poetry of mistress worship, as Elizabeth's court was
engaged actively in a cult of hyperbolic praise that extended to and fueled
the preoccupation with Petrarchism amongst early modern poets.[9] A 1593
collection of poetry contains a poem that highlights whiteness as the
primary source of female beauty:

> The Lily in the field,
> That glories in his white:
> For pureness now must yield,
> And render up his right:
> Heaven pictured in her face,

Doth promise joy and grace.
Fair Cynthia's silver light,
That beats on running streams;
Compares not with her white,
Whose hairs are all sunbeams;
Her virtues so do shine,
As day unto mine eine.[10]

The relationship between virtue and whiteness is obvious from the poem's references, such as to heaven shining in the mistress's face; neither the lily nor the moon's light ("Cynthia's silver light") can come close to the whiteness of the lady. Thus, notions of female beauty as being illustrative of a kind of white virtue are embodied in the poetry of the period as well as the visual representations of beautiful women, particularly Elizabeth I, whose portraits demonstrate that the construction of whiteness was indicative of Christian European power. Such constructions of whiteness helped to shape the symbolic and cultural resonances of its supposed opposite.

If white is virtue then black must be vice; indeed, the Vice figure in medieval drama would arguably be appareled black, the Vice being a precursor to the fool and the stage malcontent and/or revenger of Elizabethan tragedy.[11] In a recent study, Robert Hornback observes the significant legacy of blackface in the premodern period: "blackface comic types employing stereotypical dialects while impersonating African slaves appeared widely in the drama of Western Europe" and underpinned the "belief that black people were less rational, hence less human, and thereby rendered especially suited to inhumane servitude." Thus by the time Shakespeare and his contemporaries were writing plays for the commercial theatre, there had been a long tradition that linked blackface to various forms of foolery, inferiority, and other racist stereotypes: "pan-European blackface allegorical types from the middle ages and the Renaissance associating blackness with folly, sartorial pride, and ignorant speech, proved to be particularly effective in disseminating the proto-racist stereotypes that have recurred successively in differing contexts in colonialism, antebellum minstrelsy, and modern racism today."[12] When actors wore blackface or black masks on the early modern stage, they would signal to the audience racial difference and inferiority despite the fact that the meaning of blackface does shift in nuanced ways over time. Historically, mainstream scholarship tended to avoid arguments that race is the key issue in *Othello*; however, when we realize the symbolic meaning of color in the early modern imagination, it becomes impossible to separate Othello's treatment and his fate from the structures of racist ideology inherent in not only Renaissance Venice, but also Shakespeare's England.

To begin the work of exploring the numerous meanings blackness makes onstage and the materials used to create it, we have to remind ourselves of iconographic representations that extended throughout Europe. From medieval poetic and visual representations of death as black,[13] to the many allegories of "good versus bad" in depictions of the Last Judgement – the white bodies of Christ and the ascendant are deliberately juxtaposed with the black bodies of the devil and other demonic inhabitants of hell (see, for example, Fra Angelico's *Last Judgement*, ca. 1425) – we see the establishment of this binary through the powerful and emotionally evocative imagery of Christianity. Richard Dyer has observed that the white "body is the basis of Christian imagery,"[14] viewed for centuries as a site representing salvation and purity. In a Western European context, the relationship between skin color and Christianity is hard to miss in light of its history of artistic representation. Considering its European representations and practices, Dyer argues that Christianity "has been thought of and felt in distinctly white ways for most of its history," evident in relation to, among other things, "the gentilising and whitening of the image of Christ and the Virgin in paintings."[15] Shakespeare's original audiences would have been familiar with these meanings and therefore when encountering characters of color would have reacted with racist fear, judgement, and even wonder.

However, what is often neglected is that it is not beyond the realm of possibility that Shakespeare and his contemporaries encountered non-white people in London during this period. By uncovering documentary evidence of their presence, Imtiaz Habib has shown the extent to which traditional historiography erased people of color in sixteenth- and seventeenth-century London.[16] Early modern England has been white-washed by historians and literary critics for centuries in their assumption that there were only white people residing permanently in London. In the past twenty years more attention has been given to archival research that has shown pure white London to be a false narrative. This research might prompt us to question or re-evaluate the composition and demographic of the early modern theatre audiences. We already know that there were many playgoers who were tourists and travelers from Germany, Italy, Spain, Holland, etc. as well as communities of immigrants who were living in London at the time.[17] The addition of people of color to our visual picture of a 1599 theatre audience in London is, therefore, not fanciful. For example, Robert Hornback points out that there were black Africans residing in Southwark, such as a silk weaver (re)named "Reasonable Blakemore"; it is possible that he attended shows in the playhouses in

Southwark, perhaps even supplied the acting companies with costume items. This kind of archival recovery is of use to a discussion of theatre technology and racial impersonation because we ought to consider the reception and interpretation of such performances and how the materials of theatre then mediated identities real or imagined.

Theatre Technology and Race

It has been established that various forms and prosthetics of cosmetic embellishment were available during Shakespeare's time and it is plausible that these would have been employed in the theatre. To be sure, there is evidence to suggest that not only would boy actors have painted their faces with white lead and vinegar base foundations to play the parts of women, but also the same white base would have been used to depict ghosts, to create the illusion of identicality (such as Viola and Sebastian in *Twelfth Night*), and to depict monarchy.[18] The paradox of cosmetic whiteness however, lies in its artificiality. While whiteness symbolized a virtuous and superior racial ideal, cosmetic whiteness was considered by some (mainly Puritans and anti-theatrical moralists of the period) to be a lie, seen as yet another material of the theatre which depended upon illusion and falsehood. Pretending to embody the ideal complexion seems to have been considered almost as bad as, if not worse than not having white skin at all. The Puritan polemicist Philip Stubbes notoriously criticized women for wearing makeup: "Thinkest thou that thou canst make thyself fairer than God, who made us all?"[19] The question Stubbes poses resonated with a number of anti-cosmetic writers, who complained about not being able to recognize a virtuous woman from a prostitute who also painted her face to hide syphilis scars. Shakespearean and early modern plays comment frequently on this debate, mostly with a sense of irony given the fact that theatre itself relied upon makeup to achieve its vast array of illusions.[20] The widespread use of poisonous ingredients was another point of contention for anti-cosmetic writers: If women were applying poison to their faces to create the white glistening complexions so widely admired, so too were the professional boy actors in order to convincingly play women. The irony then of Monticelso's description of "whores" in his characterization of Vittoria in John Webster's *The White Devil* (1612) is obvious:

> They are first,
> Sweet-meats which rot the eater; in man's nostril
> Poisoned perfumes. They are cozening alchemy,
> Ship wrecks in calmest weather! What are whores?
> (3.2.98–101)

This passage comments upon the metaphorical significance of poisonous makeup, which is figured as the deception of women and the dangers they pose.

These negative associations that clustered around white face paint, which was used largely to create the illusion of femininity and ideal beauty, were also doubly racially motivated because of the fear of blackness. We have learned that for medieval and early modern people, in addition to folly, diabolism, and anger, blackness was linked with aggressive sexuality or deviance. Kate Lowe has shown how, throughout Western Europe, "Black Africans were . . . routinely stereotyped as sexually promiscuous."[21] Additionally, a woman who was branded a whore in Elizabethan England was "blackened" in reputational terms. Shakespeare's *Othello* refers to Desdemona's own "black and begrimed" face, not just as a metatheatrical allusion to the potential smearing of Richard Burbage's black face paint upon the painted white face of the boy actor playing Desdemona, but also because encoded within the language of black and white is a value system that rates sexual morality in precisely these linguistic terms.

A few scholars have attempted to identify what materials might have been used to create racial identities. It is important to point out that while this essay focuses on face paint, there were multiple ways to signify race on the early modern stage, including through costume/clothing and its accessories such as hats, beards, and weaponry or swords (linked in the early modern representational fantasy to Ottoman soldiers, for example); accents were undoubtedly attempted by some early modern actors to indicate a "foreigner" onstage, and occasionally music or particular instruments would have been played to gesture toward an a hyper-racialized fantasy of the "exotic"; such music might be cued in the Egyptian court scenes in Shakespeare's *Anthony and Cleopatra*, for example. The papers of Edward Alleyn (principal actor and theatre manager for the Lord Admiral's Men) held in Dulwich Picture Gallery include a props list containing items such as "caudern for the Jewe" (a cauldron for the Marlowe play, *The Jew of Malta*); "owld Mahometes head" and "Turk's head"; "The more's lymes" (the Moor's limbs), etc. When we examine this list next to the repertory of plays put on at the Rose Theatre, owned by Philip Henslowe, it becomes apparent that staging racial difference was more common than we acknowledge and that it was popular with audiences, increasingly diverse as they probably were.

In her study of performing blackness, Virginia Mason Vaughan finds that early court performers wore masks or "vizards" to portray a variety of roles, but masks would have been limiting for actors on the commercial stage who relied less on music and dance than on the spoken word.[22] Black characters appear in a number of commercial plays throughout the sixteenth and seventeenth centuries, so the methods and materials needed for, as well as the semiotics of, the performance of race would have developed over time. Vaughan traces this evolution of blackface and its symbolic meaning, arguing that:

> The performance practice of "blacking up" thrived in religious pageants of the Middle Ages as a simple way of discriminating evil from good. Cycle and morality plays set up oppositions between black and white, damnation and salvation, evil from good. Until the latter half of the sixteenth century when the cycle plays were repressed, generations of Englishmen and women enjoyed the yearly ritual of watching good angels pitted against bad angels ... at festivals.[23]

Richard Blunt adds that "between 1522 and 1604, when Shakespeare wrote *Othello*, the meaning and representation of a black-faced character changed."[24] Both Hornback and Blunt note that the shifting meanings are very likely due to the growing population of black people in London during the late sixteenth and throughout the seventeenth centuries. As such, this growth "allowed playwrights the opportunity to see people from other cultures and introduce Moorish characters to the public stage."[25] There were approximately "23 plays between 1588 and 1637 where Moors or characters disguised as Moors" appear onstage.[26] Shakespeare's Aaron the Moor from *Titus Andronicus* and Othello are perhaps the most famous examples of characters that demonstrate a developing sophistication in the portrayal.

Just as whiteness, the dominant racial signifier and semiotic of female beauty, is constructed through white lead paint on the early modern stage, black paint would have also been used by theatre companies to portray characters across a spectrum of races, from Tamburlaine, to the "tawny moor" (the Prince of Morocco) in *The Merchant of Venice*, to Cleopatra, to the two Moors and their imitators in the play *Lust's Dominion* (1600), who are murdered by Philip and Hortenzo. To hide their identities, they disguise themselves to look like the two Moors whom they murdered. The character Isabel instructs them: "Once rob the dead, put the Moors habits on, and paint your faces with the oil of hell, so waiting on the Tyrant." The "oil of hell" no doubt refers to the black paint; this phrasing thus recalls the medieval associations between blackness and the diabolic. But it also tells us that cosmetic paint was available in the theatres. To make a cosmetic base of black pigment, one would take burnt walnut shells to grind into a powder and mix with an oil base; some recipe manuals of the period indicate that the stones of particular fruits, like cherries, could form the base of black pigment. Nicolas Hilliard's artist's manual *The Arte of Limning* (1601) recommends a powder "manufactured from ivory burnt in a crucible, ground with gum water,"[27] which has fascinating implications when we consider metaphorically the process of creating blackness out of colonialist appropriated materials that are valued because of their whiteness, such as ivory.

There is also evidence to suggest that black cloth or textiles were used to cover a white actor's body so he could play the part of a Moor. I have already cited Edward Alleyn's props list, which includes a "more's lymes." This reference is probably to sleeves for the arms and perhaps stockings or leggings for the legs. Ian Smith has made the compelling argument that "among the techniques employed to imitate the black skin of Moors or Africans on the stage was the covering of the actor's body with black cloth, its function being to materialize the imagined black bodies of real Africans existing in the world outside the theatre."[28] Smith connects his case for textiles to the handkerchief in *Othello*, arguing that given the details of Othello's handkerchief narrative and its relationship to his own identity in the play it was very likely to have been black rather than the traditionally assumed white. Onstage, this additional black textile would be in dialogue with the other materials that signify Othello's origin story, his identity in Venice as a "stranger" or outsider, and his race onstage.

Smith's work has forced us to re-evaluate our interpretation of the handkerchief as a sign and its contribution to racial subjectivity in the play. Smith's premise is that the handkerchief does not represent Desdemona but is rather a metonym for Othello himself. Testifying to this theory is Othello's narrative about the handkerchief's origins, which points to its "foreign and unique" nature: being "dyed in mummy" alludes to mummi-fication practices in Egypt; "dyed" suggests it has been stained with color, and its Egyptian feminine origins suggest the skilled labor of the female maker – the "Sybil." Later Cassio, once he has the handkerchief, asks his lover Bianca (the courtesan) to "take out the work" or make the copy, suggesting she has a particular skill as many women did. But the uniquely foreign quality of the handkerchief might make us pause to question Bianca's identity. One of the stories of a black presence in English parish records and archives tells us that names were often changed: "it appears to have been considered humorous to give black Africans the 'surname' Blanco or White or a variation of it . . . and to invent nicknames for black slaves that alluded to their skin color."[29] Bianca (whose name means "white") is the only one in the play who can "take out the work"; what if her name is ironic not just in sexual terms because she is a courtesan (so therefore her "loose" sexual morals would blacken her), but also because the character is a Moor? Perhaps the boy actor playing Bianca would have had to wear black face paint signaling not only Bianca's sexual but also her racial identity, thus aligning her more closely with the black handkerchief.

Smith's argument that actors on the Jacobean stage would have worn black masks or textiles instead of face paint isn't entirely convincing, though he is right to point out the prominence of black textiles in the theatres, including the hangings that were draped around the theatres during the performances of tragedies. Smith argues that "black cloth used to imitate skin in the theatre materializes and reproduces this idea of the black man as a 'thing,'"[30] but if in the first performance of *Othello*, the actor Richard Burbage has a black mask on, why would the boy actor playing Desdemona wear white cosmetics instead of a mask himself? We know from Jacobean scholar Henry Jackson's account of witnessing a performance of the play in Oxford in 1610 that the boy playing Desdemona "entreated the pity of the spectators by her very countenance."[31] The use of facial and manual gesture in the early modern theatre was a key component of acting before the age of technology. The actor's body was the primary tool for making dramatic meaning. A word for acting in this period was "passionating," which emphasized the role the emotions played in an actor's craft, and the face was a key transmitter of this emotional meaning.[32] It seems logical, then, that what actors used to signal racial identities, whether it was black cloth or paint, depended on the theatrical conditions, perhaps even the genre and certainly the emotional stakes within the play.

While there is still a relative paucity of evidence about theatrical props and the crafts and technologies of the stage, from surviving records and the play texts themselves we can piece together a methodology for depicting racial identities onstage, including whiteness. Through costume, makeup, textiles, and fabrics, racial subjectivity became increasingly performable as more plays contained characters from a range of backgrounds. In *The Merchant of Venice*, for example, Shylock refers to his "Jewish gabardine," indicating that the actors would have had a costume that, through its constituent parts, represented a "Jew." As we learn more about the growing population in London of people of color, it seems less and less likely that audiences were racially homogeneous. This new understanding of an early modern racially diverse audience then should force us to consider more deeply how the performance of race developed over time and how it was received, and, in turn, we should interrogate just how poorly or closely Shakespeare's actors would have held a mirror up to nature.

Notes

1 Paolo Giovanni Lomazzo, *A Tracte Containing the Artes of Curious Painting, Carving and Building*, trans. Richard Haydocke (London, 1598), 98, 113.

2 Lomazzo, 114.

3 Patricia Akhimie, *Shakespeare and the Cultivation of Difference: Race and Conduct in the Early Modern World* (New York and London: Routledge, 2018), 1.

4 See Farah Karim-Cooper, *Cosmetics in Shakespearean and Renaissance Drama* (Edinburgh University Press, 2006, rev. edn 2019).

5 Richard Dyer, *White* (London and New York: Routledge, 1997), 77.

6 Baldesar Castiglione, *The Book of the Courtier*, trans George Bull (Harmondsworth: Penguin, 1967), 86.

7 Kim F. Hall, *Things of Darkness: Economies of Race and Gender in Early Modern England* (Ithaca, NY: Cornell University Press, 1995), 9.

8 Kim F. Hall, "Beauty and the Beast of Whiteness: Teaching Race and Gender," *Shakespeare Quarterly*, 47/4 (Winter 1996): 461–75 (at 466).

9 On the cult of mistress worship and beauty, see Hall, "Beauty and the Beast"; Karim-Cooper, *Cosmetics*; and Linda Woodbridge, "Black and White and Red All Over: The Sonnet Mistress amongst the Ndembu," *Renaissance Quarterly* 40/2 (1987): 247–97.

10 Anonymous, *The Phoenix Nest* (London, 1593).

11 On the Vice in medieval drama, see Charlotte Steenbrugge, *Staging Vice: A Study of Dramatic Traditions in Medieval and Sixteenth-Century England and the Low Countries* (Amsterdam: Rodopi, 2014).

12 Robert Hornback, *Racism and Early Blackface Comic Traditions: From the Old World to the New* (Cham: Palgrave Macmillan, 2018), 24, 25.

13 See Hall, *Things of Darkness*.

14 Dyer, 15.

15 Dyer, 17.

16 See Imtiaz Habib, *Black Lives in the English Archives, 1500–1677: Imprints of the Invisible* (Aldershot and Burlington, VT: Ashgate, 2008).

17 See Andrew Gurr, *Playgoing in Shakespeare's London*, 2nd edn (Cambridge University Press, 1996), Appendices.

18 See Karim-Cooper, *Cosmetics*.

19 Philip Stubbes, *The Anatomy of Abuses* (London, 1583), 64.

20 See Karim-Cooper, *Cosmetics*, chaps. 2 and 3.

21 Kate Lowe, "The Stereotyping of Black Africans in Renaissance Europe," in *Black Africans in Renaissance Europe*, ed. Thomas Foster Earle and K.J.P. Lowe (Cambridge University Press, 2005), 17–47 (at 29).

22 Virginia Mason Vaughan, *Performing Blackness on English Stages, 1500–1800* (Cambridge University Press, 2005), 9.

23 Vaughan, 2.

24 Richard Blunt, "The Evolution of Blackface Cosmetics on the Early Modern Stage," in *The Materiality of Color: The Production, Circulation, and*

Application of Dyes and Pigments 1400–1800, ed. Andrea Feeser, Maureen Daly Goggin, and Beth Fowkes Tobin (Farnham & Burlington, VT: Ashgate, 2012), 217–34 (at 218).

25 Blunt, 218.

26 Blunt, 218.

27 Nicholas Hilliard, *A Treatise Concerning the Arte of Limning*, ed. R.K.R. Thornton and T.G.S. Cain (Ashington: Mid Northumberland Arts Group, 1981), 91.

28 Ian Smith, "Othello's Black Handkerchief," *Shakespeare Quarterly* 64/1 (2013): 1–25 (at 4).

29 Kate Lowe, "Introduction: The Black African Presence in Renaissance Europe," in *Black Africans in Renaissance Europe*, ed. Earle and Lowe, 1–14 (at 12).

30 Smith, 23.

31 Cited in Michael Neill, "Introduction," in *Othello*, Oxford Shakespeare (Oxford University Press, 2006), 125.

32 For early modern acting and gestural theory, see Farah Karim-Cooper, *The Hand on the Shakespearean Stage: Gesture, Touch and the Spectacle of Dismemberment* (London: Bloomsbury, 2016); Evelyn Tribble, *Early Modern Actors and Shakespeare's Theatre: Thinking with the Body* (London: Bloomsbury, 2017); and Miranda Fay Thomas, *Shakespeare's Body Language: Shaming Gestures and Gender Politics on the Renaissance Stage* (London: Bloomsbury, 2019).

CHAPTER 3

Barbarian Moors
Documenting Racial Formation in Early Modern England

Ambereen Dadabhoy

Harvey Mudd College

I approach the question of documentary evidence of race in early modern English culture through a well-known example: Queen Elizabeth I's 1601 draft proclamation instructing the Lord Mayor of London and one of her agents to collect and deport "divers blackamoores" from England. These documents, which announce their own rationale for the collection and expulsion of these "negars and blackamoors," expose the socially, culturally, and politically precarious position occupied by black people in Elizabethan England. Moreover, they suggest a kind of early modern xenophobia that goes beyond the fear of the foreign other to signal modes of racial awareness, racial thinking, and, therefore, an emergent construction of race.[1] The series of these three proclamations, two publicly circulated and the third contained in Robert Cecil's papers, exposes anxiety about these strangers residing in the realm, coupled with a cognizance of their racial difference, which seems to sanction their mandated expulsion from England. The draft proclamation declares:

> After our heartie commendations; whereas the Queen's majesty, tending the good and welfare of her own natural subjects, greatly distressed in these hard times of dearth, is highly discontented to understand the great number of Negros and blackamoors which (as she is informed) are carried into this realm since the troubles between her highness and the King of Spain; who are fostered and powered here, to the great annoyance of her own liege that which co[vet?] the relief which these people consume, as also for that most of them are infidels having no understanding of Christ or his Gospel: hath given a special commandment that the said kind of people shall be with all speed avoided and discharged out of this her majesty's realm; and to that end and purpose hath appointed Caspar van Senden, merchant of Lübeck, for their speedy transportation, a man that hath somewhat deserved of this realm in respect that by his own labor and charge he hath relieved and brought from Spain divers of our English nation who otherwise would have perished there.[2]

The draft proclamation expresses the potential danger these "great number of Negros and blackamoors" pose to the English body politic, for they seem to be consuming resources that would be better employed in suc-coring the Queen's native subjects, those belonging to "our English nation." Furthermore, they are referred to as "infidels," those who lack the knowledge or redemptive possibilities of "Christ or his Gospel." Not only are these foreign others black, but also they espouse a false faith, possibly Islam given the use of "infidel" here rather than "pagan."[3] Whether or not this proclamation was made public, it patently confirms the position of the state vis-à-vis blackness within the body politic: blackness is undesirable.[4]

Race, then, is in the process of being created so that it can operate as a vehicle to sanction exclusion. As an important point of clarification, I am employing Karen E. Fields and Barbara J. Fields's definition of race, which "stands for the conception or the doctrine that nature produced human-kind in distinct groups, each defined by inborn traits that its members share and that differentiate them from members of other distinct groups of the same kind but of unequal rank."[5] Moreover, they define racism as "first and foremost a social practice, which means that it is an action and a rationale for action, or both at once."[6] Thus, both race and racism are social constructs and they operate in concert in order to materially reward those who are seen to 'lack' race and punish those found to 'have' race. Precisely defining these terms, the hierarchies of power informing their design, and the inherent malleability therein, helps us observe the process through which human differences, such as skin color, become racialized in the period.

There remains, however, a further dimension of this royal document that requires some attention: the position of Spain in relation to England and to blackness. By 1601, in post-Armada England, the existential threat of a Spanish invasion of the island had abated, and yet the document makes apparent that tensions between the nations and their monarchs persist. The draft emphasizes "the great number of Negros and blacka-moors which . . . are carried into this realm since the troubles between her highness and the King of Spain," alleging a seeming connection between these black people and Spain. Indeed, the plan to transport these black people out of England involves exchanging them for English subjects delivered from Spanish control: "he hath relieved and brought from Spain divers of our English nation who otherwise would have perished there." This trade in people as goods suggests another sort of merchandise and traffic, enslaving, which was quite profitable in the early modern

Mediterranean and Atlantic, geographies in which both England and
Iberia operated. As Emily Weissbourd urges regarding the position of these
black people targeted for deportation from England, "it seems increasingly
plausible that the 'blackamoores' discussed in the warrants are indeed
being treated as commodities within an uncodified (but nonetheless present) slave economy."[7] In 1444, the first "sizable group of black Africans –
about 250" arrived in Portugal,[8] and by the middle of the seventeenth
century Spanish cities like Seville could record significant numbers of
enslaved black populations in their census.[9] Enslaving and enslavement
in Iberia predate, almost by a century, the instantiation of these activities
by the English. Therefore, the mention of the Spanish in Elizabeth's
proclamations signals both the knowledge of this market of human bondage, and, as Weissbourd highlights, the strong connection between blackness and an enslaved social position.[10] In this context, too, blackness
becomes racialized in order to signal multiple imbricated meanings that
justify servitude and bondage.

   I offer this excursus into official records as a prologue to my investigation of this same terrain in Elizabethan drama, which serves as another
relevant source of documentary evidence of race in the period. As I turn
from the royal Tudor archive to the Tudor/Stuart stage, I seek to disclose
the ways the stage constructs race in the service of nation and empire, and
how the Iberian connection to blackness and enslavement that underlies
Elizabeth I's proclamations finds a corollary on the English stage. Between
1579 and 1642 nearly fifty English plays featured characters that were
marked as racially and/or religiously different from their English audiences.[11] The popularity of this subject matter suggests an interest in
foreign locales, peoples, and cultures on the part of playwrights and
audiences and exposes the ways early modern drama helped to shape the
perception of identity and difference. Within the nexus of race and empire,
George Peele's *The Battle of Alcazar* (1594) offers a documentary case
study of the ways English identity was being constructed through these
registers of difference. The play dramatizes contemporary events: the
1578 Battle of el-Kasr el-Kabir in Morocco, which was an internecine
struggle between two rival claimants to the throne of "Barbary." These
events were broadcast in Europe because of a foreign intervention by
Sebastian, the king of Portugal, who supplied troops and was himself part
of the army supporting the deposed ruler, Muly Hamet.[12] English interest
in this spectacular contest might also have been motivated by the presence
of the privateer Thomas Stukley – a "hero of Lepanto" – who joined the
Portuguese convoy to fight on the losing side.[13]

The Battle of Alcazar stages the struggle for power in Morocco between Muly Hamet, the current king, and his uncle Abdelmelec, who arrives in Morocco with an invading army supplied to him by the Ottomans (who had been hosting him during his exile). This intergenerational dynastic struggle results from a disruption in the rules of succession, which here do not follow primogeniture, but descent through the filial line, so that the son inherits from the father and is then succeeded by his brothers.[14] In defiance of his father's will, Abdallas, Muly Hamet's father, "ordered the murder of his brothers to assure the succession of his son."[15] Not all of the brothers are so easily dispatched and two seek shelter with "the Turks."[16] Peele begins his play with the fratricides, which he attributes to Muly Hamet – furthering his villainy – and with Abdelmelec's invasion and successful routing of the usurper. In defeat, Muly Hamet turns for aid to the Portuguese king, Sebastian, promising him dominion over Morocco. Sebastian offers military support because he is galvanized by a possible crusade against the Muslims as well as an imperial expansion into Africa. To further this plot, he seizes the European privateers, including Thomas Stukley and his crew, who are currently harbored in Lisbon. Stukley is on a mission, financed by the Pope, to provide military provisions to the Irish, but that plan, potentially harmful to England, is swiftly aborted in favor of this other imperial enterprise in Africa. The final battle between these different forces results in the deaths of three kings: Muly Hamet, Abdelmelec, and Sebastian. Muly Mahamet Seth, the brother of Abdelmelec, becomes the new king of Morocco, restoring "fair sequence and succession" (*Richard II*, 2.1.199).

I sketch the basics of Peele's plot in order to emphasize my interest in the play, which is its coupling of racial formation to fantasies of imperial expansion and the strategic geopolitical location of Morocco. Scholars have made much of the play's Mediterranean geography and milieu; however, I want to make the case for linking Morocco's Mediterranean coastline to its Atlantic one, to situate it in the global economy of empire and enslavement.[17] I argue that the play offers evidence of early modern race in its dramatization of technologies of empire that facilitate the plunder of Africa and naturalize the bondage and enslavement of black bodies.

Creating Race: Negro Moors and White Moors

The term Moor in the early modern period possesses an elasticity that allows for it to be applied to a variety of people from various geographies.

As Michael Neill indicates, the term's "notorious indeterminacy" makes it problematic when employing it as a racial category:

> insofar as it was a term of racial description, it could refer quite specifically to the Berber-Arab people of the part of North Africa then rather vaguely denominated as "Morocco," "Mauritania," or "Barbary"; or it could be used to embrace the inhabitants of the whole North African littoral; or it might be extended to refer to Africans generally (whether "white," "black," or "tawny" Moors); or, by even more promiscuous extension, it might be applied (like "Indian") to almost any darker-skinned peoples – even, on occasion, those of the New World.[18]

Contained within the term "Moor," then, is a geographic distinction, religious differentiation, and color consciousness (see Figures 3.1 and 3.2). Yet even as such forms of difference are signaled within the mobilization and deployment of the term, Neill cautions that it operates as an unstable racial descriptor. Indeed, Peele's source for *The Battle of Alcazar*, John Polemon's *The Second Part of the Booke of Battailes, Fought in Our Age*, offers us some insight into the inconsistent application and fluidity of the term. Halfway through its rehearsal of the events, the text announces the fact of Muly Hamet's blackness. When Abdelmelec learns that his deposed nephew has forged an alliance with Sebastian, he tells his court, "The king of Portugall ought diligentlie to weigh and thinke with himselfe, how iust and lawfull a cause he hath to come into Africa. For séeing that he is about to take the kingedome from him, to whome it doth of right appertaine, & to giue it to the Negro."[19] This is the first time Polemon mentions Muly Hamet's race. I use race here because Negro is indicative of color, but as employed by Abdelmelec in this moment it connotes ethnic and cultural differences as well. The passage frames the racialized construction of Muly Hamet in the context of his prior usurpation and his current plans for invasion, thus, linking race with behavior. Finally, this moment connects Morocco or Barbary to Africa, the significance of which lies in Muly Hamet's lineage from his black African mother.[20] Muly Hamet's black Africanness becomes a strategy to exclude him from a Moroccan-Barbary identity and to graft onto his color traits of character and morality.

Indeed, Polemon's text transforms color into race through its descriptions of the Moorish kings. He offers another, more complete, depiction of Muly Hamet at the end of the narrative:

> of stature meane, of bodie weake, of coulour so blacke, that he was accompted of many for a Negro or black Moore. He was of a peruerse nature, he would neuer speake the trueth, he did all things subtelly and deceitfully. He was not delighted in armes, but as he shewed in all battailes,

Figure 3.1   The title page from George Sandys's 1615 book, *A relation of a iourney begun an: Dom: 1610* provides a good example of the range of visual rhetoric employed for Turks and Africans.

The true Effigies of ye Alkaid, (or Lord) Iaurar Ben Abdella.
Embassador from ye high and mighty Muly Mahamed
Sheque, Emperour of Morocco, King of Fess and Sus. &c.

Figure 3.2   The 1637 frontispiece from *The arrivall and intertainements of the embassador, Alkaid Jaurar Ben Abdella*, although a later historical example, offers another example of the range of visual rhetoric employed.

of nature cowardly, and effeminate. But he so cruelly hated Christians, that he would kil either with famine or nakednesse, those that he caught. If that in these warres he being constreined by necessitie, gaue any signification of good will towards them, he did it against the heart, & in a maner vnwillingly, that he might make them the more readie and chierfull to endaunger themselues for him.[21]

This sketch of Muly Hamet permits the tidy parallel between his physical body and his internal character, so that the demerits of height, strength, and color are matched by deceit, cowardice, and effeminacy. His "cruel" orientation toward Christians becomes another incriminating quality. Blackness, then, is called upon to perform outsized symbolic work.

An oppositional or counter description of Abdelmelec precedes that of Muly Hamet, suggesting not the capacious nature of Moor, but rather the contours of white and black as they are harnessed to connote race. Here, the text eulogizes the martyred king with complimentary language that bolsters the fluid deracinated interpretation of Moor:

> he was of a meane stature, of a fine proportion of bodie, with brode shoulders, white face, but intermixed with red, which did gallantlie garnish his chéekes, a blacke beard thicke, and curled, great eies and graie. In summe, he was a verie proper man, and verie comelie in all his actions and iestures, and verie strong: the which strength he conserued by continuallie exercising of himselfe in skirmishes, and in bending of bowes ... For he was of a singular and wonderfull wit in all things that he went about or tooke in hand. And although he professed the religion of Mahamet, yet he so loued Christians, and of them Spaniardes, that I cannot expresse with wordes the loue and good will which he shewed towards many captiues & prisoners.[22]

By literally whitening Abdelmelec, the text transforms him into the perfect picture of chivalric gallantry, not only because his rule represents the restoration of proper succession but also because of his kind disposition toward Christians and Christianity. The text presents Abdelmelec as the embodiment of a Renaissance Christian prince, even as it notes his Islamic faith. Indeed, the whiteness of his face seems to actuate and access the discourse of fairness, which Kim F. Hall has identified as imbricated within the matrix of imperial desire and racial exclusion.[23] Polemon's text whitens "the Moor" to include Abdelmelec within a symbolic and moral epistemology. The text exposes the operations of race by assigning somatic whiteness, which is rendered legible through the red cheeks, gray eyes, and his many excellencies of character.

Scholars of the play, however, have used the evidence of the "white" Moor and "Negro" Moor to argue that race and racism as we perceive them are not present in the play. Indeed, they rehearse Neill's definition to diminish the importance of race through a reliance on the inexact and incoherent language of racial discourse.[24] In other words, they argue that the fact that the text can contain Negro Moors and white Moors suggests that race is not fixed – that there are shifting and contingent definitions of race. Kyle Grady, in contrast, argues that such a critical move "presents an overt racialism crafted for the stage irrespective of historical source material; it ahistorically enacts Othello's 'far more fair than black' formulation by de-racing any Moor that stands against the 'general enemy' negro."[25] This seemingly race-neutral or race-blind argument presumes that racial discourses are stable and fixed categories. Yet as scholars of race have exposed, that is not and has not been the case.[26] As a social construct race is contingent upon relations of power, labor, and property. If Moors can be white, as Polemon suggests, then do we imagine that this whiteness is the same as European whiteness? As Fields and Fields explain, "Racecraft originates not in nature but in human action and imagination. It can exist no other way ... *racecraft* is not a euphemistic substitute for *racism*. It is a kind of fingerprint evidence that *racism* has been on the scene."[27]

Even though Peele eschews the use of the racial descriptor white for his heroic Moor characters, his bombastic antihero, the villain Muly Hamet, is explicitly called a "negro Moor" (1.1.7).[28] In fact, Peele repeatedly uses the adjective in connection to Muly Hamet, fastening blackness onto his body. From his first moment onstage, Muly Hamet confirms the meaning of his character through his race.[29] The Presenter, who serves the choral function in the play, details the nature of the conflict as well as the key players:

> Honour, the spur that pricks the princely mind
> To follow rule and climb the stately chair,
> With great desire inflames the Portugal,
> An honourable and courageous king,
> To undertake a dangerous dreadful war
> And aid with Christian arms the barbarous Moor,
> The negro Muly Hamet, that withholds
> The kingdom from his uncle Abdelmelec,
> (Whom proud Abdallas wronged),
> And in his throne installs his cruel son,
> That now usurps upon this prince,
> This brave Barbarian lord, Muly Molocco.
>
> (1.1.1–12)

The opening lines of the play introduce and instantiate the "barbarous Moor" and "negro" Muly Hamet, outlining the contours of these identity categories by contrasting them favorably or unfavorably with the Christian prince of Portugal. The lines express racial coding even as they promote the fluid circulation of *some* terms; for example, "barbarous" and "Barbarian" are used to describe both Muly Hamet and Abdelmelec (Muly Molocco), as is the term "Moor." Therefore, the play seems to encourage a capacious and seemingly value-neutral and race-free interpretation of these identities. The same, however, cannot be said about the modifier "Negro," which designates both color and culture.

In his monumental study on the presence of black people in early modern England, Imtiaz Habib problematizes benign readings of "Negro," disclosing the way in which the word signals both racial formation and racism:

> Thus, if "niger," meaning black in Latin, becomes "negro" meaning a black person in Spanish-Portuguese, and "Negre" in the middle French and

"neger" in early modern English evolve with the same meaning – that is a racialization process because it essentialized a physical attribute; a color becomes an essential determinant of a person which then is made to signify the entirety of the individual (without that happening to white people in that moment). The word cannot be neutral, irrespective of whether the negative, racializing connotations show up obviously in it.[30]

We observe this racializing process in the play through its yoking of Negro to Moor, the emphasis on Muly Hamet's color, and the play's representation of the other Moorish characters. Out of the eight occurrences of "Negro" in the play, six are directly applied to Muly Hamet and the other two instances to the retainers and slaves who flee with him.

Not only does the Presenter censure Muly Hamet through his fixation on his blackness, but also other Moors mobilize Muly Hamet's somatic difference to fuel their campaign against him. In a monologue that echoes the play's source material, Abdelmelec remarks on Muly Hamet's racial difference:

> The Portugal, led with deceiving hope,
> Hath raised his power and received our foe
> With honourable welcomes and regard,
> And left his country-bounds, and hither bends
> In hope to help Mahomet to a crown
> And chase us hence, and plant this negro-Moor,
> That clads himself in coat of hammered steel
> To heave us from the honour we possess.
>
> (3.2.1–8)

The symbolic freighting of morality uncovers ways that negro, negro-Moor, and blackamoor become a "controlling image," circumscribing black identity.[31] I employ this term, coined by the black feminist scholar Patricia Hill Collins, to expose the processes of domination that structure racialization.

Muly Hamet becomes the repository for the text's anxieties about cultural and religious differences. His blackness makes him a site through which to conjure and control the dangers of cross-cultural contact and exchange in Africa. Indeed, in a world populated by Moors, how can one distinguish good from bad, particularly if their religious identity, their Islamic religion, positions them as enemies of Christians? The play makes this most explicit at the end, when Muly Hamet's skin becomes a harbinger of treachery and betrayal:

> His skin will be parted from his flesh,
> And being stiffened out and stuffed with straw ...
> So to deter and fear the lookers on
> From any such foul fact or bad attempt.
>
> (5.1.251–54)

Separated from his body and identity, Muly Hamet's skin, his epidermis, is transformed into a "livery" to serve the interests of the newly established regime.[32] Blackness becomes a spectacle here both as a warning and as an example of difference from non-blackness.[33] While the skinning of Muly Hamet's body occurs after his death, this moment is also one of torture, where black bodies and black skins are rendered fit for violence, thereby affirming their racialization.[34]

The play offers the "negro-Moor" as a fetish object, to be demonized and destroyed. Moreover, the "negro-Moor's" blackness fastens him to Africa, abolishing the neat distinctions between the Mediterranean and the Atlantic, between Barbary and Africa. *The Battle of Alcazar*'s racecraft indicates that Negro is a pejorative that helps to maintain the primacy of the Mediterranean culture over that of Africa; yet the insistence of "negro-Moor" evinces the instability of this project.

Race and Enslavement

I would now like to turn to the imperial designs and fantasies that undergird the racial formation in this play and in the period. As I have noted above, *The Battle of Alcazar*'s plot signals its interest in imperial expansion. Thomas Stukley, the English privateer who becomes embroiled in the conflict, is initially on the Pope's payroll, heading to Ireland to supply and support the rebellion against the English crown. Stukley's fatal detour to Morocco preserves the colony for the queen and leaves England's imperial interests in Ireland intact. From the secure distance of England, Peele's play can be seen as a commentary on imperial ambition. In the play, Sebastian acquiesces to Muly Hamet's request for military aid against Abdelmelec because of the promise that Morocco will become a tributary state:

> For aid to reobtain his royal seat,
> And place his fortunes in their former height.
> For quittal of which honourable arms,
> By these his letters he doth firmly vow
> Wholly to yield and to surrender up
> The kingdom of Morocco to our hands,
> And to become to us contributary;
> And to content himself with the realm of Fez.
> (2.4.10–17)

Sebastian's zeal lies his own desire to lead a crusade – "a holy Christian War" – against the Moors in "fruitful Barbary" (2.4.66, 87). Indeed, he concludes his deliberations by noting "That cause will we direct for Barbary. / Follow me, lords, Sebastian leads the way / To plant the Christian faith in Africa" (2.4.163–65). The play, thus, disguises Sebastian's imperial desire for a strong foothold in Africa by focusing on the missionary rationale.

In fact, both Spain and Portugal were establishing and consolidating their empires in the fifteenth century, and religion served as a justification for expansion and enslavement. Kate Lowe points out that "In 1455 Pope Nicholas V in his papal bull *Romanus pontifex* pronounced that it was permissible to acquire black Africans from Guinea as long as efforts for their conversion were made, and [the chronicles] mouthed the church's line when [they] constantly justified the Portuguese enslavement of West Africans on religious grounds."[35] The enslaving economy of the early modern Mediterranean and Atlantic functioned on the principle that non-Christians and non-Muslims, depending on who was doing the enslaving, could be enslaved. The Renaissance instantiated "the first sustained influx of black African slaves into Europe, and the consequent change from the widespread use of white slaves to the widespread use of black slaves in Europe."[36] The Portuguese were at the forefront of this practice, because their maritime explorations along the west coast of Africa brought them into contact with more African peoples than other European nations operating only in the Mediterranean. Lowe notes that we can find contemporary attitudes to the arrival of enslaved Africans in Portugal in the archive of the Portuguese royal chronicler, Gomes Eanes de Zurara:

> The free, triumphant white Portuguese separated their human booty into five equal groups, in the process dividing family units, whereupon the Africans began to scream and cry, and some began an African chant. Zurara and the audience of the day supposedly were moved by the Africans' suffering ... but the behavior of Laçarote da Ilha, the commander of the slave raid and royal tax-collector in Lagos, was reinforced when Prince Henrique spontaneously knighted him on the field where the scene had unfolded. The message could not have been clearer: it was not only permissible but right for Europeans to capture and enslave black Africans, and to treat them in an inhuman way; it was also financially rewarding and led directly to royal favors. This textual representation of 'blackness' and rendition of the place of black Africans in European society forcefully articulated a link between Africa, back skin, and slavery that was to take hundreds of years to uncouple.[37]

Not only does the influx of black African people in Europe expose the lie of a homogeneous, white early modern European culture, but also it evidences the dehumanizing profit motive that underlies European ventures in Africa.

By the time of Peele's *The Battle of Alcazar*, however, Portuguese fortunes in Africa were waning. Beyond possession of cities such as Ceuta and Tangier and islands off the west coast of Africa, the Portuguese were unable to have a secure, sustained imperial presence on the continent.[38] Their attempts to consolidate power in the Congo, East Africa, and Angola were unsuccessful and so this final expedition in North Africa, which is of concern to our play, memorializes Portuguese imperial ambitions and their ultimate failure. As Chouki El Hamel details:

> The motivation for the involvement of Portugal and Spain stemmed from the fear that the Atlantic routes would be threatened by the Moroccan–Ottoman alliance. Portugal and Spain feared that 'Abd al-Malik would allow the Ottomans to occupy the Portuguese forts on the Moroccan Atlantic. Against the advice of his uncle Phillip II, Don Sebastian led a large Christian army of twenty thousand men, including a very small Moroccan contingent under the command of al-Mutawakkil, and embarked on a war against Morocco in 1578.[39]

The imperial milieu of the play and of its history exposes the interests of Iberian, North African, and Ottoman regimes, underscoring the importance of the region and its traffic and trade.

During this period, the English begin to foster imperial alliances with Africa. The Barbary Company was established in 1585 to regulate and regularize trade with the region, and as Nabil Matar has shown, Queen Elizabeth cultivated a relationship with Al-Mansur, her counterpart in Morocco and the surviving heir to the throne after the Battle of Alcazar. Through archival evidence from Arabic sources, Matar uncovers the political intrigues between London and Morocco. Matar notes that during the visit of the Moroccan ambassador to the queen in 1601:

> Al-Mansur had secretly proposed to the queen a joint operation to seize the Spanish possessions in America. The queen was not interested in building an empire, but needed well-trained troops to help her against Spain. She tried, quite underhandedly, to steal his elite force of Morisco warriors by enticing them to come to England and serve on her fleet. This desperate move on her part is known through a copy of a letter from Mulay Ahmad to her that has survived in a collection of Arabic letters in the National Library of Rabat.[40]

Such correspondence exposes a network of political exchange reliant on the contingency of national security rather than religious similitude and demonstrates the intimacies between Africa and England. In fact, the political affinities between Morocco and England were so strong that in 1601 Al-Mansur proposed a joint attack on Spanish holdings in the Caribbean:

Besides, we must treat of your armie and of our armie, which shall go to those countries, of peopling the land, after that – with the help of God – we shall have subdued it. For our intent is not onely to enter upon the land to sack it and leave it, but to possesse it and that it remayne under our dominion forever, and – by the help of God – to joyne it to our estate and yours. And therefore it shall be needful for us to treat the peopling thereof, whether it be your pleasure it shall be inhabited by our armie or yours, or whether we shall take it on our chardge to inhabite it with our armie without yours, in respect of the great heat of the clymat, where those of your countrie doo not fynde themselfes fitt to endure the extremitie of heat there and of the cold of your partes, where our men endure it very well by reason that the heat hurtes them not.[41]

This military expedition did not materialize, however, because both Elizabeth I and Al-Mansur died in 1603, interrupting England's imperial designs in and with Africa. The imperial milieu that frames the conflict of *The Battle of Alcazar* – the intervention of Portugal in North African dynastic affairs, the presence of an Englishman in a battle for the Moroccan crown, and the significance of blackness within Moorish identity – reveals the ways national and imperial identity was being framed. Moreover, this national and imperial identity was entwined with the formation of race and technologies like enslavement that created racism, domination, oppression, and subjugation.

In answering the question about what documentary evidence of race existed in the early modern world, I have presented the need to revisit, through the framework of critical race theory, the documents we already have. Their received meanings have endured primarily because they were invested in deracinating the period, in seeing whiteness when it was not there, and in refusing to see the operations of race and racism when they were very clearly on the scene. To be sure, new archival material, particularly access to non-European archives, offers us a more complete understanding of how early modern people understood and represented race and racial formation. These new archives may trouble our tidy conclusions and mandate a revision of what we think we know. Re-examining the existing archive as well as consulting new ones will open up our field to the broad and cosmopolitan reality that was the premodern past, rather than the narrow confines of our received reconstruction of it.

Notes

1 These state documents from 1596 appear in *Acts of the Privy Council, New Series* (London, 1890–1964), vol. 26, 16–17, 20–21. Emily Weissbourd

claims that these "open warrants" are not in point of fact documents calling
for the expulsion of black people from England, but rather a license for
enslaver Casper van Zeuden to collect whichever black persons he could as
repayment for freeing English captives from the Spanish. Emily Weissbourd,
"'Those in Their Possession': Race, Slavery, and Queen Elizabeth's 'Edicts of
Expulsion,'" *Huntington Library Quarterly* 78/1 (2015): 1–19.

2 *Tudor Royal Proclamations*, ed. Paul L. Hughes and James F. Larkin, 3 vols.
(New Haven, CT: Yale University Press, 1964–69), vol. III, 221.

3 I make this distinction because it connects the ways race and religion become
enmeshed as categories of exclusion and for the ways "infidel" is commonly
used in the drama and other discourses of the period to identify
Muslim people.

4 For further discussion of these edicts, see Eldred Jones, *Othello's Countrymen:
The African in English Renaissance Drama* (Oxford University Press on behalf
of Fourah Bay College, the University College of Sierra Leone, 1965); Ania
Loomba, *Gender, Race, Renaissance Drama* (Manchester University Press,
1989); Kim F. Hall, "Guess Who's Coming to Dinner? Colonization and
Miscegenation in *The Merchant of Venice*," *Renaissance Drama* 23 (1992):
87–111; and Imtiaz Habib, *Black Lives in the English Archives, 1500–1677:
Imprints of the Invisible* (Aldershot and Burlington, VT: Ashgate, 2008).

5 Karen E. Fields and Barbara J. Fields, *Racecraft: The Soul of Inequality in
American Life* (London: Verso, 2014), 16.

6 Fields and Fields, 17.

7 Weissbourd, 17.

8 Kate Lowe, "Introduction: The Black African Presence in Renaissance
Europe," in *Black Africans in Renaissance Europe*, ed. Thomas Foster Earle
and Kate Lowe (Cambridge University Press, 2005), 1–14 (at 10).

9 Weissbourd, 15.

10 Weissbourd, 15.

11 Louis Wann, "The Oriental in Elizabethan Drama," *Modern Philology* 12/7
(1915): 423–47. Jonathan Burton, *Traffic and Turning: Islam and English
Drama, 1579–1624* (Newark: University of Delaware Press, 2005), 92.

12 In the play he is also called "Muly Mahamet." I follow critical convention here
by calling him Muly Hamet.

13 Jones, 40–41. The Lepanto reference is to the Battle of Lepanto (1571) fought
between an alliance of European Christian nations (the "Holy League") and
the Ottoman Empire.

14 *The Life and Works of George Peele*, vol. II: *Edward I and The Battle of Alcazar*,
ed. John Yoklavich and Charles T. Prouty (New Haven, CT: Yale University
Press, 1961), 227.

15 *Life and Works of George Peele*, 227.

16 I put "Turks" in quotation marks here and throughout because the Ottomans
would have not have employed this term to describe themselves.

17 See Emily Carroll Bartels, *Speaking of the Moor: From "Alcazar" to "Othello"*
(Philadelphia: University of Pennsylvania Press, 2010); Nabil Matar, *Turks,*

Moors, and Englishmen in the Age of Discovery (New York: Columbia University Press, 2000); Gerald MacLean and Nabil Matar, *Britain and the Islamic World, 1558–1713* (Oxford University Press, 2011).

18 Michael Neill, "'Mulattos,' 'Blacks,' and 'Indian Moors': Othello and Early Modern Constructions of Human Difference," *Shakespeare Quarterly* 49/4 (1998): 361–74 (at 364).

19 John Polemon, *The Second Part of the Booke of Battailes, Fought in our Age Taken Out of the Best Authors and Writers in Sundrie Languages. Published for the Profit of those that Practise Armes, and for the Pleasure of such as Loue to be Harmlesse Hearers of Bloudie Broiles* (London: Printed by Thomas East for Gabriell Cavvood, 1587), 76r.

20 Jones, 43.

21 Polemon, 83^r.

22 Polemon, 82^v.

23 Kim F. Hall, *Things of Darkness: Economies of Race and Gender in Early Modern England* (Ithaca, NY: Cornell University Press, 1995), 24.

24 See, for example, Bartels, *Speaking of the Moor*; and Peter Hyland, "Moors, Villainy and the Battle of Alcazar," *Parergon* 16/2 (1999): 85–99.

25 Kyle Grady, *Moors, Mulattos, and Post-Racial Problems: Rethinking Racialization in Early Modern England*, PhD dissertation, University of Michigan (2017), 74.

26 Michael Omi and Howard Winant, *Racial Formation in the United States*, 3rd edn (New York: Routledge, 2015), 3–13.

27 Fields and Fields, 18–19.

28 George Peele, *The Battle of Alcazar* (1594) in *The Stukeley Plays*, ed. Charles Edelman (Manchester University Press, 2005). All quotations are taken from this edition.

29 Muly Hamet is often seen as a precursor to Shakespeare's Aaron in *Titus Andronicus*. See Jones, 49–59.

30 Habib, 12.

31 Patricia Hill Collins, *Black Feminist Thought: Knowledge, Consciousness, and the Politics of Empowerment*, 2nd edn (New York: Routledge, 2000), 72.

32 Frantz Fanon writes, "Willy-nilly, the Negro has to wear the livery that the white man has sewed for him." Frantz Fanon, *Black Skin, White Masks*, trans. Richard Philcox (New York: Grove Press, 2008), 22.

33 Ania Loomba, *Shakespeare, Race, and Colonialism* (Oxford University Press, 2002), 74.

34 Ayanna Thompson, *Performing Race and Torture on the Early Modern Stage* (New York and London: Routledge, 2008), 1–24.

35 Lowe, "Introduction," 12.

36 Kate Lowe, "The Stereotyping of Black Africans in Renaissance Europe," in *Black Africans in Renaissance Europe*, ed. Earle and Lowe, 17–47 (at 17).

37 Lowe, "Introduction," 10–11.

38 Malyn Newitt, *A History of Portuguese Overseas Expansion 1400–1668* (New York: Routledge, 2004), 143–45.

39 Chouki El Hamel, *Black Morocco: A History of Slavery, Race, and Islam* (Cambridge University Press, 2013), 144.

40 Nabil Matar, "Queen Elizabeth I through Moroccan Eyes," *Journal of Early Modern History* 12/1 (2008): 55–76 (at 72).

41 Quoted in El Hamel, 153–54.

CHAPTER 4

Racist Humor and Shakespearean Comedy

Patricia Akhimie
Rutgers University

JESSICA   You are no good member of the commonwealth, for, in converting
  Jews to Christians, you raise the price of pork.
LORENZO   I shall answer that better to the commonwealth than you can the
  getting up of the negro's belly: the Moor is with child by you, Lancelet!
LAUNCELOT   It is much that the Moor should be more than reason; but if she
  be less than an honest woman, she is indeed more than I took her for.

  (Merchant of Venice, 3.5.31–39)

Introduction: The Question of Genre

Shakespeare's comedies, ostensibly distinct from his tragedies and histories,
are traditionally said to include those listed as such in the first folio of
1623: *The Tempest, The Two Gentlemen of Verona, The Merry Wives of
Windsor, Measure for Measure, The Comedy of Errors, Much Ado about
Nothing, Love's Labour's Lost, A Midsummer Night's Dream, The Merchant
of Venice, As You Like It, The Taming of the Shrew, All's Well that Ends
Well, Twelfth Night,* and *The Winter's Tale.*[1] This list has been more or less
accepted with some disagreements, and a few additions and subtractions,
over the course of the plays' 400 plus years of life as cultural objects, a
period during which the comedies have repeatedly been published, edited,
revised, performed, critiqued, and adapted.[2] Critics have offered a range of
reasons to argue why some or all of these plays are recognizable as
comedies, including their common plot elements, tone or mood, language,
settings, dating (early or late), sources, and relation to the broader trends in
comedic entertainment during Shakespeare's time.[3]

Lurking behind many of these attempts at categorization is the simple
idea of opposition: Shakespeare's comedies are not tragedies. That is, the
comedies are not concerned with the rise and fall of great men, or with

their great deeds. Instead, they entertain by means of a certain atmosphere
of levity, employing laughter liberally to propel audiences toward a satis-
fyingly (by early modern standards) happy (-ish, and certainly more
ordinary) ending. In the early modern period, however, comedy and
tragedy were not so sharply differentiated. As Janette Dillon explains:

> The notion that different kinds of engagement belonged in different kinds
> of plays was alien ... Dramatists sought variety instead. They looked to
> make audiences laugh and weep from moment to moment, so that the
> experience of the play was one of plenitude rather than unity. Tragedy and
> comedy were ingredients, not definitions.[4]

Shakespeare's comedies are more serious than the name implies, activating
a wide range of emotional responses to the action and ideas that play out
on the stage or on the page. This range is particularly relevant to the study
of race in the comedies because Shakespeare's attitudes toward race include
both a callous ridicule of those marked by physical or cultural differences
and an apparent empathy for those so abused. That is, he sometimes asks
audiences to laugh at racialized figures and sometimes asks them to weep
with such figures.

Beyond debates about the categorization of particular plays as *either*
comedies or tragedies, there are also those who have made the seemingly
controversial claim that some tragedies are in fact comedic in structure and
effect.[5] *The Tragedy of Othello Moor of Venice* is perhaps the most notable
example. *Othello* seems to most readers and audiences to present a mixed
marriage as a poignant spectacle, exploring the problem of racist stereotypes by displaying its devastating effects on a "valiant Moor" and his
devoted Venetian wife. Yet critics have also noted that *Othello* is comic in
its structure and that Othello is himself a kind of stock comic character: a
puffed-up soldier, smitten with his young wife, easily fooled, oddly
obsessed with handkerchiefs, etc. Michael Bristol argues that while the
doomed lovers Othello and Desdemona seem to arouse contemporary
audiences' sympathies with their impassioned speeches, early modern
audiences would have seen onstage an impossible attraction between a
beautiful woman and a "stereotypical figure of an African, parodically
represented by an actor in blackface."[6] As Bristol explains, audiences
would have interpreted this sight not only as grotesque but as "comically
monstrous."[7] *Othello* would have seemed to show a love affair as strange
and ridiculous as that between Titania, queen of the fairies, and Bottom
with his ass's head in *A Midsummer Night's Dream*. This grotesque pair is
then subjected to increasing pain and humiliation as punishment for the

social disorder their unacceptable marriage creates in a manner that would have been familiar to early modern audiences as similar to the carnivalesque ritual of charivari.[8]

For contemporary readers and audiences, this interpretation of *Othello* may be difficult to picture, since actors have long played the coveted title role as a deeply tragic and sympathetic character rather than as a clown, and the role of Othello is now no longer played in blackface. Yet Ken Ludwig's wildly successful farce, *Lend Me a Tenor*, first performed on Broadway in 1989, demonstrates that *Othello*'s comic content is all-too-easily resurrected. *Lend Me a Tenor* draws upon the hidden comedic elements of *Othello* to fuel its fast-paced physical and visual humor. The comedic confusions begin on the opening night of *Otello*, Verdi's opera based on Shakespeare's *Othello*. Two tenors – the star who falls suddenly ill on opening night and the unassuming lackey who must suddenly prepare to take his place onstage – both suit up for the role of Otello in what one theatre critic described in 1989 as "identical costumes and chocolate makeup."[9]

The image of two Otellos, both in blackface with giant afro wigs, cavorting and leaping around the stage like clowns, is meant to elicit guffaws of laughter from the audience, as is the sight of each of the two tenors, still made up as Otello, making love to the wrong Desdemona (see Figure 4.1). But there is something deeply unsettling about the casual acceptance of the idea that the very sight of Othello, or Otello, should elicit laughter, or that the sight of *two* Otellos should have audiences rolling in the aisles.[10]

Ian Smith has written about the fact that generations of critics and readers have identified with Hamlet – Shakespeare's best-known and most beloved tragic character – as being fundamentally like themselves but not with Othello, who has been perceived instead as fundamentally alien. Smith ties this phenomenon first of all to the "unavoidably simple yet pertinent" fact that "Othello is black while the cadre of critics in Shakespeare studies has been predominantly white."[11] "In a color-conscious society," he writes, "blackness often functions too easily as the mark of unassailable difference."[12] The comedic premise of *Lend Me a Tenor* relies on an unspoken understanding that Otello/Othello is unlike "us."

The premise assumes that "we" – the audience, the cast, the theatre critics – will not see ourselves reflected in Othello, whether we understand him as a "valiant Moor," a clownish buffoon, or both. Otello's ridiculous costume and blackface makeup are then utterly alien, completely

Figure 4.1   This image of two Othellos in a 2013 German production of *Lend Me a Tenor* shows the use of blackface.

unbelievable as a disguise, and therefore silly (in the tradition of blackface minstrelsy); but the underlying truth is that it is blackness in general that is understood as alien, even inhuman. This kind of comedy distances the audience, others the comedic subject, and reproduces the stigmatized meanings of blackness. Racist humor produces social difference by teaching audiences how to hold themselves as a group apart and position themselves above another group.

Still more unsettling is the fact that Shakespeare's comedies are in fact filled with such caricatures: racist slurs pepper the witty repartee between speakers, nameless stereotypical figures populate the backstories of longer and more elaborate racist jokes, and fully realized characters, ridiculous figures whose skin color, religion, nationality, speech, clothing, or habits make them the butts of jokes, are staged purely for the purpose of eliciting on- and offstage audiences' laughter. To put it more bluntly, Shakespeare employs racist humor ... a lot. In this sense comedy and tragedy are difficult to distinguish indeed. It seems that racist humor – more than other types of humor – may push comedy into tragic territory. Few critics have addressed this aspect of the plays, but it is clear that in Shakespeare's comedies alienation, pain, and ridicule are also entertainment.[13]

As scholars of critical humor studies make clear, this jarring combination of hatred and humor is not unusual. Simon Weaver explains, "In racist humour, pleasure can be gained by making others uncomfortable, causing offence or degrading an 'other' who is not present."[14] In this kind of entertainment comedy and tragedy go hand in hand: "Racist humour is a form of racist rhetoric that supports serious racism ... Humour can be, paradoxically, both serious and humourous, and often its seriousness is what people find most funny."[15] In fact, as Weaver demonstrates, racist humor serves an important purpose in societies in which fictions about race persist. First, while racism is essentially irrational – insisting on the existence and significance of differences between groups despite the absence of any evidence supporting these beliefs, and in spite of substantial evidence undercutting them – "racist truth claims are often reinforced in humour, and contradictions removed."[16]

Humor creates divisions; it "functions politically to divide social groups, particularly in generating and reinforcing social boundaries, social distance, and inequalities."[17] Racist humour, in particular, "aids in reproducing and popularizing notions of racial superiority and inferiority."[18] Racist jokes are powerful and pernicious. As Raúl Pérez notes, "jokes targeting racial and ethnic 'others' as stupid, buffoonish, dangerous, inferior, and so on, help facilitate social bonding practices among in-group members, which in turn can (re)produce an ethnocentric worldview."[19] In addition, racist humour builds community, bringing some people together at the expense of others. Shared laughter, it has long been recognized, consolidates and maintains bonds between group members, "facilitating social cooperation, social bonding, and group formation."[20] Playing a key role in the production and maintenance of racist attitudes, racist humor is serious business.

Scholars of humor, and of racist humor in particular, have argued for this simple fact: Comedy is serious. Comedy can perpetuate misconceptions, and it can interrogate them, even break them apart. If humor has this kind of potency, what then is the impact of racist humor, comedy that relies on the deployment of implicitly or explicitly racist concepts, myths, imagery, characters (or caricatures), and situations? And what is the impact of Shakespeare's racist humor with its uncommon longevity – the plays are still read and performed worldwide after over 400 years – for a group of readers and audiences more diverse today than perhaps ever before?

One way to undercut racist humor is through analyzing it. (After all, nothing kills a joke like explaining it.) So, my aim in this essay is to offer some approaches for identifying and assessing, and therefore critiquing, racist humor in Shakespeare's comedies. In the comedies we can read for race in both the early modern period in which the plays were first written, performed, and read and in the long afterlives of the comedies in print and onstage.

Race is not real; it is socially constructed. As a society we continually invent race, producing it through language as we bridge the gap between our observations and our assumptions, mapping our theories of difference onto individuals and groups even as the nature and borders of those groups are continually in flux. Comedy is the hard edge of this race thinking because our laughter solidifies the power and reach of our prejudices. Comedy may also present the opportunity to laugh those prejudices out of fashion or to undermine their logic or their appeal, but this is less often the case. More often, comedy is the place where we acknowledge with our communal sense of humor the absurdity and the reality of social difference and all the real violence our belief in such difference suborns.

I have found it useful to define Shakespeare's comedy not only in terms of its ability to make audiences laugh (whether in the early modern period or today), but also its ability to enable audiences to think the unthinkable by speaking what might otherwise be unspeakable. In the comedies, characters voice racist attitudes and utter racist clichés. Characters (sometimes even the same characters) also voice dissent, ask pointed questions, incite rebellious thought and action, and inspire hope, though these characters are often punished for their outspokenness.

Shakespeare's comedies offer a library of stereotypes. Casual racism abounds, and epithets describing religious, national, or ethnic (somatically marked, phenotypic, regional, and genetic/biological) groups are used inventively or emphatically (with verve!) to deride some person, some behavior, or some belief. The use of stereotypes lends itself to poetic invention, with authors engaging in extended racist metaphors and clever racist conceits.[21] In *Love's Labour's Lost*, King Ferdinand and two fellow courtiers tease their lovelorn friend Berowne, who waxes poetic about his beloved Rosaline's pale beauty: "Of all complexions the culled sovreignity / Do meet, as at a fair, in her fair cheek" (4.3.230–31).

DUMAINE   To look like her are chimney-sweepers black.
LONGAVILLE   And since her time are colliers counted bright.
KING   And Ethiops of their sweet complexion crack.

(4.3.262–64)

Biron's companions suggest that rather than fair, his love is blacker than soot, blacker than coal, blacker than an Ethiopian. Casual racism is used to comic effect and fairly liberally in comedy, where otherwise noble, calm, and virtuous figures from dukes to lords to masters find themselves flabbergasted and, in their exclamations, feel free to curse Ethiopes, Tartars, Jews, Welshmen, Spaniards, and a litany of others. In the comedies these epithets also fall from the lips of characters distinguished by their speech as wits. Falstaff, Benedick, and others call upon the exotic to paint persuasive pictures for their onstage audiences, transporting them to intoxicatingly unfamiliar locales: sexy orientalism sells, endearing them to offstage audiences as well.

BENEDICK   Will your grace command me any service to the world's end? I will go on the slightest errand now to the Antipodes that you can devise to send me on. I will fetch you a toothpicker now from the furthest inch of Asia; bring you the length of Prester John's foot; fetch you a hair off the Great Cham's beard; do you any embassage to the Pygmies, rather than hold three words' conference with this harpy.

(*Much Ado about Nothing*, 2.1.241–48)

FALSTAFF   She is a region in Guiana, all gold and bounty.

(*Merry Wives of Windsor*, 1.3.65–66)

Yet Shakespeare goes beyond casual racist commentary (which might be understood as colloquial I suppose) to the creation of racialized caricatures brought to full three-dimensional life for the pure sport of onstage characters and offstage audiences. The swarthy Spaniard Don Armado of *Love's Labour's Lost* is silly, stupid, and earnest. The townspeople of Windsor gleefully disdain the dueling Welsh and French suitors in *The Merry Wives of Windsor*. Skin color, religion, accents, clothing, drinking habits, culinary preferences: all these and more are fair game in *The Merchant of Venice* and many other comedies. Like Malvolio in *Twelfth Night*, the annoyingly upright steward who secretly desires others' respect and a better life for himself (*quelle horreur!*), these characters are allowed their hopes and desires. Their pain, when they are made to feel it – and they are always made to feel it – is real to us. The most famous of these easy targets is *The*

Merchant of Venice's Shylock, whose pain is so palpable that many contemporary readers find it hard to see the comedy in that comedy at all.

Characters are reducible to their nationality, region of origin, or religion, or to the stereotypical habits (mostly bad), hobbies, modes of dress, or favorite foods of that nation, region, or religion. Racialized characters are marked by their ridiculousness and undesirability more generally, and identifiable as different not because they are unique from all others, but because they are foreign; different from some collective "us." They are identified as foreign through references to dark skin, exotic dress, unusual occupations, extravagant passions and predilections, and they are identified as foreign through references to their expendability, or their monstrosity, or their insignificance; that is, they are recognizable by their lack of humanity. Some do not even have names: Titania's "lovely" Indian boy, a pregnant Moor (Launcelot's shameful secret affair). Some are merely rhetorical as with the proverbial blackness of the anonymous "Ethiope" or heartlessness of the unidentified "Jew" who serve only as aids to hyperbolic protestations.

We can learn to recognize these elements of Shakespeare's comedy and their effects, the ways in which they participate in, perpetuate, create, and, less frequently, break down or question racist thinking. A more difficult task is to learn to read the ways the comedies explore and sometimes critique the building blocks of race and racism. The comedies are interested in difference and the regimes, discourses, and means by which difference is created and maintained. Where does race difference come from, and what is it for? Is it permanent, or can it be dissolved, and how? These difficult questions and others make for riveting plots and subplots in the comedies, where marriage matches, inheritance, successions, wars, coups, shipwrecks, sudden deaths, and power grabs of various kinds hold out the hope of some kind of change, whether for one lucky individual or for a society more broadly. The bodies of men and women of whatever rank are suddenly open to reinterpretation, and audiences are privy to the workings of the intricate processes of inclusion and exclusion that produce and maintain group membership. The plays also take such opportunities to question the meanings of the signs (bodily, sartorial, linguistic, etc.) that are read as indicative of group membership, and to question the meaningfulness of signs in general.

LYSANDER   Away you Ethiope ...
    Hang off, thou cat, thou burr, vile thing let loose,
    Or I will shake thee from me like a serpent ...
    Out, tawny Tartar, out!
    Out, loathed medicine; O hated potion, hence.
                            (*Midsummer Night's Dream*, 3.2.257–64)

Humor and Hatred: Critical Approaches to the Comedies

A look back at the history of criticism on Shakespeare's comedies reveals a recurring problem: a stubbornly optimistic determination to see the comedies as themselves optimistic and benign. This approach views the plays as aesthetically dynamic but socially inert. Samuel Johnson, an early editor of Shakespeare's plays, describes a simple economy of gain and loss, joy and sadness, where one man's comic moment of happiness is another man's misfortune.

> Shakespeare's plays are not in the rigorous and critical sense either tragedies or comedies, but compositions of a distinct kind, exhibiting the real state of sublunary nature, which partakes of good and evil, joy and sorrow, mingled with endless variety of proportion and innumerable modes of combination; and expressing the course of the world, in which the loss of one is the gain of another; in which, at the same time, the reveler is hasting to his wine and the mourner burying his friend; in which the malignity of one is sometimes defeated by the frolic of another; and many mischiefs and benefits are done and hindered without design.[22]

Shakespeare's comedies, however, are more nuanced than Johnson would have it, and moments of delight or devastation are not simply two sides of the same coin. Instead, in the comedies, happiness and sadness are communally created. That is, some are winners, yes: riding high, they are admired and desired. And some are losers, but they are made to feel so by the scorn, ridicule, and neglect of others. Comedy is a group activity. This is how racism functions as well. It, too, pits winners against losers and fosters the belief that some groups of people are better in economic, aesthetic, and/or biological terms (more valuable, more beautiful, more capable), and other groups are worse (unworthy, unlovely, inept). Racist humor relies on the affirmation of such beliefs as truths and assists in the production and maintenance of racist ideology by rationalizing real inequity, real violence, and real pain experienced by those deemed inferior.

In more recent academic studies racist humor is sometimes ignored or excused from the critical evaluation of its more detrimental effects on the grounds that humor is universally or ultimately beneficial. In this vein, François Laroque reviews early modern opinions on the positive effects of humor: mirth is "therapeutic," refreshing the body and mind, and it acts as a "safety-valve," allowing for the safe-if-temporary expression of otherwise transgressive attitudes and ideas.[23] Scholarship on Shakespeare's comedies has resisted a much-needed pivot away from this approach and toward a discussion of race in the comedies, despite the political turn in Shakespeare studies from the 1980s on.

Some recent studies of race in Shakespeare's comedies have elected to mitigate or excuse this aspect of the plays. Edward Berry confusingly proclaims that "Shakespearean comedy is not essentially a comedy of stereotypes ... although stereotyping occurs" and that "Shakespearean comedy is not essentially a comedy of abuse; although abuse occurs."[24] In Berry's reading, Shakespeare employs various strategies that undercut this type of harsh and harmful humor: "The closer one looks at 'others' in Shakespeare's comedies ... the more questionable their 'otherness' becomes."[25] For Geraldo de Sousa, too, Shakespeare's racist humor in the comedies ultimately functions as a diversity initiative, or sensitivity training: "In the comedies Shakespeare affords us glimpses of the world's ethnic, racial, and cultural diversity and affirms all humans' fundamental dignity."[26] As he attests, "Shakespeare's comedies do not ... depict white-on-black violence, as is the case in tragedies, nor do they articulate a white supremacist ideology."[27]

While I could not agree more that the comedies present extraordinary opportunities to sit with, to hear from, and even relate to, othered or racialized figures in the plays, I do not find it necessary or effective to attempt to soften the hard edges of Shakespeare's racist humor. Neither will I claim that there is no humor in hatred. Rather than working to foreclose the pain of racist humor in Shakespeare's comedies, we can explore the wound. Attending to racist humor in the comedies helps us to see how they normalize a socially constructed and violently enforced process of social differentiation through racialization and stereotyping. It reveals the production and maintenance of groups, processes of inclusion and exclusion, and of hierarchization. These are building blocks of racism.

The comedies do give us characters that object to or complain about the status quo and explain the ways the system disadvantages them. As Malvolio demands of Olivia at the end of Twelfth Night: "Tell me why!" (5.1.338). This kind of dialogue allows the plays – and by extension us – to ask difficult questions that society can't or won't answer: Why are the Dromios slaves, and why do they remain so even at the end of the play? What is so wrong with Malvolio's desire for Olivia? Why can't Shylock be forgiven, and why is his desire for justice dismissed? The answers to these and other, similar questions reveal painful truths about prejudices accepted, stereotypes believed, epistemological and physical violence justified, and insurmountable barriers to change perpetuated. The power of these unanswered questions opens up the possibility of critique.

BENEDICK   If I do not take pity of her I am a villain; if I do not love her I am
    a Jew.

(2.3.252–53)

Anti-Racist Critique

Early editors and critics, from Rowe and Pope to Johnson and Coleridge, praise Shakespeare's efforts in the comedies, extolling his unparalleled ability to create characters so unique and lifelike that readers may feel they are seeing the real world reflected. In his 1765 edition of the plays Samuel Johnson famously wrote of Shakespeare that "the poet holds up to his readers a faithful mirror of manners and of life."[28] Yet their praise assumes an English, white, male reader of the plays and projects that identity as universal, imagining that every reader will find himself equally, reliably, and comfortingly reflected in the plays. Yet claims that the plays reflect "us" perfectly in our infinite variety as humans, that the characters are perfectly lifelike, and totally unique, carefully ignore the comedies' investment in the production and proliferation of racist stereotypes through the deployment of racist humor. The feeling of uniqueness that Johnson and others extoll is not a universal experience. Rather, in the comedies in particular, Shakespeare is invested in the reduction of heterogeneity and the production of homogeneity.

Sameness, not individuality, is Shakespeare's trademark in the comedies. Duplicates abound, biological twins fool everyone, young women disguised as young men produce convincing alter egos, a bed trick in the dark replaces one female lover with another, and, perhaps most troublingly, individuals are reducible to stock characters and stereotypes, many of them racist. Characters are recognizable for their speech, yes, but because they are given clownishly exaggerated accents.

DOCTOR CAIUS   Vere is Mistress Page? By gar, I am cozened, I ha' married *un garçon*, a boy, *un paysan*, by gar! A boy it is not Anne Page. By gar, I am cozened.

(Merry Wives of Windsor, 5.5.201–03)

This kind of humor anonymizes individuals by linking them to groups with shared phenotypical, linguistic, or cultural characteristics. This kind of functional indistinctness – into which audiences sometimes seem willing to buy – reflects the racist heuristic upon which Shakespeare's comedies capitalize and frequently rely.

Through criticism, however, the comedies may yield new ways of thinking about social difference and the perpetuation of stereotypes. As an early commentator remarked,

> All such dull and heavy-witted worldlings as were never capable of the wit of a comedy, coming by report of them to his representations, have found that wit there that they never found in themselves, and have parted better

witted than they came, feeling an edge of wit set upon them more than ever they dreamed they had brain to grind it on ... It deserves such a labour.[29]

The comedies may repay our careful observation and analysis.

For example, counterintuitively, decreasing individuality – in the twinning plays for example – may have the effect of questioning the very justifications for systems of social differentiation that place some groups at a disadvantage. In the plays in which two twins are onstage the humor derives from the confusion that arises when multiple individuals are treated as indistinguishable. Watching with horror and delight, the audience is privy to revelations about the absurdity and harm caused by assuming that individuals are "the same." Each of the twins, unaware of the other's existence, experiences the highs and lows of a process of social differentiation that relies on limited signs to distinguish the identity and thus the fate of group members. Audiences are aware that each twin is in fact an individual even as the visual spectacle of their similarity reinforces the idea that they are also the same person or are indistinguishable members of the same group. Their attempts to distinguish themselves (even in their own minds) are both bitter and sweet to the audiences, presented as impossible and as heroic attempts.[30] Even the doubled Otellos of Ludwig's musical farce, *Lend Me a Tenor*, may be recognizable to audiences as more than slapstick comedy. As a critic of a recent Broadway reboot rebukes,

> The central comic device – the two Otellos – strikes a sour note in the age of Obama. Is it really so amusing that Max and Merelli, of wildly different body types and voices, would suddenly be perceived as interchangeable simply by putting on blackface and a fright wig?[31]

The buffoonish blackface Otellos are symptomatic of a social tendency toward reductively racist stereotype.

To reiterate an important point: "humor is a rhetorical and political tool that can challenge, reflect, and reproduce asymmetrical power relations in society."[32] This seems particularly apparent in dramatic performance, where the presence of the actors onstage underneath the costumes and makeup is a constant reminder of the constructedness of characters or roles as well as caricatures or stereotypes. Perhaps the thin line between empathy and ridicule has something to do with the trappings of performance. Coleridge voiced his distaste for performance, which he felt ruined the fantasy. He wrote, "We do not like to see our author's [Shakespeare's] plays acted."[33] He continued:

> Bottom's head in the play is a fantastic illusion, produced by magic spells: on the stage it is an ass's head and nothing more; certainly a very strange costume for a gentleman to appear in. Fancy cannot be embodied any more than a simile can be painted ...[34]

Where the fantasy is racist ideology, this kind of disenchantment should be highly desirable.

In performance the work of multiplication onstage may create resistance through effective disillusionment. In 2018 Shakespeare's Globe Theatre invited four actors who had each performed the role of Othello to speak about the experience. The presence of professional actors onstage worked to uncouple the caricatured "Moor" from its embodied truth as character, as each actor spoke to the limitations and contradictions inherent in the role and, in so doing, reminding the audience of the impact of racialization on real bodies and real people. Undercutting Shakespeare's "universalism" as a homogenizing machine, the presence of multiple actors onstage also allowed audiences to know actively that each Shakespeare production (and each performance of each production) works to create, re-establish, and maintain racist ideas as truth.[35]

Notes

1 François Laroque offers an overview of the most influential opinions about what it is that makes Shakespeare's comedies distinct from his other plays. François Laroque, "Shakespeare's Festive Comedies," in *A Companion to Shakespeare's Works*, vol. III: *The Comedies*, ed. Richard Dutton and Jean Howard (Oxford and Malden, MA: Blackwell, 2003), 23–46.

2 On the inclusion and exclusion of plays from this list, see Emma Smith, *Shakespeare's Comedies: A Guide to Criticism* (Malden, MA: Blackwell, 2004), 29–80; Barbara Mowat, "What's in a Name? Tragicomedy, Romance, or Late Comedy," in *A Companion to Shakespeare's Works*, vol, IV: *The Poems, Problem Comedies, Late Plays*, ed. Richard Dutton and Jean Howard (Oxford and Malden, MA: Blackwell, 2003), 129–49; Paul Yachnin, "Shakespeare's Problem Plays and the Drama of His Time: *Troilus and Cressida, All's Well That Ends Well, Measure for Measure*," in *Companion to Shakespeare's Works*, vol. IV, ed. Dutton and Howard, 46–68; Janet Dillon, "Shakespeare and the Traditions of English Stage Comedy," in *Companion to Shakespeare's Works*, vol. III, ed. Dutton and Howard, 4–22.

3 For recent work on Shakespearean comedies, see Robert Maslen, *Shakespeare and Comedy*, Arden Critical Companions (London: Bloomsbury, 2005); Bart van Es, *Shakespeare's Comedies: A Very Short Introduction* (Oxford University Press, 2016).

4 Dillon, 6.

5 On *Othello* as a comedy, see Susan Snyder, *The Comic Matrix of Shakespeare's Tragedies: Romeo and Juliet, Hamlet, Othello, and King Lear* (Princeton University Press, 1979), and Susan Snyder, *Shakespeare: A Wayward Journey* (Newark: University of Delaware Press, 2002).

6 Michael Bristol, "Charivari and the Comedy of Abjection in 'Othello,'" *Renaissance Drama* 21 (1990): 3–21 (at 4).

7 Bristol, 4.

8 Bristol, 4.

9 Frank Rich, "When One Tenor Is Much Like Another: Buffoonery, Trickery, Vanity and Greed," *New York Times*, 3 March 1989, C3.

10 In more recent productions, the two tenors have done without blackface, or the director has elected to remove references to Verdi's *Otello* altogether. In 2017, director Brad Carroll substituted Ruggero Leoncavallo's *Pagliacci*, and replaced the blackface Otellos with clowns wearing the distinctive white Pierrot costume. When the play was revived on Broadway in 2010, however, blackface was included.

11 Ian Smith, "We Are Othello: Speaking of Race in Early Modern Studies," *Shakespeare Quarterly* 67/1 (Spring 2016): 104–24 (at 107–08).

12 Ian Smith, 108.

13 For work on race in individual comedies, see Bernadette Andrea, "Amazons, Turks, and Tartars in the *Gesta Grayorum* and *The Comedy of Errors*," in *The Oxford Handbook of Shakespeare and Embodiment: Gender, Sexuality, and Race*, ed. Valerie Traub (Oxford University Press, 2016), 77–92; Courtney Lehmann, "Faux Show: Falling into History in Kenneth Branagh's *Love's Labour's Lost*," in *Colorblind Shakespeare: New Perspectives on Race and Performance*, ed. Ayanna Thompson (New York: Routledge, 2006), 69–88; Margo Hendricks, "'Obscured by Dreams': Race, Empire, and Shakespeare's *A Midsummer Night's Dream*," *Shakespeare Quarterly* 47/1 (1996): 37–60; and Dennis Austin Britton, "From *The Knight's Tale* to *The Two Noble Kinsmen*: Rethinking Race, Class and Whiteness in Romance," *Postmedieval: A Journal of Medieval Cultural Studies* 6/1 (2015): 64–78.

14 Simon Weaver, *The Rhetoric of Racist Humour: US, UK and Global Race Joking* (London: Routledge, 2016), 28. Weaver provides a useful literature review on studies of racist humor, 3–4.

15 Weaver, 8.

16 Weaver, 11.

17 Raúl Pérez, "Racism without Hatred? Racist Humor and the Myth of 'Color-Blindness,'" *Sociological Perspectives* 60/5 (2017): 956–74 (at 958).

18 Pérez, 958.

19 Pérez, 958.

20 Pérez, 958.

21 See Kim F. Hall, *Things of Darkness: Economies of Race and Gender in Early Modern England* (Ithaca, NY: Cornell University Press, 1995).

22 *The Plays of William Shakespeare*, ed. Samuel Johnson, 10 vols. (London, 1765), vol. 1, xiii.

23 Laroque, 38–39.

24 Edward Berry, "Laughing at 'Others,'" in *The Cambridge Companion to Shakespearean Comedy*, ed. Alexander Leggatt (Cambridge University Press, 2002), 136.

25 Berry, 125.
26 Geraldo de Sousa, "Shakespearean Comedy and the Question of Race," in *The Oxford Handbook of Shakespearean Comedy*, ed. Heather Hirschfeld (Oxford University Press, 2018), 172.
27 De Sousa, 188.
28 Johnson, vol. 1, viii–ix.
29 These remarks come from the Epistle to the Reader in the 1609 quarto of *Troilus and Cressida*, but are not attributed to Shakespeare.
30 See Patricia Akhimie, *Shakespeare and the Cultivation of Difference: Race and Conduct in the Early Modern World* (New York and London: Routledge, 2018).
31 Charles Isherwood, "It's Not Over Till the Zonked Guy Flings," *New York Times*, 5 April 2010, C1.
32 Pérez, 958.
33 *Coleridge on Shakespeare*, ed. Terence Hawkes (Harmondsworth: Penguin, 1969), 148.
34 Coleridge, 158.
35 See also Carol Rutter, "Kate: Interpreting the Silence," in *Clamorous Voices: Shakespeare's Women Today*, ed. Faith Evans (London: Women's Press, 1987), in which three actors discuss the problems with playing Kate and *The Taming of the Shrew*.

CHAPTER 5

Race in Shakespeare's Histories

Andrew Hadfield

University of Sussex

FLUELLEN   Captain Macmorris, I think, look you, under your correction, there
is not many of your nation –
MACMORRIS   Of my nation? What ish my nation? Ish a villain, and a
bastard, and a knave, and a rascal? What ish my nation? Who talks of
my nation?
FLUELLEN   Look you, if you take the matter otherwise than is meant, Captain
Macmorris, peradventure I shall think you do not use me with that
affability as in discretion you ought to use me, look you, being as good a
man as yourself, both in the disciplines of war, and in the derivation of my
birth, and in other particularities.
MACMORRIS   I do not know you so good a man as myself. So Chrish save me,
I will cut off your head.
GOWER   Gentlemen both, you will mistake each other.

(*Henry V*, 3.2.121–36)

This exchange, the most often cited and analyzed clash of identities in the
history plays, centers around the problem of race.[1] During the Siege of
Harfleur the four representatives of the nations in Henry's army in France,
Gower, the Englishman, Jamy, the Scotsman, Macmorris, the Irishman,
and Fluellen, the Welshman, discuss military tactics while they wait on
events in a scene replete with misunderstandings because of their different
accents and outlooks. Why does Macmorris take such umbrage at what
might seem an innocent question from Fluellen? The trigger word is
"nation," as is clear when Macmorris repeats it four times in his outraged
reply, with what is surely ever heavier emphasis and rising anger. Nation
could mean a particular territory with a unified government inhabited by a
distinct group (or groups) or people, a usage dating from 1330, according
to the *OED*.[2] It could also mean, as now, a distinct group of people who
may or may not live in a particular territory. As Falstaff complains to the
Lord Chief Justice in *Henry IV, Part Two*, "it was always yet the trick of

our English nation, if they have a good thing, to make it too common" (1.2.213–15). Here, the meaning is "people" or "race."

The same is true of Macmorris's interpretation of Fluellen's usage: he is evidently outraged at the assumption that people of his identity or race are in Henry's army and can be recognized and defined. Is this because he does not want to be identified as Irish, believing the recognition of that racial identity to be too problematic (the audience was surely being reminded of the army that had been sent to Ireland to combat Hugh O'Neill, earl of Tyrone, earlier in 1599 just before the play was first performed)?[3] Or, perhaps the key word in Macmorris's response is "bastard," and he is referring to his identity as an Anglo-Irishman, someone of mixed race who is affronted by what he thinks is Fluellen drawing attention to his lack of racial purity, his in-between status?[4] However we read the conversation, it draws attention to the issue of racial identity and the differences between the soldiers in Henry's army, as clearly as the stereotypical characteristics of the two interlocutors (Macmorris losing his temper and threatening spectacular violence as English audiences thought wild Irishman habitually did; Fluellen repeating the stock Anglo-Welsh phatic phrase "Look you").[5] Gower's conclusion that Macmorris and Fluellen "mistake each other" is true in an obvious sense, as they obviously do, but also gestures toward more significant racial misunderstandings as the two cannot easily talk to each other. Fluellen asserts that Macmorris has taken his words amiss, misunderstood them, but we never find out what he really meant, as he shifts the argument to one of his own merit rather than that of racial and/ or national identity. Macmorris is happy enough to continue in this vein and the anger of the characters becomes focused on their honor, akin to quarrels that led to duels.[6] A similar problem of misinterpretation, the play suggests, affects the audience, who may not understand the characters, in a literal sense (because of their accents) and in terms of the nature of the quarrel. Such misunderstandings have also had an impact on later critical readings, not least, I would like to suggest, because the concept of race has been absent from critical discourse.

What the debate highlights is the problematic and complicated understanding of race in the early modern period. Most historians of race argue that, despite a long period of stubborn resistance in the scholarly community, race cannot be seen as a post-Enlightenment phenomenon, and we should not equate notions of race with modern scientific racism. Ideas of race and racism were major intellectual tools in the Middle Ages and the Renaissance, but they were not consistent and depended on a number of factors and ways of marking the real and perceived differences between peoples. As Geraldine Heng has argued, before the Enlightenment race was "a structural relationship for the articulation and management of human differences, rather than a substantive content."[7] Racial differences could be imagined in terms of genealogy and inheritance, or in terms of geographical distinctions, which had determined identities. Distinctions could be based on skin color, and there was undoubtedly a wealth of prejudice directed by white people against non-white people. Nevertheless, just as often they were based on ideas of blood, an inner identity that could remain hidden until forced out into the open, as, for example, anti-Semites assumed. To cite Heng once again, race was understood as "a body-centered phenomenon: defined by skin color, physiognomy, blood, genealogy, inheritance, etc."[8]

Therefore, notions of race in the early modern period can never be clearly and easily defined and often discourses of racial identity intersect with other modes of writing and thinking. When the ghosts of the princes murdered by Richard III appear to the earl of Richmond, the future Henry VII, they urge him to "beget a happy race of kings" (*Richard III*, 5.3.152). When the Lancastrian marquess of Suffolk is insulting the Yorkist earl of Warwick, he attacks his lineage and asserts that his mother sired him with "Some stern untutored churl, and noble stock / Was graft with crab-tree slip, whose fruit thou art, / And never of the Nevilles' noble race" (*2 Henry VI*, 3.2.213–15). Both usages depend on the relationship between identity and inheritance, manifested in the bloodline, which can be pure, as in the ghosts' future projection of the lineage that will be established by Henry VII, or sullied, as in Suffolk's insulting jibe at Warwick (which may well be how Macmorris reads Fluellen's question). The race of kings and nobles defined in each case here also stand for the large groups of people they govern, reminding us that concepts of race, nation, and blood were intertwined.

It should not surprise us that references to blood occur most frequently in the history plays. Of course, they are punctuated by violent military conflict and real blood is frequently visible on the stage as well as liberally sprinkled throughout speeches relating the heroic and shameful deeds of the protagonists. In his speech before Harfleur the king urges his troops on, calling them "noble English, / Whose blood is fet from fathers of war-proof" (*Henry V*, 3.1.17–18), a pointed irony given the various identities of the soldiers who make up his army, differences that are pointed out in the subsequent scene. Henry imagines them as English, defined by a shared lineage carried in the blood, but they are also Scots, Welsh, and Irish. A related understanding of the relationship between blood and racial identity emerges in the build-up to the Battle of Agincourt. Montjoy, the French herald, addresses Henry V in prose, confident of victory because the English army is too small to threaten the might of their assembled ranks: "For our losses, his exchequer is too poor; for th'effusion of our blood, the muster of his kingdom too faint a number" (3.6.128–30). The English/British/Archipelagic army, according to the French, will not be able to spill French blood on French soil and the racial identity of the nation will remain intact. The king reverses this boast in his reply in verse, asserting that, on the contrary, "if we be hindered, / We shall your tawny ground with your red blood / Discolor" (3.6.159–61).[9] English blood will prevail, the more powerful nation triumphing over the weaker one.

On the eve of the battle, in his exchange with Williams – the loyal but skeptical ordinary soldier whose voice stands as a counterpoint to the fractious alliance of Jamy, Gower, Fluellen, and Macmorris – the connection of blood to race returns. Williams, thinking the disguised king to be a mere soldier in the ranks, refers to the heavy responsibility of the king who has led his army into battle and how the blood of his soldiers may well be on his hands:

> But if the cause be not good, the King himself hath a heavy reckoning to make when all those legs and arms and heads chopped off in a battle shall join together at the latter day and cry all "We died at such a place," some swearing, some crying for a surgeon, some upon their wives left poor behind them, some upon the debts they owe, some upon their children rawly left. I am afeard there are few die well that die in a battle, for how can they charitably dispose of anything when blood is their argument? (4.1.134–43)

The long list emphasizes the cruel and often random effects of battle, which destroys more than those killed or maimed in combat. The last line stands as a stark warning that many will suffer in the afterlife too, unable to repent properly and so secure their entrance into heaven. Williams's affective speech has often been read as a comment on the problematic justice of Henry's quarrel.[10] What has escaped critical analysis is the ambiguity of the word blood, which surely refers not simply to blood shed on the battlefield, but also to "Ties of birth or heredity, esp. those connecting a person to his or her parents or ancestors; family background, lineage, descent; (also more widely) nationality, ethnicity, race."[11] Henry's quarrel with France is about his right to rule that nation as its legitimate king: it is, therefore, a quarrel about blood that will result in blood being spilled. Henry is asserting his hereditary right – which, as the play makes clear in the first act, is by no means legally or morally secure – through his bloodline, to rule the French.[12] Henry's own claim to the English throne, as the history plays also make clear, is weak, which is why he establishes his right as the king of the English through his popular appeal. Therefore, his right to rule France, as Williams surely recognizes, is a racial one based on an English national identity, asserting the superiority of England over France, that the king needs to activate in order to inspire his troops. It is a high-risk strategy, as this scene demonstrates, but he wins the battle and all is well.

An equally startling dramatic exchange occurs in the opening scene of *King Richard II*. The conflict between Thomas Mowbray, duke of Norfolk, and Henry Bolingbroke, duke of Hereford, the future King Henry IV, is narrated in Shakespeare's sources, Hall's *Chronicle* (1548) and Holinshed's *Chronicles* (1577, 1587). Holinshed, however, does not draw attention to the matter of blood, as Mowbray does.[13] When Bolingbroke declares that Mowbray is a "traitor and a miscreant" and that "With a foul traitor's name stuff I thy throat," Mowbray responds with a long, eloquent challenge that declares that speech must now give way to "knightly trial by combat" (1.1.39, 44). Mowbray states that there is no other way of arbitration in their quarrel:

> The blood is hot that must be cooled for this:
> Yet can I not of such tame patience boast
> As to be hushed and nought at all to say.
> First, the fair reverence of your highness curbs me
> From giving reins and spurs to my free speech,
> Which else would post until it had returned
> These terms of treason doubled down his throat.
> Setting aside his high blood's royalty,
> And let him be no kinsman to my liege,
> I do defy him, and I spit at him,
> Call him a slanderous coward and a villain;
> Which to maintain, I would allow him odds
> And meet him, were I tied to run afoot
> Even to the frozen ridges of the Alps,
> Or any other ground inhabitable
> Where ever Englishman durst set his foot.
> Meantime let this defend my loyalty:
> By all my hopes, most falsely doth he lie.
>   (1.1.51–68)

Mowbray's speech is replete with deceptions, half-truths, and ironies. Mowbray had indeed committed crimes and was probably involved in the murder of the king's uncle, Thomas of Woodstock, duke of

Gloucester, in 1397, the year before this quarrel, as Bolingbroke makes clear in his response (100), and as Holinshed's *Chronicles* stated. What an Elizabethan audience would have understood is that Mowbray did not commit this and other crimes because he was a traitor, but because he had been loyal to Richard who had ordered him to murder his uncle. If Mowbray is a traitor, then so is the king he has served so loyally. Mowbray reminds the audience that he does not have the luxury of free speech and so cannot answer Bolingbroke honestly, his silence required to hide the king's crimes.

Looked at another way, the real traitor is Bolingbroke, the man who opposes the king's interests and later has him deposed and murdered so that he can assume the throne himself. The conflict we have before us – which is resolved when both Mowbray and Bolingbroke are exiled – is not between a traitor and a loyal subject, but two men who could both be classified as traitors, overseen by a judge who could also be seen as a traitor. Mowbray boasts that he will declare his loyalty wherever Englishmen set foot, appealing to a shared English identity that he represents wherever he appears. In doing so Mowbray speaks truer than he realizes: Bolingbroke will overthrow the king and take his place, the very definition of treachery, and he, Mowbray, will be exiled for his loyalty and so will have to declare his allegiance abroad to the king who used him and banished him (Mowbray died in Venice on 22 September 1399, eight days before the reign of Henry IV began: his death is noted at the start of Act 4).

Identity exists in the blood and through inherited bloodlines. Mowbray has already imagined his banishment through his image of Englishmen wandering in the frozen ridges of the Alps. When Richard pronounces the sentence of perpetual exile after he has intervened to prevent their duel, Mowbray makes clear that an Englishman in exile cannot be defined by his speech, which he will have to abandon, just as he cannot be classified as English because of his location:

> The language I have learnt these forty years,
> My native English, now I must forego,
> And now my tongue's use is to me no more
> Than an unstringed viol or a harp,
> Or like a cunning instrument cased up –
> Or, being open, put into his hands
> That knows no touch to tune the harmony.
> Within my mouth you have engaoled my tongue,
> Doubly portcullised with my teeth and lips;
> And dull unfeeling barren Ignorance

Is made my gaoler to attend on me.
I am too old to fawn upon a nurse,
Too far in years to be a pupil now.
What is thy sentence then but speechless death,
Which robs my tongue from breathing native breath?
(1.3.159–73)

Shakespeare draws attention to language and so forces the audience to think about what actually constitutes an individual's national or racial identity. Mowbray, despite having lost his home and his language, still imagines himself to be English and is determined to assert his true loyalty. He is fortunate that he dies just before the accession of Henry IV and so is never actually declared a traitor. The key element in his understanding of himself, as the exchange with Bolingbroke makes clear, is his blood.

Blood is an indication of nobility and an elevated social identity (as only those with a documented genealogy could boast of having a bloodline that defined them), and a word used to define the nature of treason. Edward Coke (1552–1634), the most significant legal figure in Elizabethan and Jacobean England, who successfully prosecuted both Robert Devereux, second earl of Essex, and Sir Walter Raleigh for treason, described the punishment of a convicted traitor:

> Implied in this judgement is, first, the forfeiture of all his manors, lands, tenements [buildings], and hereditaments [inherited property], in fee simple or fee tail [i.e., with unrestricted and restricted rent], of whomsoever they be holden; secondly, his wife to lose her dower; thirdly, he shall lose his children, for they become base and ignoble; fourthly, he shall lose his posterity, for his blood is stained and corrupted, and they cannot inherit to him or any other ancestor; fifthly, all his goods and chattels, etc. And reason is that his body, lands, goods, posterity, etc., should be torn, pulled asunder, and destroyed, that intended to tear and destroy the majesty of government. And all these several punishments are found for treason in Holy Scripture . . .
>
> Corruption of blood, and that the Children of a Traitor should not inherit, appeareth also by holy scripture.[14]

Mowbray's (noble) English identity is defined through his blood, as it cannot be defined through a language he is no longer able to speak, nor through his residence in the country he loves as a patriotic subject of the Crown. The accusations of treason draw attention to the significance of blood in imagining his race and now that blood is deemed corrupt and tainted, all that is left to him after the confiscation of his lands and property. Accordingly, Mowbray is simultaneously English and not-

English (as an enemy of the Crown), his corrupted blood leaving him between the two identities.

Throughout the history plays blood is used as a marker of race and identity, whether in a more democratic sense as in *Henry V*, or in a more restricted and elite sense as in *Richard II*. Having banished Mowbray and Bolingbroke, Richard travels to visit his uncle, John of Gaunt, who wishes to see him one last time before he dies. Before Richard arrives Gaunt declares his fears for England under Richard's rule, contrasting his vision of the ideal nation to the corrupt realm: "That England, that was wont to conquer others / Hath made a shameful conquest of itself" (2.1.65–66). Gaunt represents England in glorious terms, an ideal version that has never and will never actually exist:

> This royal throne of kings, this sceptered isle,
> This earth of majesty, this seat of Mars,
> This other Eden, demi-paradise,
> This fortress built by Nature for herself
> Against infection and the hand of war,
> This happy breed of men, this little world,
> This precious stone set in the silver sea,
> Which serves it in the office of a wall
> Or as a moat defensive to a house
> Against the envy of less happier lands,
> This blessed plot, this earth, this realm, this England,
> This nurse, this teeming womb of royal kings,
> Feared by their breed and famous by their birth . . .
>
> (2.1.40–52)

England, of course, is not a "sceptered isle," and was not when Shakespeare's play was first performed (1595). A few years later the multiple kingdoms ruled by the English Crown did mean that the island of which England is a part was ruled by one monarch, but that monarch was James VI, king of Scotland (r.1567–1625), who became king of England and Ireland too in 1603. Only by ceasing to have a line of English kings could England become equated in any meaningful sense with the whole territory of the island, the gem set in the sea, surrounded by a defensive moat.

Gaunt's famous speech, all too often read as if it could be taken at face value, points to the problem of equating land and people, and, therefore, understanding the identity of a race as a distinct and separate entity.[15] Once Richard has arrived, Gaunt and the king spar over specific words, first quibbling over the nature of the verb "flatter" and the noun "flatterer" to determine the nature of Richard's kingship (2.1.85–100), passing meanings back and forth. They then turn to blood when Richard reacts angrily to Gaunt's characterization of Richard's England as a land in which the law has been perverted to serve the king's own interests. Richard interjects:

> A lunatic lean-witted fool,
> Presuming on an ague's privilege!
> Darest with thy frozen admonition
> Make pale our cheek, chasing the royal blood
> With fury from his native residence?
>   (2.1.115–19)

According to Richard, noble royal blood must be allowed to rule as the current king sees fit. Richard casts himself as the natural ruler who should be left alone to govern. He thinks himself to be one of a "happy race of kings" (*Richard III*, 5.3.152), as the ghosts of the princes murdered in the tower by his namesake, Richard III, urge Henry, earl of Richmond, later King Henry VII, to become. Richard II sees himself as the guarantor of Englishness, the latest in a line conceived and nursed by the fertile land to protect and nurture it, as Gaunt's speech states.

Gaunt turns Richard's image against him. Richard states that if Gaunt were not Edward III's son, he would be executed for treason, a boast that proves Gaunt's point that Richard uses the law as a means of furthering his own interests:

> Now, by my seat's right royal majesty,
> Wert thou not brother to great Edward's son,
> This tongue that runs so roundly in thy head
> Should run thy head from thy unreverent shoulders!
>   (2.1.120–23)

Gaunt responds with obvious impatience:

> O, spare me not, my brother Edward's son,
> For that I was his father Edward's son.
> That blood already, like the pelican,
> Hast thou tapped out and drunkenly caroused.
> My brother Gloucester, plain well-meaning soul . . .
>   (2.1.124–28)

Gaunt's meaning is that Richard has already persecuted his own family, having had Thomas of Woodstock killed, and so he has little time for his hypocritical pieties about blood relations. The pelican was thought to nurture its young by pecking its breast and was often cited as a symbol of Christ's sacrifice on the cross for mankind.[16] Here, Richard does the opposite, behaving like the proverbially ungrateful offspring of the pelican, who drink the parent's blood. Instead of sacrificing himself for his country, Richard, according to Gaunt, sacrifices it to his own selfish desires. The current ruler from the "race of kings" is in danger of cutting off the sacred bloodline through his poor behavior, a prescient observation that an audience would have understood as a prediction of Richard's terrible fate. He is the last of the undisputed line of Plantagenet kings, a dynasty that had begun when Henry II was crowned in 1154. Although the dynasty would not finally end until 1485 with the accession of the Tudors (hence the murdered princes' plea to Richmond in *Richard III* to found a new dynasty), from the death of Richard II the throne was always disputed, as the sequence of Shakespeare's history plays that make up the first and second tetralogies record. Richard II is not the monarch who nurtures and protects the English but a foolish king whose behavior leads to centuries of bloodshed and civil war. Like Mowbray he can be seen as a traitor, who has corrupted his bloodline and, in doing so, tainted his race and the race of the English to which his family belong.

King John (before 1598) is as obsessed with notions of blood (and race) as *Richard II*. Like Richard, John is a problematic ruler. He is now best known as the incompetent younger brother of the mighty warrior, Richard I, who persecuted Robin Hood through his stooge, the sheriff of Nottingham, and waged war so ineptly against the barons that he was forced to sign the Magna Carta (1215) guaranteeing his subjects liberty. John is invariably characterized as selfish, cowardly, and conniving.[17] In the early modern period, however, he was often portrayed as a flawed king with many redeeming features, struggling to defend England against the tyranny of a corrupt, self-interested Church under the sway of the Pope.[18] It is hardly surprising, therefore, that the play is particularly concerned with issues of race and identity as it explores the complicated nature of Englishness.

John's succession was disputed. As younger brother of Richard I he had a claim to the throne, which was challenged by Arthur, his nephew and son of his deceased older brother, Geoffrey. In the opening scene of the play two different claims of legitimacy are juxtaposed. Chatillion, the French ambassador, asserts Arthur's right to the English throne through inheritance; and Robert Faulconbridge disputes the claim of his elder brother, Philip, to his father's estates on the grounds that he is the illegitimate son of Richard I. John and his mother Queen Eleanor (of Aquitaine) admit that their claim is not secure but resolve to fight the French-supported Arthur because John has one crucial advantage over Arthur:

ELEANOR   What now, my son! have I not ever said
　　　How that ambitious Constance would not cease
　　　Till she had kindled France and all the world,
　　　Upon the right and party of her son?
　　　This might have been prevented and made whole
　　　With very easy arguments of love,
　　　Which now the manage of two kingdoms must
　　　With fearful bloody issue arbitrate.

KING JOHN   Our strong possession and our right for us.
ELEANOR   Your strong possession much more than your right,
　　　Or else it must go wrong with you and me:
　　　So much my conscience whispers in your ear,
　　　Which none but heaven and you and I shall hear.

                                                    (1.1.31–43)

There is an admission that right may not be on their side, but John has possession of the crown, which, as an old proverb advised, "is eleven points of the law."[19] Moreover, a disputed claim would lead to civil war, which would do untold damage to the country, as Shakespeare dramatizes in the plays depicting the later quarrel between the houses of York and Lancaster. Eleanor and John merge selfish and practical reasons in their defense of John's right.

The solution to the Faulconbridge dispute is equally problematic. Philip abandons his claim when he realizes that there is no case to answer as he is the son of the late king, resembling him so strongly that there can be no doubt of his parentage. Instead, he accepts a knighthood granted by the king, who is impressed with his indomitable spirit and wants him to serve in his army in France. The Bastard, as he is known throughout the play, delivers a soliloquy in which he celebrates his good fortune and asserts that the times are propitious for ambitious men like him:

　　　But this is worshipful society
　　　And fits the mounting spirit like myself;
　　　For he is but a bastard to the time
　　　That doth not smack of observation;
　　　And so am I, whether I smoke or no;
　　　And not alone in habit and device,
　　　Exterior form, outward accoutrement,
　　　But from the inward motion to deliver
　　　Sweet, sweet, sweet poison for the age's tooth
                                                    (1.1.205–13)

England not only has a king with a faulty claim to the throne but one of his most able supporters is illegitimate, a sign that England was in the hands of those without the obvious support of a pure bloodline. Accordingly, we might describe Shakespeare's representation of John's realm as racially mongrel (especially if we bear in mind that his mother was French).

John's reign is hard and he is constantly beset by powerful enemies. Accordingly, he has mixed success in holding off the French and preserving England's independence. Eventually he is poisoned by a monk when staying at Swinstead Abbey, Lincolnshire. John's death is very clearly described in terms of treason and the corruption of the blood. His son, Prince Henry (about to become Henry III), states that "the life of all his blood / Is touch'd corruptibly" (5.7.1–2) and John himself later acknowledges that "the poison / Is as a fiend confin'd to tyrannize / On unreprievable condemned blood" (5.7.46–48). John is represented as a traitor, in terms that explicitly recall the words in treason acts – although the corruption of his blood dies with him and is not inherited by his son. England under John is a corrupted country, and the English are a race with a mixed identity, mingling good and bad (like the Bastard).

Shakespeare demonstrates throughout the history plays that not only are nations never inviolable fortresses with impenetrable borders, but also the peoples they contain are never pure either. John of Gaunt's description of England is a dangerous fantasy. Nations trade, accept refugees, accumulate prisoners, people choose to settle in different countries, and they intermarry. Perhaps this is most true of the ruling class, as monarchs usually marry the offspring of monarchs from other countries rather than their own subjects, which is a more dangerous practice, making a particular faction especially powerful. The point is demonstrated in the final act of *King Henry V*, when the King woos Katherine, daughter of Charles VI of France, the king he has just defeated. The scene is delivered in a mixture of English and French – Franglais – with a series of crude double entendres, highlighted through the use of the translator, Alice. Henry offers to kiss the lips of his future bride, to which Katherine replies:

KATHERINE Les dames et demoiselles pour être baisées devant leur noces, il n'est pas la coutume de France.
KING Madam my interpreter, what says she?
ALICE Dat it is not be de fashion pour les ladies of France – I cannot tell vat is baiser en Anglish

(5.2.256–60)

The French verb "baiser" means both to "kiss" and to "fuck," so this scene of fumbled and confused courtesies directs the audience's attention to what happens after a marriage takes place, and the consequent production of children. In this case, the child was Henry VI, whose story had already been represented on the stage. Henry, like his father, married into French royalty, his bride being the formidable Margaret of Anjou (1430–82). If his father's marriage led to a union and a short period of stability and peace after war, Henry VI's reign saw the loss of English possessions in France and a brutal civil war at home, in which Queen Margaret, as Shakespeare's plays demonstrated, played a vital and active role.[20] The union of the Crowns had different outcomes. Both marriages, however, are a reminder that nations and races can never be self-sufficient as they have to rely on interaction with others, sometimes to good effect, at others, rather less successfully.

Henry V probably makes the audience more aware of this need than any other Shakespeare play. The English may trounce the French against all the odds, but it is made clear that, for all their profession of mutual hostility, the two nations have been closely intertwined and will be so again in the future.[21] The French, as the Dauphin points out, had ruled England since the Norman Conquest. Now their offspring have returned to invade France:

FRENCH KING   'Tis certain he hath passed the river Somme.
CONSTABLE   And if he be not fought withal, my lord,
      Let us not live in France; let us quit all
      And give our vineyards to a barbarous people.
DAUPHIN   *O Dieu vivant!* shall a few sprays of us,
      The emptying of our fathers' luxury,
      Our scions, put in wild and savage stock,
      Spirt up so suddenly into the clouds
      And overlook their grafters?
BOURBON   Normans, but bastard Normans, Norman bastards!

      . . .

DAUPHIN   By faith and honour,
      Our madams mock at us, and plainly say
      Our mettle is bred out and they will give
      Their bodies to the lust of English youth,
      To new-store France with bastard warriors.

                                        (3.5.1–10, 27–31)

The French have helped to make England what it is and now they will pay the heavy consequences. The interbreeding of Norman-French and English has created a vigorous hybrid race who now threaten to defeat their purebred relations. The French court wishes to see them as upstarts who must and will be crushed, but the audience knows better. The Bastard Faulconbridge serves King John's forces against France well because of his royal blood; here the bastard Anglo-Normans return to France to wreak revenge, a potent combination of noble French and ordinary English bloodstock, their army joined by the Irish, Welsh, and Scots. As the history plays demonstrate, racial purity is as undesirable as it is impossible.

Notes

1 For analysis, see Philip Edwards, *Threshold of a Nation: A Study in English and Irish Drama* (Cambridge University Press, 1979), 74–86; Michael Neill, "Broken English and Broken Irish: Nation, Language, and the Optic of Power in Shakespeare's Histories," *Shakespeare Quarterly* 45 (1994): 1–32; Rebecca Steinberger, *Shakespeare and Twentieth-Century Irish Drama: Conceptualizing Identity and Staging Boundaries* (Aldershot: Ashgate, 2008), 24–30.

2 "A large aggregate of communities and individuals united by factors such as common descent, language, culture, history, or occupation of the same territory, so as to form a distinct people. Now also: such a people forming a political state; a political state" (*OED*, nation, n.1, I.1.a).

3 James Shapiro, *1599: A Year in the Life of William Shakespeare* (London: Faber and Faber, 2005), 93–118.

4 Willy Maley, "Review of David Cairns and Shaun Richards, *Writing Ireland: Colonialism, Nationalism and Culture*," *Textual Practice* 3 (1989): 291–98.

5 See David J. Baker, "'Wildehirissheman:' Colonialist Representation in Shakespeare's *Henry V*," *ELR* 22 (1992): 37–61.

6 Markku Peltonen, *The Duel in Early Modern England: Civility, Politeness and Honour* (Cambridge University Press, 2003), 3–4.

7 Geraldine Heng, "The Invention of Race in the European Middle Ages I: Race Studies, Modernity, and the Middle Ages," *Literature Compass* 8/5 (2011), 258–74 (at 268).

8 Heng, 267. See also Robert Bartlett, "Medieval and Modern Concepts of Race and Ethnicity," *Journal of Medieval and Early Modern Studies* 31 (2001): 39–56.

9 For the racial implications of "tawny," see Thompson's introduction above, p. 2.

10 See, for example, Andrew Hadfield, "*Henry V*," in *A Companion to Shakespeare's Works*, vol. II: *The Histories*, ed. Richard Dutton and Jean E. Howard (Oxford and Malden, MA: Blackwell, 2003), 459.

11 *OED*, blood, n., 2.7.a.

12 Peltonen, 99.

13 *Narrative and Dramatic Sources of Shakespeare*, ed. Geoffrey Bullough, 8 vols. (London: Routledge, 1960), vol. III, 383–94.

14 Edward Coke, *The Third Part of the Institutes of the Laws of England* (London, 1669), 211. See also J.R. Tanner, *Tudor Constitutional Documents, A.D. 1485–1603, with an Historical Commentary* (Cambridge University Press, 1930), 432; *The Tudor Constitution: Documents and Commentary*, ed. G.R. Elton (Cambridge University Press, 1960), 80.

15 Christopher Lee, *This Sceptered Isle: The Making of the British* (London: Constable, 1997), uses Gaunt's lines and applies them to the British.

16 George Ferguson, *Signs & Symbols in Christian Art* (Oxford University Press, 1961), 23.

17 Graham E. Seel, *King John: An Underrated King* (London: Anthem Press, 2012), 4–10.

18 George Peele, *The Troublesome Reign of John, King of England*, ed. Charles R. Forker (Manchester University Press, 2011), 31–50.

19 Morris Palmer Tilley, *A Dictionary of the Proverbs in England in the Sixteenth and Seventeenth Centuries* (Ann Arbor: University of Michigan Press, 1950), 487.

20 On Margaret, see Helen Castor, *She-Wolves: The Women Who Ruled England before Elizabeth* (London: Faber and Faber, 2010), 4.

21 See Ardis Butterfield, *The Familiar Enemy: Chaucer, Language and Nation in the Hundred Years War* (Oxford University Press, 2009).

CHAPTER 6

Race in Shakespeare's Tragedies

Carol Mejia LaPerle
Wright State University

The only surviving visual artifact representing a black character in Shakespeare is Peacham's 1595 sketch of Aaron the Moor in *Titus Andronicus* (Figure 6.1). The sketch is relatively bare, yet the sparse outlines reveal how ideas about racial difference operate not just in this tragedy, but also in Shakespeare's other tragedies. Aaron's skin is darkened using technologies of the stage to change a white actor into a black character. He is on the side of the imprisoned spoils of war, and yet he appears separate from them as well. Outside the Goth court's kneeling tableau, Aaron's figure disrupts the symmetry of the scene. He is the fourth figure on the right – neither compliant prisoner nor officiating victor – with the dividing line of the imperial staff separating three Romans from three Goths. Aaron is neither of these cultural identities, rendering his physical and cultural difference as a Moor central to his characterization. But this difference is complicated by his erotic affair with the Goth queen Tamora. As her lover, Aaron is an outsider who nonetheless has direct access to the highest levels of power. A black figure who looms over the white characters, he points his finger and his sword at the scene before him. Is the pointed finger a rhetorical threat? Is the raised sword a physical one? And to whom are they directed? Leaving ambivalent his reaction to the submissive Goth court or to the imperial Roman guards, the sketch nonetheless creates an impression of a threatening outsider. These aspects of race in the primitive sketch – stage prosthetics of racial impersonation, ambivalence about the allures and the dangers of social outsiders, cultural codes mobilized in the visually stark juxtaposition of dark and light, and a glimpse of early modern English society's preoccupation with those somatically and culturally different from the dominant culture – are put to relief in many of Shakespeare's other tragedies.

White actors impersonated non-white characters on Shakespeare's stage using blackening techniques inherited from the Church-sponsored

Figure 6.1   Henry Peacham's sixteenth-century sketch of *Titus Andronicus* offers one of
the earliest examples of early modern stage craft and racecraft.

morality plays of the medieval period, when demons were depicted as
black. Darkening methods, such as burnt cork rubbed on faces or fitted
black cloth to convey dark limbs, resonated with Shakespeare's audience as
an aspect of the theatrical experience.[1] Consequently, the mimetic aspect
of religious theatre filters into common language that equates blackness
with the devil himself. In a genre of extreme reactions to dire circumstances that are, in Aristotle's definition of tragedy, "serious, complete, and
of a certain magnitude," references to hell intensify the drama.[2] When Lear
curses, he equates hellish torture to a dark pit: "there's hell, there's
darkness, / There's the sulphurous pit, burning, scalding, stench, consumption!" (4.6.128–29). In *Hamlet,* as Laertes avenges his father's death,
he swears "To hell, allegiance! Vows, to the blackest devil!" (4.5.148),
indicating not just the color of hell but the hue of devils. Macbeth's
entrance into Hecate's lair is accompanied by "black spirits" (4.1.44).
His summons, "How now, you secret, black, and midnight hags?"
(4.1.48), announces the expected association between blackness and the
amplified language of dismay, anxiety, or ominousness. These examples
might seem like mere speech acts, conventionalizing in secular drama what
was a stage technology of religious theatre; but the blackening of evil, when
it comes to depicting race, is not empty rhetoric.

How does the conventional rhetoric that equates blackness with evil come to mean something beyond a linguistic curse? In Shakespeare's tragedies, it is precisely the routine portrayals of the devil as black that has inculcated into the English imagination a particular response to the prosthetics and cosmetics worn to convey non-white characters.[3] For instance, Brabantio's reference to Othello's "sooty bosom" as something "to fear, not to delight!" (1.2.71–72) articulates the expected emotional response to darkened skin. Later in the play, as Othello assesses his reaction to Desdemona's suspected infidelity, distrust alters the color of her character: "Her name, that was as fresh / As Dian's visage, is now begrimed and black / As mine own face." (3.3.441–43). In her fallen, begrimed state, Desdemona elicits scorn and suspicion.[4] Such moments are grounded in a powerful cultural memory that associated scorn and suspicion with begrimed, pigmented characters.[5] Thus, conventional curses turn into something else: instruction for how physical difference is to be perceived, especially in a genre of fraught, grim encounters. In a pivotal scene in *Titus Andronicus*, when the titular character laments the death of a fly, his brother justifies the killing thus: "it was a black ill-favoured fly, / Like to the empress' Moor. Therefore I killed him" (3.2.67–68). The quip inspires an outlandish response from Titus that exaggerates, and to an extent parodies, the madness expected of revengers:

> Oh, Oh, Oh!
> Then pardon me for reprehending thee,
> For thou hast done a charitable deed,
> Give me thy knife; I will insult on him,
> Flattering myself as if it were the Moor
> Come hither purposely to poison me.
> [*takes knife and strikes*]
> There's for thyself, and that's for Tamora.
> Ah, sirrah!
> Yet I think we are not brought so low
> But that between us we can kill a fly
> That comes in likeness of a coal-black Moor.
> (3.2.69–79)

Although trafficking in the ridiculous, the scene of killing a fly "as if it were the Moor" exhibits the pedagogical inclinations of Shakespeare's representation of blackness.[6] To be black is to be a harbinger of social disaster, to be that which "comes hither to poison." The scene literalizes the meaning of, and consequently the appropriate reaction to, a "coal-black Moor." Through the gruesome events that follow, the play teaches its audience to read the black body as a catalyst to social disruption. Indeed, prosthetic-based impersonation is a surface phenomenon that goes deep.

Because tragedies are often preoccupied with interiority as much as with outward actions, they spend a lot of time elaborating on thoughts, motivations, and passions. Some of Shakespeare's famous characterizations display this tendency to dilate contemplation: Hamlet's existential musings, Macbeth's paranoid justifications, or Brutus' personal scrutiny prior to joining Julius Caesar's assassins are some examples. In many such portrayals, looking inward reveals the burdens and conflicts of conscience. When Macbeth realizes the threat of the Prince of Cumberland to his ascendency, the shame of his immoral ambition must be hidden:

> Stars, hide your fires;
> Let not light see my black and deep desires.
> The eye wink at the hand, yet let that be
> Which the eye fears, when it is done, to see.
>
> (1.4.57–60).

Thoughts of murder render his conscience dark and doomed. When Queen Gertrude, in *Hamlet*, is made aware of her transgressions, she begs her accusing son to

> speak no more!
> Thou turn'st my eyes into my very soul
> And there I see such black and grainèd spots
> As will not leave their tinct.
>
> (3.4.90–93)

Personal flaws and secret sins emerge as the hallmark of the genre's moral inquests. The references to black tint convey the compromised aspects of one's interiority, the alteration of one's soul. Introspective tendencies – in the privileging of thought over action – belie the genre's dependence on blackness as a potent metaphor for damnation. But some plays merge the figurative with the literal, as in Aaron's villainous declaration: "Let fools do good, and fair men call for grace; / Aaron will have his soul black like his face" (*Titus Androcicus*, 3.1.203–04). In tragedy's compulsive turning inward, black becomes the outward, ocular proof of sin.

Aaron's bold declaration of evil reveals that Shakespeare conveyed overdetermined villainizations of raced characters in ways shared by others of his stage, such as Christopher Marlowe's Barabas in *The Jew of Malta* or Thomas Dekker's Eleazar in *Lust's Dominion*. However, although tragedies provide an archive of characters whose physical difference signifies ethnic, cultural, and religious dissimilarity from the white, English, Protestant norm, the genre also addresses the culture's growing fascination with racial difference beyond the stage.[7] In reality, everyday interactions in early modern life and textual accounts produced by a transnational print industry offered opportunities to complicate English understanding of others.[8] Take, for instance, Richard Knolles's 1603 *Generall Historie of the Turkes*, an important context for understanding Shakespeare's portrayal of Moors like Aaron and Othello. Beyond textual accounts, the presence of diplomatic agents such as Moroccan ambassador Abd el-Ouahed ben Messaoud reveal Mediterranean and English political, social, and economic exchanges.[9] In providing Othello with the power to speak of his "proud fortune," Shakespeare conjures the royal houses of the Mediterranean and Northern Africa:

> 'Tis yet to know
> Which, when I know that boasting is an honor,
> I shall promulgate – I fetch my life and being
> From men of royal siege, and my demerits
> May speak unbonneted to as proud a fortune
> As this that I have reached.
>
> (1.2.19–24)

Other essays in this volume develop the social, religious, and geopolitical implications of Moors, thus offering complex analyses of foreigners in the English imagination. When Othello narrates the details of courtship, of "How [he] did thrive in this fair lady's love, / And she in mine" (1.3.127–28), he recounts "She loved me for the dangers I had passed, / And I loved her that she did pity them" (1.3.169–70). Moments like this invite a more nuanced acknowledgement of how racial difference does not preclude attraction, affection, and love.[10] At the beginning of the play, Desdemona and Othello's marriage indicates that multidimensional reactions to the "extravagant and wheeling stranger / Of here and everywhere" (1.1.139–40) are possible.

Erotic attachments in *Antony and Cleopatra* portray the allures of the dark-skinned woman.[11] Cleopatra's nostalgic reference to "Phoebus' amorous pinches black" (1.5.28) characterizes the charms of her "tawny front" (1.1.6). The attractiveness of dark skin is also explored in Shakespeare's sonnet sequence. His innovation of the "dark lady sonnets" rejects the common disparagements against black femininity.[12] The poems insist that "now is black beauty's successive heir" (127, 3), arguing the dark features of his mistress are superior to light-skinned beauties'; furthermore claiming "Thy black is fairest in my judgment's place" (131, 12). However, these attachments are often tinged with suspicions of intemperate sexuality, or what the opening of *Antony and Cleopatra* depicts as "the gypsy's lust" (1.1.9). In *King Lear*, Edgar rants in the guise of Poor Tom: "Wine loved I deeply, dice dearly, and in woman out-paramoured the Turk" (3.4.91), conveying the sexual proclivity and social transgression attributed to the perceived excessiveness of foreigners. Addressing Cleopatra, Antony voices his deeper paranoia about what he does, and does not, know of his lover:

> ... besides what hotter hours
> Unregistered in vulgar fame you have
> Luxuriously picked out. For I am sure,
> Though you can guess what temperance should be,
> You know not what it is.
>
> (3.13.119–23)

His insults reveal his obsession with Cleopatra's sexual appetites. The slippage from suspicious alliances to hidden degeneracies to intemperate constitution evokes a cluster of ideas about racial difference as exotic, desirable, but ultimately suspicious.[13] Antony's attachment to Cleopatra becomes an embarrassment from which his military cause will not recover:

> Betrayed I am.
> O this false soul of Egypt! This grave charm,
> Whose eye becked forth my wars and called them home,
> Whose bosom was my crownet, my chief end,
> Like a right gipsy hath at fast and loose
> Beguiled me to the very heart of loss.
>
> (4.13.24–29)

The appeal of the Egyptian queen inspires devotion, but it is ultimately characterized as deceptive and dangerous. Adoration is tinged with an indictment of the sexual practices and social deviance of the foreign beauty.

Antony expresses an anxious paranoia about miscegenation as a challenge to social and racial stability.[14] One of the most glaring indications of this panic is the opening of *Othello*, when Iago disturbs the streets of Venice to wake Desdemona's father:

> Zounds, sir, you're robbed. For shame, put on your gown!
> Your heart is burst. You have lost half your soul.
> Even now, now, very now, an old black ram
> Is tupping your white ewe. Arise, arise!
> Awake the snorting citizens with the bell,
> Or else the devil will make a grandsire of you.
>
> (1.1.88–93)

Iago's racist insults conjoin multiple forms of transgression: social chaos (theft of property), bestiality (black ram/white ewe), and monstrous lineage (demon grandchild).[15] Miscegenation, in his malicious logic, turns humans into animals and one's kin into the damned. The formidable racism that Iago unleashes at the beginning of the play, as an attack on the lovers as well as a diminishment of their progeny, echoes the report of Aaron and Tamora's mixed-race child in *Titus Andronicus*: "A joyless, dismal, black, and sorrowful issue! / Here is the babe, as loathsome as a toad / Amongst the fair-faced breeders of our clime" (4.2.67–69). Thus, miscegenation is a lightning rod that ignites some of the worst language of dehumanization in descriptions of racial difference. However, it is worth noting that the speakers of this babble are Iago and the nurse – two characters who either mindlessly or maliciously ventriloquize xenophobic racism. In response to the nurse, Aaron conveys a devotion to protecting his son that far exceeds any other parent in the play, declaring the infant "The vigor and the picture of my youth. / This before all the world do I prefer" (4.2.109–10). A few lines after Iago's racist rant, Othello proudly and eloquently articulates the sincerity of his love, the integrity of his service, and the dignity of his countenance: "My parts, my title, and my perfect soul / Shall manifest me rightly" (1.2.31–32). In other words, as much as miscegenation mobilizes anxieties about sexual reproduction in relation to race, the tragedies provide opportunities for exploring desire across racial identities and convey moments of profound dignity by racialized characters.

Nonetheless, the domestic possibilities of mixed-race families are problematized by the state implications of their union.[16] Miscegenation is a threat to lineage that goes beyond the family line. Antony pronounces his belated esteem of Roman bonds over the lusty allures of Egyptian pleasure by regretting that he has "Forborne the getting of a lawful race" (3.13.108) when choosing Cleopatra over Octavia. In this formulation, the word race indicates the progeny of his marriage to a Roman woman, but the qualification as "lawful" implicates the question of social legitimacy. Illegitimacy is particularly relevant to the Roman tragedies, whereby racializing structures inform the genre's fixation on the politics of empire.[17] The classical world of Plutarch's *Lives of the Noble Greeks and Romans* is both setting and inspiration for *Titus Andronicus*, *Julius Caesar*, *Antony and Cleopatra*, and *Coriolanus*. Victory and conquest transform these heroes: Caesar's valor starts to look like tyranny, Antony's generosity turns to dotage, Coriolanus' military determination is civic condescension, and Titus' service – sacrificing "five and twenty sons" for the cause –

morphs into a vigilance against his own family. Thus, the time of peace harbors a different kind of conflict. Anxieties about empire, relevant to burgeoning English ambitions to be the heir to Roman ascendency, are often attributed to corruption or illegitimacy, symbolized by the language of blackened virtue or the racialized figures who infiltrate the commonweal. For instance, Aaron saves his son and maintains Tamora's honor by swapping his dark-skinned son for another mixed-race child:

> His child is like to her, fair as you are.
> Go pack with him, and give the mother gold,
> And tell them both the circumstance of all,
> And how by this their child shall be advanced
> And be receivèd for the Emperor's heir,
> And substituted in the place of mine,
> To calm this tempest whirling in the court;
> And let the Emperor dandle him for his own.
>
> (4.2.156–63)

The substitute can "pass" as a Roman and will enjoy the benefits and privileges of being an Emperor's son.[18] Therefore, the threat of miscegenation is that it contaminates lineage at the highest levels of society. English theatregoers would be reminded that victory awards the spoils of war as well as invites the ailments of enemies within.[19]

Roman tragedies dramatize early modern concerns with empire in relation to race, thereby revealing how the stage exploits interest in "strangers" beyond and within England's borders.[20] This is most evident in the vexed status of gypsies who are considered local outcasts and foreign subversives.[21] The association between Egypt and gypsies is an exceptionally glaring error in which gypsies were considered descendants of Egyptians. But this error is nonetheless relevant to stereotypes of gypsies as outlandish, nomadic, and foreign. So entrenched is the problem of gypsies in England that Edgar finds refuge in impersonating the "basest and most poorest shape" (2.3.7) of a begrimed and wandering vagrant in *King Lear*.[22] Through his guise of a gypsy, Edgar enacts the group's disenfranchisement and vexed status in England. Cleopatra likewise signifies the problematic role of the gypsy as a threat both foreign and local. The condemnation of gypsies, codified in social documents and royal proclamations circulating in sixteenth- and seventeenth-century England, reveals anxieties about a population that faced accusations akin to Antony's insults at Cleopatra: unlawfulness, degeneracy, intemperance. England's preoccupation with gypsies criminalizes the exotic, nomadic group's resistance to the priorities of dominant rule in the Roman context and in the

English commonwealth.[23] The paradox of domestic foreignness signals the racializing mechanisms that mark the aliens within one's borders.

Understanding the ambivalence of non-white characters in terms of their allure and exoticism on the one hand, and dangerous potential for undermining the project of English identity on the other, reveals attitudes about race in Shakespeare. This Janus-faced representation can be traced in the juxtaposition of dark and fair throughout the tragedies.[24] When the Duke in *Othello* grants approval of Othello and Desdemona's marriage, he does so under the premise that Othello's physical difference as a black man ultimately upholds the privileges afforded to a dominantly white Venetian state: "If virtue no delighted beauty lack, / Your son-in-law is far more fair than black" (1.3.290–91). This comment establishes "fair" as code for belonging and value. The estimation of whiteness as a reference to skin and to virtue is especially acute in Shakespeare's portrayal of erotic love. In the famous balcony scene of *Romeo and Juliet*, Romeo compares his beloved to the luminosity of heavenly bodies: "The brightness of her cheek would shame those stars / As daylight doth a lamp" (2.2.19–20). Juliet's bright form is valued, beautified, and celebrated as the epitome of the female beloved whose white skin is a sign of outward beauty and inward righteousness. But such praise is often dependent upon the heroine's gendered embodiment of whiteness in relation to black bodies. In describing her, Romeo proclaims:

> O, she doth teach the torches to burn bright!
> It seems she hangs upon the cheek of night
> As a rich jewel in an Ethiop's ear –
> Beauty too rich for use, for Earth too dear.
>
> (1.5.45–48)

Juliet's effect is intensified and rendered precious in relation to the Ethiop, the imagined African woman's skin that is the "cheek of night." That the black/white dynamic emerges as a reference to a precious ornament is no accident. Desdemona too is called a jewel that Othello recognizes as "a pearl . . . richer than all his tribe" (5.2.407). The idealization of fairness as a repository of wealth and beauty mobilizes England's self-fashioning in light of its emergent colonial project. Furthermore, gendered whiteness is the very mise-en-scène of the cathartic function of tragedy.

In drama's fixation on emotional pitch, the dead white woman as "monumental alabaster" is the pinnacle of pathos. Approaching his wife's reposed form, Othello imagines murder not as the destruction of Desdemona's fair beauty and righteous virtues, but rather as the perverted preservation of it: "It is the cause. Yet I'll not shed her blood, / Nor scar that whiter skin of hers than snow, / And smooth as monumental alabaster" (5.2.3–5). Othello's idealized reverence of his wife's flawless white body – a body he is about to murder – captures the fraught, conflicted suffering of his jealous mind and the significance of her lifeless beauty as the catalyst to emotional catharsis. The condensed pathos of tragedy in the figure of the dead white woman is captured in visual culture as well.[25] In Millais's famous painting of the drowned Ophelia, her angelic form floats over a murky, lush, shaded background. Fair face and white hands open to the sky, her beautiful innocence is epitomized and memorialized. Ophelia's death is a crucial contribution to *Hamlet*'s tragic sentiment, precisely in the description of her lifeless form. Juliet is likewise mourned. Upon entering the Capulet vault, Romeo laments "A grave? O, no. A lantern, slaughtered youth, / For here lies Juliet, and her beauty makes / This vault a feasting presence full of light" (5.3.84–86). Juliet's luminous beauty transforms a bleak tomb into a "feasting presence full of light." Expressing Juliet's effect as a "lantern" renders her radiant skin the corrective to actual darkness and antidote to psychological dismay. Again, the appraisal of light against dark condenses the tragedies' paradoxes of transformative yet frozen beauty and endless yet futile devotion. The white woman's lifelessness is not a departure, but rather the ultimate confirmation, of this paradoxical symbolism.

Thus, Shakespeare's tragic female characters are themselves preserved as alabaster monuments: luminous and still, these immortalized shrines to white innocence reinforce fairness as the unquestioned repository of goodness and grace. Through the passive pose of death, these figures are active catalysts to Aristotelian catharsis. To return to the mise-en-scène of Othello's murder of Desdemona, pathos is achieved through the visual differentiation of Othello's tortured dark figure and Desdemona's angelic fair body.[26] Visual representations of the death scene hinge on a white/black dichotomy that underwrites Othello's racial difference as a visual contrast and as a moral indictment. As heavenly rays of light bathe her white skin, Desdemona's virtuous righteousness underwrites a chromatic aesthetic. Concurrently, her husband's impassioned anguish and murderous will are conveyed through the shadows of his tortured soul and the embodied tinting of his skin.[27]

As the tableau of Othello's dismayed black form and Desdemona's restoration to monumental alabaster reveals, race is not incidental to the tragedies' moral and aesthetic claims, but rather central to the genre's attention to philosophical concerns. The scene's visual use of the black/ white binary relies on the immutable essence of blackness as a sign and spectacle of sin, inherited from a linguistic and theatrical tradition. But it also conjures the other part of the binary: the elevation of icons of whiteness. The moral claims and visual aesthetics disseminated by the figure of Othello as a dark-skinned murderer concurrently deposit his wife's fair form with the pathos of innocence lost and virtue discarded. Thus, the binary perpetuates a fundamentally anti-black orientation that underscores the perception of those racially different from, and thus perceived as a threat to, normative English ideals.[28] As if to put pressure on the overdetermined stereotypes of black figures, Aaron ventriloquizes the scripted expectations of society:

> For I must talk of murders, rapes and massacres,
> Acts of black night, abominable deeds,
> Complots of mischief, treason, villainies,
> Ruthful to hear, yet piteously performed.
>
> (5.1.64–67)

He substantiates the suspicion of his "mischief, treason, villainies" with a relish that conveys an intrinsic inclination to evil. Every imaginable infraction reinforces the worst charges against him, and yet Aaron's litany of misdeeds also alerts the audience to the constructedness – "For I must talk", "as the saying is" – of his legendary crimes. Indeed, his racialized embodiment of repulsive, essentialized evil is fundamentally constructed. We are reminded that the performance of racial difference is interpellated through clothing, rhetorical tropes, tinting techniques and, as Aaron makes apparent, the iteration of socially imagined and theatrically assembled speech acts that call attention to its own fashioning. Shakespeare's tragedies reveal how the premodern imaginary considers race as both a mimetic, ephemeral enactment and proof of an essential, inherent difference.[29] As opposed to being hampered by this contradiction, depictions of race often move between fluid, malleable, and unstable expressions of identity, providing a lexicon for the epistemological crisis of tragedy's formation of subjectivity.

Many of Shakespeare's tragedies are concerned with identity as both a social interaction and an individual, private essence, as manifested in Hamlet's theatrically conscious statement about "seeming":

> "Seems," madam? Nay, it is. I know not "seems."
> 'Tis not alone my inky cloak, good mother,
> Nor customary suits of solemn black,

> Nor windy suspiration of forced breath,
> No, nor the fruitful river in the eye,
> Nor the dejected havior of the visage,
> Together with all forms, moods, shapes of grief,
> That can denote me truly. These indeed "seem,"
> For they are actions that a man might play;
> But I have that within which passes show,
> These but the trappings and the suits of woe.
>   (1.2.76–86)

Hamlet insists that "forms, moods, shapes of grief" – the outlines of passionate expression – are ancillary to the emotions themselves. These modes of dejection are socially conscribed and can thus be mimed without true feeling. In making the distinction between "suits of woe" and "that within which passes show," Hamlet professes that a person's essential identity may or may not align with that person's bearing. In *Julius Caesar*, Brutus acknowledges what his look withholds:

> If I have veiled my look
> I turn the trouble of my countenance
> Merely upon myself. Vexed I am
> Of late with passions of some difference,
> Conceptions only proper to myself,
> Which give some soil, perhaps, to my behaviors.
>   (1.2.37–42)

Brutus articulates the problematic link between outward behavior and the passions that shape it. Like Hamlet, he recognizes that society will read external countenance as an indication of personal feeling. But while Hamlet resists this alignment, Brutus offers a way to formulate the connection of private thought to public countenance. However, this connection is unstable, as articulated in Othello's exasperated demand of Iago to "Show me thy thought" (3.3.128), as if another person's interiority could be transparently displayed. But such is the plight of the tragic worldview that no subjectivity is fully accessible. Consider, for instance, Regan's cold observation in *King Lear* that her father "hath ever but slenderly known himself" (1.1.296–97). Lear's spoken demands and public acts are driven by insecurities and desires unclear even to himself. In *Othello*, this discord is exploitable. When Iago dilates the details of his plan to pervert Desdemona's goodwill into evidence of infidelity – in his words, to "turn her virtue into pitch" – he abuses the fissure between performance and intent: "When devils will the blackest sins put on, / They do suggest at first with heavenly shows, / As I do now" (2.3.348, 339–41). While these

passages convey drama's preoccupation with scripted outward performances and problematically inaccessible interiorities, it is worth noticing
how the articulation of tragic subjectivities relies on a racialized vocabulary:
the "inky" cloak of Hamlet's solemnity, the "soiled" countenance of
Brutus' vexation, the function of "pitch" in Iago's malice.[30] Therefore, it
is not just that the language of race *accompanies* depictions of damning
guilt or secret intent or compromised conscience; rather, in the genre's
epistemological exploration of subjectivity as a publicly scripted experience
and a fundamentally separate, and at times inaccessible, essence,
Shakespeare's tragedies engage the multilayered, contradictory template
of racial impersonation.

The ultimate manifestation of tragedy's complex, fissured representation
of selfhood is in Othello's last monologue:

> Speak of me as I am; nothing extenuate,
> Nor set down aught in malice. Then must you speak
> Of one that loved not wisely but too well;
> Of one not easily jealous but, being wrought,
> Perplexed in the extreme; of one whose hand
> Like the base Indian, threw a pearl away
> Richer than all his tribe; of one whose subdued eyes,
> Albeit unused to the melting mood,
> Drops tears as fast as the Arabian trees
> Their medicinal gum. Set you down this;
> And say besides that in Aleppo once,
> Where a malignant and a turbaned Turk
> Beat a Venetian and traduced the state,
> I took by th'throat the circumcised dog
> And smote him, thus. [*He stabs himself.*]
>
> (5.2.352–66)

In his request to "speak of me" and "set you down this," he reclaims a
legacy mired by the public stigma of a jealous, violent blackamoor. Othello
insists that for surviving Venetians to reiterate the stereotype is to do so in
malice. Rather, he qualifies the conditions of his downfall as the effect of
overwrought emotion and the trials of misled judgement. In doing so, he
echoes the heightened affective performance of other noble heroes of
Shakespeare's opus. However, Othello's passionate rhetoric also evokes
exotic "Arabian trees" to convey tears that are uncommon, profound, and
medicinal. Thus, his identity is marked by the fragmented, transnational
orientations of an outsider. Othello occupies the role of a "malignant and
turbaned Turk" who "traduced the state" while simultaneously exercising
his agency the only way available to him: as protector of the Venetian state.

He draws from revenge tragedy's portrayals of bloody recompense, but since his suicide unleashes that violence onto himself, it not only distills the destruction of a wrought, divided identity, but further intensifies the racialized dimensions of tragic conflict.

Considering race as the sum of theatrical technologies, literary tropes, visual effects, or social expectations tells only part of the story of racial formations on the early modern stage. This essay's provocation, however, is that race animates some of the most fundamental issues of inclusion and exclusion that the English looked to tragedy to illuminate. By tracing the projections of savagery, illegitimacy, and villainy onto the raced characters of Shakespeare's tragedies, this overview charts the ways the genre's investments in defining civility, legitimacy, and morality are profoundly intertwined with modes of racialization. Considering early modern England's increasingly transnational engagements with new worlds, foreign states, and religious rivals, what constitutes community, belonging, and value? Whether in classical Rome, or metropolitan Venice, or exoticized Egypt, dramatizations of far-off settings are indeed a meditation on an imagined English commonwealth and its ongoing negotiations with issues of civility, legitimacy, and morality. In this context, the powerful fair/dark binary in literary tropes and visual imagery functions as a manifestation of these border formations between white Englishness and the blackened other – a conceptual border that dramatic stagings mobilize and complicate. And finally, this essay vivifies how racialization, as unstable, flexible, and contradictory as regimes and categories of race tend to be in Shakespeare's plays, nonetheless shapes the form, the performance, and the meaning of tragic subjectivity.

Notes

1 See Ian Smith, "White Skin, Black Masks: Racial Cross-Dressing on the Early Modern Stage," *Renaissance Drama* 32 (2003): 33–67; Virginia Mason Vaughan, *Performing Blackness on English Stages, 1500–1800* (Cambridge University Press, 2005).

2 In Book VI of Aristotle's *Poetics*, he states that "Tragedy, then, is an imitation of an action that is serious, complete, and of a certain magnitude; in the language embellished with each kind of artistic ornament, the several kinds being found in separate parts of the play, the form of action, not of narrative, through pity and fear effecting the proper purgation-catharsis of these and similar emotions." Aristotle, *Poetics*, trans. S.H. Butcher, 4th edn (New York: Dover, 1951), 23.

3 Farah Karim-Cooper, *Cosmetics in Shakespearean and Renaissance Drama* (Edinburgh University Press, 2006, 2012).

4 See Anthony Gerard Barthelemy, *Black Face, Maligned Race: The Representation of Blacks in English Drama from Shakespeare to Southerne* (Baton Rouge: Louisiana State University Press, 1987); Patricia Akhimie, *Shakespeare and the Cultivation of Difference: Race and Conduct in the Early Modern World* (New York and London: Routledge, 2018).

5 Lara Bovilsky, *Barbarous Play: Race on the English Renaissance Stage* (Minneapolis: University of Minnesota Press, 2008).

6 Carol Mejia LaPerle, "'If I might have my will': Aaron's Affect and Race in *Titus Andronicus*," in *Titus Andronicus: The State of Play*, ed. Farah Karim-Cooper (London: Arden Shakespeare, 2019), 135–56.

7 See Bernadette Andrea, *Women and Islam in Early Modern English Literature* (Cambridge University Press, 2007); *Religion and Drama in Early Modern England: The Performance of Religion on the Renaissance Stage*, ed. Jane Hwang Degenhardt and Elizabeth Williamson (New York and London: Routledge, 2013).

8 See Imtiaz Habib, *Black Lives in the English Archives, 1500–1677: Imprints of the Invisible* (Aldershot and Burlington, VT: Ashgate, 2008); Emily Carroll Bartels, *Speaking of the Moor: From Alcazar to Othello* (Philadelphia: University of Pennsylvania Press, 2008).

9 See, Daniel J. Vitkus, *Turning Turk: English Theater and the Multicultural Mediterranean, 1570–1630* (New York and Basingstoke: Palgrave Macmillan, 2003); Jonathan Burton, *Traffic and Turning: Islam and English Drama, 1579–1624* (Newark: University of Delaware Press, 2005); Ambereen Dhadaboy, "Two Faced: The Problem of Othello's Visage," in *Othello: The State of Play*, ed. Lena Cowen Orlin (London: Bloomsbury Arden Shakespeare, 2014), 121–47.

10 Dennis Austin Britton, "Re-'turning' *Othello*: Transformative and Restorative Romance," *ELH* 78/1 (2011): 27–50.

11 See Joyce Green MacDonald, *Women and Race in Early Modern Texts* (Cambridge University Press, 2002); Mira Assaf Kafantaris, *Royal Marriage, Foreign Queens, and Constructions of Race in the Early Modern Period* (forthcoming).

12 Fred Moten, "The Dark Lady and the Sexual Cut: Sonnet Record Frame/ Shakespeare Jones Eisenstein," *Women & Performance: A Journal of Feminist Theory* 9/2 (1997): 143–61.

13 Jyotsna Singh, "Renaissance Anti-Theatricality, Anti-Feminism and Shakespeare's *Antony and Cleopatra*," in *Antony and Cleopatra: William Shakespeare*, ed. John Drakakis (London: Macmillan, 1994), 308–29.

14 See Ian Smith, *Race and Rhetoric in the Renaissance: Barbarian Errors* (New York and Basingstoke: Palgrave Macmillan, 2009); Celia R. Daileader, *Racism, Misogyny, and the Othello Myth: Inter-racial Couples from Shakespeare to Spike Lee* (Cambridge University Press, 2005).

15 See Arthur L. Little, Jr., *Shakespeare Jungle Fever: National-Imperial Re-visions of Race, Rape, and Sacrifice* (Palo Alto, CA: Stanford University Press, 2000); Joyce Green MacDonald, "Black Ram, White Ewe: Shakespeare, Race, and

Women," in *A Feminist Companion to Shakespeare*, 2nd edition, ed. Dympna Callaghan (Malden, MA and Oxford: Wiley Blackwell, 2016), 206–225.

16 David Sterling Brown, "Blackness and Domesticity in Shakespeare's *Titus Andronicus*," in *Titus Andronicus: The State of Play*, ed. Karim-Cooper, 111–34.

17 Ania Loomba, *Shakespeare, Race, and Colonialism* (Oxford University Press, 2002).

18 Francesca T. Royster, "White-Limed Walls: Whiteness and Gothic Extremism in Shakespeare's *Titus Andronicus*," *Shakespeare Quarterly* 51/4 (2000): 423–55.

19 Noémie Ndiaye, "Aaron's Roots: Spaniards, Englishmen, and Blackamoors in *Titus Andronicus*," *Early Theatre* 19/2 (2016): 58–80.

20 See Laura Hunt Yungblut, *Strangers Settled Here Amongst Us: Policies, Perceptions and Presence of Aliens in Elizabethan England* (New York and London: Routledge, 1996); *Shakespeare and Immigration*, ed. Ruben Espinosa and David Ruiter (New York and London: Routledge, 2016).

21 See David Cressy, *Gypsies: An English History* (Oxford University Press, 2018); Sydnee Wagner, *Outlandish People: Gypsies, Race, and Fantasies of National Identity in Early Modern England*, PhD dissertation, City University of New York (2019).

22 Benjamin Minor and Ayanna Thompson, "'Edgar I Nothing Am': Blackface in *King Lear*," in *Staged Transgression in Shakespeare's England*, ed. R. Loughnane and E. Semple (New York and London: Palgrave Macmillan, 2013), 153–64.

23 Carol Mejia LaPerle, "An Unlawful Race: William Shakespeare's Cleopatra and the Crimes of Early Modern Gypsies," *Shakespeare* 13/3 (2017): 226–38.

24 Kim F. Hall, *Things of Darkness: Economies of Race and Gender in Early Modern England* (Ithaca, NY: Cornell University Press, 1995).

25 *Early Modern Visual Culture: Representation, Race, and Empire in Renaissance England*, ed. Peter Erickson and Clark Hulse (Philadelphia: University of Pennsylvania Press, 2000).

26 Arthur L. Little, Jr., "'An essence that's not seen': The Primal Scene of Racism in Othello," *Shakespeare Quarterly* 44 (1993): 304–24.

27 Ayanna Thompson, *Performing Race and Torture on the Early Modern Stage* (New York and London: Routledge, 2008).

28 Matthieu Chapman, *Anti-Black Racism in Early Modern English Drama: The Other "Other"* (New York and London: Routledge, 2017).

29 Ayanna Thompson, *Passing Strange: Shakespeare, Race, and Contemporary America* (Oxford University Press, 2011).

30 Miles Grier, *Reading Black Characters: Atlantic Encounters with Othello 1604–1855* (forthcoming).

CHAPTER 7

Experimental Othello

Matthew Dimmock
University of Sussex

Othello was designed to disappoint. For those early audiences who had been weaned on a diet of drama full of fire and fury, and who sought out plays in which vast armies ranged across distant landscapes, faiths clashed, and bombastic heroes raged, Shakespeare's play repeatedly confounded expectations. Drawn in by the promise of a play tracing the tragic exploits of *Othello, the Moor of Venice*, these initial audiences watched and waited through an opening act that ends with this "strange" protagonist dispatched to the eastern Mediterranean, leading a Venetian fleet "against the general enemy Ottoman" (1.3.50) in a bid to retain their possession of Cyprus. Shakespeare draws upon a long history of Venetian–Ottoman antagonism well known in seventeenth-century Britain to elaborately set up this great conflict only for it to then evaporate, sublimated into something else entirely. All of a sudden nothing is what it seems. Why does he challenge his audience in this way? What might this disappointment tell us about race and religion on the early seventeenth-century stage?

To answer such questions we need to understand what went before. The dramatic paradigms that Shakespeare so spectacularly defies in *Othello* may have been fewer than twenty years old, but they were nevertheless well established. These paradigms began with the huge success of Christopher Marlowe's *Tamburlaine the Great* (1587) and its sequel the following year, two plays which expanded the limits of what was possible on the early modern stage. Marlowe's defiant Scythian hero violently ripped apart the old, established monarchies of the east – destroying the Ottomans and burning the Qur'an in the process – and proceeded to chastise and reform the world in his own image, confronting transfixed theatregoers with an Asian world into which British merchant-diplomats were interpolating themselves with ever greater frequency.[1] Tamburlaine shocked and thrilled in part because he cultivated an intense identification with his audiences, who in turn drew him into a wider popular culture where he was emulated, parodied, and celebrated.[2]

The *Tamburlaine* plays inevitably prompted a swathe of imitations, in which rival dramatists and companies strove to capitalize on their success. The resulting fashion for grandiloquent, bombastic plays centered upon martial conquerors racially and religiously distinct from their largely white, Protestant, English audiences, has become known as the "Turk play" phenomenon.[3] As a term it indicates the way in which the figure of the Great Turk, the Ottoman sultan, came to dominate the genre, but it is nonetheless misleading: Tamburlaine is no Turk, and the "Turk play" is capacious enough to include those plays set in North Africa, such as George Peele's *The Battle of Alcazar* (ca. 1590), which feature no Turks at all. Between the first part of *Tamburlaine* and the first recorded performance of *Othello* (at Whitehall in November 1604) there are at least twenty examples of which evidence remains, and there were probably many more.[4] The establishment of a stock costume followed, borrowed from continental prints and costume books: elaborate, rich robes, a falchion (or scimitar), a turban, and sometimes – for the stage Turk in particular – a moustache.[5] As this suggests, Islam, or "Mahometanism," was also a prominent feature within the broader development of an explicitly spectacular, essentializing dramatic language that used costume, cosmetics, gesture, and voice to enable the expression of different races and religions. Exemplary protagonists repeatedly defined themselves in terms of these stage markers – Turk, Moor, Mahometan – and racialized taxonomies were adapted from chronicles, cosmologies, and the Bible in order to define the subject peoples of the world, as in the parade of Moors, Amazons, pygmies, cannibals, Cataians, and others that concludes the first part of *Tamar Cham* (1592).[6] The success of these plays does not solely reflect Marlowe's influence and the collaboration and competition between theatre companies that immediately followed *Tamburlaine*, but also shifting geopolitical circumstances. Indeed, the relatively rapid shift in focus from Tamburlaine's anti-Ottoman histrionics to a new fixation upon Muslim dynastic history, Islamic–Christian conflict, and later harem culture was a consequence of England's increasing engagement with the Ottomans and North Africa.

The depiction of the Muslim "Turk" Bajazeth in the first of Marlowe's *Tamburlaine* plays embodies the dominant features of long-established Christian polemics against Islam, resurgent in the wake of the Ottoman conquest of Constantinople in 1453 and westward expansion thereafter. However, subsequent plays such as Robert Greene's *Selimus* (1590) and the anonymous *John of Bordeaux* (ca. 1590) began to temper that polemical vision in a way that reflected new English priorities. English figures such as Greene's English clown Bullithrumble appear without warning or context in the Turkish hinterlands to proffer homespun advice to Ottoman princes in an example of the kinds of dislocations that the genre generated. Of course neither Turks nor Moors were ever entirely exempt from caricature, but English dramatists and their audiences were increasingly aware, particularly in the wake of the publication of Richard Hakluyt's *Principal Navigations* (1589) that their queen was conducting a regular correspondence with the Ottoman sultans Murad III and Mehmed III, and the Moroccan king Mulay al-Mansur, and that both the Ottoman Empire and Morocco were now England's commercial allies.[7] The letters and the treaties between them were themselves widely copied and circulated.[8] As one anonymous dramatist wrote in 1594, "The Turke hath sworne never to lift his hand, / To wrong the Princesse of this blessed land."[9] The result of this rush of plays was to push a very particular type of the stranger – a non-native, non-Christian, warlike male – to the fore of the English imagination as never before: so that "even occasional playgoers" became familiar "with visual or verbal images of the Ottoman Empire" and all of the prominent playing companies "maintained a repertoire of 'Turk plays' from the late sixteenth well into the seventeenth century."[10]

Shakespeare had a complicated relationship with the "Turk play" that began some years before the writing of *Othello*. Although there are no obvious examples in his early output, Shakespeare does repeatedly reference the Turk motif in his history plays, in which a rhetoric of crusade is regularly invoked, one that involves fighting for "Jesu Christ in glorious Christian field / Streaming the ensign of the Christian cross" against "black pagans, Turks, and Saracens" (*Richard II*, 4.1.94–96). This was a useful shorthand that could be used to define Christian martial valor, celebrate virtue, and demonize vice.[11] The brutal, defiant Moor Aaron seems out of place in the classical world of *Titus Andronicus* (a play probably written in collaboration with George Peele around 1590) because his character has far greater affinities with a figure like the malevolent and "barbarous" Moor Muly Hamet in Peele's *Alcazar*. Similarly, the appearance of the Prince of Morocco in *The Merchant of Venice* dressed all in white to take the casket test for Portia's hand again suggests the curious interpolation of a figure from another play: he has the benign nobility of the Ottoman Prince Selim-Calymath in Marlowe's *The Jew of Malta*, for instance. This sense of disjunction may again be intentional, suggesting that with Morocco Shakespeare was seeking to parody the speech patterns and bellicosity of the standard "Turk play" protagonist.

As a result, Morocco seems lost in the comedic world of Belmont where his "heroic visions are misplaced."[12]

A deep Shakespearean skepticism regarding the "Turk play" by the mid-1590s seems to be confirmed by a celebrated passage in 2 *Henry IV*, a play roughly contemporary with *The Merchant of Venice*, when the pompous braggart Pistol rants and rails at Doll Tearsheet before Falstaff and Mistress Quickly in the Boar's Head, an Eastcheap tavern. Pistol is more comically self-deluded than generically out of place. He thinks himself a warrior hero in the Tamburlaine mold and proves it by absurdly garbling quotations from three prominent "Turk plays" (*Tamburlaine*, *The Battle of Alcazar*, and Peele's lost play, *The Turkish Mahomet and Hiren the Fair Greek*) and in the process demonstrates that the playhouse is the source of his conceptions of masculine valor. In choosing famous lines of high tension and hubris – "hollow pampered jades of Asia, which cannot go but thirty mile a day"; "feed and be fat, my fair Calipolis"; and "Have we not Hiren here?" (2.4.140–55) – Shakespeare gently ridicules the genre whilst satirically mocking those in the wider culture, dramatists and audiences alike, who obsessively parroted the stale excesses of the "Turk play." It is a savvy, playful announcement of the death of a genre.

Shakespeare's resolution to develop the raw material of Cinthio's *Gli Hecatommithi* (1565) into what became *Othello*, his decision to foreground the race of his protagonist, and provocatively introduce Cyprus and the threatening Ottoman frame, can therefore only be understood in relation to his earlier history with the "Turk play." Others had sought to revivify the genre around the turn of the century, and plays such as *Vaivode* (1599), *The Shoemaker's Holiday* (1599), *The Spanish Moor's Tragedy* (1600), *George Scanderbeg* (1600), and *The West Indies* (1601) similarly represent a mixture of old themes and new contexts. There are other, external factors that may also have prompted Shakespeare to consider this type of material, specifically the arrival and subsequent pomp and ceremony of a Moroccan embassy under Abd al-Wahid bin Masoud bin Muhammad al-Annuri in London between 1600 and 1601 (an earlier embassy under Ahmad Bilqasim had been resident at around the time Shakespeare was writing *The Merchant of Venice*).[13]

Yet Cyprus is crucial to the action of *Othello* and it is the pivot on which the action of the play and its divergence from the established "Turk play" paradigm turns. On the Mediterranean front line, Cyprus had been a prominent location in the Christian imagination throughout the sixteenth century and, in a revealing move, Shakespeare chooses not to specify when these events take place, deliberately leaving the chronological setting of his play vague. His initial audiences would have been well aware of the long and complex relationship between Venice and the Ottomans that had been maintained despite the determined westward expansion of the Ottomans in the late fifteenth and sixteenth centuries, at great expense to the Venetians. In the extraordinary campaign of 1516–17 the Ottoman sultan Selim I had defeated the Mamluk sultanate, bringing Syria, Egypt, and much of the Arabian Peninsula under Ottoman suzerainty. Later Tunis and Algiers would fall under their control, and with Greece and its Aegean islands also largely Ottoman territories, the eastern half of the Mediterranean Sea had become effectively Ottoman by *Othello*'s first performances. The Venetians had little choice but to cajole, placate, and negotiate, retreating when it was expedient to do so. Tensions between the two erupted into open warfare only four times over this long period (1463–79, 1499–1503, 1537–40, and 1570–73) and in every case this resulted in the ceding of Venetian territory to the Ottomans. By the beginning of the seventeenth century, the dynamic on which the play is based had fundamentally changed, and Venice was no longer the commercial, military, and colonial force it had been. As a result, the play is situated in what feels like a near past, and this long, slow Venetian retreat from the eastern Mediterranean looms, unacknowledged, in the background of *Othello*'s opening. When, in the third scene, audiences watch the nervous receipt of rapid, contradictory, and "disproportioned" (1.3.2) news by the Duke and senators of Venice concerning the movements of the Ottoman fleet, in which it is unclear whether an Ottoman attack is to fall on Rhodes or Cyprus, they are left to reflect on what is likely to follow. They know that an island is probably going to fall, for the model of the "Turk play" was defined by conquest and siege warfare, with islands – Malta, Rhodes, and Cyprus – regularly conquered on the stage between the late 1580s and the first English opera, William Davenant's *The Siege of Rhodes* in 1656. Sometimes a dramatist would reverse history, enabling islands to fall that had resisted Ottoman attack (such as Marlowe's *The Jew of Malta*), and others would reimagine Ottoman victories (such as Thomas Kyd's *Soliman and Perseda*, ca. 1589, in which a pair of poisoned lips enacts revenge on the victorious Ottoman sultan).

Despite references to Rhodes (which had been captured by the Ottomans in 1522), for *Othello*'s early audiences the most likely scenario to be played out once Othello had been dispatched against "the general enemy Ottoman" (1.3.50) was the most recent. Cyprus had fallen to the Ottomans following the eleven-month siege of Famagusta in August of 1570, a loss widely reported across Christendom. Its fame was only enhanced by the ensuing Battle of Lepanto, in which a Holy League featuring a combined papal, Venetian, and Spanish galley fleet defeated an Ottoman fleet under Ali Pasha in October 1571. In England celebratory printed texts accompanied bonfires and bell-ringing to mark the victory. This connection had a particular resonance for one specific member of Shakespeare's first audience at Whitehall: King James I had mourned the loss of Cyprus and gloried in the Christian naval victory in heroic verse in *His Maiesties Lepanto*, which had initially been published in 1591 but was reprinted in London to mark his accession to the English throne in 1603, at the point Shakespeare is thought to have been writing *Othello*.[14] As the Venetian senators consider the feints and counter-feints of the Ottoman fleet they are tracking, their reflections on Cyprus make the resonances of its recent loss all the greater. The first senator notes:

> When we consider
> Th'importancy of Cyprus to the Turk,
> And let ourselves again but understand
> That, as it more concerns the Turk than Rhodes,
> So may he with more facile question bear it,
> For that it stands not in such warlike brace,
> But altogether lacks th'abilities
> That Rhodes is dressed in – if we make thought of this,
> We must not think the Turk is so unskillful
> To leave that latest which concerns him first,
> Neglecting an attempt of ease and gain
> To wake and wage a danger profitless.
>
> (1.3.19–30)

A skilled and warlike adversary, a vulnerable island: by dramatizing Venetian fears for their ability to hold Cyprus, Shakespeare intentionally draws on recent history and implies with this prelude to war that the play will center upon Othello's martial encounter with the Ottomans. That is what the Venetian senate expects, that is what Othello and his officers expect, and that is what an audience expects. In every significant respect, this appears to be a "Turk play" in action.

Instead of the clash of armies and faiths this set-up promises, an audience is given a storm, anxiously watched from the fortified walls of Cyprus. This "desperate tempest" they are told "hath so banged the Turks / That their designment halts" (2.1.21–22) and a "grievous wrack and sufferance" has been visited on "most part of their fleet" (2.1.23–24). The storm again represents a striking departure: the Turks never appear onstage (whereas previous plays had seen them dominating the stage), and when they are invoked, there is none of the antagonistic vitriol that tends to characterize the English stage in this period. Instead the "reverend and gracious" Ottoman fleet is lost, and with them the battle that has been promised. Othello then appears out of this "dangerous sea" (2.1.46) to immediately greet his new wife Desdemona as his "fair warrior" (2.1.179), a reflection back to her desire to share "the rites for why I love him" (1.3.255), with its provocative mingling of the military and the sexual.

The threat of the Turks that had so dominated the previous scenes has suddenly vanished, and the grateful Cypriot inhabitants Othello is now to rule seem as Venetian as Venice itself. This was again something of an occlusion, although Shakespeare is unlikely to have known its full extent. The ease and swiftness with which the Ottoman forces under their commander Lala Mustafa Paşa would take control of large swathes of Cyprus in June 1570 was a result of the brutality of Venetian rule; the Ottomans had been greeted by the Greek Cypriot population as liberators from Latin oppression, not as the alien enemies they are characterized as in *Othello*. In a swift and brutal retaliation, the Venetian authorities imprisoned all Ottoman Muslims and Jews residing on Venetian territory. Instead of focusing on the politics of Venetian colonialism, in the play tensions are focused on claustrophobic rivalries within the ruling elite as the easing of the pressures of the Ottoman enemy without begins to expose fractures and transformations within. As the tumult that Iago sparks to disgrace Cassio boils over, Othello angrily demands, "Are we turned Turks?" (2.3.160).

Long before the events that transpire on Cyprus, other connections to and differences from the "Turk play" paradigm become apparent. The beginning of *Othello* had borrowed an old device used by Marlowe in the first part of *Tamburlaine* to draw in an audience and build anticipation: the entrance of the protagonist is delayed until the second scene while others talk about him. Even here Shakespeare signals a divergence: Tamburlaine is given a mercurial reputation that develops out of an unlikely, unstoppable military prowess despite his lowly origins; in contrast Othello is defamed, racialized, and made monstrous, and a different kind of prowess is invoked when Brabantio is told that "you'll have your daughter covered with a Barbary horse, you'll have your nephews neigh to you, you'll have coursers for cousins and jennets for germans" (1.1.110–13). When Othello does speak, and presents his famous "travailous" history, it again has echoes of the earlier genre but simultaneously departs decisively from it, not least in what it reveals about his own history. In explaining his wooing of Desdemona, he describes how:

> ... I spake of most disastrous chances,
> Of moving accidents by flood and field,
> Of hair-breadth scapes i' the imminent deadly breach,
> Of being taken by the insolent foe
> And sold to slavery, of my redemption thence
> And portance in my travels' history:
> Wherein of antres vast and deserts idle,
> Rough quarries, rocks and hills whose heads touch heaven
> It was my hint to speak – such was the process;
> And of the Cannibals that each other eat,
> The Anthropophagi and men whose heads
> Do grow beneath their shoulders. This to hear
> Would Desdemona seriously incline ...
>
> (1.3.135–47)

Captured "by the insolent foe," Othello was sold into slavery and then experienced some kind of "redemption," which is a word redolent of a liberation from slavery and of being delivered from sin through Christian conversion. This appears all the more likely given that later in the same speech he refers to this earlier life as "my pilgrimage" (1.3.154), another explicitly Christian term that would seem to suggest redemption through conversion. He seems to have been captured by the Turks – the most likely meaning of "insolent foe" – a reference to the series of military campaigns the Ottomans had waged across North Africa in the sixteenth century.[15] He was then sold as a slave (most probably a galley slave) and then redeemed through Christian capture. What an audience is not told is anything of the faith into which Othello was born: was he was born a Muslim like most urbanized North Africans in this period? Or perhaps Shakespeare imagined him as a polytheistic Berber, or as an undifferentiated pagan? The most important thing here is that his origins are uncertain, and all we can be sure about is that he has changed from at least one religion to another, a transition that automatically rendered his identity unstable and his allegiances suspect: he is, in Roderigo's words, "an extravagant and wheeling stranger / Of here and everywhere" (1.1.134–35).

This is not a personal history, or a mode of address, typically associated with the "Turk play" protagonist, despite a shared mobility and martial emphasis. Such figures – as Pistol's parody suggests – speak in a declamatory style, their language a distinctive configuration of blank verse, superlatives, and the incorporation of unfamiliar, polysyllabic nouns. They can woo, but they do so in an altogether different fashion to Othello's ranging, lyrical, accidental courtship. The most pertinent example is Tamburlaine's wooing of the captive Zenocrate. He promises:

A hundred Tartars shall attend on thee,
Mounted on steeds swifter than Pegasus;
Thy garments shall be made of Median silk,
Enchas'd with precious jewels of mine own,
More rich and valurous than Zenocrate's;
With milk-white harts upon an ivory sled
Thou shalt be drawn amidst the frozen pools,
And scale the icy mountains' lofty tops,
Which with thy beauty will be soon resolv'd:
My martial prizes, with five hundred men,
Won on the fifty-headed Volga's waves,
Shall we all offer to Zenocrate,
And then myself to fair Zenocrate.

(1.2.93–105)[16]

For Tamburlaine his own and others' worth is appraised in terms of their acquisition of goods, peoples, and space, and love is no different. Here his hyperbolic procession of improbable gifts moves from Tartars on steeds, silks, and jewels to hart-drawn sleds and martial prizes to finally reach Tamburlaine himself. It is direct, intentionally overwhelming, and seems to require no affirmation. The invocation of geography from beyond Christendom is common to both, however, and the two warriors share a self-consciously poetic turn of phrase despite, as Othello remarks, being "rude" in speech and "little blessed with the soft phrase of peace" (1.3.82–83). Othello can "lard" his speech with "choice terms" and "unfamiliar motifs" like any other "Turk play" protagonist. This is what Étienne Balibar terms a "linguistic ethnicity" rather than a "racial (or hereditary) ethnicity."[17] Both characters repeatedly remind an audience of their difference from those around them, both define themselves solely by their military capabilities, and both are to different extents undone by love. The primary difference between them may be a religious one: as a Christian Othello is expected to eschew the fixation with material wealth that had come to define supposedly "barbarous" peoples and preoccupies Tamburlaine in particular.

As a convert to Christianity Othello represents another departure from the typical playhouse model. There had been a number of dramatic converts from Christianity to Islam on the stage in this period – and more would follow in the first decades of the seventeenth century, most notably in Robert Daborne's *A Christian Turn'd Turk* (1612) – reflecting the considerable numbers that chose the same route, but no earlier example of conversion to Christianity.[18] This is another element that Shakespeare elaborates from his source, which is silent concerning how the unnamed

Moorish captain has come into Venetian employ. At the start of the play it is difficult to be sure whether Othello's new faith has somehow conceptually whitened him for the Venetian senate in the same fashion celebrated in other Jacobean entertainments such as Ben Jonson's *The Masque of Blackness* (1605), enabling his absorption into Venetian society, or whether his becoming a Christian Moor of Venice serves only to render his racial difference more conspicuous. In an early modern English context Moors and Turks did arrive in London and convert to English Protestantism and – in terms of the official records at least – after their baptism, renaming, and explicit acceptance into an Anglican congregation, they all but vanish from view.[19] On the stage, with its investment in the spectacularity of difference, such anonymity was impossible.

* * *

In his determination to disappoint the expectations of audiences immersed in the conventions of the post-Tamburlaine "Turk play," Shakespeare produced an experimental drama that would go on to exert an extraordinary influence. He presents a protagonist from beyond Christendom, a Moorish warrior-convert whose origins are crucially indistinct, and early in the play invokes expansive Mediterranean geographies across which he is expected to battle the Turkish foe. At the very least his initial audiences would have anticipated a naval engagement redolent of Lepanto or one of the great sieges that were the stock in trade of the "Turk play" dramatists of the early 1590s. Instead of fulfilling his destiny as a man who draws "his life and being / From men of royal siege" (1.2.21–22), those geographies rapidly contract into the suffocating claustrophobia of a Venetian elite marooned on a distant colonial outpost, the Turks never appear, and Othello only draws his sword on Desdemona and himself. When considered from this perspective, it appears that, in the creation of *Othello*, Shakespeare was trying to turn the conventional "Turk play" inside out.

At the center of this experiment is the creation of the first Christian Moor to appear on the English stage. Earlier examples of the genre had become so suffused with Islam that they had become totally absurd. There were a number of different approaches to staging Islam that reflected a wider cultural uncertainty: was it monotheistic or polytheistic? Was the Prophet "Mahomet" a Christ-like divinity or a mortal? Were Muslims idolatrous or iconoclastic? Looking to its spectacular potential, English dramatists tended toward the idolatrous, and Robert Greene's odd *Tamburlaine*-imitation *Alphonsus, King of Aragon* (1588) became infamous for portraying Muslim priests ministering to a brass, fire-breathing idol that dispenses prophecy. It was widely ridiculed as "Mahomet's poo" (poll, or head).[20] Shakespeare deftly sidesteps all of this in *Othello*, doing something that seems counterintuitive, and which no "Turk play" had consistently done: he answers the uncertainties and failures in the vision of Mahometanism presented in the "Turk play" by downplaying it. After the hundreds of references to Mahomet that appear in the "Turk plays," the lack of reference to Mahomet in the context of the Ottoman threat in *Othello* (and indeed in his depiction of the Prince of Morocco in *The Merchant of Venice*) is again suggestive of a new direction. Instead of such blunt invocations Shakespeare works in hints and suggestions. Given his North African personal geography an audience may suspect that Othello was born a Muslim, but cannot be sure – the markers of early modern race so prominent in the "Turk play" have gone. They are told that the forces of Islam are never far away: indeed, they repeatedly threaten to infiltrate the Christian camp, for first Iago declares himself a Turk (2.1.114), and then Othello is forced to chastise his drunken soldiers for "doing that which heaven hath forbid the Ottomites" (2.3.161). When, in Act 4, scene 1 (32–55), Othello has his epileptic fit, an episode of "savage madness" (51) that has often perplexed critics and audiences, again we are given a hint of Islam: all Christian biographies of Mahomet foregrounded his supposed epilepsy, which he apparently manipulated to give the impression of divine revelation.[21] Furthermore, instead of a focus on the Mahometan bugbear that had come to dominate the stage, the repeated substitution of the Shakespearean neologism "Ottomites" for the traditional term "Turk" in this play implies a newly racialized conception, with its connotations of biblical taxonomy (Nazarite, Caananite).

The decentering of Islam, in conjunction with a turning away from the stale bombast associated with the "Turk play" – Jonson ridiculed its "scenical strutting and furious vociferation" – are key elements of a different approach.[22] Shakespeare's decision to Christianize his protagonist also enabled a more intense focus on the implications of racial difference. This is clear in the conclusion of Othello's final speech:

> Set you down this;
> And say besides that in Aleppo once,
> Where a malignant and a turbanned Turk
> Beat a Venetian and traduced the state,
> I took by th'throat the circumcisèd dog
> And smote him – thus.
> *He stabs himself*
>
> (5.2.350–55)

Figure 7.1   Although this broadside is from 1672, it shows the ways that both Africans and Turks were aligned imaginatively.

In a visceral act of remembrance, division, and self-retribution, Othello is simultaneously loyal Venetian and enemy of Venice; the desperate and apparently unsustainable duality of his position as a Venetian Moor can only be brought to the fore because he is Christian. As Othello smites the "circumcisèd" and "turbanned Turk" that he has become, he again does not mention Mahometanism as might be expected, but uses alternative, bodily signifiers of that religion in the process of identification. Once more the focus shifts to physical markers of difference and the reassertion rather than erasure of that difference in death (see Figure 7.1).

Mary Floyd-Wilson has argued that *Othello* "stands at a crossroads in the history of ethnological ideas," that the play reflects and brings into being new ideas about race in early seventeenth-century Britain.[23] The argument of this essay would, at least in some respects, seem to confirm that notion. Yet my contention that *Othello* emerged directly from Shakespeare's determination to challenge the outdated and old-fashioned "Turk play" formula in order to find a new language in which to explore the non-Christian geographies and trajectories that had previously been that genre's sole province suggests that thinking about race had a strong theatrical component. This in turn suggests that race was an unfinished business on the early modern stage, and that new conceptions of race were generated by generic experimentation. Marlowe had pioneered a declamatory, spectacular mode for performing different religions and races on the stage, a dramatic form that Shakespeare remodeled, turning the spectacular inwards with a focused intensity that posed new and troubling questions concerning race and racial difference.

Notes

1 See Thomas Healy, *Christopher Marlowe* (Plymouth: Northcote House, 1994), 46; Michel Poirier, *Christopher Marlowe* (London: Chatto & Windus, 1951), 112. The opposite point is made in Stephen Greenblatt, *Renaissance Self-Fashioning: From More to Shakespeare* (University of Chicago Press, 1980), 194.

2 See Matthew Dimmock, *Mythologies of the Prophet Muhammad in Early Modern English Culture* (Cambridge University Press, 2013), 118–23; Richard Levin, "The Contemporary Perception of Marlowe's *Tamburlaine*," *Medieval and Renaissance Drama in England* 1 (1984): 51–70.

3 *Three Turk Plays from Early Modern England*, ed. Daniel J. Vitkus (New York: Columbia University Press, 2000); Mark Hutchings, "'The Turk Phenomenon' and the Repertory of the Late Elizabethan Playhouse," *Early Modern Literary Studies* Special Issue 16 (September 2007): 10.1–39, http://extra.shu.ac.uk/emls/si-16/hutcturk.htm.

4 Jonathan Burton, *Traffic and Turning: Islam and English Drama, 1579–1624* (Newark: University of Delaware Press, 2005), 257–59.

5 Jean MacIntyre, *Costumes and Scripts in the Early Modern Theatres* (Edmonton: University of Alberta Press, 1992); Matthew Dimmock, "Materialising Islam on the Early Modern Stage," in *Early Modern*

Encounters with the Islamic East: Performing Cultures, ed. Sabine Schulting, Sabine Lucia Muller, and Ralf Hertel (Farnham: Ashgate, 2012), 115–32.

6 The play text of *Tamar Cham* is now lost, but the plot book of the play (now also lost) was transcribed in the nineteenth century and is reproduced in *Henslowe Papers: Being Documents Supplementary to Henslowe's Diary*, ed. Walter W. Greg (London: A.H. Bullen, 1907), 145–48.

7 Susan Skilliter, *William Harborne and the Trade with Turkey, 1578–1582* (Oxford University Press, 1977).

8 The scale of this circulation, both before and after Hakluyt published the correspondence in 1589, is suggested in the discussion of the relevant letters in Skilliter, but the practice seems to have been more widespread than even Skilliter imagined.

9 *The True Tragedie of Richard the third* (London: Thomas Creede, 1594), sig. I2^{r}.

10 Hutchings, 6–7.

11 Jerry Brotton, "Shakespeare's Turks and the Spectre of Ambivalence in the History Plays," *Textual Practice* 28/3 (2014): 521–38.

12 James Shapiro, "Which is the Merchant Here, and Which the Jew," *Shakespeare Studies* 20 (1988): 269–79 (at 273); Robert Logan, *Shakespeare's Marlowe: The Influence of Christopher Marlowe on Shakespeare's Artistry* (Aldershot: Ashgate, 2007), 156.

13 Bernard Harris, "A Portrait of a Moor," *Shakespeare Survey* 11 (1958): 89–97. See also Matthew Dimmock, *Elizabethan Globalism: England, China and the Rainbow Portrait* (London: Yale University Press for the Paul Mellon Centre, 2019), 186–87.

14 James VI and I, *His Maiesties Lepanto, or heroicall song being part of his poeticall exercises at vacant houres* (London, 1603).

15 Andrew C. Hess, *The Forgotten Frontier: A History of the Sixteenth-Century Ibero-African Frontier* (University of Chicago Press, 1978).

16 Chrisopher Marlowe, *Tamburlaine The Great*, ed. J.S. Cunningham and Eithne Henson (Manchester University Press, 1998).

17 Balibar quoted by John Drakakis in his introduction to *The Merchant of Venice* ed. John Drakakis, Arden Third Series (London: A & C Black, 2010), 85.

18 See Linda Colley, *Captives: Britain, Empire and the World, 1600–1800* (London: Jonathan Cape, 2002); Gerald MacLean and Nabil Matar, *Britain and the Islamic World, 1558–1713* (Oxford University Press, 2011); *Conversions: Gender and Religious Change in Early Modern Europe*, ed. Simon Ditchfield and Helen Smith (Manchester University Press, 2017).

19 Matthew Dimmock, "Converting and Not Converting 'Strangers' in Early Modern London," *Journal of Early Modern History* 17/5–6 (2013): 457–78.

20 See Dimmock, *Mythologies of the Prophet Muhammad*, 108–10.
21 Dimmock, *Mythologies of the Prophet Muhammad*, 50–52 and throughout.
22 Ben Jonson, *Timber, or Discoveries* (London, 1640), N4ᵛ.
23 Mary Floyd-Wilson, *English Ethnicity and Race in Early Modern Drama* (Cambridge University Press, 2003), 140.

CHAPTER 8

Flesh and Blood
Race and Religion in The Merchant of Venice

Dennis Austin Britton

University of New Hampshire

SHYLOCK   My own flesh and blood to rebel!
SOLANIO   Out upon it, old carrion! Rebels it at these years?
SHYLOCK   I say my daughter is my flesh and my blood.
SALERIO   There is more difference between thy flesh and hers than between jet
and ivory; more between your bloods than there is between red wine
and Rhenish.

(3.1.30–33)

Shylock's outrage that his daughter Jessica has left home, stolen his money, and married a Christian falls on unsympathetic ears; Solanio and Salerio respectively poke fun at the presumably elderly Shylock's ability to hold an erection, and dismiss Shylock's claim that his daughter is his "flesh and blood." Both responses nevertheless are connected to the complex interconnections between race and religion in the early modern period, and in *The Merchant of Venice*'s use of "Jew" as both a racial and religious label. Solanio's joke renders Shylock old and impotent, and thus unable to sexually reproduce. Salerio's response picks up where Solanio's leaves off; after his friend makes Shylock impotent, Salerio's suggests that Shylock is not Jessica's father because their flesh and blood differs – Jessica's flesh is like ivory and her blood is like Rhenish (a white wine), while Shylock's flesh is jet (black) and his blood is like red wine.

In many ways, *The Merchant of Venice* is a play obsessed with flesh and blood. Shylock's bond that requires a pound of Antonio's "fair flesh" (1.3.143) if the loan is not repaid places properties of the body at the center of the conflict between Jews and Christians. The terms of the bond and the adjective "fair" indicate that Antonio's flesh and Shylock's are very different from each other: Antonio's white/"fair" flesh has value, and Shylock's does not.[1] Moreover, the defense offered to save Antonio's flesh at the end of the play implies that one cannot have flesh without blood. Antonio is saved by a literal reading of the terms of the bond; although

Shylock is legally entitled to Antonio's flesh, he is not entitled to his blood – and, of course, it is impossible to take a pound of flesh without shedding blood. Just as it is with literal bodies, so it is with early modern racial and religious ideology; flesh and blood are inextricably connected to each other. Throughout *The Merchant of Venice*, the flesh and blood of Shylock, Morocco, and Jessica come under scrutiny. The play uses references to flesh and blood to interrogate the connection between external and internal, between the racialized body and religious identity. It is not at all surprising that the racialized body should be composed by flesh and blood, especially since race in the early modern period could be marked by bodily features (skin, hair, the shape and size of specific body parts) and through the blood that connects individuals to a particular line of descent. *The Merchant of Venice*, however, racializes religious identity, asserting that religious identity is also inheritable from one's ancestors, passed from parents to children through sexual reproduction, and expresses itself both on the body and through the body's behaviors (see Figure 8.1).

Shylock

The rampant anti-Semitism that circulates amongst the play's Christians undergirds the joke about old Shylock's penis. The joke nevertheless brings into focus that early modern understandings of the body and sexual reproduction lay at the foundation of the play's construction of racialized religious difference, and the very relationship between Judaism and Christianity as well. The joke betrays that Shylock's Jewish penis is a particular site of anxiety, for it has the potential to reproduce racial and religious damnation. The play renders Shylock – and Judaism by extension – as old and sexually impotent in order to imagine a future with no Jews.

To understand the interlocking of racial and religious identity in *The Merchant of Venice*, we first need to turn to Christian interpretations of circumcision. Very early on, Christians established the penis as a site that registered the difference between themselves and Jews who did not follow Jesus. Early Christians (Jewish followers of Jesus) debated whether or not non-Jewish converts to Christianity needed to be circumcised. The apostle Paul emphatically stated no:

> Behold, I Paul say unto you, that, if ye be circumcised, Christ shall profit you nothing. For I testifie againe to everie man which is circumcised, that he is bounde to kepe the whole Law. Ye are abolished from Christe: whosoever are justified by the Law, ye are fallen from grace. For we through

Figure 8.1   A late eighteenth-century drawing of the Irish actor Charles Macklin's
portrayal of Shylock.

the Spirit waite for the hope of righteousnes through faith. For in Jesus
Christ nether Circumcision availeth anie thing, nether uncircumcision, but
faith which worketh by love. (Galatians 5:1–6, Geneva Bible, 1560)

Although Paul's statement at first seems to be a prohibition of
circumcision, it is more an admonishment to early Christians not to put
their faith in the rituals of what would eventually be rendered the
"Old Testament." According to Paul, rituals like circumcision were the
old way, and faith in Christ alone was the new way – an idea that

Protestant reformers were vigorously beholden to in their insistence on *sola fide*, justification by faith alone. As differences between Jews who followed Jesus (Christians) and those who did not solidified in relation to circumcision, Christians began to read Jews as children of the flesh and themselves as children of the spirit.[2]

Theological discussions of circumcision take on racial significance when they are considered alongside why the penis was understood as a necessary site of a spiritual covenant between a people and their God. In Genesis, God establishes a covenantal relationship with one man and his descendants:

> Againe God said unto Abraham, Thou also shalt kepe my covenant, thou, and thy sede after thee in their generacions. This is my covenant, which ye shal kepe betwene me an you, and thy sede after thee, Let everie man child among you be circumcised . . . But the uncircumcised man childe, in whose flesh the foreskinne is not circumcised, even that person shall be cut fró his people, *because* he hath broké my covenant. (Genesis 17:9–10, 14)

That this covenant should be sealed on the male genitals, however, needed explication. Julia Reinhard Lupton explains, "in tradition, the real emphasis falls on the fact of genealogical propagation, the marking of the organ though which Abraham will become 'the father of a multitude of nations' (Gen 17:4) . . . by removing something of the organ of generation, generation itself is enabled."[3] Circumcision thus established a covenant between God and an entire race of people; it yoked race and religion. The covenant also created a shared identity among the descendants of Abraham based on the fact that they were unique in being the descendants of Abraham. Thus, as Janet Adelman suggests, "Insofar as Jews constituted both a lineage and a people, perhaps they were ideally situated to mediate between older and the newer senses of 'race' and hence to be early victims of racism."[4] Early modern views of Jews draw from an understanding of race as a specific line of descent and a developing understanding of race as a category that claims groups of people who share or have similar flesh and blood are also alike in character, aptitude, and behavior.

In Christian anxieties surrounding circumcision lies a belief that religious identity is primarily determined by one's race. Given that it was widely known that Jewish men were circumcised, Solanio's and Salerio's jokes obliquely point to Shylock's circumcised penis and his ability to reproduce Jewish identity. Their "solution" is to strip Shylock of sexual potency, symbolically castrating him; castration and circumcision were often elided in medieval and early modern English texts.[5] In denying

Shylock's procreative abilities, they have denied him the ability to reproduce both his racial and religious identity through his children.

The play, then, seems to double down on imagining a future without
Jews by forcing Shylock to convert to Christianity in Act 4. Yet, some
critics have questioned if Shylock can truly be considered a Christian at the
end of the play. For one, the Protestant belief that salvation comes through
faith alone rather than through rituals like baptism means that, according
to the prevailing religious views of Shakespeare's day, it is unlikely that
Shylock would be considered a Christian – it is hard to imagine that at the
end of the play Shylock suddenly has faith in Jesus.[6] Additionally, a
contemporary account of attitudes toward Christians of Jewish descent also
indicates that in England individuals who were Jewish by race were not able
to really be considered Christians. On 7 June 1594, Elizabeth I's doctor,
Roderigo Lopez, was executed for allegedly plotting to poison the queen.
Lopez denied the accusation and is accounted as saying, "he loved the queen
as well as he loved Jesus Christ."[7] His words were read as equivocal, in no
way alleviating suspicion. Moreover, Gabriel Harvey wrote in his account
that "Dr. Lopus was baptised," but "his baptism was not of the heart."[8]
Harvey's statement aligns with a Protestant view that the ritual of conversion, baptism, does not actually make one a Christian, and it also betrays a
general suspicion of Jewish converts as false converts. If Harvey's view is
indicative of the prevailing religious sentiment, there is little chance that the
audience would have considered Shylock a "real" Christian after his forced
conversion. In the end, the play refuses to let Shylock be a Jew, but
simultaneously refuses to let him be a Christian.

Morocco

Circumcision is so important to *The Merchant of Venice*'s racialization of
religious identity that it introduces another circumcised male, the Prince of
Morocco.[9] Kim F. Hall has argued that the play indeed asks us to consider
the two characters alongside each other: "The imagery associated with
Shylock in the play reveals an ongoing link between perceptions of the
racial difference of the black, and the religious difference of the Jew, and
the possible ramifications of sexual and economic contact with both."[10]
Following Hall's lead, I want to emphasize here that the play links blacks
and Jews in order to assert that both groups' racial and religious difference
resides in their flesh and blood.

Unlike Shylock, the African prince's religious identity is never pointed
to explicitly. Nonetheless, Shakespeare's audience likely would have

assumed that Morocco was Muslim, and thus circumcised, because he is from North Africa. Moreover, in addition to being dressed in white (indicated in the stage direction), given how other Muslim characters are costumed on the early modern stage, it is very likely that Morocco would have worn a turban, an article of clothing that itself was linked to circumcision.[11]

That said, the play briefly allows the audience to entertain the idea that Morocco might be a Christian. Before meeting the prince, Portia tells Nerissa, "If he have the condition of a saint and the complexion of a devil, I had rather he should shrive me than wive me" (1.2.111–13). That Morocco might "shrive" her (hear her confession) briefly lays open the possibility that a prince of Morocco could have "the condition of a saint." Yet in a play that will so strongly link religious identity to flesh and blood, the line calls into question if someone with a devil-like complexion can have a saintly condition. The line raises questions about the relationship between the body and soul, between outside and inside, most poignantly through the use of the word "complexion." Shakespeare uses this word here and in other plays to refer to humoral composition (an understanding that the body was composed of blood, black bile, yellow bile, and phlegm), temperament, the physical appearance of the body, and skin color.[12] In *Othello*, for example, the word refers to the protagonist's black skin when Iago indicates that Desdemona may now dislike Othello because he is different in "clime, complexion, and degree" (3.3.229). In *Much Ado About Nothing* and *Measure for Measure*, the word points to the way the body expresses a person's emotional and spiritual condition: in *Much Ado About Nothing*, Beatrice describes Claudio as "civil as an orange, and something of that jealous complexion" (2.1.276–77), and in *Measure for Measure*, the Duke tells Isabella, "grace, being the soul of your complexion, shall keep the body of it ever fair" (3.1.180–81), suggesting that God's grace and Isabella's spiritual and bodily purity manifest themselves in physical beauty. Read in light of other uses of "complexion" in Shakespeare, Portia's line asks the audience to think about the connection between Morocco's outside and inside, between his skin color and his religious condition.

The play troubles the ability to conceive of a black Christian Moor through Portia's imagining that the prince might specifically have "the complexion of a devil" – it is important to note that she has not seen him yet, and thus Portia is imagining what a Moroccan prince would look like. Portia's sentiment draws from a long tradition of associating black skin with sin and cursedness. Virginia Mason Vaughan has shown that devils were often depicted as black in medieval and early modern Europe.[13] Given early modern understandings of complexion and medieval and early modern connections between black skin and evil, the play makes it difficult to imagine the possibility of a black Christian Moor.

Outside of the theatre, but surely affecting what happened on the stage, were discussions of black skin by writers like the English explorer George Best. He writes in *A true discourse of the late voyages of discoverie* (1578):

> Blacknesse proceedeth of some natural infection of the first inhabitants of that Countrey, and so all the progenie of them descended, all still polluted with that same blot of that infection. Therefore it shal not be fare from our purpose, to examine the first originall of these black men, and how by lineall discente, they haue hitherto continued thus black.

The "first originall," according to Best and others, was Ham's son, Chus (or Cush): "And of this blacke & cursed Chus came al these blacke Moores which are in Africa ... the cause of the Ethiopian blacknesse, is the curse & natural infection of bloud, & not the distemperature of the clymate."[14] In addition to using "black" and "Moor" (and "Ethiopian," too) inter-changeably, Best argues that black skin is a racial characteristic, an "infec-tion of bloud" passed from Chus to all of his descendants. Having black skin was thus seen as proof that an individual was part of a cursed race. Best creates a causal relationship between the color of the flesh and the condition of the blood; he implies that one can know blood and race by looking at the skin.

Portia's statement, then, demonstrates an anti-blackness that proceeds from explications like Best's and theatrical tradition. Her anti-blackness should also be read in conversation with the play's sexual obsessions and racialization of Jewishness. Like Morocco, Shylock too is connected to the devil: Launcelot calls him "the very devil incarnation" (2.2.23), a mala-propism for "incarnate," from the Latin *incarnātus*, meaning "made flesh" or "embodied in flesh."[15] Here, however, Portia expresses her racial-sexual preference; she exposes a prejudice against black skin, his "complexion" regardless of "condition." Here race (marked by skin color) and sexual desire trump religion. Moreover, even this allusion to Portia's sexual preference does not emerge apart from religious language – the language of devils (damnation) and shriving (forgiveness). Once again we see that the play's meditations on race and religion are inextricable from sex and reproduction.

The play also draws attention to the reality of skin color prejudice. The first words out of Morocco's mouth, "Mislike me not for my complexion," indicate that Morocco knows that dark complexions are disfavored. Ian Smith asserts, "Morocco's apologetic entry … attends to his awareness of his skin colour as a disability whose remedy can be found in the linguistic rationalizations he offers."[16] To confront skin color prejudice, he attempts to assert that his condition makes him a suitable suitor:

> Bring me the fairest creature northward born,
> Where Phoebus' fire scarce thaws the icicles,
> And let us make incisions for your love
> To prove whose blood is reddest – his or mine.
>
> (2.1.4–7)

Morocco claims that it is what is inside, blood, that counts, and that his blood is redder than that of the "fairest" (i.e., whitest) northern Europeans – red blood was a conventional sign of valor. He goes on to emphasize his valor later in the scene when he swears "By this scimitar, / That slew the Sophy and a Persian prince, / That won three fields of Sultan Suleiman" (2.2.24–26). Unfortunately for Morocco, however, his identity as a Moor marks him as different. Anthony Gerard Barthelemy provides a helpful history of the word "Moor" and what it would have conjured in Shakespeare's day – among other things, black African, North African, Indian, and very often Muslim.[17] "At the simplest level," Barthelemy writes,

> they were the Other, the non-English, the non-Christian. But the history of the word *Moor* is far too complex to allow Moors to escape untainted by that name. If a stage Moor, therefore, was other than Muslim or black, he had to identify himself as such by denying his kinship with his kind. If he was not black of spirit, he had to declare himself so. Yet, while the stage Moor may have been able to divest himself of several of his inherited traits, never was he able to cast off his strangeness. Other he would always be.[18]

"Moor," then, like "black," was in no way a neutral label; it came with racial and religious prejudice. Given such prejudices, it is no surprise that Morocco enters *The Merchant of Venice* on the defensive, asserting that he is not what the audience or Portia assume him to be.

Nonetheless, Morocco's racial and religious otherness remains – he does not "deny his kinship with his kind." His description of his valor and blood indicate that he is not from Christian Europe; his weapon, the scimitar, and the victories he describes place the prince geographically in Islamic Turkey and Persia. Moreover, in a play where blood so potently signifies racial and religious difference, drawing attention to his blood works contrary to his purpose. Morocco unwittingly points to the fact that, like Shylock, both his flesh and blood are different from fair European flesh and blood. And, also like Shylock, the play denies him posterity. To "hazard" the casket test, Portia tells him, "swear before you choose, if you choose wrong / Never to speak to lady afterward / In way of marriage" (2.1.40–42). As Marc Shell argues, "His legitimate gene bloodline (if not the flesh and blood of his own body) will be cut. He will become . . . a castrate."[19]

Jessica

Solanio and Salerio are not the only characters to raise questions about Shylock and sexual reproduction, and about the biological/paternal connection between Shylock and his daughter. The play vexes the blood relationship between the Jewish father and daughter at the very point that Jessica is introduced, in Launcelot's tearful departure from Shylock's house:

LAUNCELOT   Adieu; tears exhibit my tongue. Most beautiful pagan, most sweet Jew, if a Christian do not play the knave and get thee, I am much deceived. But adieu; these foolish drops do something drown my manly spirit.

[Exit]

JESSICA   Farewell, good Launcelot
Alack, what heinous sin it is in me
To be ashamed to be my father's child!
But though I am a daughter to his blood
I am not to his manners. O Lorenzo,
If thou keep promise, I shall end this strife,
Become a Christian and thy loving wife.

Exit (2.3.10–20)

Critics have had much to say about this exchange. Adelman, for example, has pointed out that Jessica's racial and religious identity is defined in relation to both her father and future husband. Focusing on Launcelot's words in the Second Folio, "if a Christian *did* not play the knave and get thee, I am much deceived," and drawing attention to the past tense "did," she argues, "Lancelot's response fuses Christian husband and Christian father – as though Jessica's Christian husband could do away with the embarrassment of her Jewish birth by becoming her Christian father, literally re-begetting her in the present with Christian, rather than Jewish, blood."[20]

Numerous critics have seen religious conversion as a primary location through which *The Merchant of Venice* entangles racial and religious identity. Although it is easy to dismiss the idea that Shylock truly converts to Christianity, Jessica's conversion lays open the possibility that a person who is Jewish by race may become a Christian by faith. But why Jessica and not Shylock? The difference lies in her status as a white woman. Mary Janell Metzger has suggested that Jessica can more easily be incorporated into Christian Venice because she, unlike her father, is rendered "white." Her whiteness is firmly established by Lorenzo when he states, using a pun on "hand" as handwriting and body part, that Jessica has a "fair hand; / And whiter than the paper it writ on / Is the fair hand that writ" (2.4.12–14). Lorenzo draws our attention to Jessica's flesh, making her superlatively white by insisting that her hand is whiter than paper. Lorenzo, like Portia, reveals that skin color determines sexual desirability. Jessica's fairness makes her a desirable wife, and, as Metzger offers, "Jessica's 'Jewish blood' is subordinated in the course of the play to her 'fair' and hence convertible flesh."[21]

Jessica's flesh may be white, but the problem of her blood remains. Lara Bovilsky's analysis also focuses on race and religion as transmitted through blood, especially focusing on Jessica's distinction between "blood" and "manners." Through insisting that she is not a daughter "to his manners,"

> Jessica claims that the cultural breach between herself and Shylock defines her own identity and therefore makes genealogy less relevant ... Jessica's distinction between lineage and manners complicates the presumed monolithic identity of what may be called a racial group by pointing to a boundary between two distinct components of the discourse defining Jewishness in the play. The blood metaphor constructs Jewishness as a matter of literal substance and of genealogical inheritance, a "genetic" legacy in the etymological sense, while the question of "manners" points to a concept of distinctively Jewish culture, ethics, and group psychology.[22]

Bovilsky goes on to show that the difference that Jessica attempts to uphold eventually breaks down as other characters in the play identify her as a non-Christian even after her conversion.[23] Launcelot, for example, still believes that Jessica is damned to hell even after she has supposedly become a Christian and Lorenzo's wife:

LAUNCELOT Yes, truly; for, look you, the sins of the father are to be laid upon the children: therefore, I promise ye, I fear you. I was always plain with you, and so now I speak my agitation of the matter: therefore be of good cheer, for truly I think you are damned. There is but one hope in it that can do you any good; and that is but a kind of bastard hope neither.
JESSICA And what hope is that, I pray thee?
LAUNCELOT Marry, you may partly hope that your father got you not, that you are not the Jew's daughter.

(3.5.1–10).

Launcelot alludes to Genesis 20, though he (and Shakespeare) takes the passage out of context in order to focus the connection between lineage, salvation, and damnation.²⁴ Launcelot uses scripture as evidence that blood relations dictate one's status among the saved (Christian) and the damned (Jew). Moreover, Launcelot does not, nor does anyone in the play, make any reference to what Jessica might actually believe, implying the view that religious identity is formed primarily by race. Accordingly, the only hope Jessica has to be saved is that she is not Shylock's daughter. Launcelot believes that religious identity is constructed by race (lineage and blood) rather than rituals of conversion or faith.

Jessica, however, is of a different opinion. She maintains that she is a Christian because she is married to a Christian: "I shall be saved by my husband. He hath made me a Christian" (3.5.23–24). Strangely, Jessica believes that she is a Christian not because she has faith in Christian beliefs but because of her familial (and implied sexual) relationship with a Christian husband, evincing Adelman's claim that marriage to a Christian seems to resolve the problem of her Jewish blood. Jessica's belief has a biblical foundation. Paul states in 1 Corinthians 7:14, "For the unbelieving husband is sanctified by the wife, and the unbelieving wife is sanctified by the husband: else were your children unclean." The long historical controversy this passage has caused aside, Jessica places her faith in a scripture – as any good Protestant should – that upholds the play's larger message that religious identity is primarily constructed by family relations.²⁵ That said, the part of the passage she does not quote does not disprove Launcelot's initial position. Paul asserts that the unbelieving parent is sanctified for the sake of the child, "else were your children unclean," suggesting that children do indeed inherit spiritual cleanness or uncleanness from their parents. Jessica's citation of this scripture, then, does not negate a belief that religious identity, one's status as saved or damned, is a racial characteristic passed down from parents to their children. She, nevertheless, seems to have found the exception to the general rule: become part of a Christian family by marrying a Christian and having a child.

Launcelot concedes to Jessica's argument; Jessica does seem to be a Christian here. Later, however, the play undermines Jessica's newfound Christian identity. Lisa Lampert asserts that Jessica's Jewishness rather than Shylock's is the real cause of the play's anxiety; her fair skin allows her to pass as a Christian, but may conceal an inalterable Jewishness that resides within.²⁶ In Act 5, where Christian couples (Portia and Bassanio, Nerissa and Graziano) are relationally and sexually reconciled (the husbands will not neglect to value their wives' "rings"), Jessica and Lorenzo's final verbal interaction in the play makes it difficult to believe that the couple will have a happily-ever-after ending.²⁷ Lorenzo seeks to bring an end to their lovers' quarrel (which in performance can be played as a playful spat or as exposing more serious marital conflict) through telling his wife to turn her attention to heavenly harmony and music:

LORENZO   Sit, Jessica. Look how the floor of heaven
Is thick inlaid with patens of bright gold:
There's not the smallest orb which thou behold'st
But in his motion like an angel sings,
Still quiring to the young-eyed cherubins;
Such harmony is in immortal souls;
But whilst this muddy vesture of decay
Doth grossly close it in, we cannot hear it.
  Enter Musicians
Come, ho! and wake Diana with a hymn!
With sweetest touches pierce your mistress' ear,
And draw her home with music.   *Music*

JESSICA   I am never merry when I hear sweet music.
LORENZO   The reason is, your spirits are attentive:
For do but note a wild and wanton herd,
Or race of youthful and unhandled colts,
Fetching mad bounds, bellowing and neighing loud,
Which is the hot condition of their blood;
If they but hear perchance a trumpet sound,
Or any air of music touch their ears,
You shall perceive them make a mutual stand,
Their savage eyes turn'd to a modest gaze
By the sweet power of music: therefore the poet
Did feign that Orpheus drew trees, stones and floods;
Since nought so stockish, hard and full of rage,
But music for the time doth change his nature.
The man that hath no music in himself,
Nor is not moved with concord of sweet sounds,
Is fit for treasons, stratagems and spoils;
The motions of his spirit are dull as night
And his affections dark as Erebus:
Let no such man be trusted. Mark the music.

(5.1.66–96)

Lorenzo begins by heavily employing religious language and imagery; he seeks to end the quarrel by directing his wife's attention to "heaven," "angels," "cherubins," and "immortal souls." Attempting to end the dispute in this way draws marital harmony and the hope of heaven (and its music) into connection with each other. Moreover, he hopes the music will serve as a kind of aphrodisiac, calling the musicians forth to "wake Diana with a hymn!" Lorenzo links Jessica to the chaste goddess Diana, suggesting that their dispute is leading to problems in the bedroom. Music, Lorenzo hopes, will "draw her home" – her withholding sex is represented as contrary to being at home, family, belonging.

Jessica, however, is unmoved, declaring that music does not change her in the way that Lorenzo believes it should. In not being converted to merriness when she hears "sweet music," the play implies that the marital relationship between Lorenzo and Jessica will remain fraught (especially problematic in a comedy), and that she cannot see or hear the heavenly sights and sounds that her husband describes; heaven is inaccessible to her. The play does not leave it at that, however, but feels the need to explain why music does not make Jessica merry. Lorenzo tells Jessica that even the behaviors of wild animals, whose wildness "is the hot condition of their blood," are altered by music: "Their savage eyes turn'd to a modest gaze / By the sweet power of music." Lorenzo claims that the connection between blood and behavior is a natural one, exemplified in the animal world. But if Lorenzo's explanation is correct, Jessica's earlier claims that she is the daughter of Shylock's blood but not of his manners becomes suspect. Lorenzo's statement here conflicts with Jessica's earlier claim, and Jessica's current manners, her obstinance, can be read as manifesting the condition of her blood, validating Lorenzo's claim that blood governs behavior.

Lorenzo believes that music has the power to alter behavior. He says just this: "But music for the time doth change his nature." Why, then, is Jessica not altered by music? Lorenzo's explanation implies that it is because she is a Jew. Lorenzo's claim that the man "not moved with concord of sweet sounds, / Is fit for treasons, stratagems and spoils" resonates with stereotypes about Jews in general, as well as with the alleged actions of the real Lopez and the fictional Shylock. If music has the power to transform even wild animals, Jessica's lack of transformation, or conversion, here suggests that she remains a Jew. In the end, her blood and manners are like her father's despite having a Christian husband and any rituals of conversion that we are to imagine took place offstage; the text does not stage and thus allow the audience to witness and verify either Jessica's or Shylock's conversion, though this may be because the Master of the Revels (responsible for play censorship) would have objected to having a sacred Christian ritual, baptism, performed on the secular stage. Furthermore, Jessica and everyone who is unaffected by music have "motions of . . . spirit . . . dull as night" and "affections dark as Erebus." Lorenzo's explanation both damns and blackens Jessica; she will be stripped of her whiteness if she is unable to obey her Christian husband's final command to "Mark the music."

In the end, *The Merchant of Venice* speaks out of both sides of its mouth, simultaneously converting Jewish characters to Christianity while undermining our ability to believe that they are really Christians. The play provides us with no examples of Jewish flesh and blood convincingly becoming Christian flesh and blood, affirming a belief that race and religion reside in and are signified on human bodies. By making white skin desirable and black skin undesirable, the play establishes skin color as a primary way that racial difference is marked. Racist ideologies passed down through the story of Ham and Cush made black skin relatively easily to deal with: black skin signified infected blood and cursedness, establishing a correspondence between interior and exterior. White skin, however, presented special problems. When it comes to individuals like Jessica who have white skin, the play asks its audience to look deeper, into the blood.

Notes

1 The germinal study of "fair" as a racial signifier in early modern English literature is Kim F. Hall, *Things of Darkness: Economies of Race and Gender in Early Modern England* (Ithaca, NY: Cornell University Press, 1995).

2 Daniel Boyarin, *A Radical Jew: Paul and the Politics of Human Identity* (Berkeley: University of California Press, 1994), 7, 13, 29–32.

3 Julia Reinhard Lupton, *Citizen-Saints: Shakespeare and Political Theology* (University of Chicago Press), 33.

4 Janet Adelman, *Blood Relations: Christian and Jew in The Merchant of Venice* (University of Chicago Press), 116n25.

5 James Shapiro, *Shakespeare and the Jews* (New York: Columbia University Press, 1992), 114.

6 Dennis Austin Britton, *Becoming Christian: Race, Reformation, and Early Modern English Romance* (New York: Fordham University Press, 2014), 148–49.

7 Quoted in Eric Griffin, *English Renaissance Drama and the Specter of Spain: Ethnopoetics and Empire* (Philadelphia: University of Pennsylvania Press, 2009), 115. Also see Griffin's discussion of the fraught place of *conversos* (Jewish converts to Christianity) and *marranos* (Jewish converts who secretly practiced Judaism) in Christian society (113–20).

8 Quoted in Griffin, 115.

9 On circumcision as connecting Jews and Muslims in early modern England, see Lupton, 60–67.

10 Kim F. Hall, "'Guess who's coming to dinner?': Colonialism and Miscegenation in 'The Merchant of Venice,'" *Renaissance Drama*, New Series 23 (1992): 87–111, esp. 100.

11 Dennis Austin Britton, "Muslim Conversion and Circumcision as Theater," in *Religion and Drama in Early Modern England: The Performance of Religion on the Renaissance Stage*, ed. Jane Hwang Degenhardt and Elizabeth Williamson (Farnham: Ashgate, 2011), 71–86, esp. 77–79 and 83.

12 See Mary Floyd-Wilson, *English Ethnicity and Race on the Early Modern Stage* (Cambridge University Press, 2003); Gail Kern Paster, *Humoring the Body: Emotions and the Shakespearean Stage* (University of Chicago Press, 2004).

13 Virginia Mason Vaughan, *Performing Blackness on English Stages, 1500–1800* (Cambridge University Press, 2005), 19–23.

14 George Best, *A true discourse of the late Voyages of discoverie, for the finding of a passage to Cathaya by the Northwest, under the conduct of Martin Forbisher Generall: Divided into three Bookes* (1578; London: Argonaut Press, 1938), 34–35. For more on blackness and Cush, see Benjamin Braude, "The Sons of Noah and the Construction of Ethnic and Geographical Identities in the Medieval and Early Modern Periods," *William and Mary Quarterly* 54 (1997): 103–42.

15 See definition in *OED*, which notes that the word was especially used by fourth-century Christian writers when discussing the incarnation of Christ. On medieval depictions of Jews as black, see M. Lindsay Kaplan, "Jessica's Mother: Medieval Constructions of Race and Gender in *The Merchant of Venice*," *Shakespeare Quarterly* 58 (2007): 4–10.

16 Ian Smith, "The Textile Black Body: Race and 'shadowed livery' in *The Merchant of* Venice," in *The Oxford Handbook of Shakespeare and Embodiment: Gender, Sexuality, and Race*, ed. Valerie Traub (Oxford University Press, 2016), 170–85, esp. 178.

17 Anthony Gerard Barthelemy, *Black Face, Maligned Race: The Representation of Blacks from Shakespeare to Southerne* (Baton Rouge: Louisiana State University Press, 1987), 6–17.

18 Barthelemy, 17.

19 Marc Shell, "The Wether and the Ewe: Verbal Usury in 'The Merchant of Venice,'" *Kenyon Review* 1 (1979): 65–92, esp. 72.

20 Adelman, 73.

21 Mary Janell Metzger, "'Now by My Hood, a Gentle and No Jew': Jessica, *The Merchant of Venice*, and the Discourse of Early Modern English Identity," *PMLA* 113 (1998): 52–63, esp. 58.

22 Lara Bovilsky, *Barbarous Play: Race on the English Renaissance Stage* (Minneapolis: University of Minnesota Press, 2008), 83–84.

23 Bovilsky, 89–90.

24 Genesis 20 narratives God's displeasure at Israel worshiping other gods. God promises that he will curse the present and future generations, but also promises that if they repent mercy will be shown.

25 For more on this controversy and its significance within *The Merchant of Venice*, see Britton, *Becoming Christian*, 151.

26 Lisa Lampert, *Gender and Jewish Difference from Paul to Shakespeare* (Philadelphia: University of Pennsylvania Press, 2004), esp. 138–67.

27 On the quarrel alluding to the possibility of future marital conflict between Jessica and Lorenzo, see Metzger, 60; and Lampert, 165.

CHAPTER 9

Was Sexuality Racialized for Shakespeare?
Antony and Cleopatra

Melissa E. Sanchez

University of Pennsylvania

Antony and Cleopatra dramatizes the complex and mutually constitutive relations among race, sexuality, gender, and empire.[1] This tragedy is set during the final wars of the Roman Republic, which concluded with the defeat of Shakespeare's titular characters and the installment of Augustus Caesar as emperor of Rome. In *Antony and Cleopatra* these military conflicts are also presented as contests between Western, masculine self-control and Eastern, effeminate self-indulgence. Antony falls because he lacks *virtus*, a term derived from the Latin *vir*, man, which makes virility and virtue synonymous with one another. *Virtus* requires not just a male body, but a masculine spirit defined by sexual continence, martial prowess, and fair skin. Its antithesis is the promiscuous and effeminate indulgence, cowardice, and dark skin of peoples from Eastern and African nations. Usually, Caesar and Cleopatra are each taken as the embodiment – or "human personality" – of Rome and Egypt, respectively, as the two poles of racialized sexuality.[2] As Carol Chillington Rutter sums it up, "The play offers no one 'whiter' than the anti-sensualist, utterly sterile, imperialist Octavius; no one 'darker' than the constantly 'becoming' Cleopatra, whose 'infinite variety', like the Nile's, can't be mapped, contained, bounded."[3] Resisting white male direction and domination, surrounding herself with women and eunuchs, Cleopatra represents the threat of sexuality to classical Roman – and early modern English – order and virility. Antony, as the "synthetic middle figure" torn between Caesar and Cleopatra, registers the danger of attempting to reconcile Roman and Egyptian forms of gender, sexuality, and selfhood.[4] The contest between Rome and Egypt is a zero-sum game, and it serves as an allegory of seventeenth-century England's aspirations to dominate in global trade and colonialism – aspirations framed in racial and sexual terms. As Arthur Little writes, "Rome serves not only as a model for early modern England's imperial ambitions but as the primary prototype for its cultural and racial character and masculinity."[5] Read in this context, Antony's

Figure 9.1   This eighteenth-century engraving of *Antony and Cleopatra* allows one to ponder the desirability of white chastity.

self-destruction warns of the vulnerability of white manhood to the "dark" people it should subdue. Augustus Caesar's cold determination to crush those who resist him is justified as no less than the defense of a Western civilization defined by the logic of *translatio imperii*, or ruthless and continuous global expansion.

Yet *Antony and Cleopatra* in fact questions this binary vision of racialized sexuality and, by implication, the colonial and imperial projects that it legitimizes.[6] The play struggles to define "white" sexuality – and its supposed contrary, "black" sexuality – and fails conspicuously (see Figure 9.1). This failure reveals the contradictions and fissures within Roman ideals of self-mastery and self-determination that continue to shape modern ideals of respectability and responsibility. Rather than depict Caesar and Cleopatra, white masculinity and dark femininity, as absolutes or antitheses, Shakespeare's play attends to their mutual implication within one another. For along with this seemingly whitest of men and darkest of

women, *Antony and Cleopatra* includes a range of racialized sexual types
with whom Caesar and Cleopatra overlap. Most obviously, Antony, whose
attachments are torn between Roman compatriot and Egyptian paramour,
shares qualities of both. Antony's first Roman wife, Fulvia, is a domineer-
ing and dangerous warrior, as different from an ideal of passive femininity
as Cleopatra. The prominence of the eunuch Mardian and the spectral
figure of the "boy" further undermine attempts to claim a binary opposition between Roman *virtus* and its seductive and corrupting others.

Antony and Cleopatra begins in mid-conversation, as Philo and
Demetrius, two of Antony's followers, gossip about their leader's obsessive
attachment to Cleopatra. Philo's opening speech summarizes an opposition between light skin, masculinity, and sexual self-control, on the one
hand, and dark skin, femininity, and sexual self-indulgence, on the other.
This opening allows us to appreciate "the profound bias at work in the
construction of that opposition *per se*" – the very binary critics have taken
for granted, in other words, is presented by Shakespeare as part of the
massive enterprise of Augustan propaganda.[7] Philo's first words, "Nay,
but," situate his speech as an attempt at persuasion rather than an uncon-
tested or univocal Roman view:

> Nay, but this dotage of our General's
> O'erflows the measure. Those his goodly eyes,
> That o'er the file and musters of the war
> Have glowed like plated Mars, now bend, now turn
> The office and devotion of their view
> Upon a tawny front. His captain's heart,
> Which in the scuffles of great fights hath burst
> The buckles on his breast, reneges all temper,
> And is become the bellows and the fan
> To cool a gipsy's lust. Look where they come.
> Take but good note, and you shall see in him
> The triple pillar of the world transformed
> Into a strumpet's fool.
>
> (1.1.1–13)

Philo's speech sets the terms by which centuries of readers understood the
passions of the title characters. Antony's desire for Cleopatra "O'erflows
the measure," or the proper limits that Roman society imposes on erotic
feeling. His "dotage" appears to Philo as a deviation, or perversion, from
the world order that Rome fights to protect. And this perversion is not
only individual but a threat to all of Rome. If the "triple pillar of the
world" has been "transformed / Into a strumpet's fool," the Roman

Empire might well dissolve. This image of liquidity and dissolution will shortly be repeated in Antony's exclamation that, so long as he has Cleopatra, he is content to "Let Rome in Tiber melt," seemingly confirming Philo's fears and justifying Roman hostility to Cleopatra as a predatory force causing both personal and political destruction.[8]

Philo's emphasis on Cleopatra's darkness conjoins racial and sexual threats to Roman empire. The "tawny front" to which Antony's eyes "now bend, now turn" their "office and devotion" is not only Cleopatra's brown face, but also the Eastern zone of military conflict that Antony formerly sought to subdue when he was Caesar's "mate in empire, / Friend and companion in the front of war" (5.1.43–44). The world of war is not only a male, homosocial world, as Kahn and others have observed, but a *white* world. For Philo, to be "tawny," a "gipsy," and a "strumpet" are virtually synonymous. By calling Cleopatra a "gipsy" who has reduced the "third pillar of the world" to her sex toy, an instrument for both kindling and cooling her own insatiable "lust," Shakespeare locates the threat she poses in the here and now of his own day, rather than contained in the distant past – a temporality accentuated by Philo's repetition of "now." In Shakespeare's England, Egyptians and gypsies were conflated not only with one another, but also with Jews and Muslims. All of these racial and religious others were characterized by disguise, trickery, and gender inversion that threatened English governance and Christian faith. Accordingly, "from 1530 onwards, the English authorities repeatedly banished gypsies from the realm and proclaimed harsh punishments for English people who associated with gypsies."[9] English customs – and particularly gendered and sexual mores – were feared too fragile to withstand contact with foreign others.

The association of non-European peoples with sexual excess was central to Virgil's *Aeneid*, a celebration of Augustus Caesar that was central to the English grammar school curriculum. Here, the eponymous hero, Aeneas, is distracted from his destined foundation of Rome when he is shipwrecked in Carthage and falls in love with its queen and founder, Dido. Aeneas and Dido "while away the winter, all its length, in wanton ease together, heedless of their realms and enthralled by shameless passion" (4.193–95). It is only after the gods remind Aeneas of his imperial destiny that he subordinates passion to duty. Aeneas ruthlessly contains his feelings, a self-chastisement that hurts him almost as much as Dido. When the Carthaginian queen begs him to stay, "loyal Aeneas, though longing to soothe and assuage her grief and by his words turn aside her sorrow, with many a sigh, his soul shaken by his mighty love, yet fulfills Heaven's bidding and returns to the fleet" (4.393–96).[10]

Virgil explicitly conflates the suppression of male passion, the foundation of Rome, and the triumph of Augustus Caesar with the defeat of Eastern others when he depicts the future Battle of Actium on Aeneas's shield. Aeneas's military victory is an external confirmation of his conquest over his own longing for the pleasures embodied by the queen whom Virgil calls "Sidonian" Dido. This adjective associated luxury and effeminacy with the Asiatic and African peoples rightly mastered by Rome.[11] In the center of Aeneas's shield, "Antonius with barbaric might and varied arms ... brings with him Egypt and the strength of the East and utmost Bactra; and there follows him (O shame!) his Egyptian wife" (8.685, 687–88). In Virgil's treatment, Augustus is another Aeneas, one chosen by the gods for "triple triumph" against this barbaric army. Indeed, Augustus does not even need to do anything. At the sight of Apollo poised to defeat their "monstrous gods of every form," "all Egypt and India, all Arabians, all Sabaeans, turned to flee. The queen herself was seen to woo [*vocatis*: call] the winds" (8.705–07). Antony, in this scenario, is what Aeneas could have become had he stayed with Dido. In wrenching himself away from her, he has both founded the nation that will become Augustan Rome and set a pattern that will be followed by Augustus himself. The flight of Cleopatra and her barbarian forces ushers in the *Pax Romana*, the period following decades of civil war that Shakespeare's Caesar celebrates as "the time of universal peace" (4.6.4). In his *Eclogues*, Virgil presents this period of Rome's domestic harmony and foreign domination as no less than the return of the golden age, represented by the return of the goddess Astraea: "the Virgin returns" (*Eclogues*, 4.6). As the last of the immortals to leave the earth at the end of the original golden age, Astraea can finally return to earth now that it is ruled by the sexually and racially pure Augustus Caesar. Renaissance writers, Margaret Ferguson demonstrates, expand this classical justification of empire to "associate Dido with qualities of blackness, savagery, and duplicity that are important to emergent ideas of race."[12] Shakespeare's play appears at the nexus of classical and early modern idealizations which celebrated the *translatio imperii* from East to West in terms of sexual as well as racial purification.

Understood in the context of Augustan ideology, even an erstwhile enemy like Pompey is a better friend to Antony than Cleopatra. In Antony's view, Pompey's military attack on Rome has rescued him from Cleopatra's sensual assaults: "The beds i'th'East are soft; and thanks to you, / That called me timelier than my purpose hither; / For I have gained by't" (2.6.50–52). Antony here adopts the perspective taken by Philo, Caesar, Enobarbas, and others. If the East has softened him up, Pompey's advances serve as an alarm to get him out of Cleopatra's bed and back to Rome, where he re-"gains" the hard masculinity of his former self. Sexual pleasure, by this logic, can only be understood in terms of loss of agency and power. In *Antony and Cleopatra*, foreign immorality includes not only wallowing in sensual delight, but also shrinking from discomfort. Roman *virtus*, by contrast, is characterized by chastity in the etymological sense of that term. To be morally pure Romans were expected to continually *chastise* themselves.[13] The ability to endure suffering in pursuit of higher ideas appears most prominently in Roman suicide. In contrast to Cleopatra, who "pursued conclusions infinite / Of easy ways to die" (5.2.426–27), Roman men unflinchingly died by the sword, and Cato went so far as to disembowel himself rather than give in to his enemies.[14]

Such self-punishing behavior was required in life as well as death, as we see in Caesar's description of Antony's lost military strength. Caesar's recollection affirms the difficulty of sustaining *virtus*, which is threatened by the extremes of self-denial as well as those of self-indulgence:

> Antony,
> Leave thy lascivious wassails . . .
> Thou didst drink the stale of horses and the gilded puddle
> Which beasts would cough at. Thy palate then did deign
> The roughest berry on the rudest hedge.
> Yea, like the stag when snow the pasture sheets,
> The barks of trees thou browsed. On the Alps
> It is reported thou didst eat strange flesh,
> Which some did die to look on. And all this –
> It wounds thine honour that I speak it now –
> Was borne so like a soldier that thy cheek
> So much as lanked not.
>
> (1.4.55–56, 61–70)

In the "lascivious wassails" of Egypt, appetites of all kinds are conflated with one another in excessive orgies of rich food and hot sex: Cleopatra proudly recalls her youth, when she was "A morsel for a monarch," and the Romans describe her as an "Egyptian dish," a "morsel" or "fragment" for Roman consumption (1.5.31; 2.6.123; 3.13.120, 121). Indeed, in Shakespeare's day the importation and preparation of foreign ingredients for domestic consumption was part of the ideology of English empire and colonialism.[15] Located firmly on European soil, the Alps' frozen landscape affords no such imported delicacies. Here, Antony's militant celibacy – the absence of sex – is made present through the detail with which Caesar lingers over his primitive subsistence diet of horse urine, slimy puddles, unripe berries, tree bark, and the "strange flesh" of animals so revolting that weaker men "did die to look on" it. Antony not only tolerates this inhuman fare, but also eats so much that his "cheek . . . lanked not" and remains as full and fleshy as ever. Paradoxically, the extremity of Antony's stoicism requires that he set aside the values of the civilization he ostensibly defends. Read from this perspective, as Little observes, Caesar's encomium is also a "formal condemnation" exposing Antony to be "a wild animal" and evoking early modern colonial depictions of the "warring wild African or Irishman."[16] The limit and the epitome of Roman *virtus* may be one and the same.

In Acts 3 and 4, the battles between Antony's and Caesar's forces further illuminate the racial and sexual tensions inherent in the Western justification of imperial expansion as the spread of sexual civility. Antony treats his loss at the Battle of Actium as a result not of Caesar's superior strength but of Cleopatra's sexual power: "O, whither hast thou led me, Egypt? . . . Egypt, thou knew'st too well / My heart was to thy rudder tied by th'strings" (3.11.50, 55–56). Grammatically, Cleopatra is subject here, deliberately leading Antony as object to a destination that he can neither predict nor recognize. After his conclusive losses at Alexandria, Antony underscores the intertwined racial and sexual connotations of his subjection to "Egypt," asserting that "This foul Egyptian hath betrayed me . . . Triple-turned whore! 'Tis thou / Hast sold me to this novice" (4.12.10, 13–14). Much as Antony's soldiers believe his own "vantage" is the "elder" to Caesar's, Antony here accentuates the youthful inexperience of the "novice" who has beaten him (3.10.12, 13). Since Caesar could not have defeated him outright, Antony reasons, Cleopatra must have "sold" him to ensure her own safety. As a "Triple-turned whore," she both sells own her loyalties to the highest bidder and transforms Antony into an object of exchange between herself and Caesar. As a "foul Egyptian," moreover, Cleopatra embodies not only the sexual pollution of the whore, but also racial contamination. Foulness is the opposite of cleanliness and beauty, but it is also the opposite of whiteness, as in Shakespeare's sonnets, where the speaker complains of black women's custom of "Fairing the foul with art's false borrowed face" and avers that in his mistress "beauty herself is black / And all they foul that thy complexion lack" (127, 6; 132, 13–14). This vocabulary renders foulness the opposite of fairness even as it encompasses an early Spanish definition of race, or *raça*, as a blemish or stain attached to those with Jewish or Muslim ancestry. To be *sin raça* in this schema was to be Christian and white.[17] Early modern race was also understood in terms of familial and religious lineage (animal husbandry was a common analogue), and so Cleopatra's "foul"-ness does more than figuratively corrode Antony's *virtus*. It literally imperils Rome's racial purity. Enraptured by Cleopatra, Antony has forgone the "getting of a lawful race" with his legal wife, Caesar's sister Octavia (3.13.110). Instead, as Caesar complains, Antony "hath given his empire / Up to a whore" for whose services he has paid by conferring Rome's eastern and African territories on Cleopatra and the "unlawful issue" that their "lust . . . hath made between them" (3.6.66–67, 7–8). Antony and Cleopatra defy Roman (and early modern) law and custom by announcing this adulterous, "unlawful" mixture of blood and property "in the public eye" and the "common showplace" (3.6.11, 12). When they send their children's schoolmaster as messenger to Caesar, they further underscore the existence of the "unlawful issue" of foreign lust that Antony has "proclaimed the kings of kings" (3.6.13).

In *Antony and Cleopatra*, the stakes of containing such foreign lust thus extend well beyond Antony's individual manhood to Roman – and, for Shakespeare, English – empire and identity as such. Just before his suicide, Antony rejects the masculine values that founded Rome when he imagines his eternal afterlife with Cleopatra:

> Where souls do couch on flowers, we'll hand in hand,
> And with our sprightly port make the ghosts gaze.
> Dido and her Aeneas shall want troops,
> And all the haunt be ours.
>
> (4.14.51–54)

The sensuous imagery of spirits reclining on flowers and prancing before rapt audiences remakes the afterworld in the image of Alexandria, with its "soft beds" and "lascivious wassails" (1.4.56). Moreover, it repudiates the Augustan view of the Battle of Actium found in Virgil's *Aeneid*. Antony not only imagines an Aeneas who has given himself over to Dido, but also rejects the military resonances of this couple, converting their "troops" to spectators of their passion. He thereby imaginatively extends the Alexandrian coronation that so riled Caesar into an eternal show of unmarried, interracial desire.

Antony's rejection of Augustan values entails acceptance of the mutually cancelling terms in which Virgil and others had cast these options. At the same time, *Antony and Cleopatra* reveals white identity to be an impossible construct, riven with contradictory ideals. Cleopatra's own masculinity offers a case in point. Caesar comments that Antony "is not more manlike / Than Cleopatra, nor the queen of Ptolemy / More womanly than he" (1.4.5–7). Caesar means to confirm the complaints of Antony's followers that the once-great triumvir has gone soft, but he implies not that Antony has become *as* feminine as Cleopatra, but that Cleopatra is herself masculine. His lines thereby bespeak "widespread cultural fears and fantasies about powerful, emasculating, and cross-dressing women" – including the recently deceased Queen Elizabeth.[18] However, female masculinity could attract admiration as well as anxiety. In detaching masculinity and femininity from male and female bodies, Caesar participates in Roman and early modern discourses that allowed for the possibility of female *virtus* in heroic women from the biblical Judith to the Roman Lucretia to a wide array of Christian martyrs. Cleopatra's own account suggests that she is indeed "more manlike" than Antony, and that he is "More womanly" than she is. As Cleopatra recalls, "I drunk him [Antony] to his bed, / Then put my tires and mantles on him, whilst / I wore his sword Philippan" (2.3.21–23). In this instance of "double crossdressing," racial, gendered, and sexual identities are put into play.[19] Cleopatra has a better head for alcohol than Antony, and she uses this capacity to dress him in clothing that is both feminine *and* Eastern, a "cultural transvestism" that associates the threat of Cleopatra's Egypt with that of the powerful early modern Ottoman Empire.[20] At the same time, in donning the sword that Antony used to defeat Brutus and Cassius at the Battle of Philippi, Cleopatra claims military triumph for herself. Her memory of strapping on Antony's sword anticipates her determination to participate in the Battle of Actium: "A charge we bear i'th' war / And as the president of my kingdom will / Appear there for a man" (3.7.16–18).

Cleopatra performs what Jack Halberstam calls *female* masculinity, a sexual and gendered position that undermines "conventional understandings of masculinity, manliness, and, broadly speaking, the classification of gendered behavior."[21] Insofar as white men are typically understood as most properly masculine, as against the savagery and excess attributed to African men or the luxury and effeteness attributed to Asian men, female masculinity necessarily disturbs racial categories as well.[22] In *Antony and Cleopatra*, Cleopatra's suicide emulates not the Virgilian Dido, who kills herself in despair when Aeneas abandons her, but the historical Dido who led a group of Phoenicians to found Carthage and killed herself rather than submit herself in marriage to the Libyan king Iarbas.[23] It is *this* Dido – a formidable *virago*, or woman warrior – that Cleopatra emulates when she dies to elude Caesar's plan to display her as a trophy. Taking on the historical Dido's political mantle, Cleopatra urges her female attendants to group suicide, exhorting "what's brave, what's noble, / Let's do it after the high Roman fashion, / And make death proud to take us" (4.15.88–90). But she understands "the high Roman fashion" as going beyond the tradition of death by sword to encompass "knife, drugs, serpents" (4.15. 26). Just before her suicide, Cleopatra insists that "My resolution's placed, and I have nothing / Of woman in me. Now from head to foot / I am marble-constant" (5.2.234–36). This rejection appears, counterintuitively, in the powerful *maternal* role she claims for her death, comparing the asp to a "baby" that "sucks the nurse asleep" (5.2.300, 301). Cleopatra figures herself as powerful giver of life rather than passive object of penetration.

Nor is Cleopatra the only masculine woman in Shakespeare's play. Fulvia, Antony's first wife, is another Renaissance *virago*. Fulvia never appears in person, but her military exploits shape much of the play's early action. We learn early on of her initiative in contesting Caesar's dominance on Antony's behalf: "Fulvia thy wife first came into the field" (1.2.78). Fulvia's military prowess threatens not only Caesar's power, but also the Roman association of military power with male bodies. She thus can be situated amidst a long line of Amazonian figures from Homer's Penthesilea and Virgil's Camilla to Spenser's Britomart and Shakespeare's own Hippolyta. Moreover, as Kathryn Schwarz argues, Amazons signify "what is 'out there,' at the edge of the world or beyond that edge. Talking about Amazons, in early modern England as before and since, is a way of referring to the unknowable and the unreachable; Amazons are repeatedly associated with such other mythic figures as headless men, cannibals, Prester John, and the lost tribes of Israel."[24] In particular, Abraham Hartwell's *A Report of the Kingdome of Congo* locates both Amazons and headless men in Africa, thereby literalizing "the threatening/castrating freedom" of these militant foreign women.[25] As a woman warrior, Fulvia cannot be absolutely differentiated from the sword-wielding, castrating Cleopatra: the ostensibly foreign threat of female masculinity can also reside in a white woman's body. In her martial prowess, Fulvia is more like Cleopatra than she is like Antony's second wife Octavia. Octavia is arguably the whitest woman in the play, a "piece of virtue" characterized by "beauty, wisdom, modesty" and "holy, cold, and still conversation" (3.2.28, 2.2.246, 2.6.120). Cleopatra herself identifies with Fulvia: "Now I see, I see, / In Fulvia's death how mine received shall be" (1.3.64–65). Moreover, even as Cleopatra initially mocks Fulvia as an

"angry," "shrill-tongued" "scold" (1.1.21, 34), she re-evaluates the meaning of these terms. Upon hearing that Octavia is "low-voiced" rather than
"shrill-tongued," Cleopatra breathes a sigh of relief: "That's not so good.
[Antony] cannot like her long" (3.3.12, 13, 14). Better to possess a
piercing voice and grand stature than to be "Dull of tongue, and dwarfish"
(3.3.16). Surprisingly, however, the masculinity of both Fulvia and
Cleopatra is also lauded by the play's male characters: Antony celebrates
Fulvia as "a great spirit," while Caesar admits that Cleopatra was "Bravest
at the last" when her suicide thwarts his plans for triumphant display of her
foreign body to the Roman populace (1.2.111, 5.2.326). May we conclude
that *virtus* is at least as admirable as the "patience" repeatedly attributed to
Octavia, regardless of the race or gender of the body that performs it
(3.6.98, 4.12.38)?

The fact that Caesar's virility is questioned as frequently as Antony's
further strains the relationship between whiteness and masculinity. If
Cleopatra is first introduced through Roman eyes that see her as a "tawny"
"gipsy" and "strumpet," Caesar is first introduced through Cleopatra's
dismissal of him as the "the scarce-bearded Caesar" (1.1.22). As Patricia
Parker has discussed at length, beards in both classical Rome and
Shakespearean drama were "indices of masculinity," while the lack of a
beard was associated with "the smoothness of the catamite or
Ganymede."[26] This association accentuates Caesar's soft penetrability as
well as the "thrice barber'd" Antony's emasculation. Antony underscores
Caesar's lack of virility by deriding him as "the young man" (3.11.61)
inexperienced in the martial combat for which Antony is famous:

> He at Philippi kept
> His sword e'en like a dancer, while I struck
> The lean and wrinkled Cassius; and 'twas I
> That the mad Brutus ended. He alone
> Dealt on lieutenantry, and no practice had
> In the brave squares of war.
>
> (3.11.35–40)

In Antony's characterization, it is Caesar who is effeminate, keeping his
sword sheathed as though it were part of a costume rather than a real
weapon, ducking behind the lieutenants who do the real fighting. More
specifically, Antony's comparison of Caesar to a dancer recalls Plautus'
"depilated player and transvestite male dancer or saltator, the well-known
Latin word for 'leaper' or 'dancer' echoed in the condemnation of 'wanton'
dancers" in such antitheatrical early modern tracts as Philip Stubbes's
Anatomy of Abuses.[27] This "boy Caesar," Antony charges, is afraid "To

lay his gay caparisons apart, / And answer me declined, sword against sword, / Ourselves alone" (3.13.16, 26–27). "The young Roman boy" is all show, whereas Cleopatra herself enters battle rather than deal "on lieutenantry" and, we recall, straps on the Philippan sword that Caesar can only watch in action, not use himself (4.13.48).

It is not only Caesar's youth and hairlessness that Antony and Cleopatra mock, but also his fair complexion: he "wears the rose / Of youth upon him," "blossoming" like a maiden (3.13.19–20, 4.12.23). Caesar's smooth, pale skin may associate him with women as well as eunuchs. Dympna Callaghan argues that "Onstage, whiteface was probably the primary way of signifying femininity," while Anston Bosman explains that "one visible effect of castration before puberty is indeed a pale, smooth skin: modern medicine confirms classical and Renaissance observations that a eunuch is beardless and looks bleached."[28] As Bosman further shows, the eunuch was almost invariably, and paradoxically, paired with the blackamoor in Christian, classical, and Renaissance writing. Not only a foreign gender but also a foreign sexuality, the eunuch is "unseminared," or sterile, like Augustus. Incapable of erection or penetration, the eunuch is aligned with women, and particularly with same-sex female eroticism. As Cleopatra's double entendre rejecting the possibility of billiards with Mardian has it, "As well a woman with an eunuch played / As with a woman" (2.5.5–6). Caesar's boyish smoothness, fair complexion, rosy cheeks, theatricality, and cowardice indeed render him Cleopatra's opposite, but not in the sense critics have usually thought. Rather, these insistent descriptions of his sexual immaturity and effeminacy permit Antony to indulge in a fantasy of sadistic pederasty. When Antony instructs his servants to whip Caesar's messenger, Thidias, "Till like a boy you see him cringe his face, / And whine aloud for mercy," he treats Thidias as a proxy for what he would like to do to Caesar: whip him until he reveals himself to be a mere boy, too delicate to take his beating like a man (3.13.102–03). The homoerotic valences of Thidias' whipping again contrast Caesar's virility unfavorably with that of Cleopatra. Whereas Thidias is made to sob like a child, Cleopatra twice affirms the pleasures of rough sex. Early on, she asserts that she is "with Phoebus' amorous pinches black," figuratively attributing her dark skin to the rough and continual caresses of the sun (1.5.28). Just before her death, she compares "The stroke of death" to "a lover's pinch, / Which hurts and is desired" (5.2.287–88). Cleopatra can play either top or bottom, wielding her lover's sword or succumbing to his pinches, and this erotic flexibility further resists a strict association of whiteness, masculinity, and sexual dominance.

It is, in the end, the shamefully submissive posture of the sodomized boy that Antony and Cleopatra most fear being reduced to. Both, in fact, explicitly choose suicide as the only alternative to such humiliation. Antony imagines himself displayed as an unwilling catamite:

> with pleached arms, bending down
> His corrigible neck, his face subdued
> To penetrative shame, whilst the wheeled seat
> Of fortunate Caesar, drawn before him, branded
> His baseness that ensued?
>
> (4.14.73–77)

Antony here occupies the position to which he forced Thidias and, vicariously, Caesar: bound arms, bending submissively to a penetrating sense of disgrace. The homosocial masculinity that scholars have seen as essential to *Antony and Cleopatra* appears here not as the friendship between equally virtuous men idealized by Plato and Aristotle, but as the sodomy associated with foreign perversion.[29] Cleopatra, more famously, imagines herself being depicted as a catamite:

> Antony
> Shall be brought drunken forth, and I shall see
> Some squeaking Cleopatra boy my greatness
> I'th' posture of a whore.
>
> (5.2.214–17)

Cleopatra here refers to the English theatrical practice of casting boys in women's parts. This practice made boys "available for sexual titillation in an institutional configuration more akin to prostitution than indenture."[30] Accordingly, as Little has argued, "the maturing boy actor occupies a dangerous liminal zone that pushes Antony and Cleopatra's relationship into a homoerotic space."[31] And because the boy impersonates an Egyptian queen, Roman conquest is itself presented as an act of pornographic violence, "the primal sexual encounter between East and West, between Cleopatra and Antony, as a sex scene between an inebriated man and a 'posturing' boy posing as and assuming the sexual position of a whore."[32] Little further proposes that these passages' allusions to "Antony's putative pathic homosexuality and pederasty" bespeak Antony's emasculation, his "non-Romanness" through the boy actor who "speaks less passionately about Cleopatra's fate in Rome than he does about his *vulnerable* posture, his being forced to parade his *vulnus* – that is, his wound – in front of the dirty old men in England's theater," revealing that theatre to be "quite improper in its proprieties."[33]

The sodomitical scenes that Caesar and his would-be English emulators like to watch, in other words, reveal empire to be a perverse enterprise indeed. Caesar is deprived a full sense of triumph when the lovers' suicide forecloses a mise-en-scène in which he is able to observe his captives watching their own sexual exposure and humiliation. If we accept the proposition that Caesar is the whitest man in *Antony and Cleopatra*, his sadistic, voyeuristic pleasure in the performance of a homoerotic consummation that he cannot himself achieve decouples whiteness from both *virtus* and traditional sexual morality. Among the racialized sexualities explored by *Antony and Cleopatra*, white chastity ends up being the most disturbing of all.

Notes

1 For detailed discussion, see Jonathan Gil Harris, "'Narcissus in Thy Face': Roman Desire and the Difference It Fakes in *Antony and Cleopatra*," *Shakespeare Quarterly* 45/4 (1994): 408–25; Kim F. Hall, *Things of Darkness: Economies of Race and Gender in Early Modern England* (Ithaca, NY: Cornell University Press, 1995), 153–60; Coppélia Kahn, *Roman Shakespeare: Warriors, Wounds, and Women* (London: Routledge, 1997), 110–43; Arthur L. Little, Jr., *Shakespeare Jungle Fever: National-Imperial Re-Visions of Race, Rape, and Sacrifice* (Stanford University Press, 2000), 102–76; Ania Loomba, *Shakespeare, Race, and Colonialism* (Oxford University Press, 2002), 112–34; Joyce Green MacDonald, *Women and Race in Early Modern Texts* (Cambridge University Press, 2002), 45–67; Sujata Iyengar, *Shades of Difference: Mythologies of Skin Color in Early Modern England* (Philadelphia: University of Pennsylvania Press, 2005), 192–99.
2 Barbara C. Vincent, "Shakespeare's 'Antony and Cleopatra' and the Rise of Comedy," in *Antony and Cleopatra*, ed. John Drakakis (Basingstoke: Macmillan, 1994), 212–47 (at 217).
3 Carol Chillington Rutter, *Enter the Body: Women and Representation on Shakespeare's Stage* (New York and London: Routledge, 2001).
4 Marilyn French, "'Antony and Cleopatra,'" in *Antony and Cleopatra*, ed. Drakakis, 262–78 (at 265).
5 Little, 102.
6 For this view, see Kahn; Loomba; Harris; and Patricia Parker, "Barbers, Infidels, and Renegades," in *Center or Margin: Revisions of the English Renaissance in Honor of Leeds Barroll*, ed. Lena Cowen Orlin (Selinsgrove, PA: Susquehanna University Press, 2006), 54–87.
7 Kahn, 112. See also Carol Cook, "The Fatal Cleopatra," in *Shakespearean Tragedy and Gender*, ed. Shirley Nelson Garner and Madelon Sprengnether (Bloomington: Indiana University Press, 1996), 241–67.

8 See Loomba; Margot Heinemann, "'Let Rome in Tiber melt': Order and Disorder in 'Antony and Cleopatra,'" in *Antony and Cleopatra*, ed. Drakakis, 166–81.

9 Loomba, 129; more broadly, 118–20 and 127–31. On the long-standing European confusion between Egyptians and gypsies, as well as the associations between Romani gypsies and Jews, see Geraldine Heng, *The Invention of Race in the European Middle* Ages (Cambridge University Press, 2018), 421–22, 431–35.

10 All quotations from the *Aeneid* are from the Loeb Classical Library edition, trans. H.R. Fairclough: *Virgil I: Eclogues, Georgics, Aeneid 1–6* (Cambridge, MA: Harvard University Press, 1999) and *Virgil II: Aeneid 7–12, the Minor Poems* (Cambridge, MA: Harvard University Press, 1998), cited parenthetically by book and line.

11 See Ralph Hexter, "Sidonian Dido," in *Innovations of Antiquity,* ed. Ralph Hexter and Daniel Selden (New York and London: Routledge, 1992), 332–89.

12 Margaret Ferguson, *Dido's Daughters: Literacy, Gender, and Empire in Early Modern England and France* (University of Chicago Press, 2003), 22.

13 On the etymological and conceptual relations between chastity and chastisement, see Stephanie Jed, *Chaste Thinking: The Rape of Lucretia and the Birth of Humanism* (Bloomington: Indiana University Press, 1989).

14 See Kahn, 125–27.

15 See Jennifer Park, "Discandying Cleopatra: Preserving Cleopatra's Infinite Variety in Shakespeare's *Antony and Cleopatra*," *Studies in Philology* 113 (2016): 595–633.

16 Little, 138.

17 L.P. Harvey, *Muslims in Spain, 1500–1614* (University of Chicago Press, 2005), 7n4.

18 Loomba, 121.

19 On the tradition of "double crossdressing" in Renaissance drama, see Simone Chess, *Male-to-Female Crossdressing in Early Modern English Literature* (New York and London: Routledge, 2015), 9, 39–70.

20 See Parker.

21 Jack [Judith] Halberstam, *Female Masculinity* (Durham, NC: Duke University Press, 1998), 45.

22 Halberstam, 267–77.

23 See Hexter, 336–38.

24 Kathryn Schwarz, *Tough Love: Amazon Encounters in the English Renaissance* (Durham, NC: Duke University Press, 2000), 13.

25 See Hall, *Things of Darkness*, 43.

26 Parker, 56.

27 Parker, 56.

28 See Dympna Callaghan, *Shakespeare without Women: Representing Gender and Race on the Renaissance Stage* (New York and London: Routledge, 2000);

Anston Bosman, "'Best Play with Mardian': Eunuch and Blackamoor as Imperial Culturegram," *Shakespeare Studies* 34 (2006): 123–57.

29 See Jonathan Goldberg, *Sodometries: Renaissance Texts, Modern Sexualities* (Stanford University Press, 1992); Valerie Traub, "Sexuality," in *A Cultural History of Western Empires in the Renaissance*, ed. Ania Loomba (London: Bloomsbury, 2019), 147–80.

30 Callaghan, 70. See also Stephen Orgel, *Impersonations: The Performance of Gender in Shakespeare's England* (Cambridge University Press, 1996).

31 Little, 174.

32 Little, 175.

33 Little, 176.

CHAPTER 10

The Tempest *and Early Modern Conceptions of Race*

Virginia Mason Vaughan and Alden T. Vaughan

Clark University

Although *The Tempest* is set on an uninhabited island located implicitly but unmistakably between Italy and North Africa, it is often considered Shakespeare's American play.[1] The opening scene's tumultuous storm recalls William Strachey's description of a 1609 hurricane that battered a fleet taking settlers and supplies to England's beleaguered colony in Virginia. The flagship *Sea Venture*, carrying a new governor and colonists from a cross section of English society, barely survived "A most dreadfull Tempest" and lodged upright on an outcrop of the uninhabited Bermuda Islands. Presumed dead, the castaways remained on Bermuda for nearly ten months while they constructed two small ships and completed the voyage to Virginia. News of their miraculous "wracke, and redemption" reached England in the autumn of 1610 and was widely celebrated.[2] Shakespeare's *Tempest* begins with a terrifying storm and calamitous shipwreck, and, like the English settlers aboard *Sea Venture*, the crew and passengers all survive. In the ensuing action, they wander about the island, fomenting conspiracies and schisms that roughly parallel Strachey's account of events on Bermuda. Like many of the castaways who returned to England soon after their Bermuda adventure, in *The Tempest*'s final moments the Europeans plan their voyage back to Italy.

The island's chief inhabitant, Prospero, the deposed duke of Milan, is not there to establish a colony, but in essential ways he resembles a European imperialist. Twelve years before the play commences, Prospero and his three-year-old daughter were marooned on the uncharted island where they encountered two inhabitants, Ariel, a "spirit" with some human characteristics, and Caliban, the son of an African woman who arrived on the island shortly before she gave birth. Prospero's settlement of the island and his interactions with Ariel and Caliban fit the colonial paradigm: he appropriates the island's natural resources and makes Ariel his servant, Caliban his slave.

Prospero's daughter Miranda, who has lived most of her life on the island, is astounded when she sees the king of Naples and his companions at the play's finale. "O brave new world," she cries, "that has such people in't" (5.1.183–84). The "people" are all Europeans, but Miranda unwittingly echoes more than a century of Spanish, Portuguese, French, Dutch, and English reactions to newly discovered lands and peoples across the seas. Ominously for natives of these new worlds, Europeans rarely considered them as equals. Unlike Miranda, explorers and colonists routinely disparaged and exploited newly encountered peoples of the Americas, Africa, and Asia.

An exchange between King Alonso and his brother Sebastian underscores the Europeans' distinction between themselves and indigenous Africans, such as Caliban's ancestors. Sebastian blames Alonso for the loss of Alonso's son Ferdinand, who is presumed drowned in the storm. If Alonso hadn't arranged the marriage of his daughter Claribel to the king of Tunis, there would have been no journey to her wedding and no shipwreck:

> Sir, you may thank yourself for this great loss,
> That would not bless our Europe with your daughter
> But rather loose her to an African.
>
> (2.1.124–26)

Shakespeare's spelling – "loose" – has sexual undertones, as if Alonso had pandered his daughter for financial or political gain. Sebastian reminds Alonso that he was "kneeled to and importuned otherwise / By all of us" (2.1.129–30), who argued against the union of a white European with an African. Claribel herself, Sebastian recalls, was torn "between loathness and obedience" at the prospect of such a marriage (131).

Prospero, too, deplores miscegenation. He wants an appropriate marriage for Miranda and contrives the shipwreck partly to provide his daughter with a suitable mate in Ferdinand and to thwart Caliban, the island's only alternative. Prospero explains in 1.2 that Caliban's mother Sycorax, a "witch" who was banished from Algiers for an unspecified crime, had twelve years before Prospero and Miranda's arrival landed on the island and given birth to Caliban. According to Prospero, he was fathered by the devil (1.2.320). His name, an anagram of "cannibal," may highlight his African origins, as rumors circulated in Europe of the continent's repugnant man-eaters.

Prospero claims to have treated Caliban humanely, lodging him "In mine own cell, till thou didst seek to violate / The honour of my child" (1.2.348–49). Miranda shares Prospero's sense of betrayal:

> I pitied thee,
> Took pains to make thee speak, taught thee each hour
> One thing or other. When thou didst not, savage,

Know thine own meaning, but wouldst gabble like
A thing most brutish, I endowed thy purposes
With words that made them known. But thy vile race
(Though thou didst learn) had that in't which good natures
Could not abide to be with; therefore wast thou
Deservedly confined into this rock,
Who hadst deserved more than a prison.

(1.2.354–63)

Initially, then, the native and the newcomers enjoyed a symbiotic relationship. Caliban introduced the father and daughter to "all the qualities o'th' isle" (1.2.338); they taught him their language and rudiments of astronomy. But Caliban's sexual attack on Miranda shattered European standards of decorum and, more portentously, raised the specter of mixed-race descendants. "Oh, ho!" Caliban boasts, "Would't had been done; / Thou didst prevent me, I had peopled else / This isle with Calibans" (1.2.350–52).

This essay looks behind and beyond Shakespeare's text of *The Tempest* to reveal how it reflects his era's understanding of race, especially the impact of Europe's encounter with America. Race had numerous meanings then as it does now, depending partly on rhetorical contexts, partly on regional customs, and partly on the word's evolution from long before Shakespeare's time to, presumably, long beyond our own. The task at hand is to examine how Shakespeare's last solo play evokes notions of race that had evolved in Europe over several centuries and, after 1492, were further complicated by the complex and expanding encounter with the western hemisphere, as well as, after 1554, by an influx of Africans into the British Isles.

We have already discussed the very revealing banter about Claribel, who has no further role in the play. Most of the remaining racial markers appear in the several pejorative categories into which Shakespeare thrusts Caliban, the island's only native: savage, slave, cannibal, pagan, and monster. Collectively those identifications condemn him to a distinctly separate and inferior human category from the Europeans who berate and abuse him.

Caliban's Perceived Defects

Miranda's choice of "vile race" to describe Caliban's character is striking. Shakespeare infrequently uses "race" in his texts, but when he does, it usually refers to a family relationship, past or future, in accord with the

OED's first definition of its use as a noun: "A group of persons, animals or plants connected by common descent or origin." Most often, the term is combined with a modifier that establishes its meaning. The adjective can be positive: The duke of Suffolk refers to the Neville family's "noble race" in *3 Henry 6* (3.2.215), and Antony regrets that he has his "pillow left unpressed in Rome / [and] Forborne the getting of a lawful race" (*Antony and Cleopatra*, 3.13.107–08). But the modifier can also be negative. Miranda asserts that Caliban deserves to be enslaved because his inherent nature – his "vile race" – is ineluctably deficient, making him inferior, even repugnant, to "civilized" Europeans.

Caliban's otherness is not, of course, solely a matter of his ill-defined identity. Most of the text's descriptors of Caliban suggest a physical anomaly. "Names of the Actors," a cast list in the First Folio (1623), describes Caliban as "a saluage and deformed slaue" (TLN 2329). Alonso declares that he is as "strange a thing as e're I looked on" (5.1.290). The hyperbolic Trinculo and Stephano call Caliban a "mooncalf," implying to English audiences some physical and/or behavioral abnormality caused by birth under the full moon. The two shipwrecked Europeans refer to Caliban as a monster some forty times, modified by "shallow," "weak," "poor," "perfidious," "ridiculous," "puppy-headed," "scurvy," "abominable," "bully," "ignorant," and (in the seventeenth-century sense of foolhardy or blustery) "brave." On first encountering Caliban under the gabardine, Trinculo says he smells like a fish, but on further inspection concludes that "this is no fish, but an islander that hath lately suffered by a thunderbolt" (2.1.25, 34–36). In the play's final scene, Antonio calls Caliban "a plain fish" (5.1.266), which again likely refers to his smell, for he and his co-conspirators have just emerged from a "filthy-mantled pool" (4.1.181–84). Nevertheless, in illustrations and stage productions Caliban is often given fins, scales, webbed feet and hands, and other aquatic or animal appurtenances, such as floppy ears or apish fur. However Caliban is imagined, the text insists that he differs in one or more significant ways from European anatomical norms.

At the same time Shakespeare's text asserts that Caliban has an essentially human figure. Hasty readers often cite Prospero's phrase, "A freckled whelp, hag-born, not honoured with / A human shape" (1.2.283–84) to prove Caliban's non-human form, but when read in the context of the First Folio's parentheses – "Then was this Island / (Saue for the Son that [s]he did littour heere, / A frekll'ed whelpe, hag-borne) not honour'd with / A humane shape" (TLN 408–11) – it is clear that Caliban is the only human-shaped islander. Miranda seems to challenge that image when she assures Ferdinand that she has seen no more that she "may call men than you, good friend, / And my dear father" (3.1.51–52), but at 1.2.446, she calls Ferdinand "the third man that e'er I saw," presumably in addition to her father and Caliban. Prospero concurs when he chides Miranda for her sudden infatuation with Ferdinand, "Having seen but him and Caliban" (1.2.480). Despite his unspecified anomaly, Caliban is clearly human.

Caliban as Slave

More important to this discussion, Caliban is a slave. As punishment for his sexual assault on Miranda, Prospero has styed him in a cave, forced him to perform manual labor, and physically tormented him with cramps and pinches when he failed to please. In Act 1, scene 2, Prospero initially addresses Caliban, "What, ho, slave!" (314), and subsequently calls him "poisonous slave" (320) and "most lying slave" (345). To Miranda, he is "Abhorred slave" (352).

This use of "slave" lends Caliban's status an unusual resonance in the Shakespeare canon. Romantic comedies such as *Love's Labour's Lost* and *Twelfth Night* feature men who claim to be enslaved by love. *Julius Caesar* and *Antony and Cleopatra* include actual slaves as existed in ancient Rome. More often Shakespeare's characters use "slave" to demean another character and to underscore social inferiority. In *King Lear*, for example, Oswald is Goneril's steward, but Lear repeatedly refers to him as "slave," even coupling it with pejoratives, such as "dog, you slave, you cur" (1.4.80). In *The Tempest* slavery is literal, and Prospero is a slavemaster. True, Prospero forces Prince Ferdinand to pile heavy logs as a kind of "wooden slavery" (3.1.62), but only briefly and to show his power. Aaron, the black Moor who serves the queen of the Goths in *Titus Andronicus*, and Caliban are the two enslaved servants in Shakespeare who appear to be, in modern terminology, racially distinct.

The First Folio's description of Caliban as "a savage and deformed slave" invokes two of the criteria often associated with racial slavery in early modern Europe and America. His perceived deformities, whatever they may be, signal in exaggerated terms the way enslaved persons were commonly characterized. His sexual assault on Miranda, not to mention his surly attitude toward Prospero and his unintelligible (to them) language demonstrate his savagery – a failure to meet European standards of social and ethical civility. Prospero links the two slavish criteria when he complains that Caliban "is as disproportioned in his manners / As in his shape" (5.1.291–92).

Caliban's paganism fulfills a third customary criterion for enslavement. Rarely did Europeans make slaves of fellow Christians; people of other faiths were fair game. While the play largely ignores Caliban's religious beliefs, two clues suggest that he shared his mother's worship of the Patagonian deity Setebos, first mentioned in an Italian account of Ferdinand Magellan's circumnavigating expedition of 1519–22, translated into English in 1555. When Prospero threatens to punish Caliban in 1.2., the slave laments, "I must obey; his art is of such power / It would control my dam's god Setebos, / And make a vassal of him" (1.2.373–75). In the final scene, Caliban reacts to his first sight of the shipwrecked noblemen: "O Setebos, these be brave spirits indeed" (5.1.261). These lines and Prospero's insistence that Caliban's father was the devil put Caliban beyond the Christian pale in Prospero's imagination.

But nothing demonstrated savagery to Europeans so emphatically as cannibalism. Reports that some Africans, and after 1492, indigenous Americans ate human flesh either in their regular diets or in pagan ceremonies appalled Europeans. While *The Tempest* does not accuse Caliban of practicing cannibalism, numerous Shakespeare critics since at least the late eighteenth century have insisted that Shakespeare's choice of the name Caliban was intentional on the grounds that the early modern English delighted in wordplay, including the use of anagrams. Shakespeare, it can plausibly be argued, meant Caliban to be a cannibal, figuratively if not literally. In sum, Caliban's physical irregularity, savagery, heathenism, and perhaps cannibalism, justified, in Prospero's eyes, his perpetual bondage.

Ariel's Contrasting Status

The "Names of the Actors" describes Ariel as an "ayrie [airy] spirit" (TLN 2336). In contrast to Caliban, a creature associated with the earth who lives in a subterranean cave, Ariel lives in the air. He (or she – Ariel is genderless, but the sole textual descriptor is "his," 1.2.192) had freely enjoyed the island's natural wonders until Sycorax arrived. Ariel became her servant but was "a spirit too delicate / To act her earthy and abhorred commands" (1.2.172–73). Unlike Caliban, Ariel recognizes and eschews evil. Soon after her arrival, Sycorax pinioned the airy spirit in a cloven pine, where he remained in agonizing pain for twelve years until Prospero arrived and freed him. In return, Ariel serves Prospero with the promise of eventual freedom. Until then, Ariel, invisible, acts as Prospero's eyes and ears. He flits from one area of the island and one group of characters to another, then reports back to his master. Ariel also intervenes on Prospero's behalf. He wakens Gonzalo in 2.1 (preventing his murder by Sebastian), appears in 3.3 as a vengeful harpy, stage-manages the masque of goddesses in 4.1, and, at the beginning of 5.1, empathizes with Prospero's victims and urges the magician to show mercy toward his enemies. Seeing their suffering, Ariel says his affections would become tender "were I human" (5.1.20). Ariel is also the instrument of Prospero's magic. Besides producing the opening scene's tempest, through song he creates the island's haunting noises and through stagecraft he creates its wondrous spectacles.

Prospero calls Ariel a slave only once, and that is in response to the servant's demand for freedom (1.2. 270). Thereafter, the relationship is between affectionate master and faithful servant. When Ariel asks, "Do you love me, master? No?" the reply is, "Dearly, my delicate Ariel" (4.1.48–49.) Prospero fondly addresses Ariel as "my industrious servant" (4.1.33), "my bird" (4.1.184), "my dainty Ariel" (5.1.95), "My tricksy spirit" (5.1.226), "my diligence" (5.1.241), and "my chick" (5.1.314). At the play's conclusion Prospero frees Ariel to fly and sing as he pleases. In the context of early modern social structure (if one overlooks his ethereal form), Ariel is an indentured servant.

Servitude in Early Modern England

Shakespeare was surely familiar with indentured servitude for people of various European ethnicities and backgrounds and slavery for people of African (and often indigenous American) ancestry. Servants bound for terms ranging from a few years to more than a decade were common throughout England, especially in the form of apprenticeship for learning a trade, mostly for males, and of household service, mostly for females. When *The Tempest* was first staged in 1611, the Virginia colony, England's only American outpost, had many European servants – German, Italian, Polish, as well as English, Irish, and Scottish – working for the colony or for individual masters.

Some people of African ancestry had lived in the British Isles from the Roman occupation of approximately 55 BC to approximately AD 450, but not until the 1550s did English ships bring black slaves directly from Africa. In the late sixteenth century, many more arrived, especially through England's expanding involvement in the international slave trade. Although Africans did not appear in English America until the second decade of the seventeenth century, slavery's widespread practice in Europe and Iberian America was by then common knowledge.

English writers often denied that England permitted slavery within its borders, but a variety of legal, religious, and personal documents of the early modern period attest to England's many black "servants" (the generic term for people bound to service, including slaves) and an undeterminable number of "slaves" (the specific term for lifetime servitude, though some-times – as in Caliban's case – partly or entirely as punishment for serious crimes).[3] By the 1590s Queen Elizabeth's government, alarmed by "the great number of Negroes and blackamoors brought into this realme," issued proclamations for their expulsion. Her orders were largely ignored.[4] The black population, most of it apparently enslaved, enlarged the nation's extensive category of bound labor. Sometime before his death in 1617, a prominent Cambridge preacher explained that "servants are either more slavish, or else more free and liberall: the first are such whose bodies are perpetually put under the power of the Master, as Blackmores with us ... [and] the children of [such] servants are borne the slaves of their Masters." The other category ("more free and liberall"), the preacher noted, "are upon certaine termes or conditions for a certaine time onely under the power of a man: such are our Apprentises, Journeymen, maide-servants, etc."[5] Long before Shakespeare died in 1616, the year African laborers first reached the English colony in Bermuda, and three years before the arrival of captives from a Portuguese slave ship inaugurated black slavery in Virginia, imported Africans and their progeny occupied a variety of roles in England. Especially in London but also in port towns and occasionally in the hinterland, "blackamoores" appear in the records, mostly as domes-tic servants such as cooks, footmen, and laundresses; entertainers, such as drummers, dancers, and actors; or laborers, such as sailors, carters, and roustabouts.[6] When Shakespeare crafted *The Tempest* in 1610–11, he was surely familiar with the categories and conditions of servitude and slavery practiced daily in London and elsewhere in the British Isles.

The Early Modern Rationale for Racism

Underlying the nascent British Empire's adoption of slave labor was an assumption of African inferiority. It first appeared prominently in English writings on Africa that informed English readers about the hazards and opportunities of commerce with the continent, especially the western coast. Such writings frequently distinguished African commercial partners, whom they generally admired, from African slaves at home or abroad, whom the writers customarily portrayed as barely-human commodities.[7]

Stage performances reinforced the message conveyed by travel accounts. A Swiss visitor observed in 1599 that English men and women "pass their time" at theatres, "learning at the play what is happening abroad," and presumably about the people abroad.[8] Surely the pejoratives about black skin in *Titus Andronicus* (1594) and *Othello* (1604)[9], for example, reveal English conceptions of race as much as the tracts reprinted by Richard Eden (1555, 1577) or Richard Hakluyt (1582, 1589, 1599–1600).[10] And, as several authorities on early modern England's racial perceptions have repeatedly demonstrated, English assumptions about Africans' shortcomings appeared not only in narratives and plays, but also in a wide range of literary genres, in art and artifacts, and in everyday actions.[11] Shakespeare's audiences would have recognized Caliban's compatibility with prevailing characterizations of dark-hued strangers.

Some English writers were preoccupied with the darkness of African skin. A few texts deprecated "black" people, as in a poem published separately in 1568 and reprinted in Hakluyt's *Principall Navigations . . . of the English Nation*, that dubbed Africans "blacke beast[s]," "brutish blacke people," and "black burnt men."[12] Most English texts were more concerned with the reasons for Africans' dark hue. The standard explanation for it in the early sixteenth century was proximity to the sun: sub-Saharan Africans were the nearest and therefore the darkest. Virginia's Captain John Smith articulated that notion in the year of Shakespeare's death when he described, in deeply pejorative terms, a portion of western Africa as "those fryed Regions of blacke brutish Negers."[13]

Some English observers noticed that the children of Africans who moved, willingly or not, to temperate climates favored an alternative to the geographic theory. Captain George Best's description of equatorial Africans was especially persuasive. (Best did not originate the theory, but he disseminated it widely in his pamphlet of 1578 and Hakluyt's partial reprint in 1600.) The Africans' "blacknesse," Best proposed, "preceedeth of some naturall infection of the first inhabitants of that Countrey, and so all the whole progenie . . . are still polluted with the same blot of infection." Best located the source of that infection in Noah's curse on his son Cham (Ham) for impregnating his wife on the Ark, in disobedience of Noah's orders. As punishment, Cham's son Chus and his descendants "should be so blacke & lothsome, that it might remaine a spectacle of disobedience to all the World. And of this blacke & cursed *Chus* came al these blacke *Moores* . . ."[14]

For more than a century this explanation flourished, especially in preached or printed sermons. A London sermon of 1607, the year the

Virginia colony was founded, insisted that through "the accursed seed of *Cham*, the Egyptians, Moores & Ethiopians had for a stamp of their fathers sinne, the colour of hell set upon their faces."[15] In 1615, George Sandys of the Virginia Company denied that the Ethiopians' complexion came from their seed, climate, or soil, "but rather from the curse of *Noe* upon *Cham* in the posterity of *Chus.*"[16] And, along with the curse of color came the curse of slavery. The Geneva Bible of 1560, widely used in England and the colonies, defined the "servant of servantes" that Ham's son would be to his brethren in the very words that Miranda would later invoke for Caliban – a "vile slave" (Genesis 9:25). The conviction that dark-skinned Africans were eternally cursed by God and divinely ordained to serve people of light pigmentation (George Best had insisted that Noah's sons were "white and their wives also") thus had widespread currency in England before the first enslaved Africans arrived in English America. In persistent, though inconsistent, association with other imagined African shortcomings, the myth of "God's curse" contributed profoundly to England's categorical debasement of Africans at home and abroad. When in *The Tempest*'s final moments Prospero addresses Caliban as "this thing of darkness," Shakespeare's word choice likely applies to his hue as well as his character. If we accept Prospero's charge that Caliban's father was the devil, who in Christian iconography was always black, Caliban is doubly cursed. Unsurprisingly, from the second half of the twentieth century to the present, Caliban has frequently been portrayed onstage and in non-dramatic appropriations as a black man.

Caliban as an American Indian

That Caliban was simultaneously, or alternatively, an American Indian is grounded in both text and context. The textual basis lies partly in the Names of the Actors' description of Caliban as "saluage" [savage], the predominant English label for an indigenous American in Shakespeare's era, and partly in Caliban's claim to be the island's legitimate heir: "This island's mine by Sycorax my mother, / Which thou tak'st from me" (1.2.332–33). Caliban also resembles American Indians in his intimate knowledge of the island's flora and fauna (see Figure 10.1). Like natives of Caribbean islands and elsewhere in Iberian America, Caliban's sharing of that knowledge permitted clueless newcomers to survive. When Prospero and Miranda first arrived, Caliban showed them "The fresh springs, brine pits, barren place and fertile" (1.2.338–39). Later he boasts to Stephano that he will

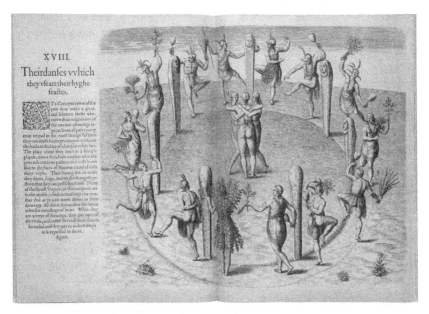

Figure 10.1   Thomas Hariot's 1590 book, *A briefe and true report of the new found land of Virginia* . . . contains many early modern English depictions of Native Americans.

> Show thee a jay's nest, and instruct thee how
> To snare the nimble marmoset. I'll bring thee
> To clust'ring filberts, and sometimes I'll get thee
> Young scamels from the rock.
>
> (2.2.166–69)

Caliban's name also strongly suggests American roots. Although some Africans reputedly ate human flesh, the customary term for them was "anthropophagi," of Greek derivation. The etymology of "cannibal", however, is strictly American. In the Taino language it designates the Caribes of the Lesser Antilles islands encountered by Christopher Columbus in 1492 – the first Americans to be accused of eating other humans' flesh. Early European illustrations of New World natives often featured scenes of them dismembering and devouring their captives. By the early sixteenth century, "cannibal" (*canibal* in Spanish) was the nearly universal term for consumers of human flesh.

In 2.1 Shakespeare drew on Michel de Montaigne's essay, "Of the Caniballes," composed after a visit to Rouen by Brazilian Indians who were thought to be man-eaters, and translated into English in 1603. The French philosopher wryly suggested that there was little moral distinction between New World cannibals and Europeans who devour each other through war and starvation.[17] In a passage closely adapted from Montaigne, King Alonso's councilor Gonzalo speculates on what he would do if he had "the plantation of this isle" (2.1.148–65). His settlement would become a new golden world, a community whose inhabitants could live well and simply off nature's bounty, where there would be no king or constable and the inhabitants were innocent and pure. But Antonio's and Sebastian's cynical interruptions undercut the aged councilor's idealism. Later, when Antonio and Sebastian secretly plan to assassinate the king and his councilor, they prove Montaigne's point. In any case, Shakespeare's use of Montaigne's relatively benign attitude toward cannibalism in the New World may have encouraged readers and viewers of *The Tempest* to recognize "Caliban" as an intentional anagram, a damning nominal emblem.

Prospero's subsequent enslavement of Caliban reinforces *The Tempest's* Indian parallels. Although early European explorers clearly distinguished indigenous Americans from Africans in appearance and culture, on their suitability to forced labor, it was a distinction without much difference. One of Columbus's first impressions of the Caribbean islanders he encountered in 1492 was "how easy it would be to convert these people – and to make them work for us."[18] During his four expeditions to the western hemisphere, Columbus shipped home hundreds of natives. Many died en route; most of the survivors became slaves in Spain or Portugal. After waves of Iberian colonists sequestered large swathes of Central and South America in the sixteenth and early seventeenth centuries, they brazenly enslaved the local peoples, using a variety of European legal and quasi-legal justifications. When American natives died in droves from imported diseases or from overwork in the fields and mines, Iberian landlords filled the void with African slaves – about 250,000 by the early seventeenth century. In 1610, when *The Tempest* began to form in Shakespeare's mind, dark-hued people in regions under European control were overwhelmingly the property of light-hued Euro-Americans, for a term of years or, usually, for life.

Caliban and England's American Colonies

English colonists did not immediately follow suit. Several perceived differences between their own imperial posture and Spain's kept the Virginia colony from attempting to enslave nearby natives. Initially, of course, Indians held the upper hand, in numbers and in resources, especially food.

Just as Caliban knew how to snare the nimble marmoset and find clear water, Virginia Indians knew how to plant and harvest maize, catch seafood, and stalk wild animals. Until the English settlements grew larger, stronger, and wiser, they relied for their very survival on native crops acquired by trade or seizure. Moreover, a major justification for the creation of English settlements was the prospect of converting American "heathens" into Protestant Christians through theological reasoning and gentle encouragement, in contrast to Catholic Spain's allegedly coercive and superstitious methods. Despite frequent assaults and occasional atrocities by both sides, the Virginia colony's lesson for Shakespeare and his contemporaries was that conflict with American Indians should be avoided: Conversion, not conquest, would eventually create a harmonious biracial society, albeit on English terms.

That goal partly explains why many English explorers in the sixteenth and early seventeenth centuries brought home one or more Indians – by capture or persuasion – for a few months or many years. Some of them, Trinculo reminds us, became posthumous curiosities. When English folk would not give a small coin "to relieve a lame beggar," he laments, "they will lay out ten to see a dead Indian" (2.2.27–32). Live Indians were usually trained as guides and interpreters for future voyages or settlements and exposed to English customs and English forms of Christianity. Shakespeare himself must have seen, perhaps spoken with, some of the dozens of Indians in London during his long residence. Near the end of his life, he may also have heard of the impending visit to England by "princess" Pocahontas of the Powhatan tribe, recently married to a colonist and christened Rebecca, living proof that Virginia's natives could become civil and Christian.

An even more immediate and applicable Indian connection surfaced at the very moment Shakespeare began *The Tempest*. Although contemporaneous narratives of *Sea Venture*'s crash on Bermuda in 1609 did not mention Indians among the castaways, other evidence confirms the presence of two young Powhatan men returning to Virginia from a diplomatic mission to London. One reached his homeland with the English survivors in the spring of 1610; the other, slain by his countryman, lay in a shallow grave on the islands. That autumn, Shakespeare could have mined oral reports of the episode for some of Caliban's characteristics and lines in Trinculo's and Stephano's reactions to Caliban under his gabardine.[19]

Caliban's negative qualities may also reflect the skepticism of the many colonists and their backers at home who insisted that Indians differed from themselves in crucial ways. During Shakespeare's life those differences rarely included skin color. The earliest European explorers, beginning with Columbus, were surprised to find that in latitudes parallel to sub-Saharan Africa, indigenous Americans were not "black" but brown, olive, or tawny. A century later, observers in the temperate latitudes of English settlement shared the European fascination with pigmentation but added a new twist. The natives in areas of English settlement were innately white, eyewitnesses insisted; the prevailing tawny hue came from nurture rather than nature. Captain John Smith, for example, reported in 1607 (orally at first and in print by 1612) that indigenous Virginians are "of a colour browne when they are of any age, but they are born white."[20] They were quickly darkened by protective stains and ointments applied at infancy and renewed as needed. William Strachey described American natives in 1610–11 as "generally of a Colour browne, or rather tawnye which the Mothers cast them into ... with red tempered oyntements of earth, and juyce of certayne scrused [twisted] rootes, so soon as they ar born."[21] Leading colonists in New England and neighboring provinces would report similar findings in the 1620s and 1630s.

English belief in the Indians' congenital whiteness helped to shield them from Noah's curse on Cham, thereby enhancing the likelihood of peaceful assimilation into colonial society. It did not, however, protect them from accusations of savagery on other grounds, such as the long-held belief among English explorers and settlers that Indians were incorrigibly treacherous and under Satan's thrall. But encounters with Indians along the North Atlantic coast in the late sixteenth and early seventeenth centuries ameliorated most derogatory images. Indigenous Americans in areas of English settlement appeared to be less numerous, less fierce, and less hostile than those the Iberians had subdued in many of the hemisphere's southerly regions.

At about the same time, English hopes for the conversion to civility and Christianity of indigenous Americans were also boosted by a growing conviction that they were analogous to England's British ancestors. When Roman occupiers introduced them to civility and Christianity, the argument went, the ancient Britons shed their barbarity and paganism in favor of new ways and beliefs. That idea circulated in many publications and in illustrations of nearly naked, heavily tattooed figures. A caption in 1590 explained "how ... the inhabitants of great Bretannie have bin in times past as sauvage as those of Virginia."[22] The Reverend William Crashaw elaborated in a sermon of 1610 to the Virginia Company of London: "time was when wee were as savage and uncivill, and worshipped the divell, as now they [the Indians] do, then God sent some to make us civill, others to make us Christians ... [S]hall we not be sensible of those that are still as we were then?"[23] Many Virginia colonists opened their doors to neighboring Indians in tacit acceptance of that challenge.

A sudden Powhatan uprising in 1622 shattered English optimism. The massacre of nearly 350 colonial men, women, and children, nearly a third of the Europeans in Virginia, convinced the Virginia Company to call for such a thorough retaliation that the enemy would no longer be "a people upon the face of the Earth."[24] Colonial troops should seize the Indians' land and kill resisters; the rest "may now most justly be compelled to servitude and drudgery," especially, the writer insisted soon after the slaughter, on "inferiour workes of digging in mynes, and the like."[25] The Iberian model was vindicated. English colonists' subsequent enslavement of indigenous Americans would reinforce the point.

Shakespeare in 1610–11 could not have foreseen these changes of perception and policy. An emerging but far from universal English view of Virginia's natives in the *Tempest*'s moment of creation was of rough but redeemable savages, as susceptible to civility and conversion as their own ancestors had been. That is arguably what Shakespeare had in mind when in the play's closing moments a chastised Caliban forswears his prior misdeeds and vows to "be wise hereafter / and seek for grace" (5.1.295–96). But after the 1622 massacre, commentators berated American Indians, especially Virginia's, as incorrigibly savage and immune for the foreseeable future to social and religious redemption. Readers of the 1623 Folio and audiences at London playhouses thereafter may have doubted Caliban's prospects for grace. Some critics of Virginia natives even stripped them of whiteness's protective (non)coloration. A longtime booster of the Virginia enterprise complained in 1623 that conversion of "the Infidels" was now impossible, "they being descended of the cursed race of Cham."[26]

If English readers and viewers saw Caliban as an American Indian, an African, or a fusion of the two ancestries, he reflected the widely held conviction on both sides of the Atlantic that those people were inherently dark, savage, and eminently suitable for slavery. Certain strands of English thought seem pervasive: that God, according to the Old Testament, had darkened and demeaned most Africans; that indigenous Americans were perhaps similarly cursed and innately savage and thus inferior to white Europeans; and that the insatiable demand for cheap labor in the Americas justified the exploitation, even enslavement, of vulnerable people.

Not everyone in the anglophone world shared those beliefs; racial thought was never monolithic. Individual ideas about race adjusted to changing local and national experiences, new information, and a host of other variables. That instability of perception is reflected in Caliban. He is the most abusive character in the play, determined to rape Miranda and murder Prospero, and yet he is the most egregiously abused in word and deed by the Europeans. He is the most savage and seemingly "uncivilized" character, and yet he speaks some of the play's most moving poetic lines. He appears unredeemable through much of the play, and yet in the end, he promises to reform. Mostly in his complex portrait of Caliban but also in Antonio's and Sebastian's revealing banter about Claribel's marriage, Shakespeare appears to have drawn a rough template for the racial conceptions of his time.

The Tempest's Afterlife

Unlike most of the colonists who founded Virginia, Prospero abandons his overseas settlement and resumes his role as duke of Milan. The other Europeans also return to Italy, and presumably stay there. Miranda will marry Ferdinand, uniting Milan with the kingdom of Naples. On the island, after Ariel assures the ship's safe passage home, he will be free. Caliban has the island to himself again.

For three centuries readers and viewers took this happy ending for granted and ignored the text's colonial resonance. In William Dryden and William Davenant's popular adaptation (1667), transformed soon after into a musical by Thomas Shadwell, *The Tempest: The Enchanted Island* was a comic opera, with a fairy-like female Ariel trilling embellished arias and Caliban parodied as a monstrous buffoon. Although Shakespeare's text, albeit drastically cut, was revived on the stage in 1838 and after, the publication of Charles Darwin's evolutionary theories later in the nineteenth century often led directors to make Caliban into a "missing link" in apish costumes. As late as 1892, the comprehensive variorum edition of *The Tempest* by Horace Howard Furness ignored what might be called Caliban's racial roots. In that year, however, the biographer-critic Sidney Lee proposed that Shakespeare had American natives in mind when he fashioned Caliban. Six years later in his biography of Shakespeare, Lee declared that "Caliban is an imaginary portrait, conceived with matchless vigor and vividness, of the aboriginal savage of the New World," a theme he expounded in many publications until his death in 1926.[27]

Lee's Americanization of *The Tempest* was prescient. During the twentieth century, as Europe's colonies in Africa and the Americas struggled for, and eventually gained, independence, commentators increasingly saw Prospero as a prototype of a European colonist, Caliban as a black man of African or mixed origins, Ariel as a light-skinned mulatto or an indigenous American. In 1969, for example, Aimé Césaire was inspired by his native Martinique's colonial past and the American Civil Rights Movement to adapt Shakespeare's *Tempest* to contemporary concerns. All of Shakespeare's characters remain the same, except Ariel is now "a mulatto slave", Caliban, "a black slave." In Césaire's adaptation, Caliban's and Ariel's interactions pose two ways of dealing with the white man's (i.e., Prospero's) oppression. Ariel argues for peaceful accommodation in the mode of Martin Luther King, Jr., while Caliban, like Malcolm X, asks to be called, simply, X, and promises to resist violently if necessary.[28] In the same year the Barbadian poet Edward Kamau Brathwaite used African rhythms to express Caliban's heritage and traced his journey to the Americas through the torments of the Middle Passage.[29] Also in the 1960s and 1970s, the Cuban writer Roberto Fernández Retamar hailed Caliban as the symbol of mestizo Latin Americans: "Prospero invaded the islands, killed our ancestors, enslaved Caliban, and taught him his language ... What is our history, what is our culture, if not the history and culture of Caliban?"[30]

Finally, Marina Warner's fictional appropriation, *Indigo, or Mapping the Waters* (1992), made Sycorax a wise woman, native to the island of St. Kitts. When she discovers a black baby among a pile of corpses, detritus from a slave ship, she raises him: "he was the first African to arrive in the islands, and he came to be known later, to the settlers from Europe, as Caliban."[31] Sycorax also adopts a homeless girl, Ariel, an Arawak Indian brought to the Caribbean island by European settlers.

Numerous examples could be cited of the ways writers, from the late nineteenth century to the present, have reimagined Caliban and Ariel as racially distinct victims of Prospero's (i.e., European and American) imperialist expropriation and exploitation. Some early modern scholars now consider *The Tempest* to be one of Shakespeare's "race plays." Although contemporary critics and artists inevitably see *The Tempest* in light of their own preferences and circumstances, the seeds of many modern interpretations, as this essay demonstrates, are embedded in Shakespeare's original language. He, too, was shaped by England's substantial African and indigenous American presence, by England's growing involvement in the transatlantic slave trade, by Europe's devastating conquest of the brave new world, and by the increasingly racialized discourse of his own time.

Notes

1 Quotations from *The Tempest* are taken from the Third Arden Series, ed. Virginia Mason Vaughan and Alden T. Vaughan, rev. edn (London: Bloomsbury, 2011), except for quotations from the First Folio, which are from *The Norton Facsimile of the First of Folio of Shakespeare*, ed. Charlton Hinman (New York: W.W. Norton, 1968), which uses "through line numbers" (TLN) instead of act, scene, and line numbers. We have adhered to the spelling used in the sources we cite except where they reverse "u" and "v", "i" and "j", which we have modernized, the First Folio excepted.

2 Quoted in Samuel Purchas, *Hakluytus Posthumus, or Purchas his Pilgrimes*, 20 vols. (1625; New York: AMS Press, 1965), vol. XIX, 5.

3 See Imtiaz Habib, *Black Lives in the English Archives, 1500–1667: Imprints of the Invisible* (Aldershot and Burlington, VT: Ashgate, 2008); Paul Baynes, *An entire Commentary upon the Whole Epistle of the Apostle Paul to the Ephesians* (London: R. Milbourne and I. Bartlett, 1643), 695.

4 *Tudor Royal Proclamations*, ed. Paul L. Hughes and James F. Larkin, 3 vols. (New Haven, CT: Yale University Press, 1964–69), vol. III, 221–22. See also Habib, 112–17.

5 Baynes, 695.

6 Peter Fryer, *Staying Power: The History of Black People in Britain since 1504* (Atlantic Highlands, NJ: Humanities Press, 1984), 1–6. See also, Habib, 302–41.

7 April Lee Hatfield "A 'very wary people in their bargaining' or 'very good marchandise': English Traders' Views of Free and Enslaved Africans, 1550–1650," *Slavery and Abolition* 25/3 (2004): 1–17.

8 Thomas Platter, *Thomas Platter's Travels in England, 1599*, ed. Clare Williams (London: Jonathan Cape, 1937), 170.

9 Virginia Mason Vaughan, *Performing Blackness on English Stages, 1500–1800* (Cambridge University Press, 2005).

10 Richard Eden, *The decades of the Newe Worlde or West India* (London: William Powell, 1555); Richard Eden and Richard Willes, *The History of Travayle in the West and East Indies* (London: Richard Iugge, 1577); Richard Hakluyt, *The Principall Navigations, Voiages and Discoveries of the English Nation* (London: George Bishop and Ralph Newberie, 1589); Richard Hakluyt, *The Principal Navigations, Voyages, Traffiques and Discoveries of the English Nation*, 12 vols. (1598–1600; New York: Augustus M. Kelley, 1969).

11 See Kim F. Hall, *Things of Darkness: Economies of Race and Gender in Early Modern England* (Ithaca, NY: Cornell University Press, 1995), 211–53; David Bindman, "The Black Presence in British Art: Sixteenth and Seventeenth Centuries," in *The Image of the Black in Western Art*, vol. III: *From the "Age of Discovery" to the Age of Abolition*, Part 1: *Artists of the Renaissance and Baroque*, gen. ed. David Bindman and Henry Louis Gates, Jr. (Cambridge, MA: Harvard University Press, 2010), 235–70.

12 Hakluyt (1589), 130–35.

13 John Smith, *The Complete Works of Captain John Smith (1581–1631)*, ed. Philip L. Barbour. 3 vols. (Chapel Hill: University of North Carolina Press, 1986), vol. I, 327.

14 George Best, *A true discourse of the late Voyages of Discouverie, for the finding of a passage to Cathaya by the Northwest, under the conduct of Martin Forbisher Generall: Divided into three Bookes* (London: Henry Bynnyman, 1578), 30–32.

15 Richard Wilkinson, *Lot's Wife. A Sermon Preached at Paules Crosse ...* (London: John Flasket, 1607), 42.

16 George Sandys, *A Relation of a Journey Begun An. Dom: 1610*, 2nd edn (London: W. Barrett, 1615), 136.

17 Michel Eyquem de Montaigne, *Essays*, trans. John Florio (1603), intro. L.G. Harmer, 3 vols. (London: J.M. Dent, 1910), vol. I, 215–29.

18 Samuel Eliot Morison, *The European Discovery of America: The Southern Voyages, 1492–1616* (New York: Oxford University Press, 1974), 67.

19 See Alden T. Vaughan, *Transatlantic Encounters: American Indians in Britain, 1500–1776* (Cambridge University Press, 2006, rev. 2008), chaps. 2–4; Alden T. Vaughan, "Namontack's Itinerant Life and Mysterious Death: Sources and Speculations," *Virginia Magazine of History and Biography* 126 (2018): 170–209.

20 Smith, vol. I, 160–61.

21 Willliam Strachey, *The Historie of Travell into Virginia Britania* (1612), ed. Louis B. Wright and Virginia Freund (London: Hakluyt Society, 1953), 70.

22 Thomas Hariot, *A Briefe and True Report of the New Found Land of Virginia: The Complete 1590 Theodore de Bry Edition* (New York: Dover, 1972), 75.

23 William Crashaw, *A Sermon Preached in London before the Right Honourable the Lord La Warre ...* (London: William Welby, 1610), sig. C4ᵛ.

24 Quoted in *The Records of the Virginia Company of London*, ed. Susan Myra Kingsbury, 4 vols. (Washington, DC: Government Printing Office, 1906–34), vol. III, 683.

25 Quoted in *Records of the Virginia Company*, vol. III, 558–59.

26 Quoted in *Records of the Virginia Company*, vol. II, 397.

27 Sidney Lee, *A Life of William Shakespeare* (London: Smith, Elder, 1898), 257.

28 Aimé Césaire, *A Tempest* (1969), trans. Richard Miller (New York: TCG, 1992), 20–21.

29 Edward Kamau Brathwaite, *Islands* (Oxford University Press, 1969).

30 Roberto Fernández Retamar, "'Caliban': Notes towards a Discussion of Culture in Our America," *Massachusetts Review* 15 (1973–74): 21–32 (at 24).

31 Marina Warner, *Indigo, or Mapping the Waters* (London: Chatto & Windus, 1992), 85.

CHAPTER II

Shakespeare, Race, and Globalization
Titus Andronicus

Noémie Ndiaye
University of Chicago

It has often been remarked upon with some degree of wonder that the playwright who arguably has the most established global reach and fame today never set foot outside England during his lifetime. Yet Shakespeare certainly was obsessed with "the great globe itself" (*Tempest*, 4.1.153). Using the word "world" at least 650 times,[1] Shakespeare's works manifest, from the very start of his career, a strong interest in what Roland Robertson calls "the compression of the world and the intensification of consciousness of the world as a whole" otherwise known as "globalization."[2] In *The Comedy of Errors*, one of Shakespeare's earliest plays, Dromio of Ephesus – an enslaved young man owned by a merchant who sails and trades across the Mediterranean world too often for his own good – describes a kitchen wench as "spherical like a globe, I could find out countries in her" (3.2.115–16). Besides Ireland, Scotland, France, England, and Spain, those countries include "America, the Indies" (3.2.134), which lay "upon her nose, all o'er embellished with rubies, carbuncles, sapphires, declining their rich aspect to the hot breath of Spain, who sent whole armadas of carracks to be ballast at her nose" (3.2.135–38). In that moment, Dromio's words are eerily reminiscent of the 1588 portrait of Queen Elizabeth I who, covered in pearls and gems, extends her hand over a globe – specifically over the Americas – while in the background, the Spanish Armada is defeated and drowned. The globe as Dromio, and perhaps Shakespeare, imagined it aligned with the world as Elizabeth I envisioned it: open to England for colonial plunder, rivalry, and conquest – a world where expansion was driven by trade, lucre, and interests.

The last twenty years have seen the rise in early modern studies of an entire subfield devoted to that vision: "Global Renaissance studies," a field naturally informed by post-colonial theory, which focuses, in Jyotsna Singh's words, on the "historical phenomenon of an expanding global world, one which includes the discovery of America to the West, growing interactions and encounters with the East ranging from the Ottoman empire on Europe's borders to the far East, forays into North and sub-Saharan Africa, and even explorations to the North Seas."[3] Shakespeare's plays and their global imagination have held a central position in that field. Global Renaissance studies, because they focus on intercultural encounters, often raise questions relevant to early modern critical race studies. That double critical framework informs the present account of Shakespeare's first tragedy, written circa 1591 – just a couple of years before Dromio's lusty musings on global goods and bodies – *The Lamentable Tragedy of Titus Andronicus.*

Shakespeare wrote *Titus Andronicus* while or shortly after completing the three parts of *Henry VI* – in other words, while or shortly after inventing the genre of the history play, a genre invested in the fashioning of England and English history. That project of national fashioning reverberates in *Titus Andronicus*, which, haunted by visions of a Rome infiltrated by Barbarians, Goths, and Blackamoors, displaces onto a weakening Roman Empire ongoing cultural reflections about past, present, and future English identity. A play devoid of direct source texts, *Titus Andronicus* best reads as a surrealist collage patching together within dream (or nightmare) logic bits of Roman history (such as the overthrow of monarchy following the rape of Lucrece in the sixth century BC, and the fall of the Empire in the fifth century AD), Roman values (such as stoicism, patriotism, patriarchy, and so-called decadence), and Roman imperial literature (such as Virgil's *Aeneid*, Ovid's *Metamorphoses*, and Senecan tragedy). Like all dream-like surrealist collages, the play's rendition of Roman culture often seems absurd and jarring, but it is not arbitrary: it is immensely poetic, invested in a formal quest for modernity, and permeated with an urgent sense of futurity. I argue that this quest for modernity and this sense of futurity in the early global age involve, in the play, the creation of a racial regime informed by the needs of early capitalism.

Titus Andronicus is a play that simultaneously deploys and foils various racial narratives and rituals in a dialectic attempt to represent the racial regime ushered in by early modern globalization. That new regime, forged in the furnace of early capitalism, was predicated not upon the elimination of racialized others, but on their strategic and contingent inclusion into a hierarchized multicultural society – be it Rome or London. To understand that new racial regime, we must first explore the various overlapping historical forms of early modern globalization indirectly reflected in Shakespeare's anamorphic Rome. Only then will we be able unpack the seemingly contradictory dynamics of exclusion and inclusion that underlie the play's new racial regime, and point out the unifying logic that actually requires their continuous push and pull. Finally, we will pay attention to the global afterlives of *Titus Andronicus* in early modern continental Europe before returning to Restoration England: the racial tropes cathected in the English context went global with *Titus Andronicus*, and so did the mold it provided for inventing a new racial regime.

Forms of Globalization: Empire, World-Economies, Colonization, Cosmopolitanism

The first historical form of globalization represented in *Titus Andronicus* is empire. The play seems to start in late imperial Rome, in a climate that evokes its impending fall at the hands of Barbarians at the end of the fifth century AD. The play opens with a succession crisis, as Saturninus and Bassianus both lay claim to their late father's imperial throne – the crisis is soon resolved by general Titus Andronicus, who returns victorious from battle against the Goths, as part of a war started ten years earlier, whose definitive issue remains undecided throughout the play. Titus declines the offer to take the throne for himself, and rules in favor of Saturninus, along the lines of primogeniture. The play thus opens on a stage where crucial decisions must be made that condition the future of the Empire. This proleptic orientation must have resonated with the play's first spectators, not only because in the early 1590s, given their unmarried queen's age, the English could fear a future crisis that might bring back the dark days of the Tudor succession wars, but also because, by virtue of the *translatio imperii*, a long-lasting concept of medieval historiography that posits the westward transfer of imperial rule across ages and cultures, the English (like most European nations) thought of themselves as heirs to the Romans.[4] Given this widespread identification between Romans and Englishmen, staging a future-oriented crisis in imperial Rome was a way of asking questions about a late sixteenth-century England that was by no means imperial, yet, as Elizabeth's 1588 portrait points out, aspired to be someday.

   While an empire's unity is primarily political – and thus administrative and military – what world-system theorists refer to as a "world-economy" dispenses with heavy political superstructures as it is primarily economic in nature (although punctual state interventions are vital to its well-being). That model describes the processes of globalization as England experienced them in the 1590s more accurately than the model of empire. One premise of world-system theory is that globalization is not just a multiplication and intensification of commercial exchanges between various points around the globe: rather it is a process that supports a specific economic system coeval with (early) modernity, namely, capitalism, understood as a system that "gives priority to the *endless* accumulation of capital."[5] In Immanuel Wallerstein's words, it was in "the long sixteenth century" that "our modern world-system came into existence as a capitalist world-economy," that is, "a large geographic zone within which there is a division of labor and hence significant internal exchange of basic or essential goods as well as flows of capital and labor," which primarily included "parts of Europe and the Americas" in Shakespeare's time.[6]

> Three things were essential to the establishment of such a capitalist world-economy: an expansion of the geographical size of the world in question, the development of variegated methods of labor control for different products and different zones of the world economy, and the creation of relatively strong state machineries in what would become the core-States of this capitalist world-economy ... the second and third aspect were dependent in large part on the success of the first.[7]

In other words, the colonization of the Americas was the indispensable key that enabled the European capitalist project, and globalization cannot be understood without colonization.

The early colonial aspirations of England, instrumental in claiming Western imperial rule ultimately, haunt the play. David Goldstein has compellingly shown that Iberian narratives of the American conquest are pervasive in *Titus Andronicus* – a play written as the feverish anti-Spanish propaganda operation known as the Black Legend climaxed in England. Indeed, "narratives of New World conquest [especially those by Francisco López de Gómara and Bartolome de Las Casas] circulate in the background of the structure and plot of *Titus*," and create a vertiginous set of shifting associations between Goths, Romans, Spaniards, and Native Americans that reflects Shakespeare's interest in "how the emerging paradigms of American travel narratives help his compatriots see themselves."[8] Goldstein focuses on ritualized cannibalism – a trope often associated with representations of Native Americans in conquest narratives – deployed in a play set under the aegis of Saturn (the god that eats his own children), especially in the scene where the Andronici have the Gothic queen feed upon her own sons' flesh. While the circulating motif of cannibalism points out the risks of "going native" in the symbolical realm, one must also keep in mind that, concretely, accounts of early English colonial forays in North America speak of English cannibalism. Archeological evidence of human remains discovered in 2012 confirmed without a doubt that

"Jamestown colonists cannibalized each other" during the "Starving Time," a sign of duress and famine that would register in the vanishing banquet scene of *The Tempest* in 1611, and that may very well have afflicted the 1587 colony of Roanoke whose disappearance hit English consciousness around the same time as Shakespeare wrote *Titus Andronicus*.[9]

We must add to Goldstein's account of the spectral presence of intercultural encounters between Spaniards and Native Americans in *Titus Andronicus* an account of encounters between Spaniards and enslaved Afro-diasporic people of Sub-Saharan descent. Indeed, the practice of color-based slavery had famously started in the Iberian Americas about a century before Shakespeare wrote *Titus Andronicus*, and that cultural context registers in Bassianus' decision to call Aaron the Blackamoor a "swart Cimmerian" (2.3.66). Indeed, that term is probably a distortion of the Spanish term *cimarrón*, which designated runaway slaves rejecting white masters' authority, societies, and so-called civilization in the Americas.[10] *Titus Andronicus* thus reckons with the Iberian colonial experience and evokes, in this ever proleptic sensibility, the various risks entailed by trafficking with Africans and Indigenous people in the New World.

Finally, early globalization took the form of English cosmopolitanism, understood as a financially interested form of "cultural accommodation and understanding" not only overseas, but also domestically.[11] While, in the 1590s, London was nowhere near as attractive to foreign traders and investors as other continental cosmopolitan capitals such as Venice, Paris, or Amsterdam, it was still a very dynamic economic center and a multicultural society in the making. Indeed, London's demographic boom gathered not only English people displaced by the enclosure movement, and foreigners, including entrepreneurial merchants, but also refugees often displaced by the wars of religion in continental Europe. Among them, one could find crypto-Jews of Portuguese or Spanish descent (*conversos* and *marranos*) who had found refuge from the Inquisition in England, yet still had to hide their faith since the Edict that had expelled Jews from England in 1290 was still in effect in the 1590s. Because domestic slavery had long been part of Iberian lifestyle, those refugees – whose number Gustav Ungerer approximates at 80–90 at the end of Elizabeth I's reign[12] – often had enslaved Afro-diasporic people of sub-Saharan descent in their service London, and Shakespeare seems to echo this association by giving his Blackamoor character a Jewish name, and not any Jewish name: Aaron, Moses' brother, a central figure in Hebrew diasporic history. Succinctly put, early globalization did not only mean that England came to the world, but also that the world itself was coming to England, and, in the process, turned London into a cosmopolitan world city replete with foreigners, Jews, and Afro-diasporic people, among others. *Titus Andronicus*, by means of a Roman anamorphosis, dreams of London as a cosmopolitan capital with imperial aspirations within a proto-colonial world-economy. In the possible futures that the play dreams up for England, defining and prescribing the most profitable forms of intercultural trafficking is a priority. The smart device used for establishing such prescriptions is called race.

Worldly Matters: *Titus Andronicus* and the Uses of Race

As Ania Loomba cogently puts it, "by definition, empires need to expand, to annex territories and people outside themselves into their boundaries, and as they do so, to underline differences between themselves and those they conquer."[13] In *Titus Andronicus*, those imperial needs occasion an acute identity crisis. *Titus Andronicus* seems to dramatize in the proleptic mode the entrance of cultural others into a world city, and the terrible consequences for a European body politic of absorbing foreign bodies that become, as Tamora eloquently puts it, "incorporate in Rome," or as Romans "now adopted happily" (1.1.462–63). But does it?

When one considers the Andronici's barbaric course of action throughout the play, any allegedly immovable difference between Romans and Barbarians proves baseless. To give but one example among many, Lucius, his father's best hope and final ruler of Rome, enthusiastically performs a human sacrifice in the opening scene of the play, before any commixing has taken place; he impiously denies funerary rites to a queen; he decides without batting an eyelash to lynch a defenseless baby in breach of the law;[14] and we get a glimpse of his rich sadistic imagination when he devises Aaron's torturous punishment. When, at the very start of the play, the Gothic brothers comment that Rome is even more barbarous than Scythia, they are on to something:

CHIRON   Was ever Scythia half so barbarous?
DEMETRIUS   Oppose not Scythia to ambitious Rome.

(1.1.131–32)

Nowhere is the sameness of Romans and Goths more transparent than in the moment when Lucius marches into Rome leading a Gothic army.

In that context of radical sameness, racial narratives come into play to do what they do best: draw artificial essentializing lines that organize and justify the power relations of a multicultural society in the making. The most authoritative racial narrative used in the play to frame the absorption of foreign bodies into the body politic as an invasion and the source of all evils is the story of the Trojan horse recounted in the *Iliad* and in the *Aeneid*. As Heather James notes, the Andronici "virtually claim the *Aeneid* as family history" throughout the play.[15] Thus, the myth operates in the background of the play from its start, long before a railing Marcus Andronicus evokes it in Act 5: "Tell us what Sinon has betwitched our ears, / Or who has brought the fatal engine in / That gives our Troy, our Rome, the civil wound" (5.3.83–85). This strategic mobilization of a popular myth directly associated with the foundation enshrines the racial work of this narrative within Roman political mythology in ways that will likely orient Lucius Andronicus' reign at the end of the play. The kaleidoscopic image of Lucius leading a Gothic army clearly shows not only that narratives of racial difference are baseless, but also that they can be mobilized or ignored at will, for their deployment is entirely strategic.

The dreaded "incorporation" of Barbarians into the Roman body politic is political, since Goths and Blackamoors become subjects to the Roman emperor, but it is also biological, since Tamora, as we soon find out, is still of reproductive age and will likely give a mixed Romano-Gothic heir to Saturninus. Moreover, although that possibility is, curiously, never discussed in the play, Lavinia might very well have been impregnated by Chiron or Demetrius during the gang rape that she suffered. There could be another mixed child in this play. Having Tamora conceive a child with Aaron rather than her husband and Titus murder a potentially pregnant Lavinia as an honor killing, the play's plot consistently works to foreclose the possibilities of Romano-Gothic miscegenation. Such anti-miscegenation politics are in line with what the early moderns perceived as the ancient rejection of Barbarians as Others, and the primacy of civilization as the category organizing racial boundaries imagined as immutable in antiquity.

The threat of miscegenation does materialize, however, when it is displaced onto the Gothic-Moorish baby fathered by Aaron – in his nurse's words, "A joyless, dismal, black, and sorrowful issue . . . As loathsome as a toad / Amongst the fairest breeders of our clime" (4.2.65–67). This displacement is in line with the evolution of racial hermeneutics, since, for the early moderns, phenotype – for which skin tone quickly became a shorthand – was on the rise as one of the paradigms in the racial matrix, overtaking "barbarity" as a conceptual basis to organize human difference. The consternation that the black–white miscegenation evokes both among Romans and Goths problematizes Tamora's racial status: Tamora is not civilized enough to give birth to a Roman child, but she is too white to give birth to Aaron's child. Yet even her whiteness is put in question in the play. Indeed, some twenty years ago, Francesca Royster pioneered the now booming field of early modern whiteness studies by pointing out that, given her moral darkness and ethnic difference, Tamora's visually striking "hyper-whiteness" is dissociated from its usual implications, capital, and affordances in early modern English culture, and thereby "denaturalizes whiteness as a cultural signifier."[16] Highlighting the fact that whiteness is a socially constructed category, the very presence of Tamora, her sons, and her Gothic retinue in Rome puts pressure on the meaning of whiteness, occasioning a semiotic crisis.

As Joyce Green MacDonald pithily puts it, "the world of *Titus Andronicus* is afflicted by categorical disarray."[17] Besides barbarity and whiteness, a last category must be mentioned that is equally put "in disarray": the category of subjectivity. Indeed, Matthieu Chapman reads the character of Aaron through the lens of Orlando Patterson's definition of slavery as a "social death" and through the Afro-pessimistic vision of blackness as a condition of radical isolation and incommunicability. Chapman convincingly argues that Aaron starts in the play in the scripted position of the slave, "the abject of humanity," only to reject that position and to impose it onto characters usually equated with human subjects.[18] In that sense, to quote Ian Smith, "Lavinia is barbarized" by Aaron and the Andronicus clan follows in her footsteps.[19] Symmetrically, Aaron becomes a human interlocutor, and his transformation "coincides with the destruction of Roman civil society."[20] In that sense, "the incorporation of a black into civil society" brings about "the collapse of that society."[21] Who is civilized? Who is white? Who is a human subject? So many fundamental questions that the play simultaneously raises and seeks to answer in reassuring and stabilizing ways.

Stabilization operates in the play not only through the use of racial narratives such as the previously discussed myth of the Trojan horse, but also through rituals – specifically, cathartic rituals with high production value instigated by the Andronici in the name of Rome. Imtiaz Habib insightfully reads *Titus Andronicus* as Shakespeare's early engagement with the cultural politics of Greco-Roman tragedy, a genre historically involved in the construction of specific notions of civilization for imperial metropolises, which relies on catharsis:

> The metropolitan location of tragedy, within the confines of an urban community practice and implicated in the project of writing a national culture, dictates its interest in social construction . . . Tragedy is the cultural

form of the metropolis's exclusionist self-construction ... As the imperial
metropolis defines itself by who or what it excludes, tragedy images
that self-definition by personifying the exclusion of the barbarian that
invents it.[22]

The symbolical cathartic exclusion of the Barbarian that Habib mentions
takes a literal turn at the end of *Titus Andronicus* – a play where human
bodies notoriously literalize political tropes and metaphors – when Lucius
orders that Tamora's corpse be thrown outside of the city's walls: "as for
that heinous tiger, Tamora, / No funeral rite, nor man in mourning weeds,
/ No mournful bell shall ring her burial, / But throw her forth to beasts
and birds of prey" (5.1.193–96). The foreign body, the Trojan horse that
had found its way through Rome's wall, is eventually expelled in an
attempt to heal the body politic. Another sensational cathartic ritual meant
to reaffirm Rome's cultural walls is the murder of Lavinia, which Arthur
Little reads as the answer to "Rome's sacrificial crisis, that is, its need for a
sacrifice, for a symbolic act that would establish the difference between,
say, pure and impure blood."[23] In Little's luminous analysis:

> Rome's crisis becomes evident in its confusion of categories: the Roman and
> the barbarous (as Tamora becomes "incorporate in Rome"), piety and
> impiety, war and peace, civil war and national war, enemy and ally
> (Saturninus marries Tamora, Titus kills his son Mutius, the brothers
> Bassianus and Saturninus struggle with each other for Rome's imperial
> seat), Tamora's allegiance to both a racial whiteness and a racial blackness,
> and murder and sacrifice. Lavinia quickly emerges as Rome's symbolic
> sacrificial object, a body in crisis, caught in its own confused signification
> between being virginal and being raped.[24]

The large-scale semiotic crisis embodied by Lavinia (whose mutilation was
designed to ensure that she could not signify anymore) should be resolved
by her dramatic elimination. Women's bodies thus serve as highly visible
sites for the cathartic rituals of civility.

In line with the play's continuous push and pull in matters of racial
politics, those narrative and ritualistic attempts at stabilizing identity
binaries fail by the end of the play. Namely, Rome's new emperor orders
the high production-value cathartic ritual of expelling Tamora's corpse, on
a stage where he stands surrounded by the Gothic soldiers who have just
delivered him his victory over Rome – and the play does not say what he
will or can do with this vengeful Gothic army. Similarly, after promising
Aaron to save his son's life in exchange for information, Rome's new
emperor is a slave to his own word, for he swore by his own god "to save
[Aaron's] boy, to nourish, and bring him up" (5.1.84). In Lucius' race war,

eliminating Tamora's family was a pyrrhic victory, and high production-value rituals can hardly hide it.

It is very tempting to read that pyrrhic victory as a Shakespearean sign of resistance to clear-cut racist politics and simplifications: several scholars – myself included – have done so in the past. Yet we have to reckon with the fact that, in a capitalist world-economy such as the early modern society anamorphically depicted in *Titus Andronicus*, it is not a profitable move at all to eliminate and expel foreign bodies. As Immanuel Wallerstein explains:

> Xenophobia in all prior historical systems had one primary behavioural consequence: the ejection of the 'barbarian' from the physical locus of the community, the society, the in-group – death being the extreme version of ejection. Whenever we physically eject the other, we gain the 'purity' of environment that we are presumably seeking, but we inevitably lose something at the same time. We lose the labour-power of the person ejected and therefore that person's contribution to the creation of a surplus that we might be able to appropriate on a recurring basis. This represents a loss for any historical system, but it is a particularly serious one in the case of a system whose whole structure and logic are built around the endless accumulation of capital. A capitalist system that is expanding (which is half the time) needs all the labour-power it can find, since this labour is producing the goods through which more capital is produced, realized and accumulated. Ejection out of the system is pointless. But if one wants to maximize the accumulation of capital, it is necessary simultaneously to minimize the costs of production (hence the costs of labour-power) and minimize the costs of political disruption (hence minimize – not eliminate, because one cannot eliminate – the protests of the labour force). Racism is the magic formula that reconciles these objectives.[25]

Wallerstein spells out the reason why racism can reconcile those objectives in a structural account of racism that is very much in line with the pillars of critical race theory:

> Racism, sexism, and other anti-universalistic norms perform important tasks in allocating work, power, and privilege within the modern world-system. They seem to imply social exclusions from the social arena. Actually they are really modes of inclusion but of inclusion at inferior ranks. Those norms exist to justify the lower ranking, to enforce the lower ranking, and perversely even, to make it somewhat palatable to those who have the lower ranking.[26]

Simply put, capitalism is incompatible with the expulsion of foreigners – at least as long as foreigners remain efficiently kept at the bottom of the social hierarchy, as a cheap labor force, by the multifaceted socio-ideological apparatus of racism. In the new racial regime informed by the needs of early global capitalism that the play dramatizes, Tamora and her sons, who have made it to the top of Roman social hierarchy through marriage, must be eliminated at all costs, while expendable Gothic soldiers and a potential Afro-diasporic servant of sub-Saharan descent such as Aaron's baby boy must be "included at inferior ranks." Francesca Royster insightfully notes that Aaron's initial plan to save his son hinges on him having "made contact with the Moorish community" in imperial Rome,[27] but that community, we might add in light of Wallerstein's analysis, will only thrive as long as it stays "in its place." Thus, while it is certainly true that "the play reminds us that new national identities were being forged in Europe at the same time as external frontiers were opening up," the play also reminds us that early modern processes of national identity formation accommodated the racial demands of global capitalism in the making.[28]

Emily Bartels made the controversial argument that Shakespeare's Rome is not a world city obsessed with racial purity to the extent that "Titus is not the only one setting the terms here . . . The play not only critiques the Rome he would create as dangerously self-centered but also juxtaposes it to a contrasting reality, which increasingly displaces and replaces Titus's untenable ideals."[29] Bartels does have a point that the play does not ultimately embrace the politics of cathartic expulsion idiosyncratically championed by the Andronici and enacted via narratives and rituals: the play actively foils those politics. Yet it would be a mistake to assume that the pragmatic politics of "inclusion at the inferior ranks" which the play ultimately embraces are not as racist as the Andronici's agenda. As a matter of fact, Rome *needs* the Andronici to push their exclusionary racial agenda just as much as it needs them to fail, for it is in that very push and pull between exclusion and conditional inclusion of racialized others that the early modern world-economy can thrive. The roots that Aaron is growing in Roman soil as he remains buried neck-deep in the ground at the end of the play – his symbolical implantation – and the implantation of his seed in Rome are no signs of a hypothetical Shakespearean resistance to racism.[30] Rather they manifest the play's earnest representation of racism's entanglement in the demands of the global capitalist project born in Shakespeare's time.

Conclusion: The Global Afterlives of *Titus Andronicus*

The inclusion of racialized others into inferior ranks in Roman society at the end of the play was not lost on its first spectators, both inside and outside of England. Indeed *Titus Andronicus* was a major success in London and it quickly moved to continental Europe via English traveling players. In the anonymous German adaptation of the play published in a collection of plays and interludes in Leipzig in 1620, Vespasianus (Lucius) agrees to spare the life of Morian (Aaron) and Aetiopissa's (Tamora's) baby boy in a movement of inclusion at the inferior rank: "I will have pity on your child and bring him up as a warrior" (*Tito Andronico*, 222).[31] Vespasianus sees that the child will prove a good soldier – a cheap, devoted, and expendable labor force – for the Roman imperial army. However, in *Aran en Titus*, the popular Dutch version of the play written by Jan Vos in 1641, signs of implantation and inclusion of others at the inferior rank are erased: the mixed baby is excised from the plot, and Aaron is burned onstage, rather than buried neck-deep into the ground.[32] This Dutch version eliminates plot elements that I read as signs of engagement with racism's entanglement in the demands of early capitalism. This elimination is quite surprising in the light of the Low Countries' well-known involvement in the slave trade and color-based slavery in the 1640s.[33] Or maybe not. There might be a reason for this erasure, and going back home, to Restoration England, might help us pin that reason down.

Vos's play had 100 performances before 1665, and at least 34 editions, as well as translations into Latin and German.[34] It is quite possible, then, that Vos's version circulated across Dutch borders, furthering the global dissemination of Shakespeare's play. It is even possible that it influenced Edward Ravenscroft's 1679 rewriting of *Titus Andronicus*, given the fact that, in Ravenscroft's version, after being tortured at the rack, Aaron is burned onstage – as he was in Vos's version. Ravenscroft – whose other plays attest to a familiarity with continental theatrical traditions – would not even have needed to read Dutch to get that idea:[35] the engraving on the title page of Vos's 1641 play shows Aaron burning onstage (Figure 11.1). Ravenscroft painstakingly removed all traces of racial confusion and admixing at the end of the play by excising all the lines that explicitly depict Lucius' army as Gothic, by killing Aaron's baby, and by disappearing Aaron's corpse with fire. As Ayanna Thompson compellingly argues, those moves are part of a larger strategy to "stabilize Roman society in a way that was impossible in Shakespeare's original" by "reading the racialized body in an explicitly linguistic and physical way" that hinges on essentialism.[36] This attempt at "reinscribing a notion of essentialism through a clear linking and unity between the signifier and the signified" must, Thompson insists, be understood in the context of "the growing

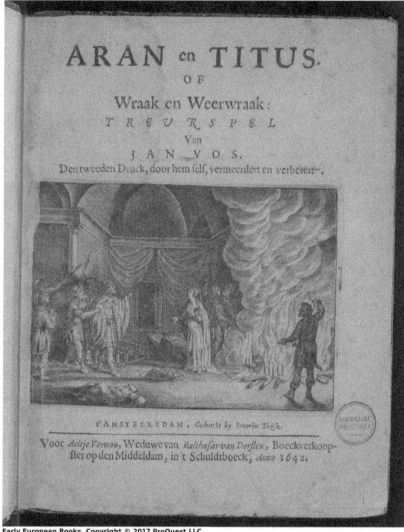

Figure 11.1   This 1641 Dutch adaption of *Titus Andronicus* shows Aaron the Moor
burning on a pyre.

violence experienced in the British colonies."[37] In that context, slavery-
based economic prosperity directly depended upon the policing of the
color-line, which itself depended upon unambiguous and essentialist racial
hermeneutics. Why, then, does a play so clearly informed by the concrete

ideological needs of British colonial slavery in the 1670s embrace the Andronican "idealist" politics of racial exclusion rather than the pragmatic inclusive racism so constitutive of early modern world-economies? Why does this play seemingly depart from the mindset of racial capitalism?

What appears to be a contradiction, both in Vos's and Ravenscroft's versions, might actually hide a deeper causal connection. We might venture that, in fact, the more explicitly and brutally an early modern society relied on the new racial regime mandated by early capitalist global thinking, the less likely its theatrical and cultural productions were to transparently stage those processes. This is by no means an absolute claim (the surviving English Restoration repertoire does include fascinating plays about colonization and slavery) – more of an invitation to consider the multifaceted relations that can exist between the stage and the sensitive worldly matters to which it attends. It might ultimately be the case that Shakespeare's original *Titus Andronicus* staged the push and pull processes at play in the creation of a new racial regime fit to support the project of early modern global capitalism more transparently than any of its avatars precisely *because*, in 1594, racial capitalism was only a project and not a reality. In 1594, the mechanisms of shame and denial that would later permeate European reckonings with the moral bankruptcy of racial traffics in the age of slavery had not crystallized yet. At the opening of this essay, I mentioned that *Titus Andronicus* functions like a surrealist collage ruled by the logic of dreams. Let me conclude then. The global history of the play's rewritings best reads as a process in which, little by little, the mechanisms of self-censorship commonly known as "repression" forced this nightmarish Shakespearean dream of a play to bend and hide the unspeakable object of desire: racial capitalism.

Notes

1 Andrew Dickson, "Why Shakespeare is the World's Favourite Writer," *BBC Culture*, 21 October 2014, www.bbc.com/culture/story/20140422-shake speare-the-worlds-writer.

2 Quoted in Anston Bosman, "Shakespeare and Globalization," *The New Cambridge Companion to Shakespeare*, ed. Margreta de Grazia and Stanley Wells, 2nd edn (Cambridge University Press, 2010), 285.

3 *A Companion to the Global Renaissance: English Literature and Culture in the Era of Expansion*, ed. Jyotsna G. Singh (Chichester and Malden, MA: Wiley-Blackwell, 2009), 5. See also Bernadette Andrea, *Women and Islam in Early Modern English Literature* (Cambridge University Press, 2007); Jonathan Burton, *Traffic and Turning: Islam and English Drama, 1579–1624* (Newark:

University of Delaware Press, 2005); Jerry Brotton, *The Renaissance Bazaar: From the Silk Road to Michelangelo* (Oxford University Press, 2002); Matthew Dimmock, *New Turkes: Dramatizing Islam and the Ottomans in Early Modern England* (New York and London: Routledge, 2005); Jonathan Gil Harris, *Sick Economies: Drama, Mercantilism, and Disease in Shakespeare's England* (Philadelphia: University of Pennsylvania Press, 2004); Gerald MacLean and Nabil Matar, *Britain and the Islamic World, 1558–1713* (Oxford University Press, 2011); Nabil Matar, *Turks, Moors, and Englishmen in the Age of Discovery* (New York: Columbia University Press, 2000); Su Fang Ng, *Alexander the Great From Britain to Southeast Asia: Peripheral Empires in the Global Renaissance* (Oxford University Press, 2019); Daniel J. Vitkus, *Turning Turk: English Theatre and the Multicultural Mediterranean* (New York and Basingstoke: Palgrave Macmillan, 2003).

4 See Thomas James Dandelet, *The Renaissance of Empire in Early Modern Europe* (Cambridge University Press, 2014); Anthony Miller, *Roman Triumphs and Early Modern English Culture* (Basingstoke: Palgrave Macmillan, 2001); Jonathan Goldberg, *James I and the Politics of Literature: Jonson, Shakespeare, Donne, and Their Contemporaries* (Stanford University Press, 1989); Freyja Cox Jensen, *Reading the Roman Republic in Early Modern England* (Leiden: Brill, 2012).

5 Immanuel Maurice Wallerstein, *World-Systems Analysis: An Introduction* (Durham, NC: Duke University Press, 2004), 24.

6 Wallerstein, *World-Systems Analysis*, x, 23.

7 Immanuel Maurice Wallerstein, *The Modern World-System I: Capitalist Agriculture and the Origins of the European World-Economy in the Sixteenth Century* (Berkeley: University of California Press, 2011), 38.

8 David B Goldstein, "The Cook and the Cannibal: *Titus Andronicus* and the New World," *Shakespeare Studies* 37 (2009): 99–133 (at 111, 115).

9 Rachel B. Herrmann, *To Feast on Us as Their Prey: Cannibalism and the Early Modern Atlantic* (Fayetteville: University of Arkansas, 2019), 9.

10 Noémie Ndiaye, "Aaron's Roots: Spaniards, Englishmen, and Blackamoors in *Titus Andronicus*," *Early Theatre* 19/2 (2016): 59–80 (at 66–67).

11 Allison Games, "England's Global Transition and the Cosmopolitans Who Made It Possible," *Shakespeare Studies* 35 (2007): 24–31 (at 29).

12 Gustave Ungerer, "The Presence of Africans in Elizabethan England and the Performance of *Titus Andronicus* at Burley-on-the-Hill, 1595/96," *Medieval & Renaissance Drama in England* 21 (2008): 20–55 (at 20). See also Imtiaz Habib, *Black Lives in the English Archives, 1500–1677: Imprints of the Invisible* (Aldershot and Burlington, VT: Ashgate, 2008).

13 Ania Loomba, *Shakespeare, Race, and Colonialism* (Oxford University Press, 2002), 82.

14 Ndiaye, 69.

15 Heather James, "Cultural Disintegration in *Titus Andronicus*: Mutilating Titus, Vergil, and Rome," in *Violence in Drama*, ed. James Redmond (Cambridge University Press, 1991), 123–40 (at 124).

16 Francesca Royster, "Whiteness and Gothic Extremism in Shakespeare's *Titus Andronicus,*" *Shakespeare Quarterly* 51/4 (2000): 432–55 (at 442).

17 Joyce Green MacDonald, "Black Ram, White Ewe: Shakespeare, Race, and Women," in *A Feminist Companion to Shakespeare,* ed. Dympna Callaghan (Oxford: Blackwell, 2000), 206–25 (at 223).

18 Matthieu Chapman, *Anti-Black Racism in Early Modern English Drama: The Other "Other"* (New York and London: Routledge, 2017), 19.

19 Ian Smith, *Race and Rhetoric in the Renaissance: Barbarian Errors* (New York and Basingstoke: Palgrave Macmillan, 2009), 130.

20 Chapman, 157.

21 Chapman, 178–79.

22 Imtiaz Habib, *Shakespeare and Race: Postcolonial Praxis in the Early Modern Period* (Lanham, MD: University Press of America, 2000), 88–89.

23 Arthur L. Little, Jr., *Shakespeare Jungle Fever: National-Imperial Re-Visions of Race, Rape, and Sacrifice* (Stanford University Press, 2000), 48.

24 Little, Jr., 49.

25 Immanuel Maurice Wallerstein, "The Ideological Tensions of Capitalism: Universalism Versus Racism and Sexism," in Étienne Balibar and Immanuel Maurice Wallerstein, *Race, Nation, Class: Ambiguous Identities* (London: Verso, 1991), 29–36 (at 33).

26 Wallerstein, *World-Systems Analysis,* 40–41.

27 Royster, 451.

28 Loomba, 85.

29 Emily Carroll Bartels, *Speaking of the Moor: From Alcazar to Othello* (Philadelphia: University of Pennsylvania Press, 2008), 75.

30 Ndiaye, 73.

31 I am grateful to Maria Shmygol for introducing me to this play, and I look forward to using the critical translation and edition of the play that she is currently preparing in collaboration with with Lukas Erne as part of the Early Modern German Shakespeare project, www.unige.ch/emgs/plays/tito-andro nico-und-der-hoffertigen-kayserin-tito-andronico-and-haughty-empress.

32 Helmer Helmers, "The Politics of Mobility: Shakespeare's *Titus Andronicus,* Jan Vos's *Aran en Titus* and the Poetics of Empire," in *Politics and Aesthetics in European Baroque and Classicist Tragedy,* ed. Jan Bloemendal and Nigel Smith (Leiden: Brill, 2016), 344–72 (at 353).

33 On the Dutch history of engagement with color-based slavery and racism, see Pieter Emmer, *The Dutch in the Atlantic Economy, 1580–1880: Trade, Slavery and Emancipation* (Aldershot: Ashgate, 1998); Kwame Nikamo and Glenn Frank Walter Willemsen, *The Dutch Atlantic: Slavery, Abolition and Emancipation* (London: Pluto Press, 2011); and Allison Blakely, *Blacks in the Dutch World: The Evolution of Racial Imagery in a Modern Society* (Bloomington: Indiana University Press, 1993).

34 Ton Hoenselaars and Helmer Helmers, "The *Spanish Tragedy* and Revenge Tragedy in Seventeenth-Century Britain and the Low Countries," in *Doing*

Kyd: Essays On *The Spanish Tragedy,* ed. Nicoleta Cinpoes (Manchester University Press, 2016), 144–67 (at 148). See also Helmers, 345.

35 Ravenscroft based *The Citizen Turn'd Gentleman* (1672) upon Molière's *Le bourgeois gentilhomme* (1670) and *Monsieur de Pourceaugnac* (1669); he based *Scaramouch a Philosopher* (1677) upon Molière's *Le mariage forcé* (1664) and *Les fourberies de Scapin* (1671); and he based *The Anatomist or the Sham Doctor* (1696) upon Noël le Breton de Hauteroche's popular play *Crispin médecin* (1680). See Louis A. Knafla, "Ravenscroft, Edward (fl. 1659–1697), playwright," *Oxford Dictionary of National Biography* (accessed 27 December 2019).

36 Ayanna Thompson, *Performing Race and Torture on the Early Modern Stage* (New York and London: Routledge, 2008), 62, 63.

37 Thompson, 55, 52.

CHAPTER 12

How to Think Like Ira Aldridge

Scott Newstok

Rhodes College

Ira Aldridge (1807–67) was not the first black performer of Shakespeare –
that honor goes to an (unnamed) actress in Scotland, who is reported to
have played Juliet around 1770.[1] Nor was Aldridge the first professional
African American actor of Shakespeare – that honor goes to James
Hewlett, "Shakespeare's proud Representative."[2]

However, we remember Aldridge today as the first black Shakespearean
to achieve international professional renown. Indeed, he's the first
American actor to do so. Frustrated, we presume, by his lack of advancement in the United States, he arrived in London in 1825, where he was the
first black actor to perform Othello, the role with which he became
intimately identified.[3] Over the next four decades, his reputation grew,
and he eventually toured throughout England and Europe. Just before his
death in 1867, he was on the cusp of a return to North America, with
plans to visit scores of Canadian and American theatres. After all, the Civil
War had just ended in the United States, and Aldridge assumed his return
would be triumphant in the face of the Union's win.

Throughout his life Aldridge was lauded with awards, including an
honorary commission as Captain in the Haitian Army (ca. 1828) and
the title Chevalier Ira Aldridge, Knight of Saxony (1858). At the height of
his celebrity, he was familiar to Hans Christian Andersen, Sir Edward
Bulwer-Lytton, Charles Dickens, Alexander Dumas (père), George Eliot,
Théophile Gautier, Alexander von Humboldt, Jenny Lind, Franz Liszt,
Tyrone Powers, Sir Walter Scott, Taras Shevchenko, Leo Tolstoy, and
perhaps even Richard Wagner. Born to free blacks in New York at the turn
of the nineteenth century, naturalized as a British citizen in 1863, and
buried in Łódź, Poland in 1867, Aldridge's cosmopolitan life was marked
by triumphs as well as persistent racist responses to his performances.

Tracing the "bypaths and indirect crook'd ways" of his career (2 Henry
IV 4.3.315), which spanned three continents and countless theatres, has
consumed more than one Aldridge biographer: Bernth Lindfors's

four-volume series (2011–15) runs to over 1,300 pages! While records for his early years are scant, we have a surfeit of reviews from his final decades. A further complication in recounting Aldridge's life is his tendency to self-mythologize in his promotional materials. For instance, he often stated that he was the child of an exiled African prince, and when he visited Shakespeare's Stratford birthplace in 1851, he listed his residence first as London, then as Senegal, where he sometimes claimed he had been born. Rather than exhaustively cataloging every instance of his Shakespearean performances, this essay surveys seven of Ira Aldridge's strategies for succeeding on the nineteenth-century stage – strategies which can still inspire us, students, performers, scholars, artists, teachers, innovators, and researchers alike.

Educate

The first strategy for Aldridge's success was his adherence to his education. Aldridge studied at the second African Free School, established in 1787 by the New York Manumission Society, whose founders included Alexander Hamilton and John Jay. While it started as a one-room schoolhouse with only about forty students, by the time Aldridge attended, its expansion required a second location.[4] Ultimately absorbed into the city's public schools in 1835, the African Free School educated thousands, many of whom went on to become active in the abolitionist movement. Alumni were praised as "prodigies of genius,"[5] including Dr. James McCune Smith, a pathbreaking physician; minister Alexander Crummell, who founded the American Negro Academy (ANA); and Charles Lewis Reason, who co-founded the Society for the Promotion of Education among Colored Children, and who was himself the first African American professor appointed at a majority-white college.[6] The African Free School aspired to prepare its graduates to become fully equal, active citizens, which has long been the ambition of liberal arts institutions.

What kind of curriculum might Aldridge have pursued? An 1816 plan for another "African School," proposed by the Presbyterian Synod of New York and New Jersey, gives us a sense of Aldridge's course of study:

> The usual term of study shall be at least four years, and longer if the Board deem it expedient. The first year shall be devoted, as the Principal may find necessary, to Reading, Writing, Spelling and learning the definition of English words, but chiefly to English Grammar, Arithmetic and Geography; the second to the elementary principles of Rhetoric, Mathematics, Natural Philosophy, and Astronomy; the third to

Theology; the fourth to Theology, the elements of Ecclesiastical History, the more practical principles of Church Government, and the Composition of Sermons. The exercises in public Speaking and composition shall be kept up through the whole course.[7]

As Aldridge's father Daniel Aldridge wanted his son to become a preacher, like him, this would have been excellent training for the ministry. However, as with Shakespeare's own humanist education, exercises in *grammar*, *rhetoric*, and *public speaking* inadvertently prepared Aldridge for a different path – toward the stage. Students at the African Free School learned to publicly recite dialogues and to compose poems for special occasions.[8] Lessons might well have included excerpts from Shakespeare, a mainstay of the era's elocutionary instruction.[9]

An 1833 letter by Aldridge states that he enrolled in Schenectady College (forerunner to today's Union College), a claim reiterated in the anonymous 1849 *Memoir and Theatrical Career of Ira Aldridge*, which was likely written by Aldridge himself. The *Memoir* maintains that prejudicial treatment led him to withdraw, and instead to enter "the Glasgow University, where, under Professor Sandford, he obtained several premiums and the medal for Latin composition."[10] While records from neither institution confirm Aldridge's enrollment, attendance at either would have furthered his acquaintance with the classical liberal arts as well as Shakespeare, whose use "in university education began in Scotland" in the 1750s.[11] Aldridge's rise to international fame as a Shakespearean actor, then, may very well have been tied directly to the history of education in the antebellum United States and the imperial aspirations of Great Britain.

Emulate

If education was Aldridge's first strategy, emulation was his second. Aligned with the history of educational practices in Shakespeare's own time, Aldridge benefited from learning and studying the art of emulation. Aldridge's *Memoir* explains how the theatre first captured his imagination:

> At school he was awarded prizes for declamation, in which he excelled; and there his curiosity was excited by what he heard of theatrical representations – representations, he was told, which embodied all the fine ideas shadowed forth in the language he read and committed to memory. It became the wish of his heart to witness one of these performances, and that wish he soon contrived to gratify. His first visit to a theatre fixed the great purpose of his life, and established the sole end and aim of his existence. He would be an actor. He says at this hour that he was bewildered, amazed,

dazzled, fascinated, by what to him was splendor beyond all that his mind had imagined, and mimic life so captivating, that his own real existence would be worthless unless he in some way participated in such imitations as he witnessed.[12]

As many Shakespeare scholars have pointed out, imitation and emulation were foundational practices of Shakespeare's education; practices that lent themselves well to imitating and creating new works of secular theatre.[13] Aldridge, following in this educational model centuries later, was also learning that imitation could lead to mimicry, a tool frequently used in acting.

With British actors regularly touring through New York, and with potential access to the segregated balcony seating in the Park Theatre, Aldridge would have had an opportunity to see Shakespearean tragedies, along with the eclectic blend of comedy, melodrama, and declamation that would characterize his own later traveling productions. With the 1821 founding of the African Grove Theatre, the first black professional company, Aldridge likely saw (and perhaps even apprenticed with) James Hewlett and other actors of color.[14] Here, according to his former classmate Phillip Bell, was "where Shakespeare seduced young Aldridge."[15]

Hewlett, the star of the African Grove Theatre, sought to align himself with the popular English Shakespearean Edmund Kean, with an 1820s engraving captioned "Mr. Hewlett as Richard the Third in imitation of Mr. Kean."[16] While the most common form of cross-cultural mimicry at the time was white actors imitating black masculinity in productions like *Othello*, Hewlett appropriated a form of cross-cultural mimicry for his own benefit. Here was a black American actor imitating a white British one for status recognition and financial gains. Cross-cultural mimicry took an even more bizarre turn when, in an 1824 London revue, Charles Mathews mocked a black Shakespearean actor he had encountered in his *Trip to America*, presumably at the Grove.[17] Mathews's sketch transposed the last lines of Hamlet's "To be or not to be" soliloquy – "And by opposing end them" – into a minstrel song that became highly popular with his audiences, "Opossum up a gum tree": "Well den, ladies and gemmen, you like Opossum up a gum tree better den you like Hamlet? me sing him to you."[18] In an indignant letter, Hewlett criticized how Mathews "burlesqued me ... mimicked our styles – imitated our dialects – laughed at our anomalies."[19] Fascinatingly, Aldridge had the last laugh. While audiences later clamored for him to perform "Opossum," presuming that Mathews had been imitating *him*, Aldridge always insisted that "I never attempted the character of Hamlet in my life."[20] And yet he eventually *did* incorporate "Opossum" into his repertory, thereby imitating Mathews imitating Hewlett imitating Kean.

The first Shakespearean role that we believe Aldridge to have played was Romeo. As Aldridge's *Memoir* affirms:

> But fancy a black Juliet! And why not? May there not be an Ethiopian Juliet to an Ethiopian Romeo? So reasoned and so *felt* the coloured members of the amateur corps, when Mr. Aldridge undertook to perform the love-sick Swain in a sable countenance.[21]

Capitalizing on the presumed universality of the *Romeo and Juliet* love story, Aldridge promoted the notion of an Ethiopian version of the young lovers. Maintaining the notion of emulation, Aldridge figures himself as performing the role in a "sable countenance."

Circulate

As Paul Robeson, himself an itinerant actor, stressed: "The right to travel has been a virtual necessity for the Negro artist."[22] Reflecting on the fact that the US State Department revoked his passport in 1950 unless he signed an affidavit declaring that he was not a member of the Communist Party, Robeson noted how important it was for Aldridge to travel:

> A century ago it was not possible for a Negro actor to appear on the American stage in any role – not even as a buffoon. (Such parts were reserved for "whites only" in the days of black-face minstrel shows, and only toward the end of that era was "progress" made to the point where a Negro face was permitted to appear in the traditional burnt cork of that happily now-dead form of American theatre.) Hence, there was no place on our stages for one of the greatest actors in theatrical history – Ira Aldridge, a Negro.[23]

Given the resistance the African Grove Theatre faced in New York – Aldridge said his *Romeo and Juliet* was disrupted, and we know that the Grove's *Richard III* induced envious rioting from a rival theatre – travel became a necessity: "go *east*, young man."[24] Thus, Aldridge's third strategy was circulation. If you cannot make audiences come to you, then you must find them and go to them. Aldridge traveled to Europe in the hopes of securing a more amenable audience.

During his 1824 transatlantic voyage, Aldridge fell in with James Wallack, a British actor who had performed Macbeth at the Park in 1818, and whose brother Henry had previously engaged Aldridge as a dresser. It seems plausible that Wallack helped introduce Aldridge to the

London theatrical world, although they parted ways when Wallack referred to him as his servant. This association would dog him for years; "I never was his servant, – nor the servant of any man," Aldridge wrote in an 1833 letter to the editor, after receiving hostile reviews that dismissed him as "Mr. Henry Wallack's black servant."[25]

Since London critics were initially difficult to satisfy, Aldridge spent several years touring provincial theatres, with engagements in Aberdeen, Belfast, Beverley, Brighton, Carlisle, Chepstow, Colchester, Coventry, Devonport, Dublin, Edinburgh, Exeter, Glasgow, Gloucester, Hull, Kendal, Lancaster, Lamington, Ledbury, Leicester, Lichfield, Liverpool, Lyon, Manchester, Newark, Newcastle, Norwich, Nottingham, Portsmouth, Preston, Salisbury, Southampton, Stratford, Surrey, Wolverhampton, Worcester, and Yarmouth. As his reputation grew, he began launching European itineraries in the 1850s, including in modern-day Austria, Belgium, Czech Republic, Denmark, France, Germany, Holland, Hungary, Ireland, Moldova, Poland, Russia, Scotland, Serbia, Sweden, Switzerland, Turkey, Ukraine, and Wales – Aldridge proved to be "an extravagant and wheeling stranger / Of here and everywhere" (*Othello*, 1.1.133–34). Just as the provincial touring of Shakespeare's own theatre company helped them refine their art and performance strategies, Aldridge's constant circulation exposed him to a wide range of audiences and theatres, making him a nimble artist who could suit the action to the world. If Aldridge had already mastered imitation and emulation from his schooling at the African Free School, then his decades on tour throughout most of Europe enabled him to master an artistic receptiveness and responsiveness to a variety of audiences and their expectations.

Nominate

What's in a name? For a shrewd self-promoter like Aldridge, naming is one of his other strategies for success. When Aldridge first performed at London's Royal Coburg Theatre in 1825, the playbill announced him as "Mr. KEENE Tragedian of Colour, from the African Theater, New York." It wasn't unusual for a young performer to adopt a moniker that (keenly!) resembled a better-known actor like Edmund Kean. By 1831, he was slowly phasing out "Keene" by blending it with his own surname: "F.W. Keene Aldridge, the African Roscius." Fascinatingly, in 1831 his old Grove Theatre peer James Hewlett "was calling himself, perhaps in tribute to an old hero and pupil alike, after both Kean and this new 'Keene': 'Hewlett for this night styles himself Keen. I am myself alone!'"[26]

The intriguing renaming and repurposing here hearkens back to Colly Cibber, who incorporated "I am myself alone," originally from *3 Henry VI*, into his *Richard III*, a role associated with the original Kean. As Shane White shrewdly observes:

> in Hewlett's notice the word "Keen" is spelled incorrectly – it is exactly halfway between "Kean," the famous white actor, and "Keene," the name under which the increasingly famous Aldridge was performing. In a context in which Aldridge had stolen some of Hewlett's past, and in which a reference had perhaps been made to the name Aldridge was currently using, the line "I am myself alone" took on another, more pointed, meaning.[27]

In a twist of fate, Aldridge replaced Kean in an 1833 production of *Othello*. Just a few years after Aldridge had stopped calling himself "Keene," he was now standing in for Kean. It gets even more complicated: the 1858 *New American Encyclopedia* confusedly claimed that Aldridge's "real name . . . was said to be Hewlett."

And what about that "Roscius"? This first-century BC Roman actor's name became a kind of byword for thespian success, as when Richard Burbage was praised as "England's great Roscius."[28] Born into slavery, the Roman Roscius earned his freedom through his theatrical renown. Though the Roman Roscius was famed as a comedian, Shakespeare refers to him as a tragedian in *3 Henry VI*: "What scene of death hath Roscius now to act" (5.6.10). An astute imitator of Shakespeare, Aldridge knew that the Roman moniker would help to market himself to unfamiliar audiences who were potentially skeptical of a black American's ability to perform classical pieces.

Innovate

Like his circulation strategy that fostered his audience receptiveness and performance adaptability, Aldridge was also attentive to innovation. Some of Aldridge's most notable innovations derived from his drive to expand the range of Shakespearean roles he could perform. While the Prince of Morocco's lines – "Mislike me not for my complexion, / The shadowed livery of the burnished sun" (*Merchant of Venice*, 2.1.1–2) – serve as the epigraph for his *Memoir*, Aldridge didn't limit himself to playing Shakespeare's handful of Moorish characters. Aldridge's decision to play both black and white roles led him to experiment with whiteface in his versions of Macbeth, Richard III, Shylock, and ultimately King Lear – a precedent invoked in 1945 by the theatre critic Samuel Sillen's defense of Canada Lee's controversial whiting up to play Bosola in *The Duchess of*

Malfi.[29] Aldridge's Shylock deployed other racial prostheses, as one 1853 reviewer observed:

> our African guest put on quite a European face . . . The stubby black nose disappeared and was replaced by a white hawk nose; the Negro wool was replaced by a white-skinned bald head.[30]

Aldridge's European performances also featured verbal ingenuity. While he initially hired a troupe of English actors to tour with him, he eventually settled on the unorthodox scheme of hiring local performers, who would speak in their native language while Aldridge delivered his lines in English. Sometimes multilingual incongruity was justified through the plot (e.g., as a way to underline Shylock's alienated status). One Russian actor who worked with Aldridge, Davydov, said that "his mimicry, gestures, were so expressive that knowledge of the English language for the understanding of his acting was not needed at all."[31]

However, Aldridge's greatest Shakespearean innovation was surely his adaptation of *Titus Andronicus* (see Figure 12.1), which took even more radical liberties than Ravenscroft's Restoration version. As early as 1849, Aldridge began collaborating with the playwright Charles A. Somerset to elevate Aaron the Moor's nobility. In Aldridge's performances of *Titus*, Aaron became the hero. Entire scenes are expunged (including all of Act 3), and a scene was imported from the drama *Zaraffa, the Slave King*, which had been written for Aldridge.[32] While the script is lost, one contemporary review indicates the extent of the modifications:

> The deflowerment of Lavinia, cutting out her tongue, chopping off her hands, and the numerous decapitations and gross language which occur in the original are totally omitted and a play not only presentable but actually attractive is the result.[33]

Another reviewer carped: "his *Titus* has nothing in common with Shakespeare's."[34] Aldridge made *Titus Andronicus* his own, and he kept remaking Shakespeare until his death. An 1867 letter describing his plans for a North American return mentions: "My Shakespearian Repertoire is as follows, *Othello*, *Shylock*, *King Lear*, *Macbeth*, and *Caliban*." Aldridge never performed in *The Tempest*. We can only speculate if Aldridge's Caliban would have been reconceived like his Aaron, turning a villain into the protagonist. What we know is that Aldridge did not shy away from innovating his Shakespearean performances.

Disseminate

Aldridge was savvy about shaping the perception of his persona. Again, because he was so attentive to the marketing of his performances, he was

Figure 12.1   Ira Aldridge's innovation as Aaron the Moor is memorialized in this
1852 image.

also attentive to the marketing of his own visual image. Aldridge grew into
something of an icon through his deployment of an array of visual media:
portraits, playbills, posters, engravings, lithographs, photographs. Art histo-
rian Earnestine Jenkins suggests that Aldridge was "probably one of the most
visually documented public black figures of the mid-nineteenth century in
Europe."[35] In fact, a number of paintings that were formerly titled with a
generic "Slave" or "Negro" or "Othello" have since been reidentified as ones
that depict Aldridge. Some of the most notable artworks include:

- 1826: William Mulready, *Ira Aldridge, Possibly in the Role of Othello*,
  Walters Art Museum
- 1827: James Northcote, *Head of a Negro in the Character of Othello*,
  Manchester Art Gallery[36]

- 1827: John Philip Simpson, *The Captive Slave*, Art Institute of Chicago[37]
- 1830: Henry Perronet Briggs, *Ira Frederick Aldridge as Othello*, National Portrait Gallery

And an 1868 marble and bronze sculpture of Othello by Pietro Calvi is thought to have been made from an Aldridge photograph, in memory of his death the year before.

Already during his lifetime, Aldridge's celebrity was established as one that could be capitalized upon if imitated. For instance, a Philadelphia minstrelsy group named itself the "Ira Aldridge Troupe" in 1863.[38] Following his death, a number of companies paid tribute to Aldridge's legacy by naming groups after him: Ira Aldridge Dramatic Association (Washington, DC, 1883); Aldridge Dramatic Club (Philadelphia, 1885); Aldridge Dramatic Association (New Haven, 1889); Ira Aldridge Club (Howard University, Washington, DC, 1916); Aldridge Players (St. Louis, 1920s); Ira Aldridge Dramatic Club (Johnson C. Smith University, Charlotte, 1940s).[39] To this day, the Ira Aldridge Repertory Players still perform in San Diego, and the Ira Aldridge Players continue at Morgan State College in Baltimore. The Black Theater Alliance has been offering the Ira Aldridge Award for decades. Shaw University (Raleigh, NC) used to award an Aldridge Prize; the Southern Illinois University–Carbondale's Department of Theater still offers a scholarship in his name. In 1929, James Weldon Johnson persuaded the NAACP to raise funds to endow the Ira Aldridge Memorial Chair in Stratford's Shakespeare Memorial Theatre – the only actor of color so honored.[40] Blue plaques in honor of Aldridge have been erected in London (2007) and Coventry (2017). The unveiling of the latter was attended by actor Earl Cameron, who was trained in elocution by Amanda Aldridge – Ira's youngest daughter, who had earlier worked with Paul Robeson.[41]

Like many black actors, Paul Robeson found Aldridge an inspiring precedent. In the 1930s–40s, Robeson even made plans for a movie about Aldridge, with his biographer Herbert Marshall.[42] Applauded by W.E.B. Du Bois and Langston Hughes,[43] Aldridge keeps circulating in popular culture, including in the Season Two premiere of PBS's *Victoria*, in which the queen watches Aldridge perform Othello. Djanet Sears's *Harlem Duet* (1997) has a character boast: "I'll not die in black-face to pay the rent. I am of Ira Aldridge stock. I am a classical man" (2.6.312). And Aldridge has frequently inspired playwrights to dramatize his life and legacy:[44]

- Ossie Davis, *Curtain Call, Mr. Aldridge, Sir*, 1963
- Henry Kemp-Blair, *Long Way from Home*, 1969

- Ted Lange, *Born a Unicorn*, 1981
- David Pownall, *Black Star*, 1987
- Jack Shepherd, *Black to Play . . . or Othello's Occupation*, 1987
- Alexander Simmons, *Sherlock Holmes and the Hands of Othello*, 1987
- Lonne Elder III, *Splendid Mummer!* 1988
- William Hairston, *Ira Aldridge (The London Conflict)*, 1988
- Robin Scott Peters, *The African Tragedian*, 1994
- Eddie Paul Bradley, Jr., *Evening with Ira Aldridge*, 1998
- Maciej Karpinski, *Othello Dies*, 2002
- Thomas L. Harris and Henri D. Franklin, *Before There Was Broadway*, 2006
- Remigiusz Caban, *The Negro Must Leave*, 2010
- Jacqueline E. Lawton, *Ira Aldridge: The African Roscius*, 2010
- Maureen Lawrence, *Speak of Me As I Am*, 2011
- Lolita Chakrabarti, *Red Velvet*, 2012
- Levi Frazier, *For Our Freedom and Yours*, 2015
- Yara Arts Group, *Dark Night Bright Stars*, 2016
- Anchuli Felicia King, *Keene*, 2020

Back in 1998, when Lolita Chakrabarti began researching *Red Velvet*, she found that discovering "any information about him proved very difficult . . . In the end there was only one book I could find" – Herbert Marshall and Mildred Stock's 1958 biography. Happily, this is no longer the case. The twenty-first century has seen a renewed interest in his life, his performances, and his career, an interest which has no sign of abating. Perhaps a biopic will finally be made.

ELABORATE

If you are keen to learn the strategy of elaborating upon Aldridge's legacy, extensive scholarly resources are now available. One could consider starting with a visit to one of the research libraries with strong collections of Aldridge-related material, including Northwestern University, the New York Public Library's Schomburg Center, Southern Illinois University–Carbondale (which holds Lindfors's papers), and the Folger Shakespeare Library, or one can begin by reading some of the resources below or in the footnotes. It is imperative that we not forget Ira Aldridge's complicated history and legacy at this point when the Shakespearean world is expanding.

Andrews, C.B., *Black Ebony –The Diaries, Letters and Criticism: The Story of Ira Aldridge (Known as the African Roscius)* (Charles Deering McCormick Library of Special Collections, Northwestern University).

Dewberry, Jonathan, "The African Grove Theatre and Company," *Black American Literature Forum* 16/4 (1982): 128–31.

Howard, Tony, and Zoë Wilcox, "'Haply, for I am black': The Legacy of Ira Aldridge," in *Shakespeare in Ten Acts*, ed. Gordon McMullan and Zoë Wilcox (London: British Library, 2016), 121–40.

Kujawinska Courtney, Krystyna, and Maria Lukowska (eds.), *Ira Aldridge 1807–1867: The Great Shakespearean Tragedian on the Bicentennial Anniversary of His Birth* (Frankfurt am Main: Peter Lang, 2009).

Kujawinska Courtney, Krystyna, "Ira Aldridge, Shakespeare, and Color-Conscious Performances in Nineteenth Century Europe," in *Colorblind Shakespeare: New Perspectives on Race and Performance*, ed. Ayanna Thompson (New York and London: Routledge, 2006), 103–22.

Lindfors, Bernth (ed.), *Ira Aldridge: The African Roscius* (University of Rochester Press, 2007).

MacDonald, Joyce Green, "Acting Black: Othello, Othello Burlesques, and the Performance of Blackness," *Theatre Journal* 46 (1994): 231–49.

Malone, Mary, *Actor in Exile: The Life of Ira Aldridge* (London: Cromwell-Collier Press, 1969).

Marshall, Herbert, *Further Research on Ira Aldridge, the Negro Tragedian* (Center for Soviet and East European Studies, Southern Illinois University at Carbondale, 1973).

Roberts, Brian Russell, "A London Legacy of Ira Aldridge: Henry Francis Downing and the Paratheatrical Poetics of Plot and Cast(e)," *Modern Drama* 55/3 (Fall 2012): 386–40.

Ross, Alex, "Othello's Daughter," *New Yorker*, 29 July 2013.

Walters, Hazel, "Ira Aldridge and the Battlefield of Race," *Race and Class* 45/1 (2003): 1–30.

Notes

1 John Jackson, *History of the Scottish Stage* (London, 1793), 349–51, cited by Paul Edwards and James Walvin, *Black Personalities in the Era of the Slave Trade* (Baton Rouge: Louisiana State University Press, 1983), 149, 245n9.

2 An 1825 playbill, cited by Henry Reed Stiles in *A History of the City of Brooklyn*, vol. III (Brooklyn, 1870), 906.

3 "From Othello is torn the deep cry 'O misery, misery, misery!' and in that misery of the African artist is heard the far-off groans of his own people, oppressed by unbelievably slavery." Russian critic K. Zvantsev, quoted in Michael Neill, "Introduction," in *Othello*, ed. Michael Neill (Oxford University Press, 2008), 52. As Francesca Royster observes, it's "sometimes impossible to distinguish between the self-image that Aldridge knowingly performed and the image that the audience projected onto him." Francesca Royster, "Playing with a Difference: Early Black Shakespearean Actors, Blackface and Whiteface," in *Shakespeare in American Life*, ed. Virginia Mason Vaughan and Alden T. Vaughan (Washington, DC: Folger Shakespeare Library, 2007), 35–47 (at 45).

4 Charles C. Andrews, *The History of the New-York African Free-Schools* (New York: Mahlon Day, 1830), 15.

5 *Letters From John Pintard to His Daughter Eliza Noel Pintard Davidson, 1816–1833*, vol. I: *1816–1820* (New York Historical Society, 1940), 300.

6 Eve Thurston, "Ethiopia Unshackled: A Brief History of the Education of Negro Children in New York City," *Bulletin of the New York Public Library* 69/4 (1965): 211–31 (at 218).

7 Edward D. Griffin, *A Plea for Africa: A Sermon Preached October 26, 1817, in the First Presbyterian Church in the City of New York, before the Synod of New York and New Jersey, at the Request of the Board of Directors of the African School Established by the Synod* (New York: Gould, 1817), 67.

8 See Anna Mae Duane, "'Like a Motherless Child': Racial Education at the New York African Free School and in *My Bondage and My Freedom*," *American Literature* 82/3 (2010): 461–88.

9 See Heather Nathans, "'A Course of Learning and Ingenious Study': Shakespearean Education and Theatre in Antebellum America," in *Shakespearean Educations: Power, Citizenship, and Performance*, ed. Coppélia Kahn, Heather S. Nathans, and Mimi Godfrey (Newark: University of Delaware Press, 2011), 54–70 (at 56).

10 Anonymous, *Memoir and Theatrical Career of Ira Aldridge, the African Roscius* (London: Onwhyn, 1849), 12.

11 Kate Flaherty, "Shakespeare and Education: The Making of an Unlikely Marriage," in *The Shakespearean World*, ed. Jill L. Levenson and Robert Ormsby (New York: Routledge, 2017): 361–76 (at 362). See also Jeremy B. Dibbell, "'A Library of the Most Celebrated & Approved Authors': The First Purchase Collection of Union College," *Libraries and the Cultural Record*, 43/4 (2008): 367–96 (at 380–82).

12 *Memoir and Theatrical Career of Ira Aldridge*, 10.

13 See, for example, Lynn Enterline, *Shakespeare's Schoolroom: Rhetoric, Discipline, Emotion* (Philadelphia: University of Pennsylvania Press, 2012). See also Scott Newstok, *How to Think Like Shakespeare: Lessons from a Renaissance Education* (Princeton University Press, 2020).

14 George Thompson, *A Documentary History of the African Theatre* (Evanston, IL: Northwestern University Press, 1998).

15 Philip A. Bell, "Men We Have Known: Ira Aldridge," *Elevator*, 20 September 1867, 2.

16 See Marvin McAllister, *Whiting Up: Whiteface Minstrels and Stage Europeans in African American Performance* (Chapel Hill: University of North Carolina Press, 2011), 57–59; this production was memorably reconstructed in Carlyle Brown's play *The African Company Presents Richard III* (1994).

17 See Peter Buckley, "Obi in New York: Aldridge and the African Grove," in *Obi*, ed. Charles Rzepka (College Park: University of Maryland, 2002); and David Worrall, *Harlequin Empire: Race, Ethnicity and the Drama of the Popular Enlightenment* (New York: Routledge, 2015), 58–62.

18 See Nicholas M. Evans, "Ira Aldridge: Shakespeare and Minstrelsy," *American Transcendental Quarterly* 16/3 (September 2002): 165–87.

19 James Hewlett, *National Advocate*, 8 May 1824.

20 *Memoir and Theatrical Career of Ira Aldridge*, 11. The first major African American playwright, William Wells Brown, claims he saw Aldridge perform Hamlet the evening after he staged *Othello*. William Wells Brown, *The Black Man: His Antecedents, His Genius, and His Achievements* (Boston: James Redpath, 1863), 118–24.

21 *Memoir and Theatrical Career of Ira Aldridge*, 11.

22 Paul Robeson, *Here I Stand* (Boston: Beacon Press, 1958), 71.

23 Robeson, 71.

24 Henry Louis Gates, Jr., "Who Was the 1st Black Othello?" *The Root*, 31 March 2014, www.theroot.com/who-was-the-1st-black-othello-1790875144.

25 Cited by Sarah Meer, "Melodrama and Race," in *The Cambridge Companion to English Melodrama*, ed. Carolyn Williams (Cambridge University Press, 2019), 192–206 (at 196).

26 Robert Hornback, "Black Shakespeareans vs. Minstrel Burlesques: 'Proper' English, Racist Blackface Dialect, and the Contest for Representing 'Blackness,' 1821–1844," *Shakespeare Studies* 38 (2010): 125–60 (at 141).

27 Shane White, *Stories of Freedom in Black New York* (Cambridge, MA: Harvard University Press, 2009), 170.

28 *A Funeral Elegy on the Death of the famous Actor Richard Burbage who died on Saturday in Lent the 13th March 1618* [i.e., 1619].

29 See McAllister, 150.

30 Gabor Egressy, cited by Bernth Lindfors, *Ira Aldridge: Performing Shakespeare in Europe, 1852–1855* (Woodbridge: Boydell & Brewer, 2011), 110.

31 Cited by Melissa Vickery-Bareford, "Aldridge, Ira Frederick," in *African American Lives,* ed. Henry Louis Gates, Jr. (Oxford University Press, 2004), 14.

32 J.J. Sheahan. "*Titus Andronicus*: Ira Aldridge," *Notes and Queries* 4th series 10 (1872): 132–33.

33 *The Era*, 26 April 1857.

34 *Brighton Herald,* 6 October, 1860. Cited by Thomas D. Pawley, "The First Black Playwrights," *Black World* 21 (April 1972): 16–25 (at 19).

35 Earnestine Jenkins, "Painting Ira Aldridge as Othello in James Northcote's 1827 Manchester Portrait," *Spectacles of Blackness: Representing Blacks in European Art of the Long Nineteenth Century*, ed. Adrienne L. Childs and Susan H. Libby (Farnham: Ashgate, 2014): 105–23 (at 105).

36 See *Black Victorians: Black People in British Art, 1800–1900*, ed. Jan Marsh (Manchester Art Gallery, 2005).

37 Martin Postle, "'The Captive Slave,' by John Simpson (1782–1847): A Rediscovered Masterpiece," *British Art Journal* 9/3 (Spring 2009): 18–26.

38 Jack Shalom, "The Ira Aldridge Troupe: Early Black Minstrelsy in Philadelphia," *African American Review* 28/4 (Winter 1994): 653–58.

39 Bernard L. Peterson and Lena McPhatter Gore, *The African American Theatre Directory, 1816–1960: A Comprehensive Guide to Early Black Theatre Organizations, Companies, Theatres, and Performing Groups* (Westport, CT: Greenwood Press, 1997): 8–9; Errol Hill, *Shakespeare in Sable: A History of Black Shakespearean Actors* (Amherst: University of Massachusetts Press, 1986), 45.

40 James Weldon Johnson, *Black Manhattan* (New York: A.A. Knopf, 1930), 86–87.

41 Earl Cameron quoted in Stephen Bourne, *Black in the British Frame: The Black Experience in British Film and Television* (London: Bloomsbury, 2005), 106.

42 Dick Russell, "All the World's Their Stage: Paul Robeson and Ira Aldridge," in Dick Russell and Alvin F. Poussaint, *Black Genius: Inspirational Portraits of African American Leaders* (New York: Skyhorse, 2009), 133. Andrea Chalupa has recently called for an Aldridge biopic: "We Need a Movie about Ira Aldridge, the Black Shakespearean Who Fought Racism from the Stage," *The Wrap*, 14 July 2018, www.thewrap.com/we-need-a-movie-about-the-black-shakespearean-no-ones-ever-told-you-about-podcast.

43 W.E.B. Du Bois, *The Gift of Black Folk: The Negroes in the Making of America* (Boston, MA: Stratford, 1924): 310; Langston Hughes, "Prelude to Our Age: A Negro History Poem," Part 4: "Yet Ira Aldridge played Shakespeare in London," *The Collected Poems of Langston Hughes* (New York: Knopf, 1994), 381.

44 See Bernth Lindfors, *Ira Aldridge: The Early Years, 1807–1833* (University of Rochester Press, 2011), 294n46.

CHAPTER 13

What Is the History of Actors of Color Performing in Shakespeare in the UK?

Urvashi Chakravarty

University of Toronto

Who gets to play Shakespeare, and why? What is the range of characters that can be performed by actors of a certain embodiment – in terms of race, gender, or physical ability? And how might these possibilities differ across nations? This essay considers the particular conditions and contingencies of performing Shakespeare as an actor of color in Britain, where the force of "national heritage" sometimes presses against the urgency of reimagining what Shakespeare can mean for different audiences at different times, and where the imperative to lead the way critically and performatively for a global audience competes with the pressure to preserve the tradition (a freighted, troubled term) of Shakespeare as a literary and theatrical touchstone and as an industry that stands in for a constructed and changing sense of "Englishness."

A question arises at the beginning of tracing this particular performance history: What does it actually *mean* to be an actor of color in the United Kingdom? And how does it relate to the particular histories of race, migration, labor, and slavery in Britain? A careful consideration of the particular racial frameworks that limn these performative enactments and their reception in the UK may be useful here. Whereas, for instance, in the United States, the term Asian often refers to a person of East or Southeast Asian heritage, in UK contexts it generally designates someone of South Asian descent. The term black, meanwhile, has traditionally been used in Britain and North America to refer to those of African and African-Caribbean heritage; in the UK, however, political coalitions between Commonwealth subjects from African, Caribbean, and South Asian nations who immigrated to Britain in the aftermath of the Second World War were mobilized toward an understanding of "political blackness," which extended to British residents of both Asian and African heritage as part of a larger anti-racist movement which registered and negotiated shared experiences of racism. Although the term political blackness still has some purchase today – the National Union of Students

Black Students' Campaign, for instance, still "represents students of African, Asian, Arab and Caribbean descent at a local and national level on all issues affecting Black students"[1] – the force of political blackness has, according to many, been complicated and eroded since the 1990s. Political blackness, critics argue, both erases the particularities of different experiences, in particular eliding the specific experiences of black, African-Caribbean peoples, and accords disproportionate importance to a recentered whiteness, a tension both acknowledged and contested in the current descriptive designation of BME or BAME (Black, Asian and Minority Ethnic) for non-white people in the UK.

At the same time, the presence of actors of color in the UK is often framed within the contexts of post-Windrush migration – a significant part of the story, but not all of it. Indeed, the presence of black Britons has been discernable throughout British history, and scholars of pre-twentieth-century British history and culture have made considerable efforts to unearth and illuminate this genealogy. Yet Britain's history of slavery remains curiously elided in many contexts. Because slavery was, officially, never permitted on English soil, a convenient fiction has arisen around Britain's (non-)involvement in the slave trade and its imperial violence. The fiction argues that slavery was marginal, rather than, as in the United States, central to its national history, and that in consequence it has played a smaller role in structuring the current conditions and the historical trajectory of BAME life in the UK.

The history of both race and slavery, however, is critically bound up with the genealogies of Shakespearean performance and the theatre. At least as early as the eighteenth century, black servants, including the boy attendants of aristocratic, white Englishwomen, visited the theatre, as did independent black people; it is likely that these performances may have included plays by Shakespeare.[2] The eighteenth-century writer Ignatius Sancho, a formerly enslaved person who was born on a slave ship and brought to England at the age of two years old, and who, as a male property owner, was the first known black Briton to vote in a general election, was a friend of the renowned Shakespearean actor and theatre manager David Garrick.[3] Meanwhile, Julius Soubise – an enslaved person from St. Kitts, formerly named Othello, who was himself a friend of Ignatius Sancho – performed excerpts from Shakespeare in London "spouting clubs," including selections from *Othello*, *Richard III*, and *Romeo and Juliet*.[4] As these examples illustrate, and as we shall see, the history of black people in Britain is thus closely connected to the history of British theatre and, specifically, the history of Shakespeare.

But what about the role of black Britons and other actors of color in commercial and theatrical performances of plays by Shakespeare? The earliest extant formal records of Shakespearean performances by actors of color, as I shall discuss, date from the early nineteenth century. But early modern plays themselves staged "blackamoors" and "Moors" (a capacious term which included black people, Indians, and other dark-skinned peoples), and although these figures have traditionally been understood as having been performed by white actors in blackface (both cosmetic and textile), recent critical scholarship has proposed that (at least some of) these black characters – often unnamed or silent – may in fact have been performed by black people. Between 1587, when the first black character appeared on the English commercial stage in Marlowe's *Tamburlaine Part I*, and the closure of the theatres in 1642, at least seventy plays featured black characters.[5] Given that there was at least one black musician in the royal court, and that black people were staged during a court performance of Jonson's *Masque of Blackness* in 1605, and especially given the relative expense of cosmetic blackface, the theatre scholar Matthieu Chapman proposes that "Nothing in history explicitly excludes or forbids black performers on the early modern English stage, and the evidence, together with the acknowledged role of blacks in court and the history of black court performers, allows for the presence of actual blacks on commercial and court stages."[6] Although this performance genealogy is speculative, based on what the archival evidence might allow rather than what it explicitly includes, it affords the exciting possibility that black actors may have appeared in plays by Shakespeare as early as the sixteenth century. This possibility also underscores the kind of critical scholarship that is necessary to excavate the histories of people of color, who are already marginalized in the annals of performance history. In other words, the speculative work proposing the early modern staging of people of color, and their role in Shakespeare performance from its earliest days, usefully frames the disciplinary and methodological questions that underpin our excavation of the history of actors of color performing Shakespeare in the UK.

Although there is little record of actors of color in Shakespeare in the eighteenth century (including Julius Soubise's recitals, and the tantalizing possibility of Ignatius Sancho's involvement in David Garrick's theatre company), there is considerable archival evidence of the impact and success of one of the most famous nineteenth-century Shakespearean actors, the American actor Ira Aldridge, who moved to England in 1824 and performed in theatres across the country before touring

Figure 13.1   A poster announcing Ira Aldridge's first appearance at Covent Garden in *Othello* in 1833.

the continent to great acclaim (see Figure 13.1). An advertisement from the *Bristol Mercury* commented on the groundbreaking nature of Aldridge's appearance, suggestively if strategically confirming the absence of actors of color in contemporaneous and previous productions, when it announced:

> the most singular Novelty in the Theatrical world, viz., an African
> Tragedian (a native of Senegal, Africa), known by the appellation of *THE*
> *AFRICAN ROSCIUS*: The unprecedented novelty of a Native African,
> personating Dramatic Characters, has excited a degree of interest unparal-
> leled in the annals of the Drama.[7]

This advertisement tellingly locates Aldridge's African provenance in
Senegal, although Aldridge himself was born in New York City in 1807.

Likewise, in a review in 1848, the critic's final comments on Aldridge
are striking:

> It was interesting to witness the acting of Mr. Ira Aldridge, a native of
> Africa, giving utterance to the wrongs of his race in his assumed character,
> and standing in an attitude of triumph over the body of one of its
> oppressors. England has, however, done its duty, and perhaps gone a little
> beyond – witness the millions paid for the manumission of the blacks in the
> British settlements, and the present ruined position of our West India
> possessions. Mr. Ira Aldridge is an intelligent actor, and his elocutionary
> powers are admirable. There is considerable impulse, but we discovered no
> genius; yet, compared with the people by whom he was last night sur-
> rounded, he might with strict justice be considered a true Roscius. The
> range of characters open to Mr. Ira Aldridge are of necessity restricted in
> consequence of his complexion; there are but Othello, and Aaron the
> Moor, in *Titus Andronicus*, in the loftier walks of the drama, and some
> few comic characters quite unworthy his delineation.[8]

This review serves as a crucial reminder that Aldridge's presence on the
commercial stage occurred in the context of Britain's imperial practices,
coinciding with the abolitionist movement and the emancipation of
enslaved peoples in Britain's West Indian colonies and its aftermath. The
author's annoyance at England's supposedly excessive reparations ("the
millions paid for the manumission of the blacks" were paid, in fact, not to
formerly enslaved people but rather to the plantation owners who had
enslaved them) underscores the way in which the most notable early
appearance of a Shakespearean actor of color was informed by the historical and imperial frameworks of race and slavery within which it was
implicated. This particular review, however, also raises the crucial question
of who gets to play Shakespeare, and *which* Shakespearean characters
certain actors are permitted to embody. For this critic, Aldridge's complexion was an impediment which must necessarily limit the range of
characters he might enact. This is a problem that has led in modern times
to the understanding of an "unofficial black canon," a term which refers to
the corpus of characters to which black actors have access, and that often

excludes major and conventionally canonical roles such as Hamlet and Lear in favor of "Moorish" characters and minor, supporting or secondary roles which serve the leading part in the play.[9]

In 1866, the year before Aldridge's death, a notice in the *English Leader* appeared to announce his dramatic successor:

> Considerable interest is just now felt in the appearance upon the English stage of Mr. S. Morgan Smith, a coloured actor from America, who is said to have very great gifts for the dramatic profession. He appears not only in parts with which he is allied by complexion, such as Othello, Oroonoko, Gambia, &c., but also in Macbeth, Shylock, and Hamlet. He has a noble voice, great facial expression, and renders with singular delicacy, naturalness, and power, a very wide range of sentiment and passion. Not the least of his merits is his high artistic ambition, and his desire to prove that the race to which he belongs is capable of successful exertion in the arduous walks of the Theatrical Profession. – July 7th.[10]

Samuel Morgan Smith was born in Philadelphia in 1832 and moved to England in 1866. The notice emphasizes Smith's American provenance, like that of Aldridge, underscoring the greater freedom for actors of color in Britain as opposed to America – and also, perhaps, rather gloating in that distinction – even as it continues to note the relative novelty of witnessing actors of "the race to which he belongs" on the stage. The *English Leader* explicitly comments on the "parts with which [Smith] is allied by complexion" – the "Moorish" characters whom actors of color were assumed to personate more convincingly – but it is striking that as early as the mid-nineteenth century, the idea that actors of color were limited to playing black and brown characters was being at once proposed and challenged – and that Aldridge was not alone in expanding that repertoire. Contemporary reviews confirm that Smith staged some of the most prominent Shakespearean tragic characters to considerable acclaim, including a review printed in 1867 which noted that:

> Mr. Smith is the second actor of colour who has become favourably known to European audiences for his clever and effective representation of Shaksperian [sic] characters. He is a fitting successor to the mantle of Ira Aldridge … His impersonation of Hamlet was forcible and dignified, and his elocution was clear and expressive. Frequent bursts of applause testified to his success with the audience.[11]

The Prince of Wales Theatre in Glasgow, meanwhile, advertised its 1871 performance of *Richard III* with Smith ("The only Actor of Colour of Shakespeare's Characters on the Stage") in the title role of Richard.[12]

The Queen's Royal Theatre in Dublin announced "Shakspeare's [sic] celebrated Play of the MERCHANT OF VENICE. Shylock, Mr. Morgan Smith"; two days later, the same theatre advertised a performance of *Othello* starring Smith – in the role of Iago, not Othello.[13] Although this may have been a misprint, it offers the intriguing possibility of a repertoire wherein actors of color could not only play parts to which they were not "allied by complexion" but could enact them even within plays which featured "Moorish" characters. In other words, it presents the specter of playing against type, of offering new perspectives on the contingencies of racial embodiment and spectacularity. It also proffers the possibility of a relatively capacious black canon at this point, at least for these exceptionally celebrated black performers.

Smith's racialized identity continued to prove an object of intense interest. In describing him as "a negro of the purest blood," for instance, the *Derbyshire Times* revealed a fascination with, and a desire to capitalize on, a "real" racial provenance rooted in a conception of purity of blood.[14] Smith's appearance in performances of *Othello*, meanwhile, sometimes took part alongside his wife in the role of Desdemona.[15] It is tempting to imagine the audience's reception not only of an actor of color on the stage – the novelty of which, as I have noted, was repeatedly emphasized in reviews and advertisements which sought to profit from it – but also of a black actor alongside his white wife in the role of Desdemona, especially at a moment when Smith's country of origin was roiled by the aftermath of civil war. Several newspapers, indeed, seemed to strike a somewhat self-congratulatory note as they recounted to their readers the reason for Smith's appearance – and that of Aldridge before him – on the British stage: that his "colour has been a bar to his appearing in any theatre of his own country."[16]

Even as the English stage repeatedly announced the opportunities it provided to actors of color who were prevented from displaying their talent in the United States, and celebrated its apparently liberatory possibilities, it also capitalized on the history of slavery to advertise its attractions. Sandwiched between an advertisement for "CHRISTY'S MINSTRELS" and "DWIGHT'S MARYLAND MINSTRELS" (both, presumably, all-white troupes in blackface) in a British newspaper in 1868, for instance, was a notice for "GEORGIA MINSTRELS, the GREAT AMERICAN SLAVE TROUPE and BRASS BAND, from the United States"; the "Georgia Minstrels," the notice explained helpfully, consisted of "Sixteen Talented *Artistes*, who, prior to June, 1865, were Slaves in America."[17]

At the turn of the twentieth century, there was another novel kind of staging at the Shaftesbury Theatre in London: an entirely non-white cast. Under the decidedly tongue-in-cheek headline of "A COLOURED CASTE," the *Nottingham Evening Post* asserted that:

"In Dahomey," now appearing at the Shaftesbury Theatre, London, is the first play in this country in which all the characters have been represented by coloured ladies and gentlemen. But more than a century back prominent parts in our theatres were occasionally taken by negroes; it is extremely probable that their first appearance on the stage was made in the British Isles. Barrington, in his "Recollections of his Own Times," mentions that the character of Mungo in Dibden's "Padlock" was played with great success by a real negro in Dublin in 1770. Nor was the negro actor confined to the representation of coloured persons, for Jackson, in his "History of the Scottish Stage," relates that in Lancashire he saw a performance of "The Beggar's Opera," in which a negress played very creditably the part of Polly Peachum.[18]

This notice from 1903 affords a tantalizing glimpse into the stage history of actors of color in the British Isles, firstly suggesting the longevity of this history, tracing it to the late eighteenth century or even earlier, and secondly noting the presence of *female* actors of color. It is difficult to know whether or not any of these actors – or the performers and entertainers mentioned earlier – might have appeared in plays by Shakespeare as well. What *is* clear is that although actors of color appeared onstage in the UK throughout the nineteenth century, and (according to this review) perhaps even earlier, the archives of Shakespearean performance are mostly confined to only two prominent actors: Aldridge and Smith.[19]

Perhaps even more poignant are those glimpses in the archive of actors of color whose only record remains in the legal annals when they were accused of a crime. In 1886, the *Northern Echo* reported that "Joseph Jones, a coloured member of a theatrical company at Spennymoor," was accused and tried for "stealing his manager's gold watch."[20] The fact that (according to the newspaper) he initially "accused a black colleague" of the crime before finally confessing perhaps suggests the more widespread presence of black actors. In 1907, meanwhile, "Wm. Gordon Masters, 19, an actor, of colour" was accused of housebreaking and theft.[21] A news item in the *Nottingham Evening Post* reported the early release of Benjamin Curnaerspursong, "a coloured actor" who "said he was born in slavery in North Carolina," who had been convicted of assault.[22] In Blackburn in 1895, "Two members of the 'Old Kentucky' company, performing at the theatre, named William Henry Shearwood and John Albert Wilson, both coloured men" were charged with "malicious wounding" after defending themselves from an attack by a bystander who had seen them speaking with two (presumably white) girls.[23] More troubling still are the multiple legal cases where actors of color stood accused of kidnapping presumably white, young English women. In 1901, for instance, "Eldridge Adolphus Patterson, a man of colour, described as an actor, was charged with the abduction of two Halifax mill girls."[24] A decade earlier, "James Travis, a coloured man belonging to the Uncle Tom's Cabin Company, at present playing at the Doncaster Theatre, was brought up charged with having abducted Mary Havern, a girl of the age of 15 years, from the custody of her parents, with intent to have carnal knowledge of her."[25] Travis and Havern, the report alleged, "lived together as man and wife" for several days before Travis was arrested. In a similar case in 1893, "Louis Rock, a coloured man" stood accused of "acting illegally towards Jane Ellen Price, 14 years old"; according to the account, and as in the case of Travis and Havern, Price had been been passed off as Rock's wife.[26]

In explicitly emphasizing the race of the accused, these headlines deliberately invoke the salacious trope of interracial sexual contact. One wonders whether and how pre-existing narrative tropes from Shakespeare, particularly from *Othello*, might frame these stories; in the instances of both Travis and Rock, the female victims are both young and are presented as their abductors' wives.[27] It is important to note, of course, that in none of the three cases above are the actors of color explicitly described as having appeared in productions of Shakespeare, although as I have suggested, *Othello* might provide a narrative lens for these cases. But in *all* these cases of actors of color who only appear in the annals of legal history, one glimpses a lost dramatic archive. One wonders whether they could, or did, appear in Shakespearean productions, and one realizes, with dismay, that if not for these accusations of theft, assault, and abduction, we would not even know their names.

The nineteenth-century history of Shakespearean actors of color on British stages concludes with one final, relatively unknown figure: the American actor Paul Molyneaux Hewlett, who moved to England in the early 1880s and performed as Paul Molyneaux. Molyneaux did not find the success of his American predecessors, Aldridge and Smith. On the contrary, in an account titled "A CREOLE TRAGEDIAN," one reviewer wrote:

> Some are born to greatness; others attain it; some have it thrust upon them; while a large number inconsistently assume it. In the last category we may place Mr Paul Molyneaux, the "great American tragedian and black Roscius," who invited us last Saturday evening to the Kilburn Town Hall

to witness his rendering of the rôle of Richard the Third. Though we could not discern the eminence thus boldly advertised, we are ready to admit that Mr Molyneaux possesses acting ability of a commonplace and conventional order ... but if he wished to impress us with his greatness his method of doing so was certainly suicidal, and we should think he would [be] the first to admit that the ridiculous farce enacted on Saturday evening would have blasted even the reputation of his Roman prototype.[28]

This scathing account received an extraordinary response from Paul Molyneaux a week later, in a printed letter to the editor in which Molyneaux reminded his readers that, "The night previous *Othello* was performed to the entire satisfaction of the audience, who, though few, were lavish with their rounds of applause, and at the close we had again to raise the curtain," and revealed both his overreliance on amateur actors as he "was endeavouring to get a start in England" and the monetary disputes with a costumier which scuppered the performance. The letter concluded with a poignant plea that drew on a perhaps familiar final request: "I only state this," Molyneaux wrote, "in order that you may deal justly with me. I crave no favours. *I simply wish you to speak of me as I am*" (emphasis added).[29] Molyneaux's letter, thus, strikingly relied on Othello's final words to stake his claim to a narrative legacy that might do him justice: "When you shall these unlucky deeds relate, / Speak of me as I am. Nothing extenuate, / Nor set down aught in malice" (5.2.339–41).[30] Sadly, it was not to be: there remains very little record of this third American-born actor of color on the British stage.

Molyneaux returned to America in 1889, and we have little record of further Shakespearean performances by black actors over the next few decades; one exception is the Egyptian-born actor, author, and founder of the Hull Shakespeare Society, Dusé Mohamed Ali (also known as Dusé Mohamed), who appeared in *Anthony and Cleopatra* in 1890 and in scenes from *Othello* and *The Merchant of Venice* in the early years of the twentieth century.[31] The year 1930, however, saw a notable Shakespearean performance, by the renowned American concert vocalist and actor Paul Robeson. Robeson was already well known to London audiences from his roles in productions of *Show Boat* and *The Emperor Jones*.[32] His performance of Othello at the Savoy Theatre met with generally favorable reviews, with *The Times* remarking that Robeson

teaches us anew that Othello on the stage means something more to us than Macbeth, Hamlet, or Lear ... Undeniably Mr. Robeson plays thrillingly upon the nerves and knocks at the heart. His performance is blemished here and there but nowhere seriously flawed ... Mr. Robeson's interpretation may not accord in every detail with our own, but it is consistent with itself, it produces an Othello pulsating with life, and so makes its way with us, irresistibly.[33]

Oddly, however, this review also saw fit to remark on Robeson's complexion in order to situate his performance within a longer British stage tradition of enacting, and embodying, Othello: "Mr. Robeson is a negro, and thus revives the stage tradition that held down to the time of Edmund Kean of a coal-black Othello."[34]

Despite Robeson's success in England, he would not play Othello in the United States until 1943. Othello, indeed, was the only Shakespearean character Robeson would perform, and he did so in only three productions, concluding with a Royal Shakespeare Company production in 1959 which received somewhat mixed responses, like: "His performance is occasionally exciting; it hardly ever touches the heart."[35] Robeson's 1959 *Othello*, however, also featured a starry cast, including Albert Finney and Sam Wanamaker as well as Robeson himself. But it also included another actor of color, in the role of Lodovico: Edward de Souza. De Souza, an English film and television actor of Portuguese Indian descent, appeared in twenty theatrical and audio productions of Shakespeare plays from 1958 to 1998, mostly in secondary roles, but including Bertram in *All's Well that Ends Well* at the Shakespeare Memorial Theatre in 1959 and the role of Theseus in *A Midsummer Night's Dream* at the National Theatre in 1982.[36]

But Robeson was not the only actor of color to perform on the British stage in the 1930s. The Burmese-born British actor Abraham Sofaer appeared in numerous productions throughout the decade, including in the title role of *Othello* at the Old Vic in 1935, as well as in a range of other roles during this time, from Berowne in *Love's Labour's Lost* (Westminister Theatre, 1932) to Bolingbroke in *Richard II* (Old Vic, 1934), Henry IV in *Henry IV, Part II* (Old Vic, 1935), and the title role in the BBC's radio production of *King Lear* (1939).[37] Sofaer had in fact already been playing a wide array of Shakespearean parts throughout the early 1920s, but he is not described or noted as an actor of color in the newspaper advertisements or reviews of these plays. Although this might be read as a potentially democratizing omission, it may also reflect Sofaer's status as a British subject, as opposed to his American predecessors; Burma (now Myanmar), where Sofaer was born, was at the time part of the British Empire. But this omission also underscores some of the difficulty of recovering the presence of actors of color on the British stage. How can we know when actors *are* people of color, and are British actors of color elided precisely by their status as imperial subjects? Sofaer himself, it seems, played a large and eclectic range of roles to consistent and considerable acclaim in a number of locations around England, including Hull, Exeter, Derby, and Gloucester, many as part of the Charles Doran Shakespeare Company. His appearances included an unnamed part in *The Merchant of Venice*, and later, the dual roles of the Prince of Morocco and Tubal (Hull, 1922; Derby, 1923); Caesar and Cassius in *Julius Caesar* (Hull, 1922 and 1924); Amiens and Jacques in *As You Like It* (Derby, 1923; Gloucester, 1925); Iago (Hull, 1924; Exeter, 1925); Banquo (Hull, 1924); Gremio in *The Taming of the Shrew* (Hull, 1924); Theseus in *A Midsummer Night's Dream* (Exeter, 1925); Sir Toby in *Twelfth Night* (Gloucester, 1925); and the Friar in *Romeo and Juliet* (Gloucester, 1925).[38]

Sofaer also starred in the 1947 BBC television production of *The Merchant of Venice* in the role of Shylock. This production was notable for featuring in the role of the Prince of Morocco the first black actor to play a Shakespearean role on television, the British Guyanese actor Robert Adams. A decade earlier, Adams had been the first black actor to appear on British television in any role.[39] Meanwhile the first black woman to appear on television (in a production of a Eugene O'Neill play), Pauline Henriques, performed as Emilia in an Arts Council production of *Othello* in 1950 to great acclaim.[40] The actor who performed the title role in this production, the African American artist Gordon Heath, received somewhat more mixed reviews, but reprised the role in the 1955 BBC television production of the play, which remains the earliest surviving British television version of *Othello*.[41]

The history of the migration of British citizens from the West Indies to Britain in the aftermath of World War II (commonly referred to as the "Windrush generation") is also perhaps reflected by and preserved within the British performance archives of the mid-to-late twentieth century, in the histories of actors such as Robert Adams and, in the early 1950s, the Jamaican-born Lloyd Reckord.[42] Reckord moved to England in 1951 and played minor roles in the Old Vic's productions of *Romeo and Juliet* and *The Merchant of Venice* in 1952 and 1953; a few years later, the actor Edric Connor, who was born in Trinidad and Tobago and moved to England in 1944, was the first black actor to perform at Stratford, playing Gower in the Shakespeare Memorial Theatre production of *Pericles* (1958); the Guyana-born Cy Grant, who would go on to become "the first black artist to appear regularly on British TV," appeared in a minor role in the Bristol Old Vic's production of *The Comedy of Errors* in 1960, and, more

prominently, as Othello at the Phoenix Theatre Company in Leicester in
1965; and the actor and playwright Errol John, who was born in Trinidad
and Tobago and moved to England in 1951, appeared in a few Old Vic
productions in the early 1960s, including in the role of Barnadine
(*Measure for Measure*, 1963), the Prince of Morocco (*The Merchant of
Venice*, 1962) and even Othello (1963).[43] Errol John was "the first black
actor to play Othello on a London stage since Paul Robeson," although the
reviews of this production were highly critical.[44] Meanwhile, one of the
first black television actors to appear on British screens consistently,
Rudolph Walker, appeared in ten theatrical productions of Shakespeare
from 1966 to 1991 – but mostly in the role of either Othello or Caliban.[45]
Another Trinidad-born actor, Oscar James, appeared in eleven productions between 1967 and 1999, many of them as part of the Royal
Shakespeare Company and the National Theatre, but most of these roles
were secondary or minor parts; James's only leading role was as Mbeth
(Macbeth) in the Roundhouse Theatre's 1972 staging of *The Black
Macbeth*, an adaptation of *Macbeth* set in Africa and starring an all-black
cast.[46]

Although the 1960s and, especially, the 1970s saw a slightly higher
number of Shakespearean roles staged by actors of color, there was still
significant unemployment among actors of color from Britain and the
Commonwealth, and in 1968 the British Actors' Equity Association (also
known simply as Equity) committed to promoting integrated casting.[47]
The 1970s in fact saw very few actors of color in Shakespearean leading
roles; indeed, even though 1972 appears to have been a bumper year for
Shakespearean roles for actors of color, twenty-one of these parts were in
The Black Macbeth, and many of the rest were minor roles ("Slave,
Ensemble, Citizen") for seven black actors as part of the RSC's *The
Romans* season.[48] In the 1980s and 1990s, there were a larger number of
roles for actors of color; in 1981, the National Theatre's production of
Measure for Measure represented "the first time either national theatre
company had employed a majority of ethnic minority actors for their main
stage Shakespeares."[49] Urgent national conversations around race were
precipitated by the Brixton Uprisings of 1981 and 1985 and, especially,
by the murder of Stephen Lawrence in 1993. These conversations, in
concert with thoughtful and deliberate attempts toward integrated and
inclusive casting, have led to a rise in parts for actors of color since the
1990s: tracing the development of casting practices in the RSC, for
instance, Jami Rogers has observed that while "In the 1980s five black
actors (no Asians) played a total of six prominent roles including the RSC's

first black Othello," "The 1990s were static with a further six prominent roles played by black or Asian actors. However, in contrast with the previous decade, the majority of those actors were playing leads" and "In the twenty-first century the number of black and Asian actors employed to play prominent Shakespearean roles at the RSC has increased exponentially."[50]

Despite these promising developments and the possibility of a more capacious "unofficial black canon," there is much work that remains to be undertaken. As the number of BAME actors in Shakespearean roles – many of them quite high-profile – have increased, the size of casts has shrunk, and regional theatre companies have downsized as well. Moreover, whilst the use of cross-cultural casting can serve to contextualize and focus the semiotics of race, in less adept dramaturgical hands it can also work to other-ize BAME actors, suggesting that British actors of color in Shakespearean productions must be explained away by situating them in "exotic" or foreign locations and contexts.[51] And although the part of Othello was played by actors of color in eighty-five British productions of the play between 1980 and 2018, the number of major, canonical leading parts played by BAME actors is far smaller.[52] During those years, only seven productions of *King Lear* featured an actor of color in the role of Lear; two of those productions employed the same actor, St. Lucia-born Joseph Marcell, in Shakespeare's Globe's productions in 2013 and 2014; one production was performed in Chinese as part of the RSC's Complete Works Festival in 2006, with Zhou Ye Mang in the role of Lear; and two were productions staged by Talawa, a black British theatre company, with Ben Thomas and Don Warrington in the leading roles in 1994 and 2016, respectively.[53] Only eight productions of *Hamlet*, meanwhile, featured a BAME actor in the title role during that time period; of those, one was a revived production starring the same actor, Paapa Essiedu, two represented the same touring production as part of Shakespeare's Globe to Globe initiative, and one was the first *Hamlet* ever to be performed with an all-black cast in the UK (Black Theatre Live, 2016).[54]

Meanwhile, since 1980, there have been only two actors of color cast to play Henry V (Adrian Lester, at the National Theatre in 2003, and Sarah Amankwah, at the Globe in 2019), one actor of color in the role of Richard III (David Lee-Jones, as part of the Festival Players Theatre Company in 2012), and no actors of color playing Prince Hal in either *Henry IV Part I* or *Henry IV Part II*.[55] This notable omission of BAME actors from these leading roles in Shakespearean history plays troublingly situates actors of color outside of dramatic imaginings and reconceptualizations of English history and genealogy; until 2019, no actor of color had played the role of Richard II. In that year, however, the Globe staged, for the first time, a Shakespearean play with a cast comprised entirely of women of color. This extraordinary production, which starred Adjoa Andoh in the title role, explicitly invoked the cast members' lived connections to Britain's histories of empire as well as the tenuous futures of a post-Brexit nation, and concluded with a striking image. As the play ended, the red cross of the English flag suddenly appeared in the backdrop, heralding the challenge, and the promise, of excavating the genealogies of black and Asian performance histories to generate new theatrical possibilities, and of renewing and reconceiving the knotty nexus of nation and race, Shakespeare and the stage.

Notes

1 See www.nus.org.uk/en/who-we-are/how-we-work/black-students (accessed 25 February 2020).
2 See Gretchen Holbrook Gerzina, *Black London: Life before Emancipation* (New Brunswick, NJ: Rutgers University Press, 1995), 14.
3 "Sancho even made an abortive attempt at acting the role of Oroonoko in the 1760s." Gerzina, 14.
4 Colin Chambers, *Black and Asian Theatre in Britain: A History* (New York: Routledge, 2011), 36–37; and Vincent Carretta, "Soubise, Julius [formerly Othello] (c. 1754–1798), man of fashion." *Oxford Dictionary of National Biography* (accessed 14 July 2020).
5 Matthieu A. Chapman, "The Appearance of Blacks on the Early Modern Stage: *Love's Labour's Lost's* African Connections to Court," *Early Theatre* 17/2 (2014): 77–94 (at 86).
6 Chapman, 80.
7 *Bristol Mercury*, 14 March 1846. In employing the term "actor of color," this essay reflects historical usage.
8 *Morning Post*, 21 March 1848.
9 The term "unofficial black canon" is coined by Jami Rogers, who defines it as "not – save Othello – leading roles of the Shakespearean canon but the small-to-medium-sized parts that are nevertheless enough for an actor to sink his or her teeth into" but from which actors rarely "graduate to the leading roles in those plays." See Jami Rogers, "The Shakespearean Glass Ceiling: The State of Colorblind Casting in Contemporary British Theatre," *Shakespeare Bulletin* 31/3 (2013): 405–30 (at 425–26); and Jami Rogers, "Is the Door Really Open for Black Actors to Star in Shakespeare?", *The Stage*, 6 October 2016): https://www.thestage.co.uk/features/is-the-door-really-open-for-black-actors-to-star-in-shakespeare. Rogers has undertaken extensive work on the history

of Black British and Asian performances of Shakespeare since the 1930s and developed an invaluable performance database, the British Black and Asian Shakespeare Performance Database (BBASPD): https://bbashakespeare .warwick.ac.uk.

10 Quoted in *The Era*, 22 July 1866.

11 *Freeman's Journal*, 21 September 1867.

12 *Glasgow Herald*, 11 November 1871.

13 *Freeman's Journal*, 17 September 1867. This advertisement is quickly followed by one for a traveling American minstrel company, reminding readers of the racial (and racist) economy of theatrical entertainment which continued to thrive contemporaneously. See also *Freeman's Journal*, 19 September 1867.

14 *Derbyshire Times and Chesterfield Herald*, 24 April 1875.

15 A review of the play at the Theatre Royal in Ludlow, for instance, commended both his enactment (a very interesting performance, wanting, perhaps, a little toning down, but decidedly intelligent) and that of "Mrs Morgan Smith," "whose plaintive and tender acting of Desdemona was highly appreciated." "Provincial Theatricals," *The Era*, 30 October 1870.

16 *Belfast Morning News*, 2 July 1866.

17 *The Era*, 19 April 1868.

18 *Nottingham Evening Post*, 19 May 1903.

19 For further discussion, see Errol Hill, *Shakespeare in Sable: A History of Black Shakespearean Actors* (Amherst, MA: University of Massachusetts Press, 1984), 17–38.

20 *Northern Echo*, 30 April 1886.

21 *Chelmsford Chronicle*, 31 May 1907.

22 "Negro Actor Released," *Nottingham Evening Post*, 8 September 1903.

23 *Pall Mall Gazette*, 18 October 1895.

24 *Manchester Courier and Lancashire General Advertiser*, 16 April 1901.

25 "Abduction of a Barnsley Girl. Serious Charge against a Coloured Actor," *Sheffield Evening Telegraph*, 12 December 1890.

26 "Grave Charges at Southport. A Coloured Actor Involved," *Manchester Courier and Lancashire General Advertiser*, 3 June 1893.

27 Tellingly, in the case of Travis and Havern, it is unclear whether or not the kidnapping comprised a mutual relationship; racial and gendered assumptions collide in the narration of this story.

28 *The Era*, 3 February 1883.

29 *The Era*, 10 February 1883.

30 William Shakespeare, *Othello: Revised Edition*, ed. E. A. J. Honigmann, with a new Introduction by Ayanna Thompson, Arden Third Series (London: Bloomsbury, 2016). Errol G. Hill suggests that while Aldridge's and Smith's appearances on the British stage coincided with particularly pressing moments in the history of slave emancipation in, respectively, the British Empire and the United States, Molyneaux's did not, and that therefore he did not benefit from a heightened interest on the audience's part for witnessing the liberatory

potential of American émigrés. See Errol G. Hill and James V. Hatch, *A History of African American Theatre* (New York: Cambridge University Press, 2003), 67.

31 Chambers, 66–70; *Hull Daily Mail*, 10 October 1902, 22 October 1902, and various.
32 *The Times*, 5 September 1929.
33 *The Times*, 20 May 1930.
34 *The Times*, 20 May 1930.
35 "Miscasting Handicaps Robeson's Othello," *The Times*, 8 April 1959.
36 "Edward de Souza," BBASPD, https://bbashakespeare.warwick.ac.uk/people/edward-de-souza (accessed 21 February 2020).
37 "Abraham Sofaer," BBASPD, https://bbashakespeare.warwick.ac.uk/people/abraham-sofaer (accessed 21 February 2020). Indeed, Sofaer features prominently in the Database until 1947, appearing in roles as varied as Philip, King of France in *King John* in 1941 (the Old Vic), Ross in *Macbeth* in 1942 (Piccadilly Theatre), Malvolio in *Twelfth Night* and Lear in *King Lear* (Shakespeare Memorial Theatre, 1943), and Agamemnon in a BBC radio production of *Troilus and Cressida* (1946).
38 *Hull Daily Mail*, 27 October 1922; *Derby Daily Telegraph*, 18 September 1923; *Hull Daily Mail*, 1 November 1922; *Hull Daily Mail*, 27 March 1924; *Derby Daily Telegraph*, 12 September 1923; *Gloucester Citizen*, 25 February 1925; *Hull Daily Mail*, 25 March 1924; *Exeter and Plymouth Gazette*, 16 February 1925; *Hull Daily Mail*, 26 March 1924; *Hull Daily Mail*, 29 March 1924; *Exeter and Plymouth Gazette*, 10 February 1925; *Gloucester Citizen*, 26 February 1925; *Gloucester Citizen*, 27 February 1925.
39 Sarita Malik, *Representing Black Britain: Black and Asian Images on Television* (London: SAGE, 2002), 135, 154.
40 "Pauline Henriques," BBASPD, https://bbashakespeare.warwick.ac.uk/people/pauline-henriques (accessed 21 February 2020).
41 "Gordon Heath" and "Othello (1955)," BBASPD, https://bbashakespeare.warwick.ac.uk/people/gordon-heath and https://bbashakespeare.warwick.ac.uk/productions/othello-1955-bbc (accessed 21 February 2020).
42 Pauline Henriques, who was born in Jamaica in 1914, moved to England at the age of five (see BBASPD, https://bbashakespeare.warwick.ac.uk/people/pauline-henriques).
43 "Lloyd Reckord," "Edric Connor," "Cy Grant," and "Errol John," BBASPD, https://bbashakespeare.warwick.ac.uk/people/lloyd-reckord; https://bbashakespeare.warwick.ac.uk/people/edric-connor; https://bbashakespeare.warwick.ac.uk/people/cy-grant; and https://bbashakespeare.warwick.ac.uk/people/errol-john (accessed 21 February 2020). See also www.theguardian.com/music/2010/feb/17/cy-grant-obituary.
44 "Errol John," BBASPD, https://bbashakespeare.warwick.ac.uk/people/errol-john (accessed 21 February 2020).
45 "Rudolph Walker," BBASPD, https://bbashakespeare.warwick.ac.uk/people/rudolph-walker (accessed 21 February 2020).

46 "Oscar James," BBASPD, https://bbashakespeare.warwick.ac.uk/people/oscar-james (accessed 21 February 2020).

47 "Protest over Coloured Actor Rejected," *The Times*, 2 September 1964; Rogers, "Shakespearean Glass Ceiling," 411; and Chambers, 128.

48 Rogers, "Shakespearean Glass Ceiling," 412–13; and BBASPD. Rogers points out (412) that the RSC's casting of seven black actors in 1972 "was to be the largest intake of ethnic minority actors in a single season at the RSC for thirty years, until 2002 when Adrian Noble directed a *Pericles* that used the racial mix to set the production in foreign climes." This last point also underscores the way in which some productions which feature a number of actors of color deliberately situate them in specific cultural contexts – what Ayanna Thompson calls "cross-cultural casting." See Ayanna Thompson, *Passing Strange: Shakespeare, Race, and Contemporary America* (Oxford University Press, 2011), 79–80.

49 BBASPD, https://bbashakespeare.warwick.ac.uk/productions/measure-measure-1981-national-theatre-lyttelton-theatre (accessed 21 February 2020).

50 Rogers, "Shakespearean Glass Ceiling," 419.

51 Rogers, "Shakespearean Glass Ceiling," 421–23.

52 "Othello," BBASPD, https://bbashakespeare.warwick.ac.uk/roles/Othello (accessed 3 July 2020).

53 "King Lear," BBASPD, https://bbashakespeare.warwick.ac.uk/roles/King%20Lear (accessed 21 February 2020).

54 "Hamlet," BBASPD, https://bbashakespeare.warwick.ac.uk/roles/Hamlet (accessed 21 February 2020).

55 "Henry V," "Richard III," "Henry IV, Part One," and "Henry IV, Part Two," BBASPD, https://bbashakespeare.warwick.ac.uk/roles/Henry%20V; https://bbashakespeare.warwick.ac.uk/roles/Richard%20III; https://bbashakespeare.warwick.ac.uk/plays/henry-iv-part-one; and https://bbashakespeare.warwick.ac.uk/plays/henry-iv-part-two (accessed 3 July 2020).

CHAPTER 14

Actresses of Color and Shakespearean Performance
The Question of Reception

Joyce Green MacDonald

University of Kentucky

As far as I can tell, the first time that the names of black actresses performing Shakespeare appeared on a playbill was in 1821, advertising the African Company's *Richard III* in New York. A "Miss Welsh" doubled as the Prince of Wales and Lady Ann, and "Miss J. Welsh" played Queen Elizabeth.[1] The story of the suppression of the African Company is familiar enough by now as a primal scene in the Atlantic history of race and representation, and as an illustration of how violently policed black people's attempts to speak for themselves, as themselves, could be. But before the arrests and before the company's dispersal, it did nevertheless exist, inserting black performance into the urban self-making of the early nineteenth century, and making its own argument for the inescapably hybrid quality of American cultural production.

Here, though, the names of those two women stand out. Were "Miss Welsh" and "Miss J. Welsh" related? Did they play other roles in African Company productions? The unnamed actress the African Company had cast as Juliet in a *Romeo and Juliet* they would never get to perform complained that "nothing but envy" made New York's white theatrical authorities deny them the opportunity to produce the play. Given the opportunity, the company would have put "the whites completely out of countenance" – that is, shattered their assumption that black actors were creatively and intellectually incapable of performing Shakespeare.[2] Was this frustrated Juliet one of the Welshes?

We know that James Hewlett, the male star of the African Company, continued performing for a few years after its dissolution until his early death, and that Ira Aldridge – who grew up in the city and acted at the company's Mercer Street theatre – eventually left the United States in 1824 and built a long career in Europe. But we know nothing of the African Company actresses besides their names, and in the case of the Juliet who never got to play the role, we don't even know that. That uncertain presence in the American theatrical record seems like an

208

appropriate place to begin a discussion of how non-white actresses have appeared in the history of Shakespearean casting and reception. The fate of the African Company tells us that even if the front door to Shakespearean roles was barred to actors like Hewlett and Aldridge, they nevertheless found ways to keep performing them. But what of the early anonymous black Shakespearean actresses?

One of the aims of this essay is simply to include some of these early actresses in the history of Shakespearean production and performance. Yet, in beginning with the story of a nineteenth-century black singer and elocutionist who never got to perform in a full Shakespearean production, the chapter also intends to identify some of the forces that particularly worked to inhibit black women's public performances, and to outline ways in which these early actresses worked with and around these forces. Their race is what ultimately prevented them from achieving the kind of public dramatic careers they wanted, but the fact of their blackness is also what enabled and nurtured their ambitions.

Henrietta Vinton Davis (1860–1941; see Figure 14.1) neither expected nor, apparently, wanted her auditors to forget she was black. Indeed, her race – as it was acknowledged by the mixed-race audiences for whom she sang, recited, and acted in a career that lasted from 1883 until after World War I – was a source of pride and affirmation. Her first performance, before an audience "comprising many of the best white and colored people" of Washington, DC, included comic and dramatic pieces as well as a "selection from the *Merchant of Venice* (Portia)" and one of Juliet's speeches from *Romeo and Juliet*. A newspaper reviewer judged her to have "wrapped the whole audience so close to her, that she became a queen of the stage in their eyes. One moment all was serene and quiet, deep pathos – the next all was laughter."[3] Another reviewer was even more enthusiastic. In Davis, audiences had "discovered real histrionic genius."[4]

Born in Baltimore to free black parents, Davis earned her teaching license at fifteen, and began working at the District of Columbia's Office of the Recorder of the Deeds at eighteen. A student of the well-known Washington elocution teacher Marguerite Saxton, she also trained in New York and Boston before making her professional debut. At that first performance, she was introduced by Frederick Douglass, the head of the deeds office, who had become a family friend and knew of her talent.

Against the larger backdrop of the failure of Reconstruction after the end of the Civil War and the violent repression of legal attempts to establish black Americans' status as full citizens, Davis's career traces a path of black self-expression and creativity that flowered even under such

HENRIETTA VINTON DAVIS.

Figure 14.1   Henrietta Vinton Davis is one of the first black Shakespearean actresses
about whom we have any archival information.

harsh circumstances.[5] Although she performed scenes from *Macbeth* and *Richard III* opposite black actor Powhatan Beaty in 1884, as well as public recitations of speeches by Portia, Ophelia, Cleopatra, Rosalind, and Juliet in tours all over New England and the Midwest, she never appeared in a full production of a Shakespeare play. But her work as a Shakespearean elocutionist, reciting passages from the plays in demonstration of her mastery of the ability to discipline her body and voice in the service of the text, speaks to her participation in creating a culture of black performance that would thrive in black communities eager to proclaim their moral worth and defend their civil rights even under renewed racial terror. That Frederick Douglass himself introduced her to Washington audiences speaks to the public role that all examples of black excellence could play under a civic order that was rapidly re-embracing principles of white supremacy after Reconstruction. In the same column that reported Davis's debut, the *New York Globe* also included a story about the call for a "National Colored Convention" to be held in the city the following fall: both political and artistic advances mattered to the progress of the race.

Dwight Conquergood is among those critics pointing to the subversive potential of black elocutionary practice; mastering the rules of elocution meant that the speaker had successfully disciplined "body and voice to accrue class distinction," and could thus possibly counterfeit their way toward social plausibility.[6] (I will be returning to this notion of expressive discipline as an index of moral worth later in this essay.) The rules of elocution and public oratory were also carefully gendered, emphasizing how women could practice these speech arts in order to proclaim the perfection of their domestic roles as wives and mothers.[7] As a black female elocutionist and would-be Shakespearean sponsored by Frederick Douglass, Vinton no doubt carried these racial, gendered, and class expectations of sanctioned and elevated public speech with her. Born free to free parents, she was educated and had received specialized training in her field. And yet, despite the potential Conquergood sees for escape and transformation, the ways in which her race conditioned the kind of reception she could expect from the racially mixed audiences for which she often performed were not always within her control. Very much approving of the "really remarkable entertainment" that Davis and friends presented in Buffalo, an anonymous reporter for the city's Sunday *Truth* newspaper lingered over her looks: "Miss Davis is a singularly beautiful woman, little more than a brunette, certainly no darker than a Spanish or Italian lady in hue, with big, lustriously [sic] expressive eyes and a mouth" like that of touring English actress Adelaide Neilson. This reviewer could not help imagining "what a magnificent Cleopatra she would make to a competent Anthony."[8] Her "deep, sonorous voice . . . reminded one very much of Charlotte Cushman," the much-admired white American Shakespearean reader and actress active into the 1870s, another asserted.[9]

The role of Shakespeare's Cleopatra is perhaps the female counterpart for his Othello, the part all modern black classically trained actresses are destined to play just as Celia Daileader observed that black stage actors all seem to be destined for the Moor.[10] But it is striking that this reviewer, while praising Davis's performance, also finds it necessary to tell their readers that Davis isn't really all that black. She could be Spanish, or Italian; she sounded like Charlotte Cushman, and even looked a little like Adelaide Neilson. Despite her light complexion and her well-received recitals, Davis was black enough to keep her from ever getting a contract with a professional company or doing a full Shakespearean performance. When in 1893 she organized a company of black actors to perform

William Easton's *Dessalines*, a verse melodrama about the Haitian Revolution, at the 1893 Chicago World's Fair, it was her first appearance in a full play in ten years.

In a move that directly took up the effect that Davis's physical appearance as a light-skinned black woman might have on her dramatic plausibility, she collaborated on the 1898 play *Our Old Kentucky Home* with journalist and editor John Edward Bruce, touring with it in the eastern United States and reviving it in 1903.[11] This extraordinary work dramatized the particular position of a mixed-race heroine, with its first-act portrayal of a brutal slave auction that includes the sale of the "Creole" heroine Clothilde, obviously brought to the block as a sexual object for white men. (Clothilde evades rape by her new owner and escapes his plantation, disguised as a man, to help her black lover escape from imprisonment in a Confederate prison camp. After the war, they marry and return to Kentucky to purchase the plantation where they had been enslaved.) Acknowledging the ugly sexual history of enslaved women, Davis succeeded in remaking the story audiences thought they knew about women who looked like her, endowing her Clothilde with dignity, courage, and the capacity for a faithful married love.

With *Dessalines* and *Our Old Kentucky Home*, Davis moved away from Shakespeare and other recital pieces, instead producing her own work that explicitly took up subjects from black history. But by 1919, she was leaving the stage altogether, after she became an officer in Marcus Garvey's pan-African Universal Negro Improvement Association.[12] Her decision to give up the life of a touring performer for full-time political advocacy shouldn't seem completely surprising; Davis's stepfather George Hackett helped lead the successful resistance to an 1859 proposal that would have expelled free blacks from Maryland, and Frederick Douglass had been her mentor. However, her choice to stop performing may not have been entirely free. Only two years after the largely self-generated success of *Our Old Kentucky Home*, Davis's professional situation was so "desperate" that she signed to appear in a musical farce called *The Country Coon*, put together by the author of the popular hit song "All Coons Look Alike to Me."[13] Her choice to leave performing and help build what she and other Garveyites believed would be a unified and independent black counterculture could certainly have seemed like a positive alternative to appearing in a coon show. For Davis, Shakespeare perhaps finally became irrelevant in the face of larger questions about dignity and survival.

In 1895, two years after Davis's *Dessalines*, Adrienne McNeil Herndon (1869–1910) was appointed to teach elocution at Atlanta University (AU).

Born the daughter of a former slave in Augusta, Adrienne McNeil grew up in Savannah and was educated at AU. She would later claim that even as a schoolgirl, she'd won praise for her excellence at recitation and oratory, but her mother didn't think these were practical skills for girls, so she trained to be a teacher. Atlanta University hired her as its first African American female faculty member two years after her marriage to Alonzo Herndon, a young businessman born into slavery who would become the city's first black millionaire. As a condition of their marriage, Herndon agreed that Adrienne could pursue her dramatic career, and she earned degrees from the Boston School of Expression and the American Academy of Dramatic Arts in New York.

In 1904, Herndon made her stage debut as a dramatic reader in Boston with a performance of *Antony and Cleopatra*, compressed to fifteen scenes, in which she played twenty-two roles – "the first time that an impersonation of the entire play has ever been given in Boston by one person."[14] It may be difficult for contemporary audiences to imagine such a performance as much more than some kind of metatheatrical stunt, but the virtuosity Herndon displayed was part of what the elocutionary arts aimed to develop. In a series of lectures in 1885, a Boston-area professor asserted that "The art of dramatic reading, in its newest phase of character-sketching and personation, requires the very highest order of the conceptive and imaginative faculties."[15] While exhibiting his or her aesthetic sensitivity, a skilled elocutionist also performed an ethical function. Certainly, oratory "arouses feeling," but its true role lay in its power "to influence the actions of men."[16]

Oratory's ethical power had been on full display during the abolitionist movement, which Dwight Conquergood identifies as the affective origin of the elocution craze of the late nineteenth and early twentieth centuries. Black speakers achieved a particular kind of moral authority, even as their public addresses were mediated through the sponsorship and rhetorical framing of white sponsors, and as black bodies and black modes of speech remained subject to white discipline.[17] But onstage at Steinert Hall, without the props or "stage trappings" that would accompany a full production, Adrienne Herndon was alone with her text and her audience. "It was the artist and her work that was constantly before the eyes of those who listened," and the "great charm" of her reading was her "absolute ease and naturalness," her "lack of straining for effect" as she smoothly transitioned from one role to the next, and the next, and the next.[18]

Adrienne Herndon's powers of impersonation were both more impressive and more circumscribed than her audience knew. She appeared under the name of "Anne Du Bignon," having told the Boston press that she was a member of an old French and Creole family from South Carolina, and it was as Du Bignon that her performance was widely praised. The director of her Boston school had known she was married to Alonzo Herndon the black Atlanta businessman (he paid her tuition) and urged her to try to begin her career in London so she would bring an established reputation with her when she tried to work in Boston or New York. Instead, Herndon chose to try to pass, apparently believing she could lead a double life – "Creole" Shakespearean recitalist on tour in the northeast, Alonzo Herndon's light-skinned black wife and Atlanta University teacher at home. Earlier, her uncle Thomas Fleming and her father George Stephens had both left their birth families to pass as white. Although she did book an appearance in Lynn, Massachusetts after her Boston success, the only other engagement she could manage was in Bellows Falls, Vermont. Despite having been assured before her Boston debut by the New York impresario David Belasco that she would "undoubtedly make a fine character actress," her career in the north effectively stopped right after it began.[19]

Both Henrietta Vinton Davis and Adrienne McNeil Herndon were light-skinned enough to pass as white, although Davis never tried to. The racial disguise Herndon tried to put on in Boston ultimately failed her – not because she didn't look "white" enough, but because no matter what she called herself or how well she fulfilled the aesthetic and ethical demands of her public reading, her blackness (which included, but also exceeded, her skin color) stubbornly peeped through. It is easy to imagine that someone – one of her Boston or New York teachers, a member of Belasco's staff – realized and revealed her secret. Even if she was mastering the rules of elocution and the concomitant rules of class standing that those vocal disciplines worked to proclaim and uphold, and even if her own family's experience had taught her that the rules of racial identity as embodied by skin color were, under the right circumstances, nothing but a self-serving fraud, the professional ghosting Herndon experienced after Boston indicates that there were firm limits to what she could successfully pretend to be.

Although she would not be permitted to act, Herndon's path toward Shakespeare would remain wide open in other ways. Her job at Atlanta University quickly involved her teaching elocution and public reading to her students; Jacqueline Jones Royster has pointed toward how important training in rhetoric, logic, and oratory could be, especially to female students, at a university founded to help teach the descendants of slaves and fit them for places in the modern world.[20] In 1905, the year after her Boston disappointment, Herndon directed *The Merchant of Venice*, the first of what would become an annual Class Day Shakespeare production by AU students. She mounted a new Shakespeare play every year until her death, convinced that black people were capable of full response to the work of the artist whom she considered "the greatest of all dramatists." Because they had "lived and suffered, and striven" so intensely, black people might even have a special affinity for him. After all, she argued, "A more dramatic life than the one given the American Negro can hardly be imagined."[21] What could fit them more deeply to communicate the intensity of Shakespearean scenes?

Herndon's AU faculty colleague W.E.B. Du Bois also believed in "the tremendous emotional wealth of the Negro," and hoped that a truly modern black theatre could "resurrect forgotten ancient Negro art and history . . . and . . . set the black man before the world as both a creative artist and a strong subject for artistic treatment."[22] Rather than rediscovering "forgotten ancient Negro art," however, Herndon simply asked for space for black people to approach Shakespeare on their own, as themselves, combining their shared physical resources of "hands, face, and body, as well as . . . voice" together to build culture in their own communities. She invoked the power of a specifically black physicality, "unmarred by the conventional training of more highly cultured races," thereby disputing the negative valence attached to her own body as an instrument for Shakespearean performance, and implicitly denying the relevance of the conventional training she had so eagerly pursued to realizing the distinctive potential of black performance in particular.[23]

The year after Herndon's *Merchant*, black people in Atlanta suffered two nights of violent attacks from mobs of the city's whites in the so-called "Atlanta Race Riots." No one is sure how many blacks were killed in a spasm of terroristic violence generated in part by white rage at the increasing visibility of a new black elite in the city, an elite which certainly included Adrienne and Alonzo Herndon and their son. Still reeling from the hate unleashed in the September attacks, the following February she sadly wrote to Booker T. Washington to decline his request to include her in an article he was planning on the notable black women of Atlanta: "Sometimes I doubt whether there is any spot in this country where one with Negro blood can plant a home free from prejudice, scorn & molestation . . . I should like to hide from the eyes of the Southern white man the things I, as a Negro woman hold most sacred for fear they pause & look to jeer and ridicule."[24] As boldly as it was asserted that Shakespeare belonged to black people too, the Shakespeare Herndon built at AU also mattered as a cultural expression of home and community, quietly aimed at disproving white assumptions of black criminality, inferiority, and incompetence.

Adrienne Herndon died in 1910 at the age of only forty. Atlanta University hired 1912 graduate Caroline Bond Day to teach public speaking and English, and she continued Herndon's tradition of an annual Shakespeare play. Hired to teach English and drama at Atlanta's Spelman College in 1928, Anne Cooke would later consolidate student actors from Spelman, AU, and Morehouse College into a group called the University Players, which regularly included Shakespeare among the plays it performed on campus and for the city at large during summers. When Cooke left Spelman in 1942 for Hampton University and later Howard University in Washington, DC, she continued and extended the tradition of black college Shakespeare begun by Adrienne Herndon Davis, and by the young actors she recruited and mentored.[25]

Both Henrietta Vinton Davis and Adrienne McNeil Herndon were barred from playing Shakespeare, although Herndon did keep her hand in the game as a teacher and director. While Davis ultimately reacted to life under the conditions that kept her from becoming the Shakespearean she may well have yearned to be by joining a movement that wanted to remake the conditions under which blackness accrued such negative meanings in the years after Reconstruction, Herndon sought to bring her Shakespeare inside the southern urban black community that nurtured both her and her husband. In light of that community's constant threatening surveillance by whites, she came to believe that self-representation for black audiences was ultimately more important and more worthwhile than the kind of fame she had sought as a reader before the general public.

In the rest of this chapter, and inspired by the examples of both Davis and Herndon – one trying to remake the world in which art might matter, the other importing the art she craved into the world that mattered most to her – I want to discuss aspects of the careers of some other actresses of color as they encountered Shakespeare, and the institutional circumstances under which these encounters happened.

Jane White (1922–2011) was born into the same kind of activist tradition that nurtured Henrietta Vinton Davis, as the daughter of Walter White, executive director of the National Association for the Advancement of Colored People from 1931 until his death in 1955. Walter White had been born in Atlanta in 1893 as the grandson of an enslaved woman named Dilsia fathered by William Henry Harrison, who

would become the ninth President of the United States, and White lived
through the 1906 white riots against the city's blacks that so shook
Adrienne Herndon. A graduate of Atlanta University, he looked "white,"
with fair skin, blond hair and blue eyes, and, beginning undercover
investigations of lynchings for the NAACP in 1918, he used his appearance to gather information from police officers and white participants,
until he was revealed to be black and had to flee the south for his life.

   As Henrietta Vinton Davis's first appearances were sponsored by
Frederick Douglass, Jane White was recommended for her first
Broadway role, in 1945's *Strange Fruit* – a play based on Lillian Smith's
novel of a tragic interracial romance – by her father's friend, Paul Robeson.
Jane White was not as light-skinned as her father, and she was often
considered too dark for the roles she wanted to play. Producers often
thought her "too black for white roles and – this really hurt – too white for
black roles. I lost two good parts well into rehearsal when it was decided
I wasn't identifiable enough as a Negro."[26] Her contemporary Geraldine
Page started out at the same time, and White observed that Page "was
getting to be a star, while I was playing 'exotics' – Hindus, Polynesians,
Mexicans – on TV."[27] In 1959 she auditioned for the part of the haughty
Queen Aggravain in the Broadway musical *Once Upon a Mattress* and was
told by a nervous member of the production team that although they'd
loved her tryout, they'd found her looks "too . . . uh . . . Mediterranean"
for the part. White asked the aide if they meant "Negro," and was told yes,
that was it. At her second meeting with the producers, she used pale
powder on her face and exposed body parts and got the role.[28]

   Her success in *Once Upon a Mattress* brought her to the attention of
Joseph Papp, who cast her as Kate in *The Taming of the Shrew* in 1960 for
the New York Shakespeare Festival. Papp used her again as the Princess of
France in *Love's Labour's Lost* in 1965 and as Volumnia in *Coriolanus* in
1966, roles for which she won an Obie Award for best lead actress. She was
later cast in other Shakespearean roles – Cymbeline's evil Queen at the
New York Shakespeare Festival in 1971, Goneril with the American
Shakespeare Festival in 1975, Queen Elinor from *King John* in 1988,
Volumnia again for the Elizabethan Theatre at the Folger Shakespeare
Library in 1991 – as well as in plays like *The Trojan Women*, *Iphigenia in
Aulis*, and Garcia Lorca's *Blood Wedding*. All of these roles call for an
actress of a certain physical presence and vocal command, and White's
work in them was highly praised. Ironically, however, she apparently never
particularly yearned to play Shakespearean roles above all others. She just
wanted "to be responded to as a woman, and an actress, and a Negro, and

an American – all those things at once. I don't want to play just queens . . .
People have got to get used to the idea that Negroes come in all shapes and
sizes and personalities."[29] She and her husband, restaurateur Alfredo
Viazzi, left New York to spend three years in his native Italy in the mid-
1960s, and she continued to act onstage and in television through the
early 2000s.

Davis and Herndon were light-skinned black women, living emblems of
a recent history of slave rape and miscegenation that gave the lie to rigid
racial categories that proclaimed the necessity of separation and distinction
between black and white. While White's career demonstrates the move
from treating actresses' blackness as a quality that disqualified them from
communicating Shakespearean meanings to regarding it as a quality that
was irrelevant to Shakespeare being produced in a modern, multiracial
world capital, the question of an actress's race did still cling to certain
Shakespearean roles. Francesca Royster has traced the racing of Cleopatra,
for example, through the 1946 film of George Bernard Shaw's *Caesar and
Cleopatra* with Vivien Leigh and Claude Rains, the failed Broadway
musical *Her First Roman* starring Leslie Uggams and Richard Kiley, and
into American popular culture in such films as *Cleopatra Jones* and *Set it
Off.*[30] Royster notes the degree to which portrayals of Cleopatra as a kind
of modern black heroine work within and against a US framing of black
girls and young women as insistently sexualized and socially deviant – a
framing whose origins lay in the sexual abuse of enslaved women, and
resistance to which we can see in the way Henrietta Vinton Davis's
Clothilde refuses concubinage. The Buffalo reviewer who imagined "what
a magnificent Cleopatra she would make" was perhaps imagining such self-
authorizing pride and dignity transferred to Shakespeare's Egyptian queen.
When in the wake of racial terror in Atlanta Adrienne Herndon mourned
the violation of black women's attempts to preserve their families' homes
as emotional havens safe from "prejudice, scorn & molestation," she was
mourning the apparent triumph of a social order determined to deny her
ability to define herself for herself, much less to become a character of
infinite variety onstage.

The possibility of Cleopatra thus haunts Davis's and Herndon's careers
(as far as I can tell, Jane White never played her). I am convinced that their
physical presence in the role – the presence of actresses who identified
themselves as black (or "Creole," in Herndon's case, for the consumption
of white audiences) shown in romantic congress with a male character who
was supposed to be white and imperially Roman – would have been
impossible to stage at that turn-of-the-century moment of white

supremacist reaction. A black actress didn't play Cleopatra opposite a white Antony for the Royal Shakespeare Company until 1992, and then only by accident when understudy Claire Benedict appeared for the ill Claire Higgins in a preview.[31] While black Cleopatras are much more common in American productions (e. g., Shirine Babb in the 2017 production at Washington's Folger Theatre), the Shakespearean role that has become far more frequently cast with a non-white actress in the last thirty years or so has been *Othello*'s Bianca, in a theatrical move that I would argue serves as another example of how black women's bodies can be racially pre-contextualized before they ever enter casting discussions. Although Bianca never identifies herself by color or race, and in fact denies that she is a courtesan (as Iago insists she is), casting her with a non-white actress not only allows for a rather lazy visual pun on the character's name, but also silently works to reinforce racialized notions of Desdemona's moral as well as physical "fairness." Seeing Bianca as evidence of Cassio's double standards in sexual matters – "he idealizes the divine Desdemona but relieves himself with a harlot" – Trevor Nunn cast the black American actress and singer Marsha Hunt as Bianca in his 1989 *Othello* at The Other Place.[32] Although Hunt had played at least one Shakespearean role before this (Hippolyta in the 1982 *Midsummer Night's Dream* at the Royal National Theatre), she was far better known for having been photographed nude by Patrick Lichfield a few months after appearing in the London production of *Hair*, for singing in rock and blues bands with Marc Bolan and John Mayall, and for having a baby with Mick Jagger. Did this extravagant personal history inflect her casting in the role, so that she exceeded it in ways that had become more socially acceptable than Davis's and Herndon's non-white bodies could have done around the turn of the twentieth century? Or did her casting only add a modern gloss to the policing of black female bodies onstage that kept the African Company's anonymous Juliet from taking her shot at the role?

Ultimately, however, a more interesting question than why Bianca has become a common role for non-white actresses is whether, as Lynette Goddard asks, we will "ever have a black Desdemona."[33] Casting someone who is not white as "fair Desdemona" would mean dislodging cultural equations between moral probity and beauty and between beauty and whiteness, equations that probably started taking root before Shakespeare's day and that reasserted themselves at moments of particular racial crisis, as we saw in the reactionary anti-blackness dominating US civic life in the decades after Reconstruction. Reading the 1980s career of black actress Josette Simon, who followed the traditional Royal Shakespeare Company path of beginning in small parts and being called back in repertory to eventually take leading roles like Rosaline in *Love's Labour's Lost* and Isabella in *Measure for Measure*, Goddard suggests that the lack of analysis of Simon's career illustrates a continuing cultural ill-ease with interracial couples consisting of a white man and a black woman. As Celia Daileader argues, Atlantic audiences already "know" that black men are dangerous company for white girls to keep. By restaging its foreordained tragic outcome, *Othello* can work in performance to justify principles of white male supremacy. On the other hand, a black woman playing the object of a white man's romantic desire – not merely his lust, as in the case of Nunn's Bianca – would too deeply unsettle the convictions of black women's sexual abjection that enabled notions of white women's fairness and moral superiority. (Adrienne Herndon writing to Booker T. Washington that she experienced the 1905 Atlanta terror as an assault on black women's commitment to creating loving homes for their families speaks to the strength of these stereotypes of defective femininity.) Following Daileader's notion of how *Othello* endlessly restages white supremacy, we might argue that portraying what might happen in an interracial love affair between a white man and a black woman would restage the history of slave rape, a history that enacted white male supremacy in the sexual domain. Even though their birth parents were all black, light-skinned black people like Henrietta Vinton Davis and Adrienne Herndon were living reminders of violent cross-racial intimacies that white society would rather have left unspoken.

In contemporary productions, companies like the Classical Theatre of Harlem or Britain's Talawa Theatre (for which Doña Croll played Britain's first black Cleopatra in 1991) not only routinely cast black actresses in Shakespearean roles, but also have participated in a reimagining of the cultural work Shakespeare does for us and of the role of raced bodies in performing that work. The racial prohibitions imposed on the African Company's black Juliet have not remained in full force and were challenged early on by pioneers like Davis and Herndon. Black actresses have continued to play Shakespeare and have also directed and designed and rewritten him. The question of all these works' reception remains open, but it is plain that we have at least moved beyond the silencing of Miss Welsh and Miss J. Welsh. What happens next turns in large part on audiences' willingness to comprehend new ways of embodying Shakespeare.

Notes

1 G.C.D. Odell, *Annals of the New York Stage*, vol. iii (New York: Columbia University Press, 1928), 35.

2 Anonymous, *Memoir and Theatrical Career of Ira Aldridge, the African Roscius* (London: Onwhyn, 1849), 11.

3 *Washington Bee*, 21 July 1883.

4 *New York Globe*, 5 May 1883, 1.

5 For a full account of Davis's career, see Errol Hill, *Shakespeare in Sable: A History of Black Shakespearean Actors* (Amherst: University of Massachusetts Press, 1984), 64–76.

6 Dwight Conquergood, "Rethinking Elocution: The Trope of the Talking Book and Other Figures of Speech," *Text and Performance Quarterly* 20/4 (2000): 325–41 (at 328).

7 For more on black American women's public rhetorical practices, see Shirley Wilson Logan, *'We Are Coming': The Persuasive Discourse of Nineteenth-Century Black Women* (Carbondale: Southern Illinois University Press, 1999).

8 Reprinted in *New York Freeman*, 4 April 1885, 2.

9 *New York Globe*, 4 August 1883, 3.

10 Celia Daileader, "Casting Black Actors: Beyond Othellophilia," in *Shakespeare and Race,* ed. Catherine M.S. Alexander and Stanley Wells (Cambridge University Press, 2000), 177–202.

11 Thomas Robson, "A More Aggressive Plantation Play: Henrietta Vinton Davis and John Edward Bruce Collaborate on *Our Old Kentucky Home*," *Theatre History Studies* 32 (2012): 120–40.

12 Natanya Duncan, "'If Our Men Hesitate then the Women of the Race Must Come Forward': Henrietta Vinton Davis and the UNIA in New York," *New York History* 95/4 (2014): 558–83.

13 Hill, 73.

14 *Boston Globe*, 29 January 1904, 3.

15 Anonymous, "Elocution: The Elements of Expression in Reading, Oratory, and Acting," *National Journal of Education* 5/10 (8 March 1877), 116, citing a series of lectures by Moses T. Brown of Tufts College.

16 Joseph Carhart, "Elocution – An Exposition Of," *Educational Weekly* 5/1 (18 July 1885), 6.

17 Conquergood, 326–29.

18 *Boston Globe*, 29 January 1904, 3.

19 Carole Merritt, *The Herndons: An Atlanta Family* (Athens: University of Georgia Press, 2002), 19–23, 28–31. Merritt quotes Belasco at 16.

20 Jacqueline Jones Royster, *Traces of a Stream: Literacy and Social Change among African-American Women* (University of Pittsburgh Press, 2000), 176–238.

21 Adrienne E. Herndon, "Shakespeare at Atlanta University," *Voice of the Negro*, July 1906, 482–86 (at 482, 485).

22 Quoted in Hill, 81.

23 Herndon, 485.

24 Quoted in David Ford Godshalk, *Veiled Visions: The 1906 Atlanta Race Riot and the Reshaping of American Race Relations* (Chapel Hill: University of North Carolina Press, 2005), 232.

25 Leslye Joy Allen, "The Birth of Queen Anne: Re-discovering Anne M. Cooke at Spelman College," in *The Routledge Companion to African American Theatre and Performance*, ed. Kathy A. Perkins, Sandra L. Richards, Renée Alexander Craft, and Thomas F. DeFrantz (New York: Routledge, 2019), 134–39.

26 Quoted in Dan Sullivan, "Determined Jane White Gets off a Racial Treadmill," *New York Times*, 25 March 1968.

27 Quoted in Sullivan.

28 Quoted in Sullivan.

29 Quoted in Sullivan.

30 Francesca Royster, *Becoming Cleopatra: The Shifting Image of an Icon* (New York and Basingstoke: Palgrave Macmillan, 2003), 122–31, 138–49, 171–95.

31 Carol Chillington Rutter, *Enter the Body: Women and Representation on Shakespeare's Stage* (New York and London: Routledge, 2001), 57–103.

32 Quoted in Virginia Mason Vaughan, *Othello: A Contextual History* (Cambridge University Press, 1994), 229.

33 Lynette Goddard, "Will We Ever Have a Black Desdemona? Casting Josette Simon at the RSC," in *Shakespeare, Race, and Performance: The Diverse Bard*, ed. Delia Jarrett-Macauley (New York: Routledge, 2017), 80–95.

CHAPTER 15

Othello
A Performance Perspective

Adrian Lester

One of the most compelling elements of this tragedy is the inexorable speed with which Othello moves from being possibly the noblest character ever created by Shakespeare to a character who, consumed by jealousy and pain, carries out one of the most brutal and violent murders seen in one of his plays. The major problem any production has, whatever its setting, is getting the audience to believe Othello's journey from one state of mind to the other. If a production gets it right, the audience is in for a captivating and upsetting performance. If not, well, they can always leave at the interval.

As we become more and more aware of society's underlying tensions around race and sex, the innocence needed to convey this compelling and difficult progression is nearly impossible to achieve with any sense of integrity on the part of the actor playing Othello. In this sense, the play's most compelling element, this journey from one state of mind to the other, is its curse.

I played the role in 2013 at the National Theatre in London, and as I began to tackle playing the character I found myself having to deal with an important lack of logic. Othello seems to trust and fall too easily. He takes for granted everything that Iago seems to be telling him. So much so that his absolute belief is almost comical within the structure of the play. Why not examine the evidence and scrutinize the facts? It is this lack of logic that led the actor Hugh Quarshie to say that Shakespeare had been "lazy" in his characterization of Othello.[1] Quarshie goes on to say:

> My suspicion is that Shakespeare was never really interested in the psychology of Othello or his behavioural credibility – in a way, he was much more interested in Iago. But when a conscious black actor comes to play the role, he's got to address those issues and ask, "Is this a plausible thing for me to say?" Sometimes the answer is "I'm not sure" and sometimes the answer is "no."[2]

In an earlier essay Quarshie wrote that, "Perhaps Othello is the one (part) which should definitely not be played by a black actor. Does he not risk making racial stereotypes legitimate and true?"[3] It's an interesting point of view. There is a risk. A very clear and present danger that those who choose to play the role must be aware of.

Finding a way through a plot that marries Othello's intellect as a strategic commander to what might appear to be a gullible, blind passion for his wife is very difficult. Passion that unseats reason is a staple of many a great play, but such gullibility in the face of racism is much more difficult. And if you add Othello's gullibility to the idea that Western racist thinking has found leverage in Shakespeare's treatment of the character – the hot-blooded black man who is welcomed into refined society before running off with a nobleman's daughter only to murder her in a violent, jealous rage – we present the modern black actor with something that is, with these considerations, almost impossible to play with intellectual rigor and deep-seated logic. No wonder Hugh Quarshie thought it should be left to white actors to play, thereby forcing the role to become ridiculous and old-fashioned.

Most discussions about whether or not *Othello* is a racist play center around Shakespeare's intentions in writing it and the culture he wrote it for. The culture of the time we can research, but Shakespeare's intentions are much harder to pin down. So we must draw our own conclusions. The celebrated Elizabethan literary critic Thomas Rymer wrote, "This may be a caution to all Maidens of quality how, without their parents consent, they run away with Blackamoors."[4] Well, that's certainly one, uncomfortable way of looking at it. If we assume that the entire Elizabethan cast and audience were white then it is easy to see it as a racist, cautionary tale warning "us" of the danger of Blackamoors: "Look, this is what they're really like!" But I have always wondered what the play becomes when performed by a racially mixed cast in front of an entirely black audience. Or, if it were played in front of an entirely female audience. What then? What does this uncomfortable cautionary tale become in *those* contexts? "Look, this is what they're really like," changes its meaning. It inverts itself.

I don't particularly like the play. If it is done very well and I have to watch it, I find it deeply upsetting and I come away angry. If on the other hand, it is done really badly then I come away angry for all sorts of different reasons. This is mainly because of Iago's seeming and easy manipulation of the other characters onstage. A manipulation in which the audience is made to feel complicit. I have sat in a few theatres filled with audiences who have gently laughed at Iago's ability to control the fate of those around him. It's a complicity that should make us feel very uncomfortable but the audible reaction of some people in the audience would make you believe that this isn't the case. I have found it remarkable that certain members of an audience could find humor in Iago's manipulation as he takes an active role in the murders of Desdemona and Emilia and the suicide of Othello.

Perhaps the reason we are uneasy about the play, and the reason it is one of Shakespeare's most controversial and brilliant pieces of work that seems to resist easy analysis, is because it continues to reflect distressing elements of our modern reality. I think the play shows us a truth about our attitudes toward race, gender, and violence that even after four hundred years we still have trouble dealing with.

When I played Othello, I was directed by Nicholas Hytner. It was a modern-dress production performed in the 1,100 seat Olivier theatre at the National Theatre for a run of roughly six months. Nick is a fantastic director who didn't shy away from any of the themes in the play. With a modern setting we distanced ourselves from courtly romance. No expressions of emotion were coated inside an older performance form. The brutality we found in the play could be expressed openly and honestly in attitudes that were in sync with our modern sensibility. We were in camouflage gear with backpacks and automatic weapons. In this production it made sense for Emilia to be a lower-ranking soldier who could be commanded by her husband. When Othello asks Iago to make sure Desdemona is looked after by Emilia, it is accepted as a soldier following orders and doing her duty for her uniform. This made it slightly easier for our production to handle outdated ideas of a wife's obedience to her husband. As Emilia was outranked by Iago, his ordering her around seemed ugly, and yet the uniform gave that element of their relationship a military foundation.

Early on in my research to prepare for the role I came across an article written for *The Independent* by Maeve Walsh about reactions to Laurence Olivier's 1964 portrayal of Othello. The *Guardian* wrote that, "this Othello compels you to accept him, not merely as a coloured man, but as a negro, with a negroid speech."[5] I listened to an interview where Paul Robeson said that "Shakespeare poses this problem of a black man in a white society."[6] Robeson is later quoted as saying "This play is about the problem of minority groups – a blackamoor who tried to find equality among the whites."[7] In the original story by Giovani Battista Giraldi (Cinthio), Disdemona complains, "You moors are so hot by nature that any little thing moves you to anger."[8] The editor of the New Cambridge

Shakespeare edition of *Othello* notes: "Mary Floyd-Wilson observes that there were competing theories regarding the effect of the extreme heat of the sun on African natures: in one model, it produced both sunburned, blackened skin and a jealous, lustful disposition."[9] It seemed that everywhere I looked the idea that Othello is an example of his race was being repeated by critics, actors, and academics.

When James Hewlett performed Othello in the 1820s, Ira Aldridge in the 1830s, or Paul Robeson in the 1930s, people from the African diaspora were dealing with life-threatening, day-to-day violence in Western societies as they tried to gain rights and establish social change. Even as late as 1987, when John Kani, the actor and activist, played the character in apartheid South Africa, it was a very risky undertaking for him. He had been put on the Assassination List and had survived a murder attempt two years before.

If this is the world in which the play is being performed, it is in many ways useful to try and make Othello and Iago emblematic of their races. The productions would reflect contemporary themes of prejudice within the story of the play. But, because of the presence of other white characters onstage, we are always encouraged to see Iago as an individual, while an isolated Othello is looked upon and treated as a racial example. This is where we run the danger of making Iago's bitterness and scheming a character trait, while making Othello's gullibility and murderous anger a racial trait. Suddenly we encounter the same problems of interpretation and truth that Hugh Quarshie spoke of. These were exactly the kind of problems I was determined to avoid.

I felt the best way of dealing with this was to make sure that Othello was not racially isolated in the play. There should be other black soldiers onstage too. I spoke about the idea to Nick during one of our early conversations and he took the concept on board straight away. I wanted Othello to be seen as an individual with unique past experiences and intellect. This could only be achieved if we made sure that there were black and white soldiers onstage who were all equally shocked and saddened by Othello's actions. In our production one example of this occurred in the first scene of Act 4, when Ludovico brings Othello a letter from Venice. Othello enters to find a group of soldiers doing basic army duties. They stop what they are doing in the general's presence and stand to attention, Emilia among them. When Othello becomes angry and hits Desdemona, her knees buckle as the force of the slap sends her to the floor. The shocked soldiers immediately break ranks to try and help her, but a noise from Othello forces the soldiers, black and white, male and female, to maintain their military formation, leaving only Ludovico to try and get

Desdemona back on her feet. Only after Othello leaves the stage could Emilia help too. It was a small moment but this and other moments like it were important. Othello is not a racial example. He is lost, but he is himself.

A modern setting had a huge effect on my starting point for researching the character. In Act 1, scene 3 Othello is brought before the council and asked to justify his actions with Brabantio's daughter. He tells them a little of his history:

> For since these arms of mine had seven years pith,
> Till now some nine moons wasted, they have us'd
> Their dearest action in the tented field;
> And little of this great world can I speak
> More than pertains to feats of broil and battle.
>
> (1.3.84–88)

Since Othello was seven years old, he has used his arms for fighting, for war. They have known "their dearest action in the tented field." I am sure that scattered across the history of this production people have attributed valiance and honor to the feats of someone who has been in battle for so long, but in our modern-dress production it meant that, for me, Othello must have been a child soldier. This was crucial for my approach to understanding him. I began to wonder what it must have been like for him growing up and learning to be an adult around the atrocities of a battlefield. Surely even the Elizabethan audience must have found some-thing wrong with a boy of seven fighting in this way.

Othello's description of himself and our modern setting led me to the human rights activist and former child soldier, Ishmael Beah. In order to promote a book about his life in Sierra Leone, Ishmael has recounted his experiences in many television interviews:

> When the war started and it came to my part of the country, I started running from it. Between 12 and 13 I had lost so much. I lost my immediate family. I started to see firsthand what this war was doing to people ... This landscape that I had come to know as a child became very scary. We were forcibly recruited into this army. We were not given a choice. If we left, we would be killed by the rebels who would consider us the enemy. Joining was not in our best interests but it was a way to stay alive ... Basically the life of a child soldier is that you go out, you shoot people and you do whatever the commanders want you to do. If not, they will kill you. You are fed drugs. There are all these ways of killing people in front of you ... Exhibition Killings ... to desensitise you, then you are given more drugs. This becomes your life.[10]

On being rehabilitated, Ishmael describes losing himself and not trusting adults at all.

> For us to regain (ourselves), we needed somebody who was compassionate and selfless. The staff we had at the rehabilitation centre were that. The phrase they would repeat, "It's not your fault, it's not your fault," upset us in the beginning but after a time it wasn't the words themselves, it was the genuine care behind it ... We would hurt these people – stab them ... They would go to hospital and when they returned they would say, "Oh, it's not your fault, have you eaten?" We thought they were crazy, but they looked at us as children ... Regaining your humanity ... is a very difficult process. I came to understand that people had a very romantic notion of war and violence and that they had very little understanding of what that really means ... and how that deeply affects people. It only brings about suffering, nothing more. [11]

Ishmael's first-person account of his time as a child soldier gave me a clearer picture of Othello's possible state of mind than all of the research I had previously done.

One of the first things any actor will take care of when rehearsing a role is "self-consciousness." It happens instinctively. Whatever acting techniques or methods an actor uses, they will slowly connect their belief, moment by moment, to the imagined circumstances of their character. In this way the actor can slowly lose themselves in a role and not feel in the slightest way awkward or tense because they are being watched. In Othello's early scenes, I tried to engage with this same process. But no matter how much I worked on each moment in rehearsal, I realized that I was, in fact, becoming more and more self-conscious, more and more aware of being watched and noted. I eventually spoke to Nick, our director, about it as it began to be a bit of a problem for me. Maybe the role was too big a deal for me, maybe I was just too tense and needed to find a way to relax.

After a few days Nick observed that Othello *is* being watched. The people around him are waiting to judge him. As we went back over the play, Nick's observation made complete sense. The reason why I was feeling self-conscious was because Othello is actually engaged in the act of playing Othello. The person in the street confronted by Brabantio and his men, the man who delivers a beautiful speech to the council defending his actions with Brabantio's daughter, and the man who asks leave for his new wife to join him in Cyprus is engaged in a subtle performance as he is very conscious of being watched and judged. If a person, in fear of what others might think of them, tries to control everyone's perception of who they really are, they will in turn slowly increase the insecurity they are trying to manage.

I imagine Othello sitting with Brabantio and perhaps a few friends, after a meal, recounting some of the things he has seen during the many conflicts he had been engaged in. The days spent narrowly avoiding death. Travelling across deserts on foot, fighting a hard, bloody battle only to lose and be taken as a prisoner, sold from one party to another as a slave. Some of the rebel forces when capturing other child soldiers would use them for exhibition killings and if not, they would be tied by the neck or ankles and forced to clean boots, mend clothes, or cook to keep the army on its feet. I imagine the distress and torment Othello must have felt. The loss of family. I imagine him telling his stories to Brabantio and friends while they react in awe, excited to hear more of the gruesome details, thinking Othello is brave, skilled, and fearless. Then I think of this man meeting his friend's daughter and at her request, telling her the story she had till now only partly overheard while Othello spoke to her dad and his mates. I imagine Othello's wonder as she begins to cry, deeply moved by the danger he had to face as a young child and teenager. She would have asked him if he was scared. If he thought he was going to die. She would cry for that little orphaned boy forced to do unspeakable things. On seeing this, something inside Othello must have cracked open and melted. No matter how many times he has told his story no one was ever truly concerned for him and how he felt. No one worried for him. And now suddenly, in an instant this young woman could see more of him than anyone else has ever done. She tells him how "wondrous, pitiful" and "strange" his life has been, and she tells him she wished she had never heard his story and at the same time "she wished heaven had made her such a man." Othello, still in wonder at her reaction, listens as she wipes away tears, earnestly thanks him, and tells him that if there were a man that loved her, he should simply learn to tell Othello's story "and that would woo her."

As Desdemona leaves the room I see Othello sitting, not moving, contemplating her words. A life of hardship and military service behind him, a life of military service stretched out in front of him. The belief that he would continue to do all of it alone, now shifts, changes and slowly reveals something . . . incredible.

As I map out this previous circumstance in my head it makes absolute sense to me why Othello would fall so completely in love with Desdemona. But I do wonder why Desdemona would fall in love with him. I could delve deeper into this question, but, as an actor playing the role, I see that it is not a useful thing for me to understand. Iago plays

Figure 15.1   Here I am playing Othello opposite Olivia Vinall as Desdemona in Nicholas
Hytner's 2013 modern-dress production at the National Theatre.

upon the insecurity Othello has about his wife's love during the play. If
I too richly understand this circumstance then I can't fully enter into the
dilemma of doubt, the unsettling need to search for answers. Shakespeare
spends a lot of time exploring doubt in some of his strongest leading roles.
Along with betrayal it is a great driving force. I sometimes find it useful to
leave major questions open in my mind. In this way each performance
becomes a re-examination of those questions alongside an active search for
answers. I think this is what an audience comes to watch. Not a cold
retelling of resolved conclusions.

Olivia Vinall had not long left drama school when she played
Desdemona in our production at the National Theatre. After meeting
Olivia in audition Nick commented that not only was she wonderful in
the meeting, but also that if he were to cast her, the part of the play that
noted the difference in age would be real and alive again (Figure 15.1).
Olivia was 24, and in the production looked like a student who had just
completed her A levels. I was 44, and we added a little makeup to make me
look slightly older. Nick knew instinctively that each circumstance that
exists in the plot has been set by Shakespeare to unsettle the audience, to
make them uneasy. We were both happy that this particular circumstance

had been protected. I asked Olivia about the scene with Desdemona and her father in front of the council:

> The fact that they have gone off secretly to get married is quite powerful. It's the most exciting thing two people in love can do. That day must have been incredible to finally state their feelings in front of each other, publicly. But also, I think about how hard it must have been not to have anyone that you love with you. No father, no mother. She's so happy and in love and yet really quite sad at the same time. I think her speech to them is premeditated. It is no surprise that she is going to be asked that question. I think she's been preparing for it, probably spoke to Othello about what she was going to say. She's young, but she's not stupid.[12]

I then asked Olivia about the line "I saw Othello's visage in his mind" (1.3.254):

> They are equal, on every level. How he thinks and sees . . . is how she does. Her world's been expanded by what he has shown her of *his* world. She has matured in herself through the things she has learnt from him. It's a statement of her being her own woman and coming out and thinking as a woman, not as a young child anymore.[13]

James Earl Jones, who has played Othello four times, most famously on Broadway in 1982, commented that Othello, Iago, and Desdemona are the three pillars that hold up the play. They should be regarded as equally important to make the story work. But it is hard to do so. An unscrupulous portrayal can lead the audience away from the depth of the tragedy. James says:

> The critic (Thomas) Rymer declared it a bloody farce. I can remember one night being on tour, Chris Plummer and me, and we played a huge barn of a theatre. No chance to find any way to play subtlety. You just got it out there as big as you could and y'know, when you go big like that well . . . all of Iago's shenanigans, y'know start showing . . . bold face. Now Chris loves to get a laugh, legal or not, legitimate or not. . . But when he came off stage he was so embarrassed the audience had sorta gone crazy with the jokes. They saw everything as a joke. He said to me: "Y'know darling, it is a bloody farce after all." Well that broke my heart because I knew that he'd given up. That's the way he played it from that point on, he played it for the laughs. Got to Broadway and they loved it though.[14]

I didn't know this about their performance. I had only heard how powerful and heartbreaking James and, therefore, the production was as a whole. Listening to James talk about laughter and working with his Iago made me so grateful I had Rory Kinnear as my Iago. We achieved a great balance onstage. Rory was generous and listened to any requests I made of him during the performance. In Act 3, scene 3, the so-called "temptation scene," Rory, Nick, and I pulled the scene apart in order to make sure every step of Othello's thought process in reaction to Iago's words was protected and logical. It got to the point in performance where it felt like Rory and I were improvising Shakespeare's words. We got into a great rhythm. Every look, every gesture, and every pause for thought was felt out between us.

During the previews Nick became understandably annoyed with the audience response and their need to laugh at certain points in the play. He didn't want to give them a release from the tension they were feeling and reworked key elements of the play in order to keep them away from the safety of that reaction.

I asked James how it felt to play such anguish and pain while the audience are laughing. "Well you have to ignore it. Try to give them the other point of view." I'm nodding and listening to James, but I found the little bits of audience laughter during some of the most brutal moments in our production very difficult to ignore. James continues:

> When Paul Robeson did it, the war was on and being a General meant something. Eisenhower meant something, Montgomery meant something, they were revered. By the time I played it we'd had Vietnam and all the wars that showed Generals denigrated ... as fools. There was cynicism. Wall Street presented us with an attitude that greed is good ... there were no values really from the old school. So when this play is presented in that atmosphere ... only the cynicism works unless you're very careful.[15]

James continued to me:

> We have the right to make the play work in the context of our own culture. What I find interesting for *any* culture, the first scene of the play. It's not just the creation of the plot, the set up for everything that's going to happen, it's the creation of racism. I think it works better if Iago is a lower-class gentleman, no chance of privilege, no chance of upward mobility ... no chance. Then when he is denied that lieutenantship, that's the end of his life.[16]

It feels as though Shakespeare begins the play with an act of betrayal against Iago. It is his jealousy that sparks the plot. I asked Rory Kinnear what it felt like to perform the play each evening, and he said:

> Iago doesn't have poetry or qualities of openness. Iago is in many ways a wonderful part structurally in terms of the way that you, as the bad guy, illicit understanding, sympathy, and entertainment from the audience, their camaraderie. When you see a young girl being, over several seconds,

painfully murdered, you as an audience member are responsible. The playwright's structural ingenuity with it is why people love playing the part and why the audience finds him compelling. It's difficult in that it's physically tiring, but it employs rhetoric more than emotional veracity.[17]

In performance it was the exact opposite for me as Othello. I had about thirty minutes of performance that relied on rhetoric and an exact delivery of verse, before I had to be swallowed up by over two hours of Othello's torturous emotions.

Rory continued to talk about the structure of the play from the point of view of Iago:

> Act 3, scene 3 is probably one of the best written scenes in terms of dramaturgy that I've ever done. Where you know that one false move and you're toast. It's a painstaking build up to a revelation. Laying the seed of insecurity in Othello while at the same time garnering his trust. It is brilliantly structured. I think Othello's reaction surprises him. "The Moor already changes with my poison." He thought it would take longer than that. Iago has to re-adjust always thinking, "How do I keep going?" and it becomes addictive.[18]

Act 3, scene 3 is brilliantly structured, but it was always the scene I found most difficult to get right. I had to struggle every night to make it believable that Othello would fall so far and so hard with a little push from Iago. I asked Rory why he thinks Iago keeps pushing. As Rory started to answer this question he began to dig at the heart of Iago's racism. It is what I believe lies at the heart of all racist thinking. Color is an excuse used to exercise the fear of a deeper truth.

> You sense, as he pushes on and on and on, that he unleashes the bile that he's holding within. This terrifying loathing that he conceals from everyone, becomes scary. He feels like he's not been given his place in society, professionally and personally. He has not been afforded the respect he craves. This simmering resentment to a society that has kept him a little man, that promotes a foreigner, though I'm not sure how much this eats away at him but it's something else to hold onto, promotes a foreigner to the top of the tree and yet keeps Iago around the middle ranks and that this man could also sleep with his wife. It's like a . . . like a breakdown in his life. But it's one where . . . were it to muck up and none of it worked, he could well have killed himself, he could well have gone on a rampage. Iago behaves like he has no concern for the future.[19]

In his book, *Balancing Acts*, Nick Hytner noted that "the word that keeps pinging out of Iago's soliloquies . . . is 'now.' He works on instinct, in the moment."[20] There is a gap in Othello's logic that is left open for the actor to fill with their skill and imagination. It is difficult to do this while accepting the negative judgements that get placed upon Othello as an example of his race. This same gap in logic exists at the heart of Iago and Desdemona. In fact, as we dig and dig into the heart of each of Shakespeare's major characters in any of his plays, we reach a playground for psychological study. A space where questions have not been fully answered.

My good friend consultant psychiatrist and cognitive behavioral therapist, Dr Stephen Pereira, had never seen a Shakespeare play before he watched one of the performances of *Othello* at the National. Afterwards, over a drink, he deconstructed each of the characters with astonishing clarity. He commented that Shakespeare's powers of observation were "astounding": "Honestly, all of the characters on that stage could have benefitted from some therapy!" I laugh a little, and ask, "What, even Desdemona?" "Oh my god," says Stephen. "Especially Desdemona." It must be true that Shakespeare, the quiet man from Stratford, was a unique and incredibly gifted observer of people. When he walked the streets of London there was no clinical diagnoses given to those who were depressed, OCD, bipolar, narcissistic, megalomaniac, had addictive personalities, or were psychotic or sociopathic. They were simply people with behavioral patterns that were out of the ordinary. Behavior that would now be diagnosed and medicated.

No character who appears onstage is normal and well balanced. If that were true, they wouldn't be worth including in a play. If a character is conceived as being ordinary and balanced you can bet that although they may start that way, some development in the plot, some revelation of past history will force that ordinary character to experience extreme stress, during which they will be forced to behave in extreme ways in order to cope. An ordinary person caught up in extraordinary circumstances will behave extraordinarily and will therefore be worth watching.

So, imagine writing at a time when there was no such thing as copyright. You could grab hold of a popular story and reinvent it by placing characters you had observed in everyday Elizabethan life. Suddenly the motivations and self-expressions of each person would be more profound. The common characters in the stories that people knew and loved would have a unique reinvention not based on where they were or what they happened to be doing but based on who they thought they were and who they feared they might be.

The Elizabethan's position in the world has obviously changed and disappeared over hundreds of years, but all over the world, human nature –

who we think we are and who we fear we might be – has not changed at all. This is the territory of writers like Shakespeare. It's been over 415 years since this play was first performed. Over 400 years since Shakespeare saw something in Elizabethan England that he wanted to re-explore with characters and plot taken from Cinthio's story. It was written before the transatlantic slave trade reached its height, producing such immense profits for the countries involved that it would lead the pro-slavery lobby to do anything to justify the continuation of its existence. It is the fall-out from this lobbying that allows us to think Shakespeare wanted us to fear and loathe the character of Othello.

The play has not changed, we have, but not enough to push the play's themes into antiquity. Since the campaign for Brexit began, incidents of racial violence have risen in the UK. The Office for National Statistics recorded that 1.6 million women suffered domestic violence in the year ending March 2019. And roughly two women a week are killed by their partners due to domestic violence. Men are four times more likely to commit suicide than women in the UK; 4,903 men took their own lives in 2018. We try to find the meaning of the play by viewing it through a lens muddied by events that happened after Shakespeare wrote it. I think people would have an easier time watching this "complete tragedy" if its themes had nothing to do with our daily existence.

Notes

1 Hugh Quarshie during "Performing Othello: Adrian Lester, Hugh Quarshie, and Janet Suzman," a public event at the British Library, 15 July 2016.
2 Quoted in "Is Othello a Racist Play? RSC Actor Hugh Quarshie Is Asking the Question," *Etcetera*, 6 August 2015, www.hamhigh.co.uk/etcetera/theatre/is-othello-a-racist-play-rsc-actor-hugh-quarshie-is-asking-the-question-1-4184119 (accessed 27 February 2020).
3 Hugh Quarshie, *Second Thoughts about Othello* (Chipping Camden: International Shakespeare Association, 1999), 5.
4 Thomas Rymer, *A Short View of Tragedy* (London, 1693), in *The Critical Works of Thomas Rymer*, ed. Curt Zimansky (New Haven, CT: Yale University Press, 1956), 132.
5 Philip Hope-Wallace, "*Othello* at the National Theatre," *Guardian*, 22 April 1964.
6 Paul Robeson, 1943 television interview in New York, www.youtube.com/watch?v=-DF7YQrC7HM (accessed 27 February 2020).
7 Paul Robeson, 1943 television interview.
8 Giovanni Battista Giraldi (Cinthio), *Gli Hecthommithi* (1565). English translation in *Othello: revised edition*, ed. E.A.J. Honigmann, Arden Third Series (London: Bloomsbury, 2016), 383.

9 Norman Sanders, "Supplemental Notes," in *Othello*, 3rd edn, New Cambridge Shakespeare (Cambridge University Press, 2018), 216.

10 Quoted in "Eye to Eye: Ishmael Beah," CBS News, 4 June 2007, www .youtube.com/watch?v=ozsOLdgp_y0 (accessed 27 February 2020).

11 Quoted in "Eye to Eye."

12 Olivia Vinall interviewed by Adrian Lester, August 2013. Printed with permission.

13 Olivia Vinall interviewed by Adrian Lester.

14 James Earl Jones interviewed by Adrian Lester, October 2013. Printed with permission.

15 James Earl Jones interviewed by Adrian Lester.

16 James Earl Jones interviewed by Adrian Lester.

17 Rory Kinnear interviewed by Adrian Lester, August 2013. Printed with permission.

18 Rory Kinnear interviewed by Adrian Lester.

19 Rory Kinnear interviewed by Adrian Lester.

20 Nicholas Hytner, *Balancing Acts: Behind the Scenes in London's National Theatre* (New York: Vintage, 2017), 206.

CHAPTER 16

Are Shakespeare's Plays Racially Progressive?
The Answer Is in Our Hands

Miles Grier
City University of New York

In the late spring of 1762, actor and theatre impresario David Douglass wanted his troupe of touring British players to perform in Rhode Island. He chose *Othello*, a perennially popular play in London, but faced a problem in British America. While he was confident there was a desire for performance, the Puritan laws of New England forbade theatre as encouraging vice.[1] He secured permission from the city fathers to perform through an ingenious argument that *Othello* is not a play at all but a series of "moral dialogues." One element of this reframing, crucial for our purposes, is his claim that *Othello* combats a pervasive and heretical racism by reinforcing Christian doctrines that all humans are descended from Adam and capable of earning God's grace. Here is part of the announcement Douglas circulated:

KINGS ARMS TAVERN-NEWPORT, RHODE ISLAND On Monday, June 10th, at the Public Room of the above Inn, will be delivered a series of

MORAL DIALOGUES,
IN FIVE PARTS,

Depicting the evil effects of jealousy and other bad passions, and proving that happiness can only spring from the pursuit of virtue.
Mr. Douglass – Will represent a noble and magnanimous Moor, called Othello, who loves a young lady named Desdemona, and after he has married her, harbours (as in too many cases) the dreadful passion of jealousy.

Of jealousy, our being's bane,
Mark the small cause and the most dreadful pain . . .

Mr. Morris – Will represent an old gentleman, the father of Desdemona, who is not cruel or covetous, but is foolish enough to dislike the noble Moor, his son-in-law, because his face is not white, forgetting that we all spring from one root. Such prejudices are very numerous and very wrong.

Fathers beware what sense and love ye lack,
'Tis crime, not colour, makes the being black.[2]

Over one hundred fifty years after the first performance of *Othello*, Douglass'
advertisement offered what may be the earliest, full-throated argument that
the play is anti-racist. However, if Douglass truly thought the play would
help elevate Christian universalism and stamp out the heresy of racial
prejudice, he did not say so until he had to persuade a Puritan government
hostile to theatre. Today, some historians take a related stance, convinced
that *Othello* is a living being that "breathes contempt" for the play's racist
characters.[3] It is certainly comforting to imagine Shakespeare as a dispenser
of moral truths, unerring in his humane vision, but that view will not bear
up under textual analysis or historical investigation.

Nevertheless, even some black performers have effaced their own labors
to credit Shakespeare as the origin of their productions' anti-racist impact.
Consider the legendary Paul Robeson – an African American scholar and
activist who played Othello in London in 1930 and New York in 1943 to
great acclaim and who established the current tradition of having the part
played by a black person rather than a white man painted black. In
interviews, Robeson mused that Shakespeare had "great sympathy for the
under-dog." He added:

> as Othello I walk into the Senate, among all those people who in their
> hearts hate me, but fear me and know they must use me. I have known
> instances of the same sort of thing today; when, for example, the only
> skillful physician in town has been a Negro and the people during an
> epidemic have had to go to him to be saved from death. Shakespeare
> grasped this principle perfectly and *Othello* is, if anything, more apt today
> than when it was first written.[4]

One can certainly understand that Robeson felt that way during his performances. However – and here is a point to which I will return throughout the
essay – this feeling is not guaranteed by Shakespeare's text. Rather, it is a
product of the interaction among those plays, the cultural prestige accorded
them, and the racial regime of a particular time and locale. In fact, I will
make the argument that, whatever Shakespeare's personal beliefs about racial
equality, his works have undoubtedly been wedded to a social order in which
whiteness is to receive a disproportionate share of social goods such as
property, pleasure, prestige, and protection. The racial progress that interests
me comes not from prosecuting Shakespeare for racism but from discerning
the strategies through which anti-racist projects have been pursued in, with,
and against the industry that is Shakespeare.

When Robeson played the part, he was quite literally defying laws and
customs that might have been brought to bear were the performances not
shielded in being *just a play*. Robeson indicated how the proscription

against black–white coupling affected him in 1930: "For the first two weeks in every scene I played with Desdemona that girl couldn't get near to me, I was backin' away from her all the time. I was like a plantation hand in the parlor, that clumsy."[5] London did not have *de jure* segregation, but he heard rumblings about opposition to the performance, and Peggy Ashcroft and Sybil Thorndike – who played Desdemona and Emilia, respectively – received letters that declared them unemployable in the theatre.[6] Having faced down Jim Crow as a force in the world that had also invaded his own psyche, Robeson announced, "Othello has taken away from me all kinds of fears, all sense of limitation, and all racial prejudice. Othello has opened me to new and wider fields; in a word, Othello has made me free."[7]

Actors today, however talented, cannot duplicate Robeson's feat, as they face a different set of audience expectations in the wake of Robeson's historic triumphs as Othello. In 2018, at Shakespeare's Globe, Eammon Walker and Abraham Popoola both expressed some disappointment with the fact that audiences laughed at Othello's gullibility. Popoola, in particular, noted that he wanted audiences to see Othello's intelligence. He took the laughter personally, as a denial of his own intelligence, with which he had carefully imbued the character, through his study for the part. Yet, whatever nobility is in Shakespeare's depiction – and whatever philosophical profundity in the actor – Othello is also, inevitably, one of the play's dupes. And audiences know that he is. Popoola concluded that playing the role was such a pyschic strain that no one should undertake it without "someone close" to return to at home. Walker added physical injury to psychological risk, recalling that he developed a "blood blister" from banging his head against the stage nightly during his epileptic fit. Golda Rosheuvel noted that one side of her face would sometimes freeze after her performance of the fit.[8]

The actors said much more during this discussion, but I was struck by these moments which revealed the gravitational pull of Othello – and the risk it poses to mind, soul, and body. It is as if aspiring dark-skinned actors today cannot play Othello without fear of demeaning themselves and their people but also cannot refuse it if they want work and potential praise. As Othello slowly and unevenly became the property of actors of color in the latter half of the twentieth century, white people lost that role. At the same time, they more or less kept Hamlet and Othello became the highest role to which all but the most celebrated black actor could aspire. Yet, the roles are not equivalent: Othello is not the Black Hamlet. Nothing so physically or psychologically injurious is demanded of the actor playing Hamlet. Moreover, the performer who succeeds in Hamlet gets to keep the laurel for having mastered what we now view as a consummately intellectual part.[9] Conversely, Shakespeare gets a share of the credit for *Othello*. It is his foresight, his empathy, and his advocacy that are applauded for dramatizing the social problems that vex us today.

Therefore, I would argue that Robeson was being too modest. It was not entirely Shakespeare's sympathy – or even Shakespeare's agency – that allowed him the opportunity to confront global apartheid and to stretch himself. Rather, Robeson's hijacking of *Othello* – a term I use without negative connotation – was an unforeseen development, completely alien to the conventions of the early modern professional stage, in which British boys and men played all roles.[10] Africans, especially captives in service to aristocrats, could appear as musicians at court or in public playhouses. In civic pageants, they could be seen riding "unicorns" or bedecked in feathered crowns, serving as "exotic paraphernalia ... visible reminders of British success in trade and exploration, as do Indians."[11] These silent figures served as emblems, who did not communicate information about their own interior lives but publicized the rising affluence of the city, the theatre company, or the household that employed them.[12] The possibility that an actor descended from Africans or Indians – American or Asian – would perform the role of *Othello* was likely not imagined. Theatre companies were white male guilds, including some new bourgeois and some near-destitute apprentices.[13] Employment was a plum, and prime money-making positions were held and circulated within those guilds.[14]

Consequently, the prospect of Othellos that were not painted white men was simply not anticipated or entertained – to say nothing of women of color who have played Cleopatra, Rosaline, and even Othello. Therefore, the contributions of these performances to anti-racist social movements cannot be attributed to Shakespearean intention. Contrary to those scholars who insist there was no racism before biology invented the scientific category in the 1780s, race-making projects existed in antiquity, the Middle Ages, and the Renaissance. What did not exist in the Renaissance was an avowed collective project of white *anti*-racism. Therefore, I take Shakespeare to have been experimenting with what a racial difference constituted by a transferable black paint allowed him to convey about character – a term that includes both conventional marks such as the letters of the alphabet and invisible possessions such as rank, reputation, and moral composition. The black paint of the stage Moor – which Shakespeare and his contemporaries often compared to an ink – allowed for the staging of fascinating scenarios in which Moors have their black exteriors read, engage in reading themselves, and transfer telltale black marks to their lovers. Within such a tradition one simply cannot attribute to Shakespeare the role of social critic. Some might convict him of primitivism and xenophobia, among other failings. For my part, I find his record mixed. I do, however, feel confident in asserting that he was interested in playing out a number of possibilities with blackened Moors as villain (*Titus Andronicus*), tragic hero (*Othello*), abased fool (*The Tempest*), failed suitor (*The Merchant of Venice*), and commanding but lovesick Queen (*Antony and Cleopatra*). Clearly, the Moor was a fascinating part to him, one he moved throughout his company, assigning it to the lead tragedian, minor fools, and boy-actresses. Given the economic structure of the early modern theatre and Shakespeare's aesthetic strategies, it seems dubious to deem him an anti-racist. Therefore, I conclude that the anti-racist force of those productions arises at the intersection of racial decorum, audience expectation, and performance choices.

When Robeson played Othello in the second quarter of the twentieth century, he was performing against audience expectations, an advantage his current successors no longer have, since audiences now expect black performers in the role. These expectations were not in place during the centuries in which stage Moors were played by white men in blackface or, beginning in the nineteenth century, a lighter brown. Shakespeare's scripts have never been able to command a single response from audiences to racist structures.

Though one horrified onlooker instructs the play's shameless villain, Iago, to "look on the tragic loading of this bed" in the final scene of *Othello*, audiences have never required this urging. The corpses of the suicidal black general Othello, Desdemona, the wife he has smothered, and Emilia, her loyal maid, have provoked a flood of commentary. In 1610, six years after the play's likely premiere, an Oxford student wrote that "But truly the celebrated Desdemona, slain in our presence by her husband, although she pleaded her case very effectively throughout, yet moved [us] more after she was dead, when, lying on her bed, she entreated the pity of the spectators by her very countenance."[15] Near the end of the seventeenth century, the critic Thomas Rymer surveyed the carnage and convicted Shakespeare of disposing of his characters "against all Justice and Reason, against all Law, Humanity and Nature, in a barbarous arbitrary way."[16] He was already convinced that the play was "improbable" because of what he deemed the preposterous interracial marriage at its center:

> The Character of [Venice] is to employ strangers in their Wars; But shall a Poet thence fancy that they will set a Negro to be their General; or trust a *Moor* to defend them against the *Turk*? With us a Black-a-moor might rise to be a Trumpeter; but *Shakespear* would not have him less than a Lieutenant-General. With us a *Moor* might marry some little drab, or

Small-coal Wench: *Shake-spear* would provide him the Daughter and Heir of some great Lord, or Privy-Councellor: And all the Town should reckon it a very suitable match.[17]

Nearly another century and a half later, former US president John Quincy Adams was certain that the meaning of the play lay in its final, macabre tableau: "when Othello smothers [Desdemona] in bed, the terror and the pity subside immediately to the sentiment that she had her just deserts."[18] He concluded, "The great moral lesson of *The Tragedy of Othello*, is that black and white blood cannot be intermingled in marriage without a gross outrage upon the laws of nature, and that in such violations nature will vindicate her laws."[19]

Sentiments such as those of Adams eventually won the day, and a "Bronze Age" of Othello began, lasting from perhaps 1807 to at least 2015, when the Metropolitan Opera stopped using darkening makeup for the white singer playing Verdi's Otello. The brownface innovation forestalled the arrival of African descendants in a role that many saw as offering an opportunity to intervene against slavery and racism in its legal and cultural forms. These include Ignatius Sancho in London – a manumitted African, abolitionist, and man of letters who is said to have been prevented from playing the part by a speech impediment.[20] The first black men to play the part there were greeted with a mixture of responses, from celebration to threat and ridicule. New Yorker Ira Aldridge debuted in 1825 with a published call to prevent him from taking the stage. This situation was not unfamiliar to him, as he was an alumnus of New York's African Theatre Company, whose members were jailed for performing *Richard III* at the same time as a rival theatre owned by a British impresario. Given the desire for African descendants to play Othello – and the potential for it to be leveraged for abolitionist purposes – the move to "bronze" Othellos cannot be understood as simply honoring the ethnic group Shakespeare had in mind when he used the term "Moor." Rather, this first major attempt to excise racial blackness from the play was an attempt to avoid a political question that arose from the convergence of the prestige of Shakespearean tragedy and the abasement of enslaved Africans. If the tradition had not been to paint Moors black (noted as early as Rymer) or if the genre were something other than vaunted tragedy, then there would have been no need to keep African descendants from playing the part.

We should not assume, however, that audience members always responded to Shakespeare's tragedies with the solemnity we might imagine. In 1709, Sir John Perceval, earl of Egmont, suggested that some were indifferent to the tale: "Those who cannot be moved at Othello's story . . .

are capable of marrying again before their husbands are cold, of trampling on a lover when dying at their feet, and are fit to converse with tygers only."[21] It would appear that the earl was responding to the laughter that has dogged the gullible Moor for centuries. According to Robert Hornback, Othello's gown and signature handkerchief would have identified him as a gullible fool to the early audiences.[22] In the eighteenth century, the great David Garrick was ridiculed for resembling a black servant in a Hogarth caricature. His competitor, Quin, said "Here's Pompey, where's [his] tea kettle?"[23] Dame Maggie Smith came backstage to talk with Sir Laurence Olivier while he was undergoing the tedious procedure of blacking up.[24] Referencing an earlier conversation, he asked her if she had improved her handling of vowels, as he directed. She replied using a vocal exercise she thought apt: "How now, brown cow?"[25] The British actor Charles Mathews once lampooned the theatre company that nurtured Aldridge in a mockery of a black actor's attempt to perform Hamlet's first soliloquy:

> "To be, or not to be? That is the question; whether it is nobler in *de* mind to suffer or take'up arms against a sea of trouble and by *opossum*, end 'em." No sooner was the word *opossum* out of his mouth than the audience burst forth, in one general cry, "Opposum! opossum!" and the tragedian came forward and informed them that he would sing their favorite [blackface minstrel show] melody with greater pleasure ... When he had finished his song he walked up the stage and when he got up the stage he soon came strutting down with, "Now is the winter of our discontent made glorious summer by the sun of York."[26]

This denigrating portrait of the African Theatre Company – and its audience – indicates that there was no guarantee that black performers entering the Shakespearean field would be able to redeem the parts. The desire to laugh at black performers was high, whether the performers were painted or in their own skin – and regardless of whether the casting was color-conscious or color-blind. In these circumstances, any black performer was going to be political.

In 1987, three years before negotiations began to end South Africa's apartheid regime, John Kani was the first African man to play Othello on a professional stage in his country. Shakespeare was the cornerstone of the white elite's theatre culture. At the same time, black South Africans had been excluded from attending plays and offered a vocational education that did not include literature.[27] Kani recalled: "In 1987, Mandela was still in prison. At that time in South Africa, the struggle was bitter and violent – bombs and bullets, protesters and police, landmines and grenades. Dozens lost their lives and many more, millions of black and coloured South

Africans, suffered. So it is no surprise that during the rehearsals there was a tense atmosphere."[28]

The potential consequences were not insignificant. Peggy Ashcroft had received threats that her career was over, but she went on to be named a Dame Commander of the Most Excellent Order of the British Empire in honor of a career that, threats notwithstanding, was not derailed by appearing onstage with Robeson. The Desdemona in the South African production, Joanna Weinberg, was not so fortunate. Kani recalled: "Joanna was very courageous and prepared to explore every possible facet of the relationship between Othello and Desdemona. And for her performance she received hate mail. The letters she got, they said only a Jewish slut would behave like that, not a proper white actor. In fact, she left South Africa and today she lives in Australia. We met up a few years ago and she told me that for her, after she had worked on that particular play, it was harder to get mainstream work; she was marginalised."[29] The pity that the Oxford student felt for Desdemona in 1610 was being withheld from a Desdemona deemed insufficiently white. Even if we are convinced that Shakespeare would never have approved of racist ideas or actions, the dangers that Weinberg faced remind us again that nothing in the play can pre-empt a racist response: in this case, the view of Jewish women as deficient in the honorable chastity of a fully white woman meets with the disdain common for any white (or white-adjacent) woman who chooses a black lover.

For his part, Kani knew the consequences he faced were potentially fatal: "When I was put on the list for assassination they said I was a terrorist masquerading as an artist. They tried to kill me two years before this production. I was stabbed 11 times and left for dead. Because they said I was not an actor. A terrorist."[30] Under these conditions, Kani was able to achieve his goal: "I come from the theatre of revolution. I want to mobilise, to educate, to inform, interact and explore every moment on the stage."[31]

Although we have no direct evidence that Shakespeare would condone racism spoken and enacted, we have to acknowledge that his plays are powerless to stop those who want to wield them for racist purposes. In other words, whatever is in them cannot entirely determine whether the plays will be mobilized for racist or anti-racist ends. However, it does seem that the name of Shakespeare and the aura of artistic supremacy that accompanies it are more easily wielded by advocates of white supremacy than they are by anti-racists. To align Shakespeare with global white supremacy and political or cultural imperialism is to work with the tide of history. To turn the tide is not impossible, but it also requires reorienting work on economic, material, and ideological fronts – often from what appears to be scratch.

Additional indications that anti-racist potential lies *outside* the plays comes from social movement history. Some of the Othellos in the US with the most impact have been closely associated (either by choice or by timing) with mass social movements. Robeson aligned himself with the fight against the "color bar" on a global scale. By the 1943 debut on Broadway, he had a fully articulated global anti-racism to tout in the interviews that preceded and accompanied his performances. He then included monologues from *Othello* in concerts of spirituals and protest songs, attempting to bind Othello to his own anti-racist politics.

James Earl Jones's New York debut in *Othello* came in 1964. Civil rights activism in the United States was at its height, with organizations such as the Southern Christian Leadership Council, Student Nonviolent Coordinating Committee, and Congress on Racial Equality mobilizing nationwide. Malcolm X had broken from the Nation of Islam early in 1964, but both the Nation and Malcolm himself remained major forces in New York politics. Casting Jones, thirty-four, seemed both a nod to young insurgents and an attempt to capture some of their energy.[32] The role has come to be one of Jonese' signatures, as he is still asked to perform Othello's famous speeches, even after an illustrious career in many other notable roles.[33] Yet, as much as *Othello* has left its stamp on Jones, one could also argue that the part itself has been reconceptualized in light of the totality of Jones's career and public persona. When he performs Othello now, we see Jack Johnson and Troy Maxson and hear the voice of Darth Vader, Mufasa, and of CNN. The gravity and solemnity that have become a part of Jones's "star image" are now lent to an Othello at whom no one in the audience laughs.[34]

Although black women had to wait even longer to play Cleopatra on major British or American stages, they have not had to face demeaning laughter in a role with a very different stage history. For one thing, Shakespeare's version disappeared from the stage for many years as John Dryden's *All for Love; Or, the World Well Lost* and truncated versions dominated the London stage until the 1920s. In addition, Shakespeare seems to have been alone in having the Egyptian queen played by a boy in black paint. The practice was not revived when the theatres reopened in the 1660s. For centuries, the role was played by white women who, if anything, played it in whiteface.[35] Finally, as the only black(ened) character in Shakespeare in the role of a sovereign, a queen is granted certain privileges. In other words, her outlandish demands, undisguised sexual desire, and rapid changes of mood can, when portrayed by an appropriately regal actor, appear as royal prerogative. Placed against a character like Caliban – traditionally clothed in dirty rags at best – the crowned and bejeweled monarch can definitely read as a reclamation of black women's beauty, dignity, and command.[36] Nevertheless, I would not attribute this response to anything intrinsic in *Antony and Cleopatra*. Rather, I would say (as with *Othello*) that the timing and locale make available certain choices and audience responses.

Centuries of white women (or boys!) playing Cleopatra in black and then brown makeup would place today's black actors in quite a different situation. Instead, they are performing in the living memory of great performers like Lena Horne and Dorothy Dandridge, whose star image included their exclusion from playing Cleopatra, while white actors like Claudette Colbert and Elizabeth Taylor were deemed appealing enough to fit the queen's legendary allure. Unlike Othello, the gull, and Caliban, the bestial demi-devil, Cleopatra is no one's supplicant and, in fact, kills herself rather than suffer that fate. Therefore, the role does not call for self-abasement. A certain player can, of course, produce such a performance, but it is not demanded (as it is, arguably, in *Othello* and, undoubtedly, in *The Tempest*).

Thus, the *Observer* could review Josette Simon in a 2017 Royal Shakespeare Company production as "liv[ing] up to Enobarbus's report of her 'infinite variety.'" The reviewer raves at the "fascinating sense Simon gives ... of underlying insecurity, as though Cleopatra were shuffling selves." The final scene suits a long-standing desire of diasporic black people to reclaim beauty and dominion: "Cleopatra's [death] is beautiful as she strips to nothing and is then dressed in royal trappings. This is death as coronation – as crowning glory."[37] Simon herself said that she wanted to emphasize Cleopatra's intellect – and her intellectual attraction to Antony.

Shakespeare's text does not automatically lead to an emphasis of Cleopatra's intelligence; Simon herself notes that the queen of Egypt can easily be reduced to a strumpet. Nevertheless, the play does not thwart an approach to Cleopatra as a consummate politician by having her demonstrate utter ineptitude, as occurs with her blackamoor colleagues, Othello, Caliban, and the Prince of Morocco in *The Merchant of Venice*. Unlike these painted brothers, Cleopatra begins and ends the play as Egypt's unquestioned ruler. So, under the current circumstances, in which black women are still rarely depicted in the US or England as rulers or as objects of desire, an approach to Cleopatra like Josette Simon's can satisfy audience members who desire to see the image of black women rehabilitated. However, the very success of performers like Robeson, Simon, and Jones means that audiences are more likely to arrive at *Othello* or *Antony and Cleopatra* expecting black actors in those roles and some form of amelioration. Without the transgression of cultural codes and the flouting of audience expectation, it is unlikely that the effects of these roles will be sustained.

What are we to make of what Ayanna Thompson calls "leaving Shakespeare," departing from any sense of fidelity to his intention (especially as received wisdom)?[38] In this case, I would say that leaving the Bard means setting aside the attempt to redeem his black characters. This tactic, as well, would not be guaranteed to do progressive work forever. For instance, I saw two productions of *The Tempest* that addressed the racialization of Caliban in completely different ways. The first, Sam Mendes' 2010 production at BAM!, had Ron Cephas Jones play the character called a hag-seed and demi-devil. He was the only person of African descent in an otherwise all white-appearing production, and the choice to have him play Caliban as the missing link between ape and human was jarring. His simian movements and grotesque facial expressions seemed designed to flout decorum, to challenge both a post-colonial critique of *The Tempest* as colonialism's ur-text and color-blind casting. It was as if the production was saying: yes, Caliban is African, and Africans are beasts designed to serve. After Caliban's attempt to overthrow his captor Prospero has been suppressed, Shakespeare has Caliban refer to himself in terms that concede his demonic nature and Prospero's superiority. "What a thrice-double ass I have been," he acknowledges. It is an economical condensation of the play's accumulated insults against Caliban: thrice-double gives us six, the devil's number, which is also the ligature for stigma, the slave's mark. An ass is a beast of burden, as well as a name for a fool and, of course, an unpleasant-smelling organ of the body. Although Caliban has previously insisted that the island should be his, Shakespeare has him relinquish this claim at the end and promise to "seek for grace," the education, favor, and forgiveness of his conqueror. In this case, it seems indisputable that Shakespeare's text ends by having his character joyfully submit to colonialism.

Alternately, color-conscious casting and pointed choices can reshape colonial relationships. In 2016, at the Smith Street Stage's free performance in Brooklyn's Carroll Park, Caliban was played by a rosy-cheeked, young white blond man. They dressed him nearly as a dog, and he scampered, howled, and rubbed against other cast members much more in that style than in the ape-like manner employed by Jones at BAM! With his character white and lovably canine, Caliban no longer seemed a racist construction. This production also followed Julie Taymor's 2010 film version by changing Prospero to a woman. Indeed, it went further in purposely scrambling the warring siblings: Antonio (in this case, a black woman) was the subject of a plot by her white brother; while King Alonso (played by a black man) is the subject of a plot by his (black) sister. With no character isolated or conspired against by another sex or race, it was impossible to see the play as implicated in a history either of patriarchy or of European imperialism. With these changes and a white Caliban, the play's colonial overlay was effectively erased: not to mention that Caliban does not board the ship for Milan in this version but remains on the island as its rightful ruler (in a silent coda adapted from Taymor's film). This work could only be accomplished by leaving some elements of Shakespeare's color-coded language, his geography, and his plot behind. It was certainly an enjoyable evening – a relief, to be honest, for this black viewer who feared having my people publicly maligned again. From the vantage point of a viewing experience, it was thoughtful – perhaps the only way to stage the play for a contemporary, multicultural audience in an active public park with a seating area set aside for children.

Yet, the question with which we began was whether or not Shakespeare's plays are racially progressive. Smith Street Stage certainly *neutralized* the overt colonial and patriarchal aspects of the play. One effect is to save Shakespeare – the universal Shakespeare – from criticism of the plays that bear his name. This production concealed what feminist, anti-racist, and anti-colonial artists and scholars have found in plain sight. It is difficult to know how an audience member – child or adult – who remembers this as her first *Tempest* would respond to Sylvia Plath's *Ariel*, Aimé Césaire's *A Tempest*, Toni Morrison's *Tar Baby*, or Gloria Naylor's *Mama Day* – among many examples. The danger is that they would then wonder why these writers *imported* historical inequalities and political critique into an innocent story about family, betrayal, and forgiveness.

As someone familiar with *The Tempest*, I could appreciate the work the company did to spare the audience from seeing a lone woman and a lone black diminished. Yet, I worry that some viewers will leave crediting Shakespeare instead of the Smith Street Company. Even with all their changes, *The Tempest* is still the play in which the king of Naples finds himself in a shipwreck that his companions interpret as a judgement against his choice to take his daughter to Tunis to marry a Moor. A strategically race- and gender-proportioned production can neutralize the obvious moral in the original: Prospero, in preventing Caliban from coupling with his daughter, is the better father (while Alonso is reminiscent of Brabantio, who loses his daughter Desdemona forever). Yet, no casting can remove that dialogue from a script that represents the "bad conscience" that Fiedler ascribed to Shakespeare and the societies that have sustained his work.[39]

In the face of these difficulties, Shakespeare's liberal-humanist defenders panic. They deny that the plays have contributed to social inequality for fear that, if the works are found complicit, then they will no longer be read, taught, performed, or enjoyed. One of the ironies is that Shakespeare scholars of color do not typically call for the plays to be hidden, burned, or otherwise erased.[40] We do call for them to be approached differently: with less reverence and more attention to their encoding and spreading of white supremacist and patriarchal relationships. Though we have our internal disagreements, as any field does, few of us see any advantage in digging up Shakespeare's corpse to flog him. We are, however, quite interested in the *uses* of Shakespeare to construct the very vision of human nature, both historically and in the present. It is that ongoing history of (mis)use to which many early modern race scholars attend, and it is that there is an implication of *us* in the Shakespeare mythology that seems to produce the most panic among those who are disturbed. It is the threat of being implicated and, therefore, of losing unbothered enjoyment that generates and sustains the objections: for to the staunch defender, to read Shakespeare as something other than either transcendent spirit or clear-eyed social critic is as bad as being told to no longer read him at all. We will have to set those contemporary defenses aside if we wish to confront the question before us honestly.

The question of Shakespeare's implication in racism arouses intense passion. That passion, though, is not particularly different from controversies about whether certain nations, laws, and institutions (such as the police) are racist. Though the combatants and alignments may be different, the investments are often similar. People invest faith or devote time to a text, a philosophy, a person, or an institution that they consider to be a force for good in the world. Others note that they have not benefited from this social or cultural force but, in fact, have been its target. Unwilling to grant that such testimony is credible – or that it carries significant weight – advocates mount the desperate defenses. And so we arrive here, when Shakespeare is both "for all time" in Ben Jonson's famous epitaph and "of his time" in the framing of those who would acknowledge racist constructions in the work but consider them accidental and not integral.

They would tell us that progress has been made – but also tell us to hold on to Shakespeare's work. As I have stated, early modern race scholars, for our part, *study* these plays and have no interest in removing them from cultural life. But we cannot disentangle the knot if we keep vacillating between stances that exonerate Shakespeare or ourselves. There is no smooth story of "progress," in which racist attitudes slowly and mysteriously – but inevitably – yield to enlightenment and egalitarianism. Shakespeare does not offer the color-blind perspective toward which some mistakenly aspire, nor does his work represent a form of race talk that our own social order has entirely shed. I say so because the structuring effects of racism are not in individual beliefs but in routinized maldistribution of social goods and harms. This distribution may be carried out with or without malice; hatred is not a necessary component. In fact, it can even be compatible with feelings of great attachment and affection to one's racial subordinates, if they (like Caliban) abandon their quests for sovereignty and "seek for grace."

The issue before us when we consider progress against racism is not one of attitudes or beliefs (ours or Shakespeare's).[41] The challenge before us has to do with *decisions* we make together about how we determine who lives or dies, who is believed and who discredited, whose reputation we protect and whose we disregard, whom we hold culpable and whose faults we condone. Racism is not only the set of elaborate justifications for inequality but the preconditions for them. Thus, the final question for every teacher, actor, reader, producer, and director is: What are we going to do with Shakespeare's plays? They may not be the inheritance all of us would have chosen (in their promise and their blind spots) but, like history and the future, they are now in our hands.

Notes

1 Odai Johnson, *Absence and Memory in Colonial American Theatre: Fiorelli's Plaster* (New York: Palgrave Macmillan, 2006).
2 Reprinted in William T. Hastings, "Shakespeare in Providence," *Shakespeare Quarterly* 8/3 (Summer 1957): 335–51 (at 336–37).
3 Woody Holton, *Abigail Adams* (New York: Simon & Schuster, 2009), 225.
4 Lindsey R. Swindall, *The Politics of Paul Robeson's Othello* (Jackson: University Press of Mississippi, 2010), 28.
5 Paul Robeson, *Paul Robeson Speaks: Writings, Speeches, and Interviews. A Centennial Celebration*, ed. Philip S. Foner (New York: Citadel Press, 1978), 152.
6 Swindall, 34.
7 Martin Duberman, *Paul Robeson: A Biography* (New York: Open Road Media, 2014), 233–34.

8 All comments from the "Playing Othello" panel at the "Shakespeare & Race Festival" at Shakespeare's Globe, 17 August 2018.

9 This view of *Hamlet* was not always ascendant. See Margreta de Grazia, "Hamlet's Thoughts and Antics," *Early Modern Culture* 2 (2001), www .earlymodernengland.com/2010/02/hamlets-thoughts-and-antics;   Margreta de Grazia, "When Did Hamlet Become Modern?," *Textual Practice* 17/3 (2003): 485–503.

10 Dympna Callaghan, *Shakespeare without Women: Representing Gender and Race on the Renaissance Stage* (New York: Routledge, 2000). Africans did appear in presentational roles, which is to say they appeared in parades and even as musicians, but not as actors playing characters. See Anthony Gerard Barthelemy, *Black Face, Maligned Race: The Representation of Blacks in English Drama from Shakespeare to Southerne* (Baton Rouge: Louisiana State University Press, 1987), chap. 3; Matthieu A Chapman, "The Appearance of Blacks on the Early Modern Stage: *Love's Labour's Lost's* African Connections to Court," *Early Theatre* 17/2 (September 2014): 77–94.

11 Barthelemy, 47.

12 Kim F. Hall, *Things of Darkness: Economies of Race and Gender in Early Modern England* (Ithaca, NY: Cornell University Press, 1995), chap. 5.

13 Mark Thornton Burnett, *Masters and Servants in English Renaissance Drama and Culture: Authority and Obedience* (New York: St. Martin's Press, 1997); Elizabeth Rivlin, "Service and Servants in Early Modern English Culture to 1660," *Journal of Early Modern Studies* 4 (2015): 17–41.

14 For exceptions, see Clare McManus, "Women and English Renaissance Drama: Making and Unmaking 'The All-Male Stage,'" *Literature Compass* 4/3 (2007): 784–96; Clare McManus, "Early Modern Women's Performance: Toward a New History of Early Modern Theater?," *Shakespeare Studies* 37 (January 2009): 161–77 (at 161); Natasha Korda, *Labors Lost: Women's Work and the Early Modern English Stage* (Philadelphia: University of Pennsylvania Press, 2011).

15 First quoted in Latin in Geoffrey Tillotson, "Othello and The Alchemist at Oxford in 1610," *Times Literary Supplement*, 20 July 1933. The original Latin text, as well as the English translation used here, is from the *Riverside Shakespeare*, ed. G. Blakemore Evans (Boston: Houghton Mifflin, 1974), 1852.

16 Thomas Rymer, *A Short View of Tragedy* (London, 1693), in *The Critical Works of Thomas Rymer*, ed. Curt Zimansky (New Haven, CT: Yale University Press, 1956), 143.

17 Rymer, 91–92.

18 John Quincy Adams, "Misconceptions of Shakspeare upon the Stage," *New-England Magazine* 9 (1835): 435–40 (439).

19 Adams, 438.

20 Ignatius Sancho, *Letters of the Late Ignatious Sancho: An African, to Which Is Prefixed, Memoirs of His Life*, ed. Joseph Jekyll (London: J. Nichols, 1782).

21 Quoted in Mythili Kaul, "Background: Black or Tawny? Stage Representations of Othello from 1604 to the Present," in *Othello: New*

Essays by Black Writers, ed. Mythili Kaul (Washington, DC: Howard University Press, 1997), 5.

22 Robert Hornback, *Racism and Early Blackface Comic Traditions: From the Old World to the New* (Cham: Palgrave Macmillan, 2018), 37.

23 John Nichols, *Biographical Anecdotes of William Hogarth; With a Catalogue of His Works Chronologically Arranged; and Occasional Remarks*, 2nd edn (London: Printed by and for J. Nichols, 1782), 161–62.

24 "The Great Sir Laurence," *LIFE Magazine*, 1 May 1964; Laurence Olivier, *On Acting* (New York: Simon & Schuster, 1987); Andrea Stevens, *Inventions of the Skin: The Painted Body in Early English Drama, 1400–1642* (Edinburgh University Press, 2013), 87–88.

25 Roger Mitchell, *Tea With the Dames*, DVD, 2018. See also Julie Miller, "Maggie Smith Had No Patience for Laurence Olivier's Diva Antics," *Vanity Fair*, 25 September 2018, www.vanityfair.com/hollywood/2018/09/maggie-smith-laurence-olivier-othello-tea-with-the-dames-joan-plowright-judi-dench-eileen-atkins (accessed 11 November 2019).

26 Charles Mathews, quoted in Marvin Edward McAllister, *White People Do Not Know How to Behave at Entertainments Designed for Ladies & Gentlemen of Colour: William Brown's African & American Theater* (Chapel Hill: University of North Carolina Press, 2003), 158–59.

27 John Kani and Virginia Crompton, *Apartheid and Othello* (London: British Council, 2016), 5.

28 Kani and Crompton, 7.

29 Kani and Crompton, 7.

30 Kani and Crompton, 7.

31 Kani and Crompton, 6.

32 Howard Taubman, "Theater: 'Othello' in Park; James Earl Jones Is Cast as the Moor," *New York Times*, 15 July 1964, 29; Lewis Funke, "The Theater: 'Othello' from the Park; Festival Production Is at the Martinique; Title Role Repeated by James Earl Jones," *New York Times*, 13 October 1964.

33 "James Earl Jones Performs Shakespeare's "Othello" at the White House Poetry Jam (2009)," 2012, www.youtube.com/watch?v=DJybA1emr_g .

34 Richard Dyer, *Heavenly Bodies: Film Stars and Society*, 2nd edn (New York: Routledge, 2003), 2–3.

35 Eve Rachele Sanders, *Gender and Literacy on Stage in Early Modern England* (Cambridge University Press, 1998), chap. 3; Joyce Green MacDonald, *Women and Race in Early Modern Texts* (Cambridge University Press, 2002), 47; Pascale Aebischer, "The Properties of Whiteness: Renaissance Cleopatras from Jodelle to Shakespeare," *Shakespeare Survey* 65 (2012): 221–38; Francesca Royster, *Becoming Cleopatra: The Shifting Image of an Icon* (New York: Palgrave Macmillan, 2003).

36 Hortense Spillers, "Mama's Baby, Papa's Maybe: An American Grammar Book," *Diacritics* 17/2 (Summer 1987): 64–81.

37 Kate Kellaway, "Antony and Cleopatra Review – Josette Simon Is a Cleopatra to Die For," *Observer*, 2 April 2017.

38 Ayanna Thompson, *Passing Strange: Shakespeare, Race, and Contemporary America* (Oxford University Press, 2011), 116.

39 Leslie A. Fiedler, *The Stranger in Shakespeare* (New York: Stein and Day, 1972).

40 Hall, *Things of Darkness*; Arthur L. Little, Jr., *Shakespeare Jungle Fever: National-Imperial Re-Visions of Race, Rape, and Sacrifice* (Stanford University Press, 2000); MacDonald, *Women and Race*; Ayanna Thompson, "The Blackfaced Bard: Returning to Shakespeare or Leaving Him?," *Shakespeare Bulletin* 27.3 (2009): 437–56; Ian Smith, *Race and Rhetoric in the Renaissance: Barbarian Errors* (New York and Basingstoke: Palgrave Macmillan, 2009); Sujata Iyengar, *Shades of Difference: Mythologies of Skin Color in Early Modern England* (Philadelphia: University of Pennsylvania Press, 2005); Royster, *Becoming Cleopatra*; Patricia Akhimie, *Shakespeare and the Cultivation of Difference: Race and Conduct in the Early Modern World* (New York and London: Routledge, 2018).

41 Michelle Alexander, *The New Jim Crow: Mass Incarceration in the Age of Colorblindness* (New York: New Press, 2010); Devon W. Carbado, "Colorblind Intersectionality," *Signs: Journal of Women in Culture & Society* 38/4 (Summer 2013): 811–45; Eduardo Bonilla-Silva, *Racism without Racists: Color-Blind Racism and the Persistence of Racial Inequality in America* (Lanham, MD: Rowman & Littlefield, 2006).

CHAPTER 17

How Have Post-Colonial Approaches Enriched Shakespeare's Works?

Sandra Young

University of Cape Town

Shakespeare's plays are first and foremost creatures of the stage. They come into being afresh with each new production and even each individual staging. To reimagine a play is not a question of betraying the text but is a core part of the process of making meaning, as actors and directors seek to figure out what is at stake when a familiar play is brought to life for a contemporary audience. To reimagine the play for each new staging *is* to be "true" to the art.[1] It is also inevitable that each staging will reflect in some way its own historical moment. Productions that are attuned to the politics of a new moment have helped to shift the cultural meanings attributed to Shakespeare. New interpretations have allowed twenty-first-century Shakespeare to participate in the robust critique of the powerful and to become aligned with global movements for social change. Shakespeare, too, has had to reckon with the imperatives of contemporary movements calling for social justice such as #MeToo and #BlackLivesMatter. The commitments and creativity of contemporary theatre-makers have produced some compelling new interpretations of familiar works, as well they should.

Shakespeare's plays continue to be shaped by their historical moment and their performance histories. The impact of the new social movements on what Shakespeare's plays are understood to mean is not a new phenomenon. This refiguring of the meanings of the plays, through innovative staging and through scholarship that privileges the perspectives of the least empowered, has a longer history. As the movements against colonization gained momentum across the Global South – that is, in many parts of Africa, South Asia, and the Caribbean – in the middle of the twentieth century, Shakespeare's plays were marshaled to an anti-colonial purpose. Radical scholars and intellectuals located away from the "traditional" locations associated with Shakespeare began to reinterpret the works, using critical analysis of Shakespeare's language to underscore its subversive effects. Paradoxically, as works that had been exported as part of an imperial canon of British literature and widely taught in the British colonies, many of Shakespeare's plays were familiar in contexts of anti-colonial struggle. The plays' treatment of power and its discontents made them fair game for politically engaged scholarship, whether the plays were imagined as sympathetic to the anti-colonial movements or as part of an old cultural and political order that needed reimagining, or as a combination of both.

This was especially true of the play that most directly addresses itself to the phenomenon of colonization and its disturbing excesses, *The Tempest*. As Rob Nixon has explained, anti-colonial movements in Africa and the Caribbean "adopted the play as a founding text in an oppositional lineage."[2] For some writers, the play had to be reimagined and appropriated, before it could be celebrated and claimed for the anti-colonial movement: "through repeated, reinforcing, transgressive appropriations of *The Tempest*, a once silenced group generated its own tradition," forever changing the meanings associated with the play and demonstrating that meaning is unstable and subject to the vagaries of history.[3] A good example of this kind of anti-colonialist appropriation and deliberate revision is the 1969 play, titled in the English translation as *A Tempest*, which was written in French by Aimé Césaire, a writer born in Martinique and one of the founders of the intellectual movement, Négritude.[4] *A Tempest* refused the possibility of restoration that Shakespeare's play seemed to affirm in its final scenes. Césaire's play also stages Caliban's resistance more explicitly, not least of all in Caliban's refusal of the name Prospero imposes on him and in his clearly articulated challenge to Prospero's bullying. For Césaire, Shakespeare's play needed to be completely overhauled if it was to expose colonial violence and catalyze anti-colonial resistance. Césaire's rewriting is well known, but there have been others, such as the Cuban play, *Otra Tempestad*, by Raquel Carrió and Flora Lauten, which imagines encounters between Shakespeare's characters and figures of African mythology, such as Oshún, queen of the rivers.[5] For Carrió the twenty-first century calls for a new way of approaching the contest between colonizer and colonized, one in which a third culture can be imagined and the complex interweaving of cultures in a more mobile world acknowledged.[6]

Even without consciously rewriting Shakespeare's plays to put them more directly in conversation with contemporary global politics, the meanings of Shakespeare's work could be said to have evolved with the passage of time. Certainly, anti-colonial resistance in Africa and the Caribbean, and the related intellectual movements, have changed the interpretative environment so much that even Shakespeare's *The Tempest* reads differently today. A reader or theatregoer, fortified with the critical vocabulary and concerns foregrounded in a post-colonial framework, is likely to notice that, even in Shakespeare's version of Caliban's story, the myth of the uninhabited island is no longer convincing, and the question of sovereignty is a matter of debate.[7]

Anti-Colonial Liberation and the Work of Interpretation

Given the impact of post-colonialist thought, it is no longer possible to interpret uncritically the entanglements and betrayals that unfold on the island, not without showing oneself to be in sympathy with the colonizer. This was not always so. Older editions of *The Tempest* tended to interpret the play in sympathy with Prospero, presenting this interpretation as though it were neutral and justified and not, in itself, influenced by politics (of a conservative sort). For example, in the 1958 Arden Shakespeare edition of the play, the editor Frank Kermode casts aspersions on Caliban's offer of service to Trinculo and Stephano in Act 2, scene 2. Caliban's promise, "I'll show thee every fertile inch o'th'island . . . I'll show thee the best springs; I'll pluck thee berries; / I'll fish for thee and get thee wood enough" (2.2.154, 166–67) is glossed in a manner that reveals the editor's alignment with the perspective of the colonizer: "The colonists were frequently received with this kindness, though treachery might follow."[8] By interpreting the resistance of the colonized as "treachery," Kermode betrays his sympathy for the colonizer and assumes that the reader will be similarly aligned. In this example we see the influence of editors in guiding the interpretative process and introducing the ideological bias that reflects the publication's historical moment. Interpretation is a function of history, at least in part. The meanings attributed to this play at any given moment, as with other works of literature, are in part the result of the historical moment within which the play is being read or performed. Whether one recognizes it or not, how one interprets a play will be influenced by one's own position and politics.

Thanks in part to the lessons gained from anti-colonial resistance movements and the intellectual ideas that grew out of them, scholars are no longer likely to treat a text's meanings as self-evident and certain, as if the work of interpretation is simply a matter of excavating down to the bedrock of "true" meaning. Literary scholarship has begun to concern itself with the contestations of history as they manifest in creative works as well as in the work of scholarship itself.[9] It has become important to recognize that scholarship, too, is a product of its time, and needs to be subjected to the same kind of critical scrutiny and interpretation that one would expect to apply to primary texts. Post-colonial theory has taught us to notice some of the ways that language and creative work help to reinforce social hierarchies and secure the interests of the powerful. The work of critical analysis enables us to see what is hidden behind the magic of word craft, and to unpack how these constructions work and which interests they serve.

In the decades that followed, the impact of the anti-colonial movements on cultural forms was profound. New ideas that were responsive to the new political moment began to flourish in creative and scholarly writings. This was not only a matter of making space for a wider range of subjects, so that the experiences of the dispossessed and marginalized became visible within new literary and cultural works. It was also a question of how the works, new and old, were interpreted. That is to say, it wasn't only a matter of new *content* but also of new *methodologies* with which to interpret all literature, new and old, making it possible to recognize the racist, colonialist assumptions undergirding the appraisal of literature.

Shakespeare's plays have had to reckon with this movement and the new critical perspectives on canonical culture it has fostered. In particular, the dominance of an idea of highbrow "Englishness" with which Shakespeare has tended to be associated, historically, has been scrutinized, its ideological interests and mythologies exposed. But the critical insights and politically attuned analyses that have emerged with post-colonial studies have also helped to free Shakespeare from that association with ideas of "Englishness." Post-colonial historical analysis has made it possible to recognize that this association between Shakespeare and highbrow "Englishness" resulted in part from the ideological maneuvering of colonial administrations who turned Shakespeare into the epitome of the supposedly "superior" cultural accomplishment attributed to "Englishness," in an act of cultural warfare.[10] The recognition of the way that Shakespeare's plays were deliberately marshaled in service of these colonialist objectives and disseminated across the British Empire, along with other elements of canonical English literature, releases Shakespeare's work and makes it available for a new, more resistant moment.

Resistance to colonialism and the new scholarly approaches it inspired have freed Shakespeare and his works from a colonialist interpretative frame and have denied the kind of exceptionalism that treated Shakespeare as a special case, as though he were able to speak for all people across all ages, even as his work is used to bolster the claims of homogeneous, white, Anglocentric forms of culture. Instead, post-colonial approaches to Shakespeare have exposed the impact of political and historical context on literary interpretation and trained us all to examine the partisan assumptions underpinning the workings of language and culture. Post-colonial studies have insisted that Shakespeare, too, be understood as a product of his time, which has enabled us to recognize his plays' engagement with their own early imperial moment and the attitudes to race, gender, and class that were evolving in early modernity.

Post-Colonialist Thought and Its Impact on Shakespeare

So how, then, do post-colonial theorists help us think critically about power and language? New attention to questions of power and privilege, from the perspective of the marginalized, have made it all the more possible for the work of literary and cultural studies to engage with concerns of social justice and with the inequities that follow from the discourses of racialization entrenched through colonialism. Even the simplest methodology can disarm dominant strands of interpretation, for example by paying attention to the "spin" surrounding ideas, protecting them from further scrutiny, and creating the impression that they are true for all time. A resistant reader can intervene effectively by drawing attention to the rhetorical effects that work to create certain truisms. Armed with an eagle eye and the skepticism that refuses to accept ideas as unbiased, a reader might notice a text's dependence on pejorative assumptions and recognize that the language used privileges a particular group's interests. Far from being "universal," even the most seemingly neutral ideas emerge from a particular set of circumstances and histories. The place and time that give rise to ideas become part of their weight and meaning, and therefore available to be analyzed. Shakespeare's supposed universalism has been irredeemably called into question and the supposedly "universal" human subject he was said to embody has been exposed as modeled on a very particular subjectivity (white, male, privileged, Western) under the scrutiny of post-colonial studies.[11]

Post-colonial intellectuals have developed analytical tools with which to identify and explain the mechanisms that establish unjust hierarchies within a social system. Within these hierarchies some are marked as unworthy or somehow "inferior" within a system of meaning that appears to be beyond question and supposedly verified with reference to nature or biology. When scrutinized, however, these hierarchies are evidently mere ideas, or constructs, that serve the interests of the dominant classes. These ideas only become vivid and seemingly "true" because of the connections established and reinforced through the knowledge practices of the sciences and through the imaginative work of language and art. This is how the invention of the idea of the "Orient" as alluringly exotic but essentially inferior to the "Occident" took hold, a process that Edward Said explicated in his field-defining book, *Orientalism.*[12] Said explains the usefulness of Michel Foucault's notion of "discourse" as a vector of power and his conviction that "without examining Orientalism as a discourse one cannot possibly understand the enormously systematic discipline by which European culture was able to manage – and even produce – the Orient politically, sociologically, militarily, ideologically, scientifically, and imaginatively during the post-Enlightenment period."[13] As Said has shown, the idea of "the Orient" develops in relation to its supposed opposite, the West, which is necessarily in a dominant position of power: through Orientalist discourse, "European culture gained in strength and identity by setting itself off against the Orient as a sort of surrogate and even underground self."[14] The "idea of Europe" is an invention, operating in tandem to the myth of "the Orient," as "a collective notion identifying 'us' Europeans as against all 'those' non-Europeans" within a hierarchy that entrenches "the idea of European identity as a superior one in comparison with all the non-European peoples and cultures."[15]

Said's compelling critique of the colonialist power dynamic operating through and within Orientalist cultural forms has been shown to function, similarly, in relation to other colonized regions, such as Africa. In his influential study, *The Invention of Africa,* V.Y. Mudimbe unmasks the ways Africa was "invented" as a compelling idea that served colonialist regimes and made their global supremacy seem inevitable. Mudimbe's analysis exposes the ways that scientific thought, historically, as well as cultural discourses, placed Africa in an adverse position through racist ideologies of difference.[16] Natural historical systems, Mudimbe argued, "defined an ascending path from savagery to commercial societies" and fixed "non-Western marginality" into that hierarchy.[17] The critical work of literary studies enables us to track how language works to fix blackness to an inimical position within a pernicious, invented hierarchy of difference and render whiteness so normative it appears invisible. When subject to critical analysis, any veneer of scientific legitimacy those racist ideologies may seem to present immediately dissolves. In his essay on "New Ethnicities," Stuart Hall makes the link between racism and the dualistic thinking underlying supposedly "scientific" taxonomies that invokes paired concepts like "savage" versus "civilized" and maps them onto differentiated bodies: "Racism, of course, operates by constructing impassable symbolic boundaries between

racially constituted categories, and its typically binary system of representation constantly marks and attempts to fix and naturalize the difference
between belongingness and otherness."[18] Colonized bodies are marked as
"other" within a network of meanings that are mutually reinforcing. These
ideas are hard to refute without the powerful tools of critical analysis that can
identify the workings of imperialism and colonialism in the racist ideologies
and economic inequalities that linger long after colonialist governments have
abandoned their posts. Post-colonial critical methodologies expose the spu-
riousness of the racist logic that seemed to legitimize colonial domination.

Exposing Coloniality's Self-Justifications: The Example
of *The Tempest*

Post-colonialism has drawn attention to the deceptions of language and
alerted us to the ways that colonialist discourse, and the racist ideologies it
entrenches, legitimize the violence of colonial conquest. Scholars working
with the conceptual framework of post-colonial studies have made it possible
to recognize how language justifies that violence, recasting it as the restoration of rightful order in the face of indigenous hostility. They have also been
able to identify cracks in the edifice of colonialist self-justification and
recognize the disturbances that point to the anxieties that accompany colonial
abuse of power. Francis Barker and Peter Hulme find in Prospero's reiteration of his story about his own experience of having his dukedom usurped
and his fury in the face of Caliban's tale of dispossession ("This island's mine,
by Sycorax my mother, / Which thou takest from me," 1.2.334–35) evidence
of colonialist anxiety about colonialism's dependence on illegitimate violence,
even as it leans on the story of native violence: "Colonialist legitimation has
always had then to go on to tell its own story, inevitably one of native
violence."[19] This anxiety is evident in Prospero's persistent attempt to control
the narrative: in Act 1, scene 2, he repeatedly exhorts his listeners (Miranda,
Ariel, and then Caliban, in turn) to *pay attention* to his narrative: he
repeatedly exhorts Miranda to, "ope thine ear. / Obey, and be attentive"
(1.2.37–38); "I pray thee mark me" (1.2.67); "Thou attend'st not" (1.2.87);
and, again, this time with an emphasizing pause, "I pray thee, mark me"
(1.2.88); "Dost thou hear?" (1.2.106); "Hear a little further" (1.2.135).
Prospero's power derives from his story of "liberating" Ariel from torment:
"I must / Once in a month recount what thou hast been, / Which thou
forget'st" (1.2.263–64). Through the continual reiteration of his account of
their history, Prospero keeps alive a memory that serves to justify his ongoing
coercion and perpetuate Ariel's indebtedness to him.

The particular violence of this strategy lies not only in the forcefulness and abusiveness of the language used, such as "Thou liest, malignant thing!" (1.2.257) and "Dull thing, I say so" (1.2.286), but also in its refusal to acknowledge its own tyranny. For even as it produces fear and distress, Prospero's narrative masquerades as an account of his goodness and of his role as liberator: "Dost thou forget / From what a torment I did free thee?" (1.2.250–51) and "it was mine art, / When I arrived and heard thee, that made gape / The pine and let thee out" (1.2.292–94). Simply through the recounting of this narrative and the reminder that he could reverse the events, Prospero secures Ariel's continued compliance: "Pardon, master; / I will be correspondent to command" (1.2.297–98).

The play allows us to see how self-serving and partisan Prospero's jaundiced characterization of Caliban is. We see his attempt to reproduce the stereotype of the "wild man" as well as Caliban's complication of that stereotype. The play invokes it, then repudiates it, and ultimately unsettles it altogether by exposing it as a partisan idea rather than a reflection of reality. When Prospero describes Caliban in terms that make him more animal than human, Ariel's simple response signals a refusal of Prospero's vocabulary while acknowledging Prospero's meaning:

PROSPERO   Then was this island –
    Save for the son that she did litter here,
    A freckled whelp hag-born – not honour'd with
    A human shape.
ARIEL   Yes, Caliban her son.

                                    (1.2.282–85)

When Caliban emerges, however, his humanity is evident in his articulate command of language. Though his words carry curses and angry protest, they also present a convincing counter-narrative that Prospero is forced, in turn, to repudiate in a dance that contradicts the feigned coherence of Prospero's story and his self-serving performance of altruism. What's more, Caliban's acuity – his sharp analysis of the operations of power that play out in the island's small, embattled society – bring to our attention Prospero's utter reliance on his maligned subject for his own display of dominion: "For I am all the subjects that you have, / Which first was mine own king" (1.2.344–45).

The conflict-ridden tussle between the irascible colonizer and the resistant islander is not a straightforward matter. The islander is racialized and rendered barely human through the colonizer's lexicon, but his resistance has a destabilizing effect on the colonizer's veneer of reason and humanity. Paul Brown has drawn on Homi Bhabha's critique of Said to argue that the colonialist stereotype of the racialized "other," as explicated by Said, is a more complex phenomenon than is immediately apparent, because the stereotype of the exoticized "other" is neither secure nor stable. The "other" has to be continually produced as rebellious, in order to justify colonial violence. However, this resistance puts the colonizer's self-justifying show of calm and "civility" at risk and brings into view the possibility of a counter-narrative. The stereotype of the resistant "other" is thus not entirely useful for the colonialist: as Brown explains, "at the heart of the stereotype, a discursive strategy designed to locate or 'fix' a colonial other in a position of inferiority to the colonizer, the potentiality of a disruptive threat must be admitted."[20] For Brown the figure of Caliban is a classic case in point: "Ostensibly *produced* as an other to provide the pretext for the exercise of naked power, [Caliban] is also a *producer*, provoking reaction in the master. He does not come when called, which makes Prospero angry (1.2.315–22). Then he greets the colonizers with a curse, provoking the master to curse in reply, reducing the eloquent master of civil language to the raucous registers of the other (1.2.323–32)."[21]

These insights into the coercive and manipulative workings of colonial power make it impossible to take Prospero's self-justifying narratives at face value. They even allow us to see reason in Caliban's most threatening and discomfiting behaviors within the space of the colonial confrontation (his curses and fulminations, his murder plot, and even his fantasy of populating the isle with little Calibans, which by the time we hear of it appears to be a threat of rape). Earlier approaches tended to take at face value Prospero's denunciations of Caliban and read the play as a celebration of social order, privileging the ending's apparent resolution rather than the disquiet, disruption, and contestation in evidence through much of the play. Generations of influential scholars were blind to the political questions posed within the works: in the early nineteenth century Samuel Coleridge found in Shakespeare's plays an "organic regularity" derived from Shakespeare's intrinsic and "genius" knowledge of humankind.[22] At the start of the twentieth century, A.C. Bradley's critical approach to Shakespeare's plays involved honing in on the "recognizable psychology of character," as Emma Smith explains, as though individual characters could be examined apart from the social dynamic in which they operated, free from questions of politics and power.[23] In the 1940s E.M.W. Tillyard read Shakespeare's plays as celebrating an essentially harmonious, stable, regimented social order, reflecting what he called the "Elizabethan world picture," a worldview in which social hierarchies were understood to be ordained by God and nature.[24] Tillyard interprets Prospero as being committed to the re-establishment of a good and natural order, evaluating other characters in terms of their alignment with this order.[25]

This co-option of Shakespeare into a conservative agenda lingered for decades, even as the mid-century anti-colonial movements began to contest these readings. In the 1958 Arden edition of *The Tempest* one can see the impact of an uncritical framework, presented as though it were objective and authoritative. The editor, Frank Kermode, foregrounds the "buds of a nobler race" and the "magic of nobility," in language lifted out of context from the play itself as if they were neutral terms of study and not contested ideas that privilege the ideological biases of the colonialists. Kermode's input demonstrates the almost imperceptible influence of editors in shaping the reception of texts and the meanings ascribed to them.

But while Kermode uncritically adopted a one-sided reading of the play without recognizing how his interpretation betrayed its alignment with the privileged and powerful in the text, new perspectives on *The Tempest* and its scene of colonial contestation were beginning to circulate. In 1950, Octave Mannoni used the contest between Prospero and Caliban as a case study in his critical account of the fraught psychology at work in the colonial encounter.[26] Anti-colonial intellectuals like Frantz Fanon later took issue with Mannoni's focus on what he called "unconscious complexes" and his use of Freud's Oedipal theories to explain the damaging colonial dynamic (Mannoni explains Caliban's condition in terms of a "dependence complex," for example), because this approach obscured social injustice and the material effects of colonial conquest.[27] Even so, Mannoni's work set in place an interpretative framework that took due cognizance of colonial abuse of power and its underlying racism, and catalyzed a proliferation of critical insights into the play's preoccupation with the damaging impacts of colonization.[28] For the Cuban intellectual, Roberto Fernández Retamar, the figure of Caliban best encompasses the situation of the dispossessed: "I know of no other metaphor more expressive of our cultural situation, of our reality . . . what is our history, what is our culture, if not the history and culture of Caliban."[29] What these anti-colonial intellectuals see in Shakespeare's work is a far cry from the earlier generations of literary scholars who laid claim to Shakespeare on behalf of elite cultures.

Post-Colonialism: Liberating Shakespeare?

Responses to Shakespeare that are attuned to colonial abuses of power and committed to anti-colonial movements have thus had a profound impact on what Shakespeare's works are understood to mean. This is still felt today: post-colonial responses have invigorated Shakespeare's works and equipped theatregoers and literary scholars with important new interpretative tools with which to recognize and explode the deceptions that would seem to legitimize colonialist oppression. Post-colonial approaches to Shakespeare have enriched the works themselves and fostered critical insights into the racializations at work on Shakespearean stages across the centuries.

This is not only a matter of theory, but also a matter of performance. Contemporary theatre-makers attuned to racial injustice have been able to invite audiences to bear witness to the workings of racism. Bold and inventive contemporary performances have exploited the capacity for subversion in Shakespeare's work. Many artists have found it freeing and empowering to appropriate Shakespeare's works, and the effect of this has been to imagine the possibility of a Shakespeare who is liberated from misogyny, racism, and colonial abuses.

For example, in 2009 in a joint production by the Royal Shakespeare Company and the Baxter Theatre in Cape Town, South Africa, Caliban was imagined as a Nelson Mandela-like figure, played with dignity by veteran actor John Kani; Prospero was an irascible and disheveled patriarch whose verbal abuse of Caliban revealed nothing so much as his own bigotry. This staging drew attention not only to colonial oppression but also to the racial injustice that derives from colonialism's structures of power, by situating it within the context of South African racial stratification and invoking the post-apartheid preoccupation with forgiveness and healing.[30]

The many ways that Shakespeare's work has travelled, and continues to travel, around the world have left it much changed and have allowed for an explosion in new interpretations and new performances. The visibility of more diverse lives and experiences is significant not only for its richness but also for the decentering of mainstream cultural forms. Perhaps even more importantly, Shakespeare's travels have helped to enable critical perspectives on power and injustice.

Interpreting Shakespeare: "are you on the boat or on the shore?"

In confronting us with the entanglements and betrayals at the heart of Caliban's story, *The Tempest* bears witness to the troubling history of colonization and invites us to reflect on our own position in relation to that history. This may mean making a choice about our perspective on historical injustice, as Laurent DuBois has argued in an address to scholars of history:

> At the basis of every work of history is a question of positioning. This is also, on some level, an ethical question. Whose history are you telling? And from whose perspective? As the Haitian thinker Jean Casimir likes to put it, when you write the story of Columbus arriving in what the indigenous people then called Ayiti, you have to make a decision: are you on the boat or on the shore?[31]

The work of criticism and of theatre-making arguably confronts us with the same question: "are you on the boat or on the shore?" Whose perspective is brought into view and given credence by the work of the critic? If DuBois is right, it is not possible to sit on the fence. Any attempt to present a "neutral" reading will simply expose the critic's blindness to the ways their interpretations are influenced by unacknowledged biases.

In the case of a play like *The Tempest* the antagonism between the interests of the colonizers and those whose lands are invaded manifests especially clearly as it plays out in the battle between Caliban and Prospero: This is Shakespeare's subject. As a work of the *theatre* rather than the campaign trail or the pulpit, the play's meanings are a matter of interpretation rather than didactic intent. It requires careful, critical attention as we listen in to the conversations onstage and watch the dynamics between characters unfold. This is true for all of Shakespeare's work, even when colonial injustice is not directly in focus. Post-colonial studies teaches us that the opportunity to attend to the vulnerabilities of the disempowered is available to scholars and audiences of every work, not only of a work that addresses itself so explicitly to the contestations that emerge with colonial conquest. Any number of Shakespeare's plays will reward an interpretative commitment to considering the position of the disempowered.

Post-colonial methodologies have liberating implications for Shakespeare's plays as sites of cultural imagining and have allowed Shakespeare's work to become an ally in the struggle against racist abuse of power. At their best, post-colonial approaches do more than simply enrich and diversify the creative palette available to theatre-makers and their audiences. They provide the tools and the vocabulary to confront the operations of power and privilege and affirm the possibility of a more just world.

Notes

1 See Margaret Jane Kidnie, *Shakespeare and the Problem of Adaptation* (New York: Routledge, 2009).

2 Rob Nixon, "Caribbean and African Appropriations of 'The Tempest,'" *Critical Inquiry* 13/3 (Spring 1987): 557–78 (at 558).

3 Nixon, 558.

4 Aimé Césaire, *A Tempest*, trans. Richard Miller (New York: Ubu Repertory Theater Publications, 1969).

5 For an account of her play, see Raquel Carrió, "On *Otra Tempestad*," trans. Peter Hulme, in *"The Tempest" and Its Travels*, ed. Peter Hulme and William H. Sherman (London: Reaktion, 2000), 157–61.

6 Carrió, 159.

7 See Ania Loomba, *Shakespeare, Race, and Colonialism* (Oxford University Press, 2002).

8 *The Tempest*, ed. Frank Kermode, Arden Second Series (London: Methuen, 1958), 67n148.

9 See Francis Barker and Peter Hulme, "Nymphs and Reapers Heavily Vanish: The Discursive Contexts of *The Tempest*," in *Alternative Shakespeares*, ed. John Drakakis (London: Methuen, 1985), 191–205.

10 Gauri Viswanathan, *Masks of Conquest: Literary Study and British Rule in India* (New York: Columbia University Press, 1989).

11 Ayanna Thompson, *Passing Strange: Shakespeare, Race, and Contemporary America* (Oxford University Press, 2011).

12 Edward Said, *Orientalism* (Harmondsworth: Penguin, 1995).

13 Said, 3.

14 Said, 3.

15 Said, 7.

16 See V.Y. Mudimbe, *The Invention of Africa: Gnosis, Philosophy, and the Order of Knowledge* (Bloomington: Indiana University Press, 1988).

17 Said, 6.

18 Stuart Hall, "New Ethnicities," in Hall, *Critical Dialogues in Cultural Studies*, ed. David Morley and Kuan-Hsing Chen (New York and London: Routledge, 1996), 442–51 (at 445).

19 Barker and Hulme, 201.

20 Paul Brown, "'This thing of darkness I acknowledge mine': *The Tempest* and the Discourse of Colonialism," in *Political Shakespeare: New Essays in Cultural Materialism*, ed. Jonathan Dollimore and Alan Sinfield (Manchester University Press, 1985), 48–71 (at 58).

21 Brown, 61.

22 Samuel Taylor Coleridge, *Shakespearean Criticism*, ed. Thomas Middleton Raysor (London: Dent; New York: Dutton, 1960), 198, 197.

23 See A.C. Bradley, *Shakespearean Tragedy* (London: Macmillan, 1904); and Emma Smith, "The Critical Reception of Shakespeare," in *The New Cambridge Critical Companion to Shakespeare*, ed. Margreta de Grazia and Stanley Wells (Cambridge University Press, 2010), 253–68 (at 259).

24 See E.M.W. Tillyard, *The Elizabethan World Picture: A Study of the Idea of Order in the Age of Shakespeare, Donne and Milton* (London: Chatto & Windus, 1943).

25 See E.M.W. Tillyard, *Shakespeare's Last Plays* (London: Bloomsbury, 2013).

26 First published in French in 1950 as *Psychologie de la colonization*, Octave Mannoni's study of the play appeared in translation as *Prospero and Caliban: The Psychology of Colonization*, trans. Pamela Powesland (London: Methuen, 1956).

27 Mannoni, 361. See Frantz Fanon, *Black Skin, White Masks*, trans. Charles Lam Markmann (Sidmouth: Pluto Press, 1967).

28 See, for example, George Lamming, "A Monster, a Child, a Slave," in Lamming, *The Pleasures of Exile* (Ann Arbor: University of Michigan Press, 1960); and Frantz Fanon, *The Wretched of the Earth*, trans. Richard Philcox (New York: Grove Press, 2004).

29 Roberto Fernández Retamar, *Caliban and Other Essays*, trans. Edward Baker (Minneapolis: University of Minnesota Press, 1989), 14.

30 For a more detailed discussion of this production, see Sandra Young, *Shakespeare in the Global South: Stories of Oceans Crossed in Contemporary Adaptation* (London: Bloomsbury, 2019), 85–90.

31 Laurent DuBois, "Atlantic Freedoms," *Aeon*, https://aeon.co/essays/why-haiti-should-be-at-the-centre-of-the-age-of-revolution (accessed 15 November 2019).

CHAPTER 18

Is It Possible to Read Shakespeare through Critical White Studies?

Arthur L. Little Jr

University of California, Los Angeles

Shakespeare critical race scholarship remains committed to understanding the raison d'être of the black (and blackened) others who grace the pages of Shakespeare: Aaron, Aaron's son, "Blackamoors with music," Caliban, Cleopatra, the Dark Lady (perhaps Lucy Negro), the Indian Changeling, the "Negro" impregnated by Launcelot, Othello, and the Prince of Morocco. It is imperative that we continue to address these impersonations, since such raced embodiments in Shakespeare's works and afterlives continue to affect the *real* lives – the experiential and existential beingness – of peoples of color. Fred Moten's pithy observation puts it best: "whether we are talking about the seventeenth, twentieth, or twenty-first [century] ... it's not so much that Shakespeare [with his Othello] has given an early articulation of the Negro Problem; it's that, instead, he has given Negroes a problem."[1] Blacks hold a special place in this raced pantheon, given not just the frequency of black characters and black allusions (many of the latter arguably racialized) in Shakespeare but also those cultural habits, especially from the eighteenth century onward, that have almost reflexively made blacks synonymous with race itself.

The ideologies and hegemonies that often insist on defining and assessing the worth of people of color through the prism of race press even more arduously (and at times, religiously) to define white peoples as nonraced or, more tacitly and chillingly, as "the human race" itself. Critical white studies, a field that earned its bona fides in the 1990s in the wake of critical race studies, works to disrupt the seeming intractability and permanence of whiteness as a uniquely privileged, adjudicative cultural force. As put by legal theorists Richard Delgado and Jean Stefancic:

> One aspect of whiteness ... is its ability to seem perspectiveless, or transparent. Whites do not see themselves as having a race, but as being, simply, people. They do not believe that they think and reason from a white viewpoint, but from a universally valid one – 'the truth' – what everyone knows. By the same token, many whites will strenuously deny that they have benefited from white privilege.[2]

Many whites, living in what we might identify as predominantly white countries and/or white communities, do not see themselves operating as racial subjects or comprehend (at least in any critical way) how they do so. Ruth Frankenberg has argued that "there *is* a cultural/racial specificity to white people, [that] at times [is] more obvious to people who are not white than to white individuals."[3] And more significant still is the fact that whiteness operates with a "structural advantage" and a "structured invisibility."[4] In other words, whites' failure to perceive themselves as raced is no surprise. As commonly pointed out by critical race and critical white studies scholars, whites not seeing themselves as white, as nothing in particular, *proactively* reproduces and maintains the principles and knowledge subtending what philosopher George Yancy calls "white-world-making," that is, "the construction of a world with values, regulations, and policies that provide supportive structures to those identified as 'white,' a world that whiteness then denies having given birth to, a possible slippage between knowing and being."[5]

Some may very well ask what does white-world-making have to do with Shakespeare and Shakespeare's era. Is it possible to read Shakespeare through critical white studies? Does racial whiteness have anything to do with Shakespeare? Not surprisingly given the existence of this essay, the simple answer is an emphatic yes. Notwithstanding, the question and answer are actually far more complex, since we need to step outside any easy reading of whiteness, race, or identity politics, especially in the context of sixteenth- and seventeenth-century England. We need to engage and challenge with a different set of historical and theoretical tools since so much of the work in (critical) white studies that has set many of the parameters within which many contemporary critics operate – including, just to name a few exemplary examples of stellar work in the field, Theodore W. Allen's *The Invention of the White Race* (1994), Richard Dyer's *White* (1997), and Nell Painter's *The History of White People* (2010) – doesn't have a more culturally grounded grasp of the English early modern period. Critical white studies, like other fields, works with its own limited parameters and its own set of blindnesses.

To get to the real substance of the question, we could, for example, explore the not-so-uncanny resonances between what Yancy argues is a white "world-picture" in our contemporary world and the "world picture" described by E.M.W. Tillyard in his study of Shakespeare and his contemporaries, *The Elizabethan World Picture* (1942).[6] Tillyard doesn't talk (explicitly) about either whiteness or race in his study of "the idea of order" in the English sixteenth and seventeenth centuries, but he does argue,

"In the chain of being the position of man was of paramount interest. *Homo est utriusque naturae vinculum.* He was the nodal point ... [and that] had the unique function of binding together *all* creation, of bridging the greatest cosmic chasm, that between matter and spirit."[7] Tillyard continues, "The Elizabethans were interested in the nature of man with a fierceness rarely paralleled in other ages; and that fierceness delighted in exposing all the contrarieties in man's composition. In particular by picturing man's position between beast and angel with all possible emphasis they gave a new intensity to the old conflict."[8] Summing up his argument, Tillyard states, "the idea of man summing up the universe in himself had a strong hold on the imagination of the Elizabethans."[9]

As iterated, Tillyard doesn't discuss whiteness or race and the humanist "man" he extols seems innocent or harmless enough, but what happens when we put his humanistic man in conversation with, say, Alexander G. Weheliye's biopolitical man? Weheliye, who is interested in the biopolitics of race and the human, argues that since the Renaissance "the human as a secular entity of scientific and humanistic inquiry has functioned as a central topos of modernity": "there exists no portion of the modern human that is not subject to racialization which determines the hierarchical ordering of the Homo sapiens species into humans, not-quite-humans, and nonhumans."[10] From the perspective of critical white studies, what emerges is what Ian Smith identifies in his study of early modern rhetoric and barbarism as "humanism's role in the discursive history of race."[11] The "man" being delineated in sixteenth- and seventeenth-century humanism is certainly no less raced than he is gendered, even though early modern critics have generally bestowed upon the former their nothing-to-see-here blessings.

"White people" as a term, however, never appears in Shakespeare, and is actually used for the first time as far as we currently know in Thomas Middleton's lord mayoral pageant, *The Triumphs of Truth*, on 29 October 1613. Are critical white studies anachronistic, then, when it comes to Shakespeare? The answer is an emphatic no. Further, it's important to have a more nuanced understanding of the concept itself, not so we can proleptically make it mean what we want it to mean, but because it's crucial we try to make legible and comprehensible the processes through which "white people" came into being both through and outside what is often erroneously understood to be the more discrete contours and epistemologies of race.

To help us better understand, we need also to apprehend early modern whiteness as less fully subsumable by modern and contemporary racial identities (even though these also obtain) than as a property that increasingly *becomes* exclusively raced. There is a long and complicated history of white racial assemblaging, that is, the coming together, crisscrossing, clashes, infusions, and confusions, of various modalities and heterogeneous ideas, images, genres, genealogies, terms, elements, inter alia, to make something we can identify as "white people," something we can claim to be a thing of whiteness. In simpler language, "white people," like "black people," are not ontologically sui generis, they're made, they're always in the act of being *(re)invented*.[12]

In "Whiteness as Property," an essay very important to critical race and critical white scholars alike, Cheryl I. Harris, working within the domain of American law, has reasoned that "Slavery as a system of property facilitated the merger of white identity and property. Because the system of slavery was contingent on and conflated with racial identity, it became crucial to be 'white,' to be identified as white, to have the property of being white. Whiteness was the characteristic, the attribute, the property of free human beings."[13] In Shakespeare's England whiteness was a property to be claimed by the relative elite in whatever arena. For example, as Peter Erickson has shown, Queen Elizabeth modeled her court as "a cult of whiteness," and her whiteness presumably radiated out to others in the court, especially those closest to her.[14] In England's reformed theology, as Dennis Britton has argued, baptism "fulfill[ed] the human part of the covenant," and also solidified the relationship between the "Baptiz'd race" (language he borrows from James I himself) and the whiteness of the soul, a whiteness that could not be claimed by non-Christian others.[15] Moreover, the soul's whiteness extended beyond religion and into the realm of humanist doctrine linking one's humanness to the "light" of knowledge within.

Whiteness worked as a property, a marker, of the socially elite, who could theoretically be easily distinguished from the lower classes "whose work [would have made] it difficult or impossible for them to stay pale."[16] And, of course, it should be noted that there was much overlap among all these groups and other elites. Not all "white-skinned" individuals, or "white-skinned" English persons, had equal access and derived equal cachet from whiteness as property. Yet what seems to have happened in the later sixteenth and early seventeenth centuries, is the shift of whiteness from being an elite property to whiteness itself as the determinant, that is the signifier of one's elite status. Notwithstanding, for the early modern English not all persons with white skin were equally white. The moniker "white people" can be read at one and the same time as the maker of and the challenge to seeing and understanding white-world-making as simultaneously exclusive and encompassing.

It is fitting that a theatrical piece introduces us to this crux, since it was essentially early modern theatre that taught Middleton's 1613 spectators, "a socially and morally undifferentiated crowd of English men and women," that, indeed, they were "white people."[17] The theatre lit English bodies, painted them, and discoursed about them to the point where those looking on could with confidence and pride imagine themselves to be "white people" whether they stood pressed together in the pit or sat separately in one of the balcony's "lord's rooms."[18] The stage and the plays performed on it were instrumental to the assemblaging of white people into a singular and privileged race, more often more propagandistic or aspirational than "real," like Hal's "band of brothers" in Shakespeare's *Henry V* (4.3.60). Thinking mainly about the impersonations of Moors, American Indians, and Africans on the early modern English stage, Ayanna Thompson observes that "the *coalescence* of these performances helped to create the actual discourses for the physical construction of race."[19] Thompson's observations here are very much on point: the "coalescence" she speaks of anticipates the racial assemblaging discussed above. Nonetheless, from the perspective of critical white studies, it's worth stressing that early modern English theatre worked even more obsessively on both the physical and metaphysical construction of a white race, however much we have been taught *not* to see whiteness or its construction. The theatre brought whiteness as a property to life, to full-fledged racial embodiment and meaning.

The discursive and performative possibilities offered by the habitus of the theatre itself, especially from the late 1580s and up until the closing of the playhouses in 1642, operated as a virtual manual on how to go about constructing and laying claim to one's embodiment of a racialized whiteness. The theatre operated as a place where one could see "the ideals of education and improvement" in untold ways.[20] Ordinary spectators, like ordinary actors, could at least imagine a more *liberating* relationship to their bodies, one dramatically bolstered by an expanding corporeal vocabulary and a corporeal presentation. English wasn't a matter of linguistics in any technical sense as much it was a matter of ideology, hegemony, and embodiment. The stage and its use of language, we could say, turned being English itself into a white event.

This imaginative vocabulary with the assist of various stage technologies, including lighting, could quite literally cast a new light on the freedom and whiteness of the English body. As R.B. Graves has found, "the contrasts of darkness and light on the English Renaissance stage were first and foremost functions of the imagery in the spoken words and, hence, worked their effects most prominently in the imaginations of the spectators."[21] The stage made more real a through-line from the whiteness of divinity and a white interiority (e.g., the enlightened Christian soul) to a white cosmos (e.g., the moon, stars, snow) and on to one's own ownership of white skin (cosmeticized or no). Virginia Vaughan insists in her study of early modern blackface performance that the putting on of blackface was far less significant than its removal: these moments, she argues, read as "miraculous" and made whiteness seem all the more "normative."[22] One of the things the theatre did, more than any other medium, including the Church, was to promulgate and solidify an affinity between a miraculous (cosmological) and a normative (cosmetic) whiteness. The theatre can be argued to have repurposed and celebrated the whiteness of divinity by rediscovering and redeploying it in playworlds and on stages that were as physically corporeal as they were secular. And further still, if we consider, as does Herbert Blau, that "the erotic capacity of theater is not a matter of secondary projection. It is right there, in the bodies,"[23] we can appreciate, too, how English theatre during the early modern period *presented* the English body itself as the meeting place, the prima facie site, of a physical desire and a meta-physical divinity working in white-racial-assemblaging fashion to make a miraculous and normative whiteness more real, present, and concrete. Critical white studies offers frameworks, models, and vocabularies for exploring the contributions such image-making makes to the construction of a racialized white people.

Shakespeare is important to this story for a range of theatrical, historical, and contemporary reasons. He was one of the period's most prolific writers and was most especially active when the theatre – not just the Globe – was arguably at its height artistically and culturally. Because Shakespeare is now the most consequential founder and practitioner of what may be called modern, global English, it's imperative that we at least take account of Shakespeare, if not hold Shakespeare accountable, in the theatrical, historical, and contemporary milieus of white-world-making. Shakespeare is no mere bystander.

Thinking about whiteness in Shakespeare is as daunting a proposition as disaggregating the assemblaging histories and constructions of whiteness itself, to say nothing about analyzing Shakespeare's works themselves. In a 1935 study of Shakespeare's imagery, Caroline F.E. Spurgeon notices Shakespeare's "intense interest in the human face" as well as its color, especially its whiteness, and how it had "never . . . been adequately noticed by critics."²⁴ Spurgeon observes, "Shakespeare is just as sensitive to the colour and tint of flesh, and the contrasts of the various shades which are called 'white', as he is to the changing colour in the cheek. In his early poems this particular colour interest, is, like the changing colour in the face, very marked, and he is for ever emphasising and illustrating the fairness of a woman's skin."²⁵ While this rhetoric fills Shakespeare's poems, it's in his plays, on his stage, where he makes his most indelible contributions to white-people- and white-world-making. We can begin simply, as a way of broaching such analyses, by asking whether some of Shakespeare's characters are whiter than others, whether we are thinking about characters within a particular play or across Shakespeare's oeuvre.

Because no well-known play from the period more than *The Tempest* (1610–11) shows the relationship between whiteness and humanity being so memorably worked out onstage, it's worth demonstrating a critical white studies reading of it first. Such a reading could of course overlap at moments with critical race readings and the far more common post-colonial readings of the play, which in both instances are most often focused on the not-quite- or not-human Caliban, whom Miranda sees as belonging to a "vile race" (1.2.359) and Prospero calls his "thing of darkness" (5.1.276). What if we shifted our focus, and not only as a passing exercise, and thought less about Caliban's thingification through darkness and more consciously about the whiteness of humanity as constituted by the other characters in the play, if not by the play itself?

Tillyard claims that while Shakespeare's plays were "always concerned with man's position on the chain of being," it is only *The Tempest* that "seem[s] to consider the chain itself."²⁶ In other words, who or what constitutes the human is one of the play's distinguishing features. Tillyard summarizes: "Caliban may hover between man and beast, yet in the end he shows himself incapable of the human power of education. Prospero too learns his own lesson. He cannot transcend the terms of his humanity. In the end he acknowledges Caliban, 'this thing of darkness, mine': man for all his striving toward the angels can never be quit utterly of the bestial, of the Caliban, within him."²⁷ From this perspective even the man with *melior natura* can't be white enough, leaving said man, as I've argued elsewhere, immersed in a kind of constitutive, white melancholia.²⁸

Still, fantasies of a white, i.e., "fair," world persist, pushed off into the carefully strategized future hetero-reproductivity promised by Ferdinand and Miranda. Ferdinand swears to Prospero that he will not have sex with Miranda until after they are married – "As I hope / For quiet days, fair issue and long life" (4.1.23–24) – reminding us too of the first line of

Shakespeare's sonnets: "From fairest creatures we desire increase" (1.1). Of course, the possibility of a white progeny, of a white royal future, has already been lost by the king who has married his daughter Claribel – "the beautiful clear [i.e., white] one" – to the king of Tunis. The word "white" itself occurs only once in the play, in Ferdinand's next speech when he says to Prospero that "The white cold virgin snow upon my heart / Abates the ardour of my liver" (4.1.55–56).

The whiteness and coldness of virginity itself seem out of step with the future bodily acts that will be required to produce "fair issue." Whatever future the playworld imagines through the procreative acts of Miranda and Ferdinand sits in odd juxtaposition to the other European characters in the play. If Caliban is notable because he "shows himself incapable of the human power of education," the bedrock of early modern humanism, what is more remarkable is the motley crew, the humanistic citizens of this "brave new world" (5.1.184) who, presumably, have been successfully educated. These aspirant thieves, murderers, and traitors form less a royal coterie than they do a loose gang of self-serving thugs, each vying with each other for social and political dominance. What perhaps should trouble us at the end of the play is not only what will happen to Caliban, who will hopefully be left alone to live in peace on the island, but also what the ending says about a world "that has such people in it" (5.1.185), who praise themselves as the measure of man. Such a reading squares with the kind of lament voiced by Roger Ascham, a prominent early modern humanist and educator, who in his *Report and Discourse of the Affairs and State of Germany* (1570) found himself "particularly [appalled with] ... the ease with which supposedly enlightened Christians can degenerate to brutal inhumanity."[29] From the viewpoint of at least one *possible* white studies reading, Shakespeare's career could be said to end on a pessimistic and dystopic note with Shakespeare seeing himself as having failed in his efforts to get white people to set aside their barbaric machinations and embody more fully the category of the human.

Who are Shakespeare's white characters? Are some of Shakespeare's characters that we may uncritically think of as white not actually white? How white are Shakespeare's more explicitly non-white characters, given the fact that they were created by a white playwright? How white are Shakespeare's works? How white is Shakespeare? So much depends, of course, on how much one wishes to interrogate the racial assemblaging of whiteness. However so, it is perhaps easiest to approach the answer oppositionally – *she's white because he's black*. Shakespeare's most explicit dramatization of this oppositional-color approach is the visual and visceral clash of the black-skinned Othello with his white-skinned wife Desdemona, whose whiteness, like her husband's blackness, is more than skin-deep, more than an incidental property. To wit, after Othello confesses to killing Desdemona, Emilia responds, "O, the more angel she, / And you the blacker devil!" (5.2.130–31). By his black skin and his black actions, Othello reinforces the angelic essence of Desdemona's whiteness.

Another way to approach the character question, a way that operates in Shakespeare and the early modern period most predominantly, would be through the ongoing and almost ubiquitous negotiations (to use a neutral term) between white skin as epidermal (physical) property and a proper interior whiteness, that is, a white knowingness or white feeling.[30] Shakespeare's audience, having a white racial literacy, would know or feel the difference between one character's whiteness and another's. When the comedic heroine Rosalind ridicules the shepherdess Phebe's "cheek of cream" in *As You Like It* (3.5.47), for example, she mocks the pseudo-whiteness of the latter whose being "not for all markets" (3.5.60) leaves her body in Rosalind's diatribe floundering somewhere in a failed Petrarchan blazon or as a compromised sexual or enslave-able object. Rosalind's disparaging of Phebe presumes to reinforce for Phebe as well as Shakespeare's audience the supra-marketability and unmarkedness of Rosalind's real whiteness, a whiteness that in its essence means to supersede embodiment, to supersede being made into (someone else's) property. Rosalind is white. Phebe is not (so much). In *Romeo and Juliet* Romeo protests Benvolio's suggestion that any woman exists who is "fairer than [his] love" Rosaline (1.2.94), only to find a few scenes later that when "with tender Juliet match'd" Rosaline is "now not fair" (2 Chorus 4). Juliet is the fairest, i.e., the whitest of them all. Juliet's whiteness, when coupled with Romeo's – Juliet describes him as "Whiter than new snow upon a raven's back" (3.2.19) – promises a jouissance that only the whitest of whites can produce. Their whiteness is no incidental property: it is stressed no less by the first fifty lines of Shakespeare's main source, Arthur Brooke's *Romeus and Juliet* (1562).

It isn't always, however, a case of who presumably has the whitest skin. In *Titus Andronicus*, with its "more complex construction of whiteness", Tamora's Gothic hyperwhiteness (and hypersexuality) sits in contradistinction to Lavinia's more "temperate Roman whiteness."[31] Even while Tamora may become "incorporate in Rome" (1.1.467), her whiteness cannot compete with what Shakespeare's audience would understand to be the truly more normative and foundational whiteness of Roman (and Englished) Lavinia, however much the latter's body is raped, amputated, or silenced. Lavinia is white. Tamora (with her Gothic perversion of whiteness) not so much.

In *Antony and Cleopatra*, for a final and more nuanced example, Octavius Caesar works arduously to rewrite Mark Antony's racial history and genealogy and make Antony himself one not begot of a "lawful race" (3.13.112), to make him not Roman, not white.[32] Most ostentatiously, Caesar in his Modena speech seems to lament a "weyward" Antony who once upon a time *heroically* survived famine by drinking horse piss and eating "strange flesh" (1.4.56–72).[33] Caesar's speech resonates with the prologue opening Act 2 of George Peele's *The Battle of Alcazar* (ca. 1591) that describes Muly Hamet, the brutal "negro Moor" (3), as having been "chased from his dignity and his diadem" and made to live "forlorn among the mountain shrubs" and make "his food the flesh of savage beasts" (32–35).[34] Antony is the inverse of Othello who, according to the Duke in that play, is black on the outside but white on the inside (1.3.291–92). (Of course, the Duke turns out to be wrong.) Whiteness, argues Caesar, is far more than skin-deep and even a Roman, one as revered as Antony, may in fact lack it. What is interesting, too, about this example, is the way whiteness has less to do with skin color than with one's disposition. Antony's heroism turns out to betray a "temperate Roman whiteness." In the instances given here, what it means to be a proper white character is part of these Shakespearean characters' construction as well as that of many others. Thinking about whiteness of particular characters does not preclude us from thinking about whiteness *intersectionally*, the way white racialization works concomitantly with, for example, gender, sex, sexuality, class, religion, and nationalism, among others.[35] We could, for example, think about Portia's aristocratic whiteness versus Nerissa's gentlewomanly whiteness in *The Merchant of Venice*; Cassio's Florentine whiteness versus Iago's Venetian whiteness in *Othello*; or Antony's hypersexual whiteness versus Caesar's more sexually ascetic whiteness in *Antony and Cleopatra*. Intersectionality figures prominently in the ways whiteness is being negotiated and renegotiated not only in Shakespeare's plays but in the first decades of the seventeenth century in England.

We are not limited to thinking about whiteness only, or even primarily, in terms of characters. We may think, for example, about how whiteness functions in different Shakespearean genres, including the history plays, romantic comedies, Roman plays, and so on, and should not forget Shakespeare's non-dramatic works. Still, while thinking about whiteness in Shakespeare's plays, the most productive site for thinking about white-racialization in Shakespeare, it's important that we pull back from the stories and characters of the plays themselves and consider, too, the real bodies onstage and how their demonstration of their skills and their *capacity* for transformation undergird a culture becoming increasingly ecstatic about what it sees as its having the most proprietary claim on and right to a racial whiteness.

This essay, having focused its critical energies on Shakespeare's works and his sixteenth- and seventeenth-century England, tells only a partial story: Shakespeare as "cultural capital" is a complex assemblage of his many afterlives – extending from performance histories to performances tomorrow, from allusions to adaptations to rewritings, from classrooms to boardrooms, from slavery to post-Civil Rights, from colonial education to post-colonial (post-) protestations. Shakespeare's whiteness looms, it haunts. We arrive again at this question that is as ethical as it is intellectual, critical, and political: Is it possible to read Shakespeare through critical white studies? Unless we willfully subscribe to whiteness as transhistorical, invisible, inevitable, nonperformative, normative, natural, and neutral, it really is impossible not to.

Notes

1 Fred Moten, "Letting Go of *Othello*," *Paris Review*, 1 November 2019, www .theparisreview.org/blog/2019/11/01/letting-go-of-othello (accessed 19 March 2020).

2 Richard Delgado and Jean Stefancic, *Critical Race Theory: An Introduction*, 3rd edn (New York: NYU Press, 2017), 91–92.

3 Ruth Frankenberg, "White Women, Race Matters: The Social Construction of Whiteness," in *Theories of Race and Racism: A Reader*, 2nd edn, ed. Les Back and John Solomos (New York: Routledge, 2000), 519–33 (at 522).

4 Frankenberg, 519, 523.

5 George Yancy, "Introduction: Fragments of a Social Ontology of Whiteness," in *What White Looks Like: African-American Philosophers on the Whiteness Question*, ed. George Yancy (New York: Routledge, 2004), 1–23 (at 10–11).

6 Yancy, 10.

7 E.M.W. Tillyard, *The Elizabethan World Picture: A Study of the Idea of Order in the Age of Shakespeare, Donne and Milton* (New York: Vintage, 1959), 66.

8 Tillyard, 76.

9 Tillyard, 90.

10 Alexander G. Weheliye, *Habeas Viscus: Racializing Assemblages, Biopolitics, and Black Feminist Theories of the Human* (Durham, NC: Duke University Press, 2014), 9.

11 Ian Smith, *Race and Rhetoric in the Renaissance: Barbarian Errors* (New York and Basingstoke: Palgrave Macmillan, 2009), 71.

12 It's important to note, however, that the relationship between the assembla-ging of "white people" and the assemblaging of "black people" is not a symmetrical one: these do not simply exist as oppositional categories.

13 Cheryl Harris, "Whiteness as Property," in *Critical Race Theory: The Key Writings that Formed the Movement*, ed. Kimberlé Crenshaw, Neil Gotanda, Gary Peller, and Kendell Thomas (New York: New Press, 1996), 267–91 (at 279).

14 Peter Erickson, "Representations of Blacks and Blackness in the Renaissance," *Criticism* 35/4 (Fall 1993): 499–527 (517).

15 Dennis Austin Britton, *Becoming Christian: Race, Reformation, and Early Modern English Romance* (New York: Fordham University Press, 2014), 50.

16 Gary Taylor, *Buying Whiteness: Race, Culture, and Identity from Columbus to Hip-Hop* (New York: Palgrave Macmillan, 2005), 36.

17 Taylor, 126.

18 Andrew Gurr, *Playgoing in Shakespeare's London*, 3rd edn (Cambridge University Press, 2004), 22.

19 Ayanna Thompson, *Performing Race and Torture on the Early Modern Stage* (New York and London: Routledge, 2008), 15.

20 Tanya Pollard, *Shakespeare's Theater: A Sourcebook* (Malden, MA: Blackwell, 2004), xxii. See also Patricia Akhimie, *Shakespeare and the Cultivation of Difference: Race and Conduct in the Early Modern World* (New York and London: Routledge, 2018).

21 R.B. Graves, "Elizabethan Lighting Effects and the Convention of Indoor and Outdoor Theatrical Illumination," *Renaissance Drama* 12 (1981): 51–69 (at 69).

22 Virginia Mason Vaughan, *Performing Blackness on English Stages, 1500–1800* (Cambridge University Press, 2005), 109.

23 Herbert Blau, *Take up the Bodies: Theater at the Vanishing Point* (Urbana: University of Illinois Press, 1982), 289.

24 Caroline F.E. Spurgeon, *Shakespeare's Imagery and What It Tells Us* (Cambridge University Press, 1935), 58, 63–66.

25 Spurgeon, 66.

26 Tillyard, 34.

27 Tillyard, 34–35.

28 Arthur L. Little, Jr., "Re-Historicizing Race, White Melancholia, and the Shakespearean Property," *Shakespeare Quarterly* 67/1 (Spring 2016): 84–103.

29 Mike Pincombe, *Elizabethan Humanism: Literature and Learning in the Later Sixteenth Century* (New York: Routledge, 2013), 71.

30 See Cheryl E. Matias, *Feeling White: Whiteness, Emotionality, and Education* (Rotterdam: Sense, 2016).

31 Francesca T. Royster, "White-Limed Walls: Whiteness and Gothic Extremism in Shakespeare's *Titus Andronicus*," *Shakespeare Quarterly* 51/4 (Winter 2000): 423–55 (at 436, 444).

32 See Arthur J. Little, Jr., *Shakespeare Jungle Fever: National-Imperial Re-Visions of Race, Rape, and Sacrifice* (Stanford University Press, 2000), esp. 102–42.

33 See Ayanna Thompson, "What is a 'Weyward' *Macbeth?*," in *Weyward Macbeth: Intersections of Race and Performance*, ed. Scott L. Newstok and Ayanna Thompson (New York: Palgrave Macmillan, 2010), 3–10.

34 The language these two speeches share seems to be more than coincidental: beasts, flesh, savage(s); hedge (*AC* 65) and shrubs (*BA* 34); "daintily" (*AC* 61) and "dignity" (*BA* 33).

35 See Kimberlé Williams Crenshaw, "The Intersection of Race and Gender," in *Critical Race Theory*, ed. Crenshaw et al., 357–437.

Further Reading

CHAPTER I

Chapman, Matthieu A., "The Appearance of Blacks on the Early Modern Stage: *Love's Labour's Lost*'s African Connections to Court," *Early Theatre* 17/2 (2014): 77-94.

Coles, Kimberly Anne, Kim F. Hall, and Ayanna Thompson, "BlacKKKShakespearean: A Call to Action for Medieval and Early Modern Studies," *Profession*, Fall 2019, https://profession.mla.org/blackkkshakespear ean-a-call-to-action-for-medieval-and-early-modern-studies.

Fields, Karen E., and Barbara J. Fields, *Racecraft: The Soul of Inequality in American Life* (New York: Verso, 2012).

Habib, Imtiaz, *Black Lives in the English Archives, 1500–1677* (Burlington, VT: Ashgate, 2008).

Heng, Geraldine, *The Invention of Race in the European Middle Ages* (Cambridge University Press, 2018).

Lowe, Kate, "Introduction: The Black African Presence in Renaissance Europe," in *Black Africans in Renaissance Europe*, ed. Thomas Foster Earle and Kate Lowe (Cambridge University Press, 2005), 1–14.

Thompson, Ayanna, "Response: Shakespeare, My Sparring Partner," *Early Modern Culture* 14 (2019): 183–86.

Weissbourd, Emily, "'Those in Their Possession': Race, Slavery, and Queen Elizabeth's 'Edicts of Expulsion,'" *Huntington Library Quarterly* 78/1 (2015): 1–19.

CHAPTER 2

Akhimie, Patricia, *Shakespeare and the Cultivation of Difference: Race and Conduct in the Early Modern Period* (New York and London: Routledge, 2018).

Blunt, Richard, "The Evolution of Blackface Cosmetics on the Early Modern Stage," in *The Materiality of Color: The Production, Circulation, and Application of Dyes and Pigments 1400–1800*, ed. Andrea Feeser, Maureen Daly Goggin, and Beth Fowkes Tobin (Farnham and Burlington, VT: Ashgate), 217–34.

Hall, Kim F., "Beauty and the Beast of Whiteness: Teaching Race and Gender," *Shakespeare Quarterly*, 47/4 (1996): 461–75.

Things of Darkness: Economies of Race and Gender in Early Modern England (Ithaca, NY: Cornell University Press, 1995).

Hornback, Robert, *Racism and Early Blackface Comic Traditions: From the Old World to the New* (Cham: Palgrave Macmillan, 2019).

Karim-Cooper, Farah, *Cosmetics in Shakespearean and Renaissance Drama* (Edinburgh University Press, 2006; rev. edn 2019).

Lowe, Kate, "The Stereotyping of Black Africans in Renaissance Europe," in *Black Africans in Renaissance Europe*, ed. Thomas Foster Earle and Kate Lowe (Cambridge University Press, 2005), 17–47.

Smith, Ian. "Othello's Black Handkerchief," *Shakespeare Quarterly* 64/1 (2013): 1–25.

CHAPTER 3

El Hamel, Chouki, *Black Morocco: A History of Slavery, Race, and Islam* (Cambridge University Press, 2013).

Fields, Karen E., and Barbara Jeanne Fields. *Racecraft: The Soul of Inequality in American Life* (New York: Verso, 2014).

Grady, Kyle, *Moors, Mulattos, and Post-Racial Problems: Rethinking Racialization in Early Modern England*, PhD dissertation, University of Michigan (2017).

Habib, Imtiaz *Black Lives in the English Archives, 1500–1677: Imprints of the Invisible* (Aldershot and Burlington, VT: Ashgate, 2008).

Hall, Kim F. *Things of Darkness: Economies of Race and Gender in Early Modern England* (Ithaca, NY: Cornell University Press, 1995).

Lowe, Kate, "Introduction: The Black African Presence in Renaissance Europe," in *Black Africans in Renaissance Europe*, ed. Thomas Foster Earle and Kate Lowe (Cambridge University Press, 2005), 1–14.

MacLean, Gerald, and Nabil Matar, *Britain and the Islamic world, 1558–1713* (Oxford University Press, 2011).

Matar, Nabil, "Queen Elizabeth I through Moroccan Eyes," *Journal of Early Modern History* 12/1 (2008): 55–76.

Weissbourd, Emily, "'Those in Their Possession': Race, Slavery, and Queen Elizabeth's 'Edicts of Expulsion,'" *Huntington Library Quarterly* 78/1 (2015): 1–19.

CHAPTER 4

Akhimie, Patricia, *Shakespeare and the Cultivation of Difference: Race and Conduct in the Early Modern World* (New York and London: Routledge, 2018).

Hendricks, Margo, "'Obscured by Dreams': Race, Empire, and Shakespeare's *A Midsummer Night's Dream*," *Shakespeare Quarterly* 47/1 (1996): 37–60.

Pérez, Raúl, "Racism Without Hatred? Racist Humor and the Myth of 'Color-Blindness,'" *Sociological Perspectives* 60/5 (2017): 956–74.

Smith, Ian, "We Are Othello: Speaking of Race in Early Modern Studies," *Shakespeare Quarterly* 67/1 (2016): 104–24.

Snyder, Susan, *The Comic Matrix of Shakespeare's Tragedies: Romeo and Juliet, Hamlet, Othello, and King Lear* (Princeton University Press, 1979).

Shakespeare: A Wayward Journey (Newark: University of Delaware Press, 2002).

Weaver, Simon, *The Rhetoric of Racist Humour: US, UK and Global Race Joking* (London: Routledge, 2016).

CHAPTER 5

Baker, David J., "'Wildehirissheman:' Colonialist Representation in Shakespeare's *Henry V*," *ELR* 22 (1992): 37–61.

Baker, David, and Willy Maley (eds.), *British Identities and English Renaissance Literature* (Cambridge University Press, 2002).

Bartlett, Robert, "Medieval and Modern Concepts of Race and Ethnicity," *Journal of Medieval and Early Modern Studies* 31 (2001): 39–56.

Bradshaw, Brendan, and Peter Roberts (eds.), *British Identity and British Consciousness, 1533–1707* (Cambridge University Press, 1998).

Hadfield, Andrew, "*Henry V*," in *A Companion to Shakespeare's Works*, vol. II: *The Histories*, ed. Richard Dutton and Jean E. Howard (Oxford: Blackwell, 2003), 451–67.

Heng, Geraldine, "The Invention of Race in the European Middle Ages I: Race Studies, Modernity, and the Middle Ages," *Literature Compass* 8/5 (2011): 258–74.

Kearney, Hugh, *The British Isles: A History of Four Nations*, 2nd edn (Cambridge University Press, 2006).

Neill, Michael, "Broken English and Broken Irish: Nation, Language, and the Optic of Power in Shakespeare's Histories," *Shakespeare Quarterly* 45 (1994): 1–32.

CHAPTER 6

Akhimie, Patricia, *Shakespeare and the Cultivation of Difference: Race and Conduct in the Early Modern World* (New York and London: Routledge, 2018).

Chapman, Matthieu A., *Anti-Black Racism in Early Modern English Drama: The Other "Other"* (New York and London: Routledge, 2017).

Daileader Celia R., *Racism, Misogyny, and the Othello Myth: Inter-Racial Couples from Shakespeare to Spike Lee* (Cambridge University Press, 2005).

Hall, Kim, *Things of Darkness: Economies of Race and Gender in Early Modern England* (Ithaca, NY: Cornell University Press, 1995).

Karim-Cooper, Farah (ed.), *Titus Andronicus: The State of Play* (London: Arden Shakespeare, 2019).

MacDonald, Joyce Green, *Women and Race in Early Modern Texts* (Cambridge University Press, 2002).

Minor, Benjamin, and Ayanna Thompson, "'Edgar I Nothing Am': Blackface in *King Lear*," in *Staged Transgression in Shakespeare's England*, ed. R. Loughnane and E. Semple (New York and London: Palgrave Macmillan, 2013), 153–64.

Smith, Ian, "White Skin, Black Masks: Racial Cross-Dressing on the Early Modern Stage," *Renaissance Drama* 32 (2003): 33–67.

CHAPTER 7

Brotton, Jerry, "Shakespeare's Turks and the Spectre of Ambivalence in the History Plays," *Textual Practice* 28/3 (2014): 521–38.

Burton, Jonathan, *Traffic and Turning: Islam and English Drama, 1579–1624* (Newark: University of Delaware Press, 2005).

Dimmock, Matthew, "Materialising Islam on the Early Modern Stage," in *Early Modern Encounters with the Islamic East: Performing Cultures*, ed. Sabine Schulting, Sabine Lucia Muller, and Ralf Hertel (Farnham: Ashgate, 2012), 115–32.

Mythologies of the Prophet Muhammad in Early Modern English Culture (Cambridge University Press, 2013).

Hutchings, Mark, "'The Turk Phenomenon' and the Repertory of the Late Elizabethan Playhouse," *Early Modern Literary Studies*, Special Issue 16 (September 2007): http://extra.shu.ac.uk/emls/si-16/hutcturk.htm.

MacLean, Gerald, and Nabil Matar, *Britain and the Islamic World, 1558–1713* (Oxford University Press, 2011).

CHAPTER 8

Adelman, Janet, *Blood Relations: Christian and Jew in The Merchant of Venice* (University of Chicago Press, 2008).

Britton, Dennis Austin, *Becoming Christian: Race, Reformation, and Early Modern English Romance* (New York: Fordham University Press, 2014).

"Muslim Conversion and Circumcision as Theater," in *Religion and Drama in Early Modern England: The Performance of Religion on the Renaissance Stage*, ed. Jane Hwange Degenhardt and Elizabeth Williamson (Farnham: Ashgate, 2011), 71–86.

Griffin, Eric, *English Renaissance Drama and the Specter of Spain: Ethnopoetics and Empire* (Philadelphia: University of Pennsylvania Press, 2009).

Hall, Kim F., "'Guess who's coming to dinner?': Colonialism and Miscegenation in 'The Merchant of Venice,'" *Renaissance Drama*, New Series, 23 (1992): 87–111.

Kaplan, M. Lindsay, "Jessica's Mother: Medieval Constructions of Race and Gender in *The Merchant of Venice*," *Shakespeare Quarterly* 58 (2007): 4–10.

Shapiro, James, *Shakespeare and the Jews* (New York: Columbia University Press, 1992).

Smith, Ian, "The Textile Black Body: Race and 'shadowed livery' in *The Merchant of Venice*," in *The Oxford Handbook of Shakespeare and Embodiment: Gender, Sexuality, and Race*, ed. Valerie Traub (Oxford University Press, 2016), 170–85.

CHAPTER 9

Bosman, Anston. "'Best Play with Mardian': Eunuch and Blackamoor as Imperial Culturegram," *Shakespeare Studies* 34 (2006): 123–57.

Chess, Simone. *Male-to-Female Crossdressing in Early Modern English Literature* (New York and London: Routledge, 2015).

Heng, Geraldine. *The Invention of Race in the European Middle Ages* (Cambridge University Press, 2018).

Iyengar, Sujata. *Shades of Difference: Mythologies of Skin Color in Early Modern England* (Philadelphia: University of Pennsylvania Press, 2005).

Kahn, Coppélia. *Roman Shakespeare: Warriors, Wounds, and Women* (London: Routledge, 1997).

Little, Jr., Arthur L. *Shakespeare Jungle Fever: National-Imperial Re-Visions of Race, Rape, and Sacrifice* (Stanford University Press, 2000).

MacDonald, Joyce Green. *Women and Race in Early Modern Texts* (Cambridge University Press, 2002).

Park, Jennifer. "Discandying Cleopatra: Preserving Cleopatra's Infinite Variety in Shakespeare's *Antony and Cleopatra*," *Studies in Philology* 113 (2016): 595–633.

CHAPTER 10

Fernández Retamar, Roberto, "'Caliban': Notes towards a Discussion of Culture in Our America," *Massachusetts Review* 15 (1973–4): 7–72.

Guasco, Michael, *Slaves and Englishmen: Human Bondage in the Early Modern Atlantic World* (Philadelphia: University of Pennsylvania Press, 2014).

Habib, Imtiaz, *Black Lives in the English Archives, 1500–1667: Imprints of the Invisible* (Aldershot and Burlington, VT: Ashgate, 2008).

Kendi, Ibram X., *Stamped from the Beginning: The Definitive History of Racist Ideas in America* (New York: Nation, 2016).

Vaughan, Alden T., *Transatlantic Encounters: American Indians in Britain, 1500–1776* (New York: Cambridge University Press, 2006; rev. 2008).

Vaughan, Alden T., and Virginia Mason Vaughan, *Shakespeare's Caliban: A Cultural History* (New York: Cambridge University Press, 1991).

Vaughan, Virginia Mason, *Performing Blackness on English Stages, 1500–1800* (Cambridge University Press, 2005).

CHAPTER 11

Chapman, Matthieu A., *Anti-Black Racism in Early Modern English Drama: The Other "Other"* (New York and London: Routledge, 2017).

Goldstein, David B., "The Cook and the Cannibal: *Titus Andronicus* and the New World," *Shakespeare Studies* 37 (2009): 99–133.

Little, Jr., Arthur L., *Shakespeare Jungle Fever: National-Imperial Re-Visions of Race, Rape, and Sacrifice* (Stanford University Press, 2000).

MacDonald, Joyce Green, "Black Ram, White Ewe: Shakespeare, Race, and Women," in *A Feminist Companion to Shakespeare*, ed. Dympna Callaghan (Oxford: Blackwell, 2000), 206–25.

Ndiaye, Noémie, "Aaron's Roots: Spaniards, Englishmen, and Blackamoors in *Titus Andronicus*," *Early Theatre* 19/2 (2016): 59–80.

Royster, Francesca, "White-Limed Walls: Whiteness and Gothic Extremism in Shakespeare's *Titus Andronicus*," *Shakespeare Quarterly* 51/4 (2000): 432–55.

Thompson, Ayanna, *Performing Race and Torture on the Early Modern Stage* (New York and London: Routledge, 2008).

Ungerer, Gustav. "The Presence of Africans in Elizabethan England and the Performance of *Titus Andronicus* at Burley-on-the-Hill, 1595/96," *Medieval & Renaissance Drama in England* 21 (2008): 20–55.

CHAPTER 12

Andrews, C.B., *Black Ebony – The Diaries, Letters and Criticism: The Story of Ira Aldridge (Known as the African Roscius)* (Charles Deering McCormick Library of Special Collections, Northwestern University).

Dewberry, Jonathan. "The African Grove Theatre and Company," *Black American Literature Forum* 16/4 (1982): 128–31.

Howard, Tony, and Zoë Wilcox, "'Haply, for I am black': The Legacy of Ira Aldridge," in *Shakespeare in Ten Acts*, ed. Gordon McMullan and Zoë Wilcox (London: British Library, 2016), 121–40.

Kujawinska Courtney, Krystyna, and Maria Lukowska (eds.), *Ira Aldridge 1807–1867: The Great Shakespearean Tragedian on the Bicentennial Anniversary of His Birth* (Frankfurt am Main: Peter Lang, 2009).

Lindfors, Bernth (ed.), *Ira Aldridge: The African Roscius* (University of Rochester Press, 2007).

MacDonald, Joyce Green. "Acting Black: *Othello, Othello* Burlesques, and the Performance of Blackness." *Theatre Journal* 46 (1994): 231–49.

Walters, Hazel, "Ira Aldridge and the Battlefield of Race," *Race and Class* 45/1 (2003): 1–30.

CHAPTER 13

Bourne, Stephen, *Black in the British Frame: The Black Experience in British Film and Television* (New York: Continuum, 2001).

British Black and Asian Shakespeare Performance Database, https://bbashakespeare.warwick.ac.uk.

Chambers, Colin, *Black and Asian Theatre in Britain: A History* (New York: Routledge, 2011).

Chapman, Matthieu A., "The Appearance of Blacks on the Early Modern Stage: *Love's Labour's Lost*'s African Connections to Court," *Early Theatre* 17/2 (2014): 77–94.

Gerzina, Gretchen Holbrook, *Black London: Life before Emancipation* (New Brunswick, NJ: Rutgers University Press, 1995).

Hill, Errol, *Shakespeare in Sable: A History of Black Shakespearean Actors* (Amherst: University of Massachusetts Press, 1984).

Malik, Sarita, *Representing Black Britain: Black and Asian Images on Television* (London: SAGE, 2002).

Rogers, Jami, "Is the Door Really Open for Black Actors to Star in Shakespeare?," *The Stage*, 6 October 2016, www.thestage.co.uk/features/is-the-door-really-open-for-black-actors-to-star-in-shakespeare.

"The Shakespearean Glass Ceiling: The State of Colorblind Casting in Contemporary British Theatre," *Shakespeare Bulletin* 31/3 (2013): 405–30.

CHAPTER 14

Conquergood, Dwight, "Rethinking Elocution: The Trope of the Talking Book and Other Figures of Speech," *Text and Performance Quarterly* 20/4 (2000): 325–41.

Daileader, Celia, "Casting Black Actors: Beyond Othellophilia," in *Shakespeare and Race*, ed. Catherine M.S. Alexander and Stanley Wells (Cambridge University Press, 2000), 177–202.

Goddard, Lynette, "Will We Ever Have a Black Desdemona? Casting Josette Simon at the RSC," in *Shakespeare, Race, and Performance: The Diverse Bard*, ed. Delia Jarrett-Macauley (New York: Routledge, 2017), 80–95.

Hill, Errol, *Shakespeare in Sable: A History of Black Shakespearean Actors* (Amherst: University of Massachusetts Press, 1984).

Royster, Francesca, *Becoming Cleopatra: The Shifting Inage of an Icon* (New York: Palgrave Macmillan, 2003).

Rutter, Carol Chillington, *Enter the Body: Women and Representation on Shakespeare's Stage* (New York and London: Routledge, 2001).

CHAPTER 15

"Eye to Eye: Ishmael Beah," CBS News, 4 June 2007, https://www.youtube.com/watch?v=ozsOLdgp_yo

"Is Othello a Racist Play? RSC Actor Hugh Quarshie Is Asking the Question," *Etcetera*, 6 August 2015, https://www.hamhigh.co.uk/etcetera/theatre/is-othello-a-racist-play-rsc-actor-hugh-quarshie-is-asking-the-question-1-4184119.

Quarshie, Hugh, *Second Thoughts about Othello* (Chipping Camden: International Shakespeare Association, 1999).

CHAPTER 16

Hornback, Robert, *Racism and Early Blackface Comic Traditions: From the Old World to the New* (Cham: Palgrave Macmillan, 2019).

Kani, John, and Virginia Crompton, *Apartheid and Othello* (London: British Council, 2016).

Kaul, Mythili, "Background: Black or Tawny? Stage Representations of Othello from 1604 to the Present," in *Othello: New Essays by Black Writers*, ed. Mythili Kaul (Washington, DC: Howard University Press, 1997), 1–22.

Lindfors, Bernth, *Ira Aldridge: The Early Years, 1807–1833.* (University of Rochester Press, 2011).

MacDonald, Joyce Green, *Women and Race in Early Modern Texts* (Cambridge University Press, 2002).

McAllister, Marvin Edward, *White People Do Not Know How to Behave at Entertainments Designed for Ladies & Gentlemen of Colour: William Brown's African & American Theater* (Chapel Hill: University of North Carolina Press, 2003).

Robeson, Paul, *Paul Robeson Speaks: Writings, Speeches, and Interviews. A Centennial Celebration*, ed. Philip S. Foner (New York: Citadel Press, 1978).

Royster, Francesca, *Becoming Cleopatra: The Shifting Image of an Icon* (New York: Palgrave Macmillan, 2003).

Thompson, Ayanna, *Passing Strange: Shakespeare, Race, and Contemporary America* (Oxford University Press, 2011).

CHAPTER 17

Barker, Francis, and Peter Hulme, "Nymphs and Reapers Heavily Vanish: The Discursive Contexts of *The Tempest*," in *Alternative Shakespeares*, ed. John Drakakis (London: Methuen, 1985), 191–205.

Brown, Paul, "'This thing of darkness I acknowledge mine': *The Tempest* and the discourse of colonialism", in *Political Shakespeare: New essays in Cultural Materialism*, ed. Jonathan Dollimore and Alan Sinfield (Manchester University Press, 1985), 48–71.

Busia, Abena P.A., "Silencing Sycorax: On African Colonial Discourse and the Unvoiced Female", *Cultural Critique* 14 (1989–90): 81–104.

Césaire, Aimé, *A Tempest*, trans. Richard Miller (New York: Ubu Repertory Theater Publications, 1969).

Nixon, Rob, "Caribbean and African Appropriations of 'The Tempest,'" *Critical Inquiry* 13/3 (Spring 1987): 557–78.

Said, Edward, *Orientalism* (Harmondsworth: Penguin, 1995).

"The Tempest" and Its Travels, ed. Peter Hulme and William H. Sherman (London: Reaktion, 2000).

Thompson, Ayanna, *Passing Strange: Shakespeare, Race, and Contemporary America* (Oxford University Press, 2011).

Young, Sandra, *Shakespeare in the Global South: Stories of Oceans Crossed in Contemporary Adaptation* (London: Arden Shakespeare, 2019).

CHAPTER 18

Britton, Dennis Austin, *Becoming Christian: Race, Reformation, and Early Modern English Romance* (New York: Fordham University Press, 2014).

Erickson, Peter, "Representations of Blacks and Blackness in the Renaissance," *Criticism* 35/4 (Fall 1993): 499–527.

Harris, Cheryl, "Whiteness as Property," in *Critical Race Theory: The Key Writings that Formed the Movement*, ed. Kimberlé Crenshaw, Neil Gotanda, et al. (New York: The New Press, 1995), 276–91.

Little, Jr., Arthur L., "Re-Historicizing Race, White Melancholia, and the Shakespearean Property," *Shakespeare Quarterly* 67/1 (2016): 84–103.

Shakespeare Jungle Fever: National-Imperial Re-Visions of Race, Rape, and Sacrifice (Stanford University Press, 2000).

Moten, Fred, "Letting Go of *Othello*," *Paris Review*, 1 November 2019), www .theparisreview.org/blog/2019/11/01/letting-go-of-othello/.

Royster, Francesca T., "White-Limed Walls: Whiteness and Gothic Extremism in Shakespeare's *Titus Andronicus*," *Shakespeare Quarterly* 51/4 (2000): 432–55.

Smith, Ian, *Race and Rhetoric in the Renaissance: Barbarian Errors* (New York: Palgrave Macmillan, 2009).

Yancy, George, "Introduction: Fragments of a Social Ontology of Whiteness," in *What White Looks Like: African-American Philosophers on the Whiteness Question*, ed. George Yancy (New York: Routledge, 2004), 1–24.

Index

CPSIA information can be obtained
at www.ICGtesting.com
Printed in the USA
LVHW050229080123
736639LV00008B/497